Pascal™:
Text and Reference

second edition

John B. Moore

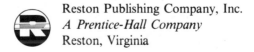
Reston Publishing Company, Inc.
A Prentice-Hall Company
Reston, Virginia

To Barb

- a very special person

ISBN 0-8359-5440-4

©1984 by Reston Publishing Company, Inc.
A Prentice-Hall Company
Reston, Virginia 22090

10 9 8 7 6 5 4 3 2 1

Printed in the United States of America

TABLE OF CONTENTS

Preface to the Revised Edition

This revised edition contains a number of enhancements and updates which reflect the evolutionary nature of modern computing.

One important change is the use of the keyboard as the default source of input data in the example programs. This change is a reaction to the growing number of personal computer users and the proliferation of interactive applications.

Appendix C has been rewritten to provide a complete description of the Waterloo Pascal implementation of the language. It reflects the latest specification of the compiler. Waterloo Pascal is being used by an ever-increasing number of educational institutions and individuals because of its comprehensive facilities, superb diagnostics, and excellent reliability.

Other improvements include: the addition of many new programming problems; over one-hundred new index entries; a consistent approach in the algorithms used in Chapter 14; and more comprehensive explanations of input-output operations in Chapters 2, 5 and 12.

I would like to acknowledge the helpful suggestions of many who have used the first edition of this book. Valuable advice concerning the typesetting of the material was received from Bruce Uttley. The material in Appendix C is taken in large part from section G of *Pascal Reference Manual and Waterloo Pascal User's Guide* by Boswell, Welch and Grove published by WATFAC Publications Ltd., Waterloo Ontario. The permission of the authors and the publisher to use this material is acknowledged and appreciated.

Waterloo Ontario Canada   John B. Moore

Preface

Pascal is rapidly becoming one of the most widely used programming languages in the world. This growth is due to a number of factors most important of which is the discipline it imposes upon the programmer. The rules of the Pascal language, coupled with good programming style, result in good programs.

Goals. The purpose of this book is to describe how to use the Pascal language correctly and effectively. It is a comprehensive description of standard Pascal although unique features of three particular implementations of the languages are summarized in the appendices. It is intended for the person who wants to make a systematic study of the language and who, when finished, requires a solid reference.

Assumptions. It assumes the reader has no previous programming experience. Readers already familiar with programming concepts and/or another programming language can quickly read those paragraphs and explanations related to algorithm development and focus on the attributes of Pascal. Problems and exercises are taken from a wide variety of subject areas.

Pedagogy. The examples chosen to illustrate each component of the language are as simple as possible. In this way the reader can focus on the programming concept without becoming enmeshed in the in logic needed to solve the illustrative problem. The examples are complete programs. All have been run and listed using the Waterloo Pascal processor which accepts standard Pascal.

The material is organized so that the reader may proceed sequentially through the entire text. Each topic is presented using a four-step sequence.(1) Here's what we are trying to do; (2) Here's how we can do it with our existing knowledge; (3) Here's a better way to do it; (4) Here's what we did. Each chapter begins with questions which the chapter answers and concludes with a summary of the key concepts and important programming skills presented.

Exercise questions are found throughout. These test the reader's understanding immediately following the presentation of new material. In the author's view, these questions are one of the most efficient ways to imbed new knowledge. A variety of programming problems is found at the end of each chapter. They range in difficulty from very simple to complex. Some involve simple mathematical peculiarities which stimulate the reader's curiosity. Others are designed to massage the programming knowledge developed in the chapter.

Throughout the book, emphasis is placed on good programming style. Indentation rules, naming conventions and commenting guidelines are explicitly stated and consistently followed.

Organization. The book is divided into three parts: Statements and Values, Data Structures and Dynamic Variables, and Appendices.

Part I describes the statements which are used to process the three basic kinds of values - numbers, characters and Boolean (true-false) values.

Chapter 1 describes the five-step sequence which is followed when a computer is used to assist the problem-solving process. The first example results in a complete program which the student may enter and run. Sufficient programming detail is presented in the three examples to allow a reader to solve a wide variety of simple problems using the examples as prototypes. Attention is devoted to the acceptance of errors and the understanding of diagnostic messages.

Chapter 2 begins the rigorous study of numeric processing. Constants, variables, value assignments and simple input-output are covered in detail.

Chapter 3 describes Boolean values and operations and then shows how they are used in the decision-making statements of the Pascal language.

Chapter 4 illustrates, compares and contrasts the three statements used to control loops.

Chapter 5 explains character and text processing. It also summarizes input-output using READ and WRITE with the standard files INPUT and OUTPUT. The difference between numeric and non-numeric input-output is one of the most difficult parts of the language to learn. Consequently, detailed examples and explanations are given.

Chapter 6, extends the readers knowledge of types to include enumerated and subrange types. A summary of the processing rules for all scalar types is provided.

Chapters 7 and 8 describe functions and procedures respectively. Functions, being simpler, are explained first. Particular attention is paid to rules of scope and the meaning of the terms global and local identifiers. Chapter 8 shows how procedures differ from functions both in form and purpose. The last section of the chapter gives guidelines for partitioning algorithms into procedures. It also suggests criteria for choosing the nesting structure of blocks.

Part II of the book begins with an overview of data structures in general and Pascal data structures in particular. Differences among arrays, records, sets and files are emphasized.

Chapters 10 through 13 describe the four predefined structures available in the language. Arrays, having the most utility, are described first. The material describing records and files builds on the knowledge already gained. Sets are described in Chapter 13. An understanding of other data structures is not necessary to use sets and this material can be studied independently of arrays, records and files.

The final chapter describes the use of pointer variables. Individuals not familiar with memory concepts and indirect addressing often find the use of pointers one of the more difficult programming ideas to grasp. Consequently, a very simple example is presented early in the chapter to show the mechanics of their use. This leads to a discussion of the two most common kinds of data structures requiring pointers, namely linked lists (of which stacks and queues are specify instances) and trees. Examples are provided which demonstrate the use of binary trees in information retrieval applications.

Part III of the book contains six appendices. The first two provide a reference for character sets, standard identifiers, operators and the syntax of the language. Appendix C describes the implementation dependencies of the Waterloo Pascal compiler. Appendices D and E summarize those features of Pascal/VS and IBM Pascal for the IBM Personal Computer which are not part of standard Pascal. Appendix F gives a number of suggestions for reducing debugging time and for improving memory and execution-time efficiency.

No one writes a book without a lot of help. I would like to thank Kay Harrison for her excellent work in entering the original, readable(?) draft of the manuscript and for making the innumerable changes in subsequent versions. Mike Ruwald designed the Script macros used to format the text. Jim Dodd found many typos and made excellent editorial suggestions. For errors that may yet be present, I take full responsibility.

To you the reader, I hope you find this a useful and enjoyable book. I have tried to keep your needs in mind from start to finish.

Waterloo, Ontario Canada   John B. Moore

Preface to the Student

This is a book that teaches you how to speak a language — a language which permits you to use a computer to help solve problems. The language is called Pascal. It was originally developed by a professor to help students learn the principles of computer programming. Because he designed the language so well, it has rapidly become one of the most widely-used languages in the world.

Reading a book about computer programming is like reading a book about playing the piano — there is only so much you can learn without intense practice. To become fluent in the use of the Pascal language, you must practise, experiment and test your knowledge continually. Good luck and good programming.

Part I:
Statements and Values

CHAPTER 1: GETTING STARTED

Questions Answered in this Chapter:

1. What is a computer?

2. Why do we use them?

3. How do we use them?

1.1 What Can a Computer Do?

Computers are attributed with many remarkable powers. However, all computers, from the large ones used to control the space flights to the micro-sized ones you can hold in your hand, are simply collections of electronic components which have three basic capabilities.

First, they have circuits which perform the four basic arithmetic operations denoted by the symbols + - * /. An asterisk or star indicates multiplication; two times three for example is written as 2*3. The slash symbol represents division. For example, the value of 7/5 is 1.4. When two integers are being divided, you can request that "integer division" be performed meaning that the remainder is ignored. Integer division is denoted by "DIV". Therefore the expression "15 DIV 4" has a value of 3, not 3.75. Chapter 2 contains a detailed description of arithmetic operations.

Second, computers have circuits which make decisions. Their decision making capabilities are not such that they can answer a question such as "Will it rain next Tuesday?" or "Who would win a war between Russia and China?" The decision making capabilities of a computer are limited to deciding

1. if one number is less than, equal to, or greater than another number

2. if one character (letter, digit or symbol) comes before, is the same as, or comes after another character in dictionary order

Third, computers have circuits for performing input and output operations. That is, they are able to accept input in the form of instructions and data from human beings. (By data we mean the numbers and characters manipulated by the instructions.) And computers would still be useless machines if we were unable to get the results out of the computer in a form that humans can understand. Thus computers have circuits for sending signals to printers and display screens.

Since all computers have only these three limited capabilities -- arithmetic, decision making and input-output, it is only natural to ask the following question.

1.2 Why Do We Use Them?
There are three reasons why computers are so widely used.

Speed. First, computers are fast. How fast is fast? A powerful computer can perform several million instructions per second. If you or I were to do five million additions of ten digit numbers it would take us -- working a forty hour week -- about four years. Speeds for decision making are also measured in MIPS (millions of instructions per second) but speeds for many input and output operations are thousands of times slower because mechanical motion of cards and paper is often involved. A typical high speed printer for example prints 1000 lines of output per minute. Information can be sent over a standard telephone line at about 10 words per second -- about 1/25 of the rate of a high speed printer.

Accuracy and Reliability. In spite of newspaper headlines such as "Computer Fails Student", incorrect statements from credit card companies and other horror stories of computer foul-ups, you and I realize that it is seldom the machines that make mistakes -- it is the people who make the errors. Computers are remarkably accurate and operate for months, performing billions of operations without an error! Because they are man-made, they occasionally break down and have to be repaired.

A Big Problem = A Set of Little Problems. The most important reason computers are so widely used is that almost all big problems can be solved by solving a set of little problems -- one after the other. If each of these little problems is so simple that it can be solved using the limited capabilities of the computer, then we end up solving the big problem. For example, doing the payroll for a large corporation is indeed a big problem. But in order to solve this problem we need only do the following kinds of things for each person on the payroll: First, input information about the employee such as hours worked, rate of pay, etc. Second, do some simple arithmetic and decision making; Third, output a few lines on a check. By repeating this process over and over again, the payroll will be finished. Since computers can do all of these operations quickly and accurately, the reason for using them is obvious.

Having seen what these machines can do and why we use them, let's find out the steps that are necessary to have them assist us in solving a problem.

1.3 The Five Steps in Problem Solving

There are five steps which must be followed when a computer is used to help solve a problem. They are:

1. Define the problem

2. Develop a procedure for solving the problem.

3. Translate this procedure into a language the computer understands.

4. Enter the instructions and data into the computer.

5. Tell the computer to execute the instructions.

Note that the computer isn't even involved until step 4! In fact, only in step 5 does it operate without human intervention. We shall look briefly at what is in involved in each of these steps and then study an example.

Step 1: Define the Problem. Unless the problem is well-defined, there is no sense even thinking about using a computer to help solve it. The people who get paid the highest salaries in the computing business are those who are trying to answer the question "What, precisely, is it that we want to use the computer to do?" Glib answers such as "do inventory control" or "type form letters" are no good. The problem must be well-defined. Before you write any program, ask yourself "Do I know exactly what the problem is?"

Step 2: Develop a procedure for solving the problem. A word which means "a procedure for solving the problem" is *algorithm*. An algorithm takes the form of a sequence of instructions which, if followed by a moron, will solve the problem. Most algorithms in this book are relatively simple.

Because an algorithm processes numbers and characters it is also necessary to describe the *data* (the objects manipulated by the instructions).

Step 3: Translate the procedure and data descriptions into a language the computer understands. The result of this process is called a computer program. There are literally hundreds of languages which computers can "understand". The programming language described in this book is called Pascal in honor of the sixteenth century Swiss mathematician by that name. It was originally invented to teach the principles of computer programming. Because it is so simple and so powerful, it has rapidly become used for all kinds of programming problems. Like natural languages, programming languages tend to grow (verbs, nouns and sentence structures are added to the language). Pascal is no exception.

Nonetheless, computers can really only understand one language. It consists of long strings of ones and zeros called bits. A *bit* is a *B*inary dig*IT*, namely a zero or a one. All programming languages are translated into strings of bits by a special program called a *compiler*. More will be said about the compiler in Step 5.

Step 4: Enter the program into the computer. Once the algorithm and data descriptions have been written in a programming language, you must enter the computer program and data into the computer. This is done in one of two ways. The lines in the program can be punched into cards, one card per line.

Then a device called a card reader reads the cards and stores the information represented by the holes in cards in computer's memory.

A more common method of data entry is to type the lines in the program directly into the computer using a device that has a typewriter-like keyboard and a television-like screen. Such devices are called computer terminals. The screen of the terminal shows the program as it is typed -- one line at a time and also displays messages generated by the data entry program which resides in the computer during the entry process. Once the program has been entered into the computer's memory, it is called a *source file.*

Step 5: Execute the program. The final step is to have the computer perform the instructions in the program. This is a two-stage process. First, the instructions in the program which are written in the Pascal language must be translated into machine language (strings of bits) which the computer can understand. This translation from the Pascal language to machine language is performed by a special program called the Pascal compiler which reads each line of your Pascal program and performs the translation. The Pascal compiler checks for errors such as missing commas, misspelled words, etc. and prints appropriate error messages on the screen and/or printer. If no errors are found by the compiler, the computer executes the machine language instructions produced by the compiler. During this execution phase an error such as division by zero may occur. If an execution-time error occurs, a message giving the cause of the error is printed and further execution of instructions is halted. The two stages -- compilation followed by execution -- are illustrated below.

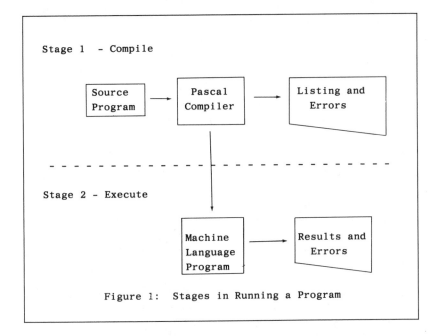

Figure 1:   Stages in Running a Program

1.4 How About an Example?

Step 1: Define the problem.

For each of the values x = 0, x = 1, x = 2, ... , x = 10, calculate the corresponding value of y using the formula:

$$y = x^2 + 2x + 3$$

Hopefully, this is a well-defined problem. We are to take each of the eleven different values of x and use the formula to calculate the corresponding value of y.

Step 2: Develop a procedure for solving the problem.

One algorithm which would solve the problem is the following thirty-four step procedure.

Algorithm A (Brute Force)

  1. Set x = 0
  2. Calculate y using the formula
  3. Write down the value of x and y
  4. Set x = 1
  5. Calculate y using the formula
  6. Write down the value of x and y
  7. Set x = 2
  8. .
  9. .
10. .
    .
    .
    .
31. Set x = 10
32. Calculate y using the formula
33. Write down the value of x and y
34. Stop

If a robot were to follow this set of instructions, one after the other, the required eleven pairs of values of x and y would be produced. Using this algorithm, each step is executed once. Observe that any algorithm which solves the problem will require a minimum of thirty-four instructions to be executed.

Is this a good algorithm? In one sense it is the best because by using this algorithm the fewest number of steps necessary to solve the problem will be executed. Suppose however that the problem required us to use the values x=0, 1, 2, ..., 9999, 10000. The algorithm would then contain 30004 intructions! The disadvantage of this Brute Force algorithm then, is that three instructions must be written down for each value of x used. Furthermore, following the first instruction

$$\text{Set } x = 0$$

which gives x its initial value, the following group of three instructions is repeated over and over:

Calculate y using the formula
Write down the value of x and y
Generate the next value of x

How long do we go on executing this group of intructions? The answer is "as long as x has a value less than or equal to 10". That is

$$\text{While } x \leq 10$$

When x is no longer less than or equal to ten, what should we do? Well, by then, we have done everything necessary to solve the problem so we stop. Thus an alternative algorithm is the following:

Algorithm B (Iterative)

1. Set x = 0
2. While $x \leq 10$ do the following
   .1 Calculate y using the formula
   .2 Write down the values of x and y
   .3 Add 1 to the value of x
3. Stop

If you are a first-time programmer, it may seem a little peculiar to set x=0 in step 1 and then immediately test if $x \leq 10$ in Step 2. You are absolutely right but remember that this test is wasted only the first time and it takes an inconsequential amount of time to execute. From then on, the test is necessary to determine if we are finished.

Note that the next value of x is generated by adding one to the current value of x. You should satisfy yourself that this algorithm does indeed solve the problem by following the instructions in a robot-like manner.

How many instructions are executed if Algorithm B is used to solve the problem? To the left of each step in the algorithm below is written the number of times that step is executed.

(1) 1. Set x =0
(12) 2. While $x \leq 10$ do
(11)   .1 Calculate the value of y
(11)   .2 Write down the value of x and y
(11)   .3 Add 1 to the value of x
(1) 3. Stop

Observe that the decision in the While statement is made 12 times -- once for each of the values of x=0 thru x=10 and also for x=11. This is necessary to decide if further processing is required. The total number of instructions executed using Algorithm B is 1+12+11+11+11+1 or 47 compared to the 34 needed for the brute-force approach of Algorithm A. Does this mean Algorithm A -- the brute force approach -- is better than Algorithm B which has a looping or iterative approach? Certainly it is more efficient to execute Algorithm A but consider the following two facts. First, the algorithm will be executed on a computer which executes hundreds of thousands of instructions per second. The extra time required to execute Alogrithm B will therefore be an insignificant fraction of a second. Are you willing to wait that much longer for the results?

Second, even more important than computer time is people time. In the brute-force algorithm we had to write down all thirty-four steps. In Algorithm B, we only had to write down 6 instructions. One last point. Suppose the problem required using values of x from 0 thru 10000. How many instructions are there in Algorithm A? How many in Algorithm B? The foregoing discussion should convince you of the advantage of an *iterative algorithm*. Almost all computer algorithms have this property. With a little practice you will find it easy to think iteratively.

How do we describe the data associated with an algorithm? For an algorithm which will be translated into a computer program, we must describe the constants and variables which are used in the algorithm. Our algorithm contains three specific constants, namely 0, 10 and 1 and two variables x and y which take on integer values. Now we shall translate the algorithm into the Pascal programming language.

Step 3: Transform the algorithm into a computer program. Shown below is the Pascal program which is a translation of the algorithm.

```
PROGRAM EXAMPLE1 (OUTPUT);

(* THIS PROGRAM CALCULATES VALUES OF
   Y = X*X -2*X +3 FOR X=0, X=1, ..., X=10 *)

VAR
  X, Y : INTEGER;

BEGIN (* EXAMPLE1 *)
  X := 0;
  WHILE X <= 10 DO
    BEGIN
      Y := X*X - 2*X +3;
      WRITELN ( X,Y );
      X := X + 1
    END
END. (* EXAMPLE1 *)
```

The Pascal program consists of two parts, namely the first line and the rest of the program. "Isn't that rather obvious?", you might say. However the first line is called the *program header* and the remainder is called the *program block*. A semicolon separates the program header and the program block.

Consider the program header.

```
PROGRAM EXAMPLE1  (OUTPUT)
```

A program header contains:

- the word 'PROGRAM', followed by

- the name of the program, followed by

- a list of the files used in the program enclosed in parentheses.

The choice of the program name is up to you. Detailed rules for names are given in Chapter 2. Any name can be used as long as it starts with a letter and contains only letters or digits thereafter.

In this example we use only one file called "OUTPUT". Whenever we tell the computer to write a line of information, it is sent to the OUTPUT file. Depending on the particular version of Pascal you are using, this may be either a display screen, a printer, or both. All of the programs in this book contain OUTPUT in the program header. The INPUT file is first used in Chapter 2 while files in general are discussed in Chapter 12.

The pair of lines:

```
(* THIS PROGRAM CALCULATES VALUES OF Y = X*X - 2X + 3
   FOR VALUES OF X OF 0, 1, 2, ..., 10                *)
```

illustrates a *program comment*. Comments are used to provide anecdotal information about the purpose of a program, the author of a program, and/or the algorithm and data. Comments are enclosed within a pair of matching delimiters. You have two choices of delimiter pairs:

$$(* \text{ and } *) \quad \text{or} \quad \{ \text{ and } \}$$

In this book, the character pairs (* and *) are used in example comments. There is no restriction on the number or kind of characters which may appear between comment delimiters except that once begun, the first occurence of the matching delimiter terminates the comment.

Consider now the program block. It contains two sections, namely a declaration followed by the body of the block. The declaration consists of the pair of lines

```
VAR
   X, Y : INTEGER;
```

This is an example of a *VAR* (pronounced "vair") declaration which defines
the variables used in the program and the type of value each may have. All
programs except those used as a hand calculator have a VAR declaration.
(The first programming problem at the end of the chapter is an example of a
hand calculator problem.) Programs may also have other kinds of declarations
which are described in later chapters. In this example, the VAR declaration
declares X and Y to be variables of the type INTEGER. That is, X and Y
can only be given integer or whole-number values.

Although it is not necessary to put "VAR" by itself on a separate line, it
is considered good programming practice. That is, the single line

```
VAR X, Y : INTEGER;
```

is equivalent in every way to the pair of lines above because in Pascal the
number of blanks between the items VAR and X (or any other two objects)
doesn't matter. Observe that the program in fact contains three completely
blank lines which could be omitted. They were included to improve the
readability of the program.

A semicolon separates the declaration from the body of the block. The
body of the program block contains the following lines.

```
BEGIN (* EXAMPLE1 *)
  X := 0;
  WHILE X <= 10 DO
    BEGIN
      Y := X*X - 2*X +3;
      WRITELN ( X,Y );
      X := X + 1
    END
END. (* EXAMPLE1 *)
```

The body of a block contains the "action statements" in a Pascal program.
These statements are contained within a BEGIN-END pair which defines a
single compound statement. This compound statement is followed by a period
denoting the end of the program. BEGIN and END are really like brackets
which delimit or enclose a sequence of one or more statements.

The statements within a BEGIN-END pair are normally indented two or
three spaces. In the example, the comment (* EXAMPLE 1 *) follows the
BEGIN and END that delimit the body of the program. This practice is
recommended and further emphasizes that comments can appear anywhere
within a program.

The statements within the body of the block have a one-for-one
correspondence with the steps in the algorithm. We shall look at each in turn.

The translation of "Set x = 0" is the Pascal statement "X := 0". It causes the variable X to be assigned a value of zero. Statements of the form

```
variable := value
```

are called *assignment statements*. In many programs, over half the statements are assignment statements. A common mistake of beginning programmers is to leave out the colon in the *assignment operator* ":=". X = 0 means something entirely different and will cause an error if mistakenly used as an assignment operator.

A semicolon separates the assignment statement from the WHILE statement which follows. Semicolons are used to separate successive statements in the body of the block.

The algorithm specifies that three things are to be done as long as the value of X is less than or equal to 10. That test is translated into

```
WHILE X <= 10 DO
```

The word WHILE is followed by an expression which is either true or false. The expression is "X <= 10". Observe that the less than or equal to relationship is written as the pair of characters "<=". Six relationships can be tested. They are:

Relationship	Usual Representation in Pascal	Alternative Representation
<	<	LT
≤	<=	LE
=	=	EQ
≥	>=	GE
>	>	GT
≠	<>	NE

Note that not equal is equivalent to "less than or greater than". The word "DO" which follows the condition being tested indicates that the *single* statement which follows is to be done as long as the condition is true. Because we want to do more than one thing when x ≤ 10, we must use a compound statement after the DO. The compound statement is the following.

```
BEGIN
  Y := X*X - 2*X + 3;
  WRITELN ( X, Y );
  X := X + 1
END
```

Within the compound statement, the first statement is:

```
Y := X * X - 2 * X + 3
```

Beginning programmers often forget that 2X is really two times X -- so remember to include the multiplication operator '*'. A semicolon separates the assignment statement from the statement

```
WRITELN ( X, Y )
```

This statement means "Write a line containing the values of X and Y on the OUTPUT file." WRITELN is the name of a predefined procedure which is built into the Pascal language. The list of values to be sent to the OUTPUT file are separated from each other by a comma and the list is enclosed in parentheses.

The third step to be performed when $X \leq 10$ is to "Add 1 to x". In Pascal, this becomes the assignment statement "X := X + 1". Remember that an assignment statement calculates the value on the right and assigns it to the variable on the left. The expression on the right adds one to X. This value then replaces the current value of X.

Before continuing, let us summarize a few important points. A Pascal program consists of a program header followed by a program block followed by a period. A program block consists of declarations and a body. The body consists of a single, compound (BEGIN-END) statement containing one or more statements.

1.   A semicolon is used to separate, not terminate, statements. This means that whatever precedes a semicolon must be the end of a statement and what follows it must be the start of a statement. This explains why there is never a semicolon after BEGIN (BEGIN is not a statement) nor before an END (END is not a statement) nor after DO (DO separates the true-false expression from the statement to be executed when the expression is true).

2.   Blanks can and should be used liberally between and within statements to improve the appearance of a program. However, blanks are not permitted between the character pairs :=, <=, >=, <>, (* and *).

3.   There are many rules of good programming style. Style guidelines are found throughout the book. If followed, they will not only improve the readability of your programs but make it easier to find and correct mistakes. Two of the style guidelines described in this chapter are to use comments and to indent the lines between matching BEGIN-ENDs and after a WHILE.

How many statements are there in the following six lines taken from the example?

```
WHILE X <= 10 DO
  BEGIN
    Y := X*X + 2*X + 3;
    WRITELN ( X, Y );
    X := X + 1
  END
```

If you said one, two or five, you're right! Collectively, all six lines can be thought of as a single WHILE statement. Or, two would be correct if you viewed the lines as a WHILE statement containing a single compound statement. Finally, you could argue that there is a WHILE statement (the whole thing), a compound statement (the lines BEGIN thru END), two assignment statements and a procedure called WRITELN. The message is simply that it depends on your point of view. Note that even viewed as five statements, only two semicolons are necessary. Any other place you might think of putting them violates the requirement that what precedes must end a statement and what follows must begin a statement.

There are two questions which may have crossed your mind which have not yet been answered. First, do you have to use upper case letters? The answer is "no", both upper and lower case can be used and are treated as being equivalent. Thus X and x are interchangeable as are "ProGraM", "pROgRAm", "PROgram", "program", "PROGRAM" or any other of the 128 combinations of upper and lower case spellings of the word.

Second, can whole numbers be written with decimal points? This will be discussed completely in Chapter 2. For the examples used in this chapter, it doesn't matter. The basic rule is that if a decimal point is used, there must be at least one digit before and one digit after the decimal point.

Step 4: Enter the Program. After the somewhat lengthy but important discussion of our first example program, we come to the fourth step in the problem-solving process -- that of entering the program in the memory of the computer so that it can be run (compiled and executed). When doing this, an additional line is entered ahead of the program header as shown below.

```
$JOB PASCAL
PROGRAM EXAMPLE1 (OUTPUT);
     .
     .  (as shown previously)
     .
END. (* EXAMPLE1 *)
```

The line "$JOB PASCAL" simply indicates that what follows is a Pascal program. The contents and format of this "job control" statement may differ slightly from one computing center to another. Some compilers may also require a second job control statement such as "$ENTRY" at the end of the program. Check with your instructor or consultant for the details which apply in your environment.

If the program is recorded on punched cards, one card is punched for each line in the program. If the program is being typed directly into a computer file using a keyboard/ screen device (a terminal) then one record in the file is created for each line in the program.

Step 5: Run the program. The fifth and final step (if no mistakes have been made!!) is to have the Pascal compiler read the source file and

1. Translate the Pascal program contained in the file into strings of ones and zeros (i.e. compile the program)

2. Execute the instructions represented by the bit strings producing the desired output.

Shown below is the printed output produced when the example Pascal program is processed by the Pascal compiler used at the University of Waterloo.

```
WATERLOO PASCAL -- ( CMS, 80/6/10 ):
    1  |    PROGRAM  EXAMPLE1  (OUTPUT);
    2  |
    3  |    (* THIS  PROGRAM  CALCULATES  VALUES  OF
    4  |        Y = X*X  -2X  +3 FOR  X=0,  X=1,  ..., X=10 *)
    5  |
    6  |    VAR
    7  |      X,  Y :  INTEGER;
    8  |
    9  |    BEGIN (* EXAMPLE1 *)
   10  |      X :=  0;
   11  |      WHILE  X <= 10 DO
   12  |        BEGIN
   13  |          Y :=  X*X  -  2*X +3;
   14  |          WRITELN ( X,Y );
   15  |          X :=  X + 1
   16  |        END
   17  |    END. (* EXAMPLE1 *)
```

Note that the compiler prints each line in the program exactly as entered. A line number is printed on the left to make references contained in error messages easy to find. Since there were no errors in our program, the computer executes the machine language instructions produced by the compiler. The run-time output is shown below.

```
Execution begins...
```

0	3
1	2
2	3
3	6
4	11
5	18
6	27
7	38
8	51
9	66
10	83

```
...execution ends
File 'ONE1': 17 lines; no diagnostics
402 bytes of object code generated
46 statements executed
10608 bytes of memory requested during compilation
```

This execution-time output consists of the message "Execution begins" followed by the results of executing the statements and a summary of computer resources used. The values of X and Y are printed two per line as specified by the WRITELN procedure. By default, twelve print positions are made available to print each INTEGER value. Each value is right-justified meaning it appears in the rightmost positions of those available.

The summary information indicates that the program has: 17 lines; that no errors or warnings were detected; that the compiler produced 402 bytes (one byte equals 8 bits) of machine language instructions; and that 46 Pascal statements were executed. (You should verify this by examining the program). The last line indicates the amount of memory used when compiling the source program.

1.5 Exercise 1.1

1. Modify the algorithm used in the example to process the following values of x:

   a) X = 0, 2, 4, 6, 8, 10

   b) X = -1, 4, 9 , 14, 19

   c) X = -10, -9, -8, ... , 9, 10

   d) X = 100, 99, 98, ... , 2, 1

2. Suppose the formula used for y in the example problem is changed. Write an assignment statement to assign y each of the following expressions in x.

   a) $x^3 - x$

b)   14(x - 7)

c) $5x^5 + 4x^4 + 3x^3 + 2x^2 + x + 8$

3.   Explain why 46 statements were executed when the example program was run.

4.   Consider the following program fragment.

```
X := 10;
WHILE X <= 5 DO
   X := X - 1;
WRITELN (X)
```

a)   How many Pascal statements does the program fragment contain?

b)   How many statements are executed if the fragment is executed?

5.   Suppose in the program EXAMPLE1 that the lines containing WRITELN and "X := X+1" are interchanged. What is the output?

6.   The lines below contain a perfectly valid Pascal program. Re-format them to demonstrate good programming style and predict the output when the program is run. Enter and run the program to verify your answer.

```
PROGRAM DUMBSTYLE   (OUTPUT);VAR MOM,
DAD:INTEGER;BEGIN MOM:=5;DAD:=25;WHILE MOM<=
DAD DO BEGIN MOM := MOM + MOM END;WRITELN(
MOM) END.
```

1.6 What Happens When An Error is Made?

There are five steps in the problem-solving process. Naturally it is possible to make a mistake in any one of them. A computer is of no help in correcting errors in the problem definition or in the logic defined by an algorithm -- that is something only you can do. If you make a mistake in programming such as writing an invalid Pascal statement however, it will be caught during the compile-time of the program. Consider the following program which contains three errors. (Can you find them?)

```
PROGRAM ERRORS (OUTPUT);

(* THIS PROGRAM CALCULATES VALUES OF
   Y = X*X -2X +3 FOR X=0, X=1, ..., X=10 *)

VAR
  X, Y : INTEGER

BEGIN (* EXAMPLE1 *)
  X = 0;
  WHILE X <= 10 DO
      Y := X*X - 2X +3;
      WRITELN ( X,Y );
      X := X + 1
END. (* ERRORS *)
```

What follows is the output produced when this program is run.

```
WATERLOO PASCAL -- ( CMS, 83/9/18 ):
   1  |   PROGRAM ERRORS (OUTPUT);
   2  |
   3  |   (* THIS PROGRAM CALCULATES VALUES OF
   4  |      Y = X*X -2X +3 FOR X=0, X=1, ..., X=10 *)
   5  |
   6  |   VAR
   7  |      X, Y : INTEGER
   8  |
   9  |   BEGIN (* EXAMPLE1 *)
********* ?????
*** Error: Incorrect syntax near 'begin' Missing ';'
  10  |      X = 0;
*** Error: 'x' is not a procedure
*** Error: Incorrect syntax near '='
'=' in input discarded - scanning for recognizable construct
  11  |      WHILE X <= 10 DO
  12  |          Y := X*X - 2X +3;
*************************** ?
*** Error: Incorrect syntax near 'x'
'x' in input discarded - scanning for recognizable construct
  13  |          WRITELN ( X,Y);
  14  |          X := X + 1
  15  |   END. (* EXAMPLE1 *)
File 'Errors': 15 lines; 4 errors, no warnings
342 bytes of object code generated
no statements executed
```

The first indication that something is wrong is the line of asterisks and question marks following line 9. The error reported is:

```
*** Error: Incorrect syntax near 'begin'  Missing ';'
```

But, you are saying the BEGIN line is exactly the same as in EXAMPLE1 which ran perfectly! A *syntax error* is an error in grammar or punctuation. The clue comes from the phrase "Missing ';'". We know BEGIN never has a semicolon after it (it is not a statement) so the missing punctuation must be required *before* the BEGIN. Looking back one line we find the problem. There is no semicolon to separate the end of the declaration from the beginning of the body of the block. Why wasn't the error detected before the BEGIN was encountered? Remember that the compiler processes the program one statement at a time. It wasn't until after the BEGIN was read that the error condition could be recognized. The lesson here is that sometimes you must look backward in a program to find the cause of an error.

The second pair of error messages follows the line "X = 0;" and is:

```
*** Error: 'x' is not a procedure
*** Error:  Incorrect syntax near '='
```

As is often the case, one message is more helpful than another. The fact that "x is not a procedure" won't mean much until we have studied PROCEDUREs in Chapter 8. On the other hand, "Incorrect syntax near '='" is much more informative. The answer is that the '=' by itself, is not the assignment operator, it is one of the six relational operators for comparing two values. Since the assignment operator is needed, the remedy is to replace the equal sign with ':='.

The cause of the third error "Incorrect syntax near 'x'" is fairly obvious. It has nothing to do with "X*X" but refers to "2X". The multiplication operator '*' needs to be inserted between the 2 and the X.

Suppose we fix the three compiler-detected errors and run the program. After the message "Execution begins ...", what do we get? Absolutely nothing!! Why? Let's do some logical thinking. Since no output was displayed, the WRITELN procedure must never have been executed. This means the program execution must have been stuck doing something else (caught in a never-ending loop of instructions) before the WRITELN procedure. The only loop we have in the algorithm is the one beginning "While x≤10". If the condition is true the algorithm says to perform the *group* of three steps which follows. In the program however, we always execute the *single* statement which follows the WHILE-DO. And what is the statement which follows the DO?. You guessed it – the assignment statement "Y:=X*X-2*X+3". In other words, the computer executed the assignment statement over and over again. After each execution it tested x≤10 and if true, executed the assignment again. Since nothing caused x to change its value, it continued to do this until either the time limit for the job was exceeded or you interrupted the process. Note that we indented what we thought were the loop statements properly. Indentation however, means nothing to the Pascal compiler -- it is for our benefit only. Remember that a WHILE statement causes a *single* statement to be executed. So if you want more than one thing done when the WHILE expression is true, you must use a compound statement. The correction for the error is therefore to enclose the three statements following the WHILE line in BEGIN-END delimiters. When this is done, the program runs correctly.

In summary, errors can occur at compile time or at execution time. Diagnosing and removing errors from a program is called *debugging* a program. If you make a logic error however, the smartest computer in the world can't help you. Top notch experienced programmers seldom make errors of either type. However while you are learning to develop algorithms and write Pascal programs, you should experiment. Try different ways of accomplishing the same thing. Make use of the full capabilities of the Pascal language. In this way you will develop your self-confidence to write readable, bug-free and efficient programs.

1.7 A Second Example

Step 1: Problem definition. Use the computer to find the average of the integer values between 1 and 50 inclusive. Is the problem clear? We are to compute the value of $(1+2+3+...+50)/50$.

Step 2: Develop an algorithm. To get the average, we must first find the total of the fifty values. So our overall algorithm will be:

1. Calculate the sum $1+2+3+...+50$
2. Set average = sum/50
3. Write down the result

How do we calculate the sum? With practice it may be easy to write down an iterative algorithm directly from a problem statement. If not, begin with a brute-force approach. This involves successively adding the values 1 thru 50 to a running total which initially is set to zero. The brute-force algorithm to find the sum is therefore:

1. Set total = 0
2. Set number = 1
3. Add number to total
4. Set number = 2
5. Add number to total
6. Set number = 3
7. Add number to total

  .

  .

100. Set number = 50
101. Add number to total

Now we ask three questions. First, "What is being repeated over and over again?" The answer:

Add Number to Total
Set Number = one more than previous value

(The reason for putting the addition step first will become clear in a moment.) Second, "What is changing each time these steps are repeated?" The answer: "The value of Number increases by 1." Third, how long do we repeat this pair of steps? Answer: "As long as Number is 50 or less." This analysis leads to the iterative algorithm shown below which, after initializing Total and Number to 0 and 1 respectively, continues to add Number to Total and add 1 to Number as long as Number $\leq$ 50. The complete algorithm is therefore:

1. Calculate sum of 1+2+3+ ... +50
    .1 Set total = 0
    .2 Set number = 1
    .3 While number $\leq$ 50 do
        .1 Add number to total
        .2 Add 1 to number
2. Set average = total/50
3. Write down the average

Observe that the algorithm has three main steps. Within the first step are three substeps and within the third substep (the while) are two more substeps. Many algorithms have this structure -- steps-within-steps- within-steps -- sometimes to a depth of twenty or more levels. When developing algorithms, always start from the outside level and work inward getting into greater and greater detail as you do. This process has the fancy name of *stepwise refinement*. A simple way of viewing this approach is to view it as a sequence of "what-how" steps. That is, first write down a sequence of simple steps of what is to be done. Then, for each of these tasks write down how it is to be done. (This is the refinement process.) Each step in the "how" becomes a "what" at the next level of detail.

Now, why is Number assigned a value before entering the while loop? The reason is that a while loop requires a condition to be tested *before* the body of the loop is executed. Therefore Number must be given a value before the loop is entered because this is the condition we wish to test for terminating the loop.

Once the logic of the algorithm is satisfactory, the next step is to examine the algorithm to determine its data requirements. In our example we see we need three variables, namely: Total, Number and Average. The first two take on integer values whereas Average may be a non-integer value.

Step 3: Translate the algorithm into Pascal. In the program below, variables of type REAL are used instead of INTEGER variables that were used in the first example. Variables of type REAL can be assigned both integer and non-integer values and it is quite possible that the average is not a whole number.

```
PROGRAM AVERAGE (OUTPUT);

(* THIS PROGRAM CALCULATES THE AVERAGE
    OF THE FIRST 50 NATURAL NUMBERS      *)

VAR
    TOTAL, NUMBER, AVERAGE : REAL;

BEGIN (* AVERAGE *)
  PAGE;
  TOTAL := 0;
  NUMBER := 1;
  WHILE NUMBER <= 50 DO
    BEGIN
      TOTAL := TOTAL + NUMBER;
      NUMBER := NUMBER + 1
    END; (* WHILE *)
  AVERAGE := TOTAL/50.0;
  WRITELN('THE AVERAGE IS',AVERAGE)
END. (* AVERAGE *)
```

Comments: There are three new programming ideas in this example. Note that the program has exactly the same overall structure as the first example.

To declare variables to be of type REAL, the list of such variables is followed by a colon and the word REAL. Numbers containing a decimal point have at least one digit on each side of the decimal point. Although this program uses only REAL values and the first example used only INTEGER values, most programs which process numbers contain a mixture of the two types.

The single line of execution-time output is shown below. Note how values of REAL variables are printed. Chapter 2 describes how to print REAL values in the more customary way.

THE AVERAGE IS 2.550000000E+01

The "E+01" means "times ten to the one". Thus the value represented is 25.5.

The second new feature is the use of the PAGE procedure to skip to the top of a page. PAGE is a standard procedure in Pascal which causes the next line of execution-time output to be written at the top of the next page.

The third new feature is contained in the line

WRITELN ('THE AVERAGE IS', AVERAGE)

The 'THE AVERAGE IS' is an example of a literal or string constant. Literals should be included in WRITELN operations to describe the values being printed or to print a TITLE as in

WRITELN ('THIS IS EXAMPLE TWO')

A literal consists of a string of characters enclosed within single quotes. If it is necessary to include a quote within a literal, put two quotes in succession. The word WRITELN all by itself can be used to print a blank line.

1.8 A Third Example

Step 1: Problem definition. One method of finding the square root of a number is the following. Make an initial estimate of the value of the square root -- say half the number. Call this estimate X1. If A denotes the number, then X1 = A/2. Given X1., a better estimate X2 is given by:

X2 = 1/2 (X1 + A/X1)

An even better estimate X3 can be obtained using X2 in the same formula. That is

X3 = 1/2 (X2 + A/X2)

In general by repeating this process over and over again, one can obtain increasingly accurate estimates of the square root of any positive value. Why does this method work? Observe that each estimate of the square root is the average of two values - one high, one low. Therefore the average is between the two. For example, the square root of 10 is 3.236. Now since 4 is a high estimate of the square root of 10 then because of what we mean by square root, it follows that 10/4 must be a low estimate. The average of these two, namely (4+2.5)/2 = 3.1 is a better estimate. That is precisely what the formula does, it takes the average of a high and a low estimate to give a better estimate.

Use this method to find the square root of 726.4. Continue calculating approximations until the change in the estimate is less than 0.001. Output the number, the final estimate and the number of estimates calculated.

Step 2: Develop an algorithm. If we are going to use an iterative algorithm, we must ask what is being done over and over again. The answer is we are calculating a better approximation of the square root using the previous estimate to obtain it. Second, what is changing each time? Answer: the previous estimate is used as the old estimate. Third, how long do we continue repetitions? Answer: until the new estimate differs from the old estimate by less than 0.001.

We will use a while loop to control the execution of the repetitive steps. It will look something like

$$\text{While difference of old and new estimate} < 0.001 \text{ do}$$

At the beginning of the algorithm, what should be used for the old and new estimates? If half the number is used as the first estimate, then we can use anything we want - even the number itself as the old estimate. This discussion indicates that occasionally we need to initialize more than one value prior to entering a loop. Our algorithm is therefore:

1. Initialize
   .1 Set Number = 726.4
   .2 Set Old Estimate = Number
   .3 Set Estimate = Number/2
   .4 Set Count = 1
2. While difference of Old Estimate and Estimate
              is greater than 0.001 do
   .1 Set Count = Count + 1
   .2 Set Old Estimate = Estimate
   .3 Set Estimate = (Old Estimate + Number/Old Estimate)/2
3. Write down the values of Number, Estimate and Count

Before writing the program, a list of variables is needed. Number, Old Estimate, and Estimate may have REAL values; Count will be INTEGER-valued. The two constants used are 2 and 0.001.

We are now ready to write the program.

Step 3: Translate Algorithm into a Pascal program. The algorithm appears in the body of the block in the following program. What are the two new ideas?

```
PROGRAM SQUARE_ROOT(OUTPUT);

(* THIS PROGRAM COMPUTES THE SQUARE ROOT OF 726.4
   BY CALCULATING SUCCESSIVELY BETTER APPROXIMATIONS
   OF THE VALUE, STOPPING WHEN THE IMPROVEMENT IS
   LESS THAN 0.001                                    *)

VAR
  NUMBER, OLD_ESTIMATE, ESTIMATE : REAL;
  COUNT                          : INTEGER;

BEGIN (* SQUARE_ROOT *)
  (* INITIALIZE *)
    NUMBER := 726.4;
    OLD_ESTIMATE := NUMBER;
    ESTIMATE := NUMBER / 2;
    COUNT := 1;
  WHILE ABS(OLD_ESTIMATE - ESTIMATE) > 0.001 DO
    BEGIN
      OLD_ESTIMATE := ESTIMATE;
      ESTIMATE := (OLD_ESTIMATE + NUMBER/OLD_ESTIMATE)/2;
      COUNT := COUNT + 1
    END;
  WRITELN('ESTIMATE NUMBER',COUNT,' OF THE SQUARE ROOT OF');
  WRITELN(NUMBER,' IS',ESTIMATE)
END. (* SQUARE_ROOT *)
```

When the program is entered and run, the output is the pair of lines below.

```
ESTIMATE NUMBER                9 OF THE SQUARE ROOT OF
7.264000000E+02 IS 2.695180884E+01
```

That is the square root of 726.4 to within .001 is 26.952. It takes nine iterations of the loop algorithm to obtain this result. Now let's look at what's new in this program.

The VAR declaration defines both REAL and INTEGER variables. Observe the syntax of the declaration namely:

```
VAR
  list of REAL variables: REAL;
  list of INTEGER variables: INTEGER;
```

More than one list of variables of any type can be used if desired. Furthermore the variables and the types can be in any order. For example, the following declaration is equivalent.

```
VAR
   OLD_ESTIMATE : REAL;
   COUNT : INTEGER;
   EST, NUMBER : REAL;
```

Chapter 2 provides complete details of the VAR declaration.

Second, consider the line

```
WHILE ABS(OLD_ESTIMATE - ESTIMATE)> 0.001
```

The expression ABS(OLD_ESTIMATE - ESTIMATE)is used to obtain the absolute value of the difference of the two estimates. ABS is one of the predefined functions built into the Pascal language. Chapter 2 describes the predefined functions available for processing INTEGER and REAL values.

1.9 Exercise 1.2

1. Modify the algorithm in Example 3 to:

    a) print the value of each estimate

    b) stop after six estimates have been obtained

    c) stop when the change in estimate is less than .1 percent of the value
        of the number. Is this a good idea?

2. Assuming that the standard function SQRT produces the correct value of
    the square root, modify the algorithm for Example 3 to determine the
    square root of seven correct to 0.001.

3. What happens if an attempt is made to use the algorithm for Example 3
    to find the square root of a negative value? What should be done to avoid
    this happening?

4. The lines below form a complete Pascal program that runs without errors.

    ```
    PROGRAM EX1_3(
    OUTPUT);VAR I,J
        :INTEGER;BEGIN I:=-5;J:=I*I+I;WHILE I
    <J DO BEGIN WRITELN(I-J
    );I:=2*I+10 END END.
    ```

    a)   What is the output produced?

    b)   Reformat the lines in the program to show proper indentation.
         (Indentation guidelines are found in the next section.)

1.10 Program Style

Good programmers not only have the ability to develop straightforward algorithms to solve complex problems, they also know how to write programs which are easy to understand and hence make it easy to find and correct errors.

Well-written programs have the following characteristics:

- comments are used liberally

- blanks are used to separate symbols and parts of the program

- names of variables are meaningful

- consistent indentation rules are followed

With respect to indentation rules, the following guidelines are provided. These are used in the example programs throughout the book. Other programming style recommendations are found in the chapters which follow.

Indentation Guidelines

- The reserved words PROGRAM, VAR, and the BEGIN-END pair defining the body of the program are vertically aligned.

- The VAR declarations begin on the line below VAR and are indented. Each list of variables of a given type begins on a new line.

- Statements within a BEGIN-END pair are indented and vertically aligned.

- The statement which is the body of a WHILE is indented.

1.11 Summary

After studying the material in this chapter you should be able to write simple programs such as those found in the programming problems in the next section.

1. The vocabulary introduced in this chapter includes the following terms which you should understand.

> computer - a   collection of electronic components used to input, process and output numbers and characters
>
> algorithm - a procedure for solving a problem
>
> computer program - a sequence of instructions written in a language a computer understands
>
> compiler - a   program which "understands" a programming language
>
> compile-time   - the time during which the compiler translates a program to machine language
>
> execution-time - the time during which the machine language instructions produced by the compiler are executed by the computer

2. There are five steps in using a computer to help solve a problem. They are:
    1. Define the problem.
    2. Develop an algorithm for solving the problem
    3. Translate the algorithm into a computer program.
    4. Enter the program.
    5. Run (compile and execute) the program.

3. Pascal can manipulate two kinds of numbers -- INTEGER and REAL. BOOLEAN (true-false) values are described in Chapter 3 and CHAR(character) value processing is discussed in Chapter 4.

4. All Pascal programs have the following structure.

```
            PROGRAM name (OUTPUT);
                  declarations;
    block
                  body.
```

5. The statements used in the example programs are:

    • BEGIN-END creates a compound statement

    • the assignment statement assigns a value to a variable

    • the WHILE statement controls the number of times a statement is executed

    • The predefined procedure WRITELN is used to display printed values. ABS and SQRT are examples of predefined functions.

PROGRAMMING PROBLEMS

1. Write a Pascal program to calculate the sum of 127 and 584.

2. Tabulate (calculate and print) the values of

    $$y = 3x^2 - 2x + 7$$
    $$\text{for } x = 1, 3, 5, .., 21$$

3. The SQR function in Pascal produces the square of a value. Use SQR to print values of x, x^2, x^4, x^8, x^{16} for $x = 1.25$. Use a looping algorithm.

4. Calculate and display the first eight values in the sequence x, $x^3/3$, $x^6/6$, $x^{10}/10$,... Observe that the exponent and the denominator in sucessive terms increase by 2,3,4,etc. Take this into account in defining the loop in the algorithm and corresponding program.

5. Calculate the sums 1^3, 1^3+2^3, $1^3+2^3+3^3$, ..., $1^3+2^3+3^3+..+9^3$. Print the square root of each sum of cubes. What general result is being illustrated?

6. In the Fibonacci sequence of numbers 1,1,2,3,5,8,..., each term after the first two is obtained by adding the values of the two previous terms. Write a program to calculate and display the first 15 terms in the Fibonacci sequence.

7. Write a program to print your name in large letters as illustrated below. (Use a sequence of 7 WRITELNs.)

8. One measure of the spread of a set of N values (called the variance)
    $X_1, X_2, X_3, .., X_N$ is given by the formula

    $$\frac{(X_1 - AVG)^2 + (X_2 - AVG)^2 + .. + (X_N - AVG)^2}{N}$$

    where AVG is the average of the N values.

    a) Develop an algorithm to calculate the variance of the set of values a,
        a+k, a+2k, .. a+(N-1)k

    b) Using a=5, k=3, N=10, translate the algorithm into Pascal and run
        the program.

9. Because the SQRT function in Pascal produces the positive root, it can be
    used with the SQR function to obtain the absolute value of any number.
    For example SQRT(SQR(-3)) is 3. Use this technique to tabulate values
    of z given by the following formula.

    $$z = \frac{x^2 + 3y^2 - 2xy}{|x^2 - y^2|}$$

    Use x = -3, -2, -1, 0, 1, 2, 3 and for *each* value of x calculate z using y
    = -2, 0, 2. Note that one of the steps in the loop which controls x will
    be an inner loop to generate the y values.

CHAPTER 2: NUMBERS, ARITHMETIC AND VARIABLES

Questions Answered in this Chapter:

1. How do we define and process REAL and INTEGER numbers?

2. What are the rules for evaluating arithmetic expressions?

3. How do we define variables in Pascal? What are the two ways of assigning values to them?

2.1 Numbers in Pascal

In the Pascal language, a number has three parts -- a whole number part, a fractional part, and an exponent part. The whole number part is required; the fractional and exponent parts are optional. Some examples of Pascal numbers follow.

> 234   (whole number part only)
> -7.65   (whole number and fractional parts)
> +41E2   (whole number and exponent parts; the exponent E2 means
>   "times 10^2" Therefore the value of the number is 4100)
> 862.5E-1 (whole number, fractional and exponent parts; the value is
> 862.5×10^{-1} or 86.25)

If a number contains only the whole number part, it is called an INTEGER number. If it contains either the fractional part, the exponent part or both it is called a REAL number. Because there are important differences in the processing of INTEGER and REAL values, we will discuss them separately. If it doesn't matter whether a value is INTEGER or REAL, we will simply use the word "number".

2.2 INTEGER Values

An INTEGER value represents a whole number and is written as a sequence of digits preceded by an optional '+' or '-'. It does not contain a decimal point or use a comma to separate groups of digits. Examples of valid INTEGERs are:

> 123   -4574   +2   0

A good way of describing the rule for a valid INTEGER constant is to use a syntax diagram. The syntax diagram for an INTEGER is shown below.

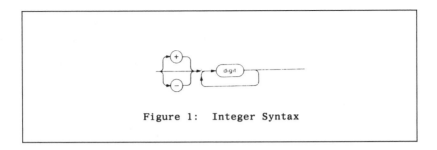

Figure 1:   Integer Syntax

These diagrams are sometimes called "railroad diagrams" because you can "get on the railroad" at the entry point and follow any path or track you like to the exit. In this example, each path that can be followed represents a valid INTEGER number. For example "+17" is a valid INTEGER because it can be obtained by going: through the plus sign; through "digit"; back around and through "digit" again before exiting. Note that "++9" and "-1,792" for example, are invalid because there is no path to create them. Note also that + 475 is invalid because the sign must immediately precede the first digit.

According to the syntax diagram, theoretically we could go around the digit loop forever. In fact however, the largest positive INTEGER value which can be used in Pascal is called MAXINT. On many large computers MAXINT has a value of 2147483647 or just over two billion. The reason for the funny value is that the binary number system is used to represent INTEGERs in the computer memory. The value 2147483647 is 2^{31} -1. The range of INTEGER values which can be used is:

```
-MAXINT, -MAXINT+1, -MAXINT+2, ...,-1,0,+1,...,MAXINT-1,MAXINT
```

Any attempt to define or create an INTEGER value outside this range causes an INTEGER "overflow" to occur. In most cases, this is undesirable but in some situations, we deliberately generate INTEGER overflows.

2.2.1 Operations With INTEGERs

There are six basic operations which can be performed with pairs of INTEGERs. These are:

```
+    addition
-    subtraction
*    multiplication
DIV division (result is an INTEGER)
/    division    (result is a REAL)
MOD remainder of an INTEGER division
```

What are the values of the following expressions?

```
  i) 3 + 2 * 4
 ii) 5 DIV 2
iii) 5 / 2
 iv) -4 * -3
  v) MAXINT * MAXINT
 vi) 3 * 5 DIV 4 * 2 MOD 7
vii) MAXINT + 1  - 1
```

We can learn all we need to know about INTEGER arithmetic by studying these examples. In some cases it might appear that more than one answer is possible. Fortunately there are absolutely unambiguous rules for evaluating all expressions. These rules will be summarized following a discussion of the examples.

Consider (i) The value of 3 +2 * 4 is 11 since multiplication has a higher priority than addition and is therefore done first.

In the second example the result is 2, not 2.5. The operator DIV requires an INTEGER dividend and an INTEGER divisor and produces the whole number part of the quotient as an INTEGER. Thus 3 DIV 4 is 0 (round off is not performed).

The value of 5/2 is 2.5. The slash symbol indicates "normal" division and produces a REAL value. It is discussed in greater detail in the next section.

In example (iv) the expression is "-4 * -3". This will produce an error message because it contains two operators in a row, namely multiplication and subtraction. To remove the error we could write it as -4 * (-3). This has the value +12 but is obtained by evaluating -(4 *(-3)) → +12. That is, a leading minus sign denotes subtraction and subtraction has a lower priority than multiplication. Note however that (-4) * (-3) expresses multiplication of two negative numbers and has a value of +12.

Example (v) is "MAXINT * MAXINT". This is an example of INTEGER overflow. Although it does not cause an error, predicting the result requires a detailed knowledge of the computer system on which the Pascal program is run.

Example (vi) has a value of 6 because multiplication, division and MOD (remainder) have equal priorities and are performed left to right. The sequence of operations leading to the result is

```
3 * 5 DIV 4 * 2 →    15 DIV 4 * 2 MOD 7
                →    3 * 2 MOD 7
                →    6 MOD 7
                →    6
```

Parentheses can and should be used to control and/or indicate the order of operations even if they are not required. For example, writing the expression as (((3*5)DIV 4)*2)MOD 7) clearly indicates how the expression is to be evaluated.

The last example is "MAXINT + 1 - 1". The result is not MAXINT! Why? Since addition and subtraction have equal priorities and are evaluated left to right, the evaluation proceeds by first computing MAXINT +1 causing an INTEGER overflow. Then 1 is subtracted from whatever value is produced.

There are four other operations with INTEGER values which produce INTEGER results. The effect of each of these can be obtained by using one or more of the operators + - * DIV but because they are so commonly used, predefined functions have been made available. In the list below, 'i' denotes an INTEGER value.

ABS(i) -absolute value of i
      e.g. ABS(-79) → 79

SQR(i) -square of i; equivalent to i * i
      e.g. SQR(2*5) → 100

SUCC(i) -successor of i; equivalent to i+1 except SUCC(MAXINT) is
      an error
      e.g. SUCC(-245) → -244

PRED(i) -predecessor of i; equivalent to i-1 except PRED(-MAXINT)
      is an error
      e.g. PRED(38) → 37

The priority of operations is summarized in the table below.

Order of Evaluation of Arithmetic Expressions

1. Function values; left to right
2. Parentheses; innermost first
3. *, /, DIV, MOD; equal priorities, left to right
4. +, -; equal priorities, left to right

Output of INTEGERS

When INTEGER values are displayed using a WRITELN statement as in "WRITELN(2, -759, MAXINT)", the Pascal processor uses a fixed number of positions (commonly 8 or 12) to display the value. The digits are shifted as far to the right as possible (right justified) in the space provided.

To control the number of spaces used to display an INTEGER value, a *format specifier* is placed after the value. The format specification consists of a colon followed by an INTEGER constant called the *field width* which denotes the number of spaces to use. An example is shown below.

```
WRITELN( 2:4, -759:8, MAXINT:20)
```

This causes the values of 2, -759 and MAXINT to be printed right justified in spaces of 4, 8 and 20 positions respectively. If the field width is too small, the width is increased to the minimum number of spaces necessary to display the value. If the number of values and/or the sum of the field widths exceed the length of line, the Pascal processor puts as many as it can on one line, prints it and continues at the beginning of the next line.

2.3 Exercise 2.1

1. Calculate the value of the following INTEGER expressions:
    ```
    a) 3 * 5 -3
    b) 3 -5 * 3
    c) 100 DIV 12 DIV 5
    d) -4 * 3 MOD 2
    e) (-17) MOD 5
    f) (-17) MOD (-5)
    g) PRED (SUCC ( -MAXINT))
    h) ABS (24 -92*SQR(5))
    ```

2. What is the error in each of the following?
    ```
    a) +20 * DIV * 3
    b) (4 * (2 - ABS (-8))
    c) 14 MOD PRED (1)
    d)  8 + PRED 7
    e)  10 DIV 3.0
    ```

3. Rewrite the expression below removing as many pairs of parentheses as is possible without changing the value of the expression.

    ```
    ((SQR((-5)*2)MOD 4)+SUCC(2DIV(5 MOD1)))
    ```

4. Using only the operators, +,-,*,DIV,MOD and the number 4, write INTEGER expressions which produce each of the values 1,2,3,...,20. For example, 4 DIV 4 → 1;

2.4 REAL Numbers

In mathematics, a number such as seven-and-three-eights can be written in many different but equivalent ways. Some of these are

$$7.375, \quad +0.007375 \text{ x } 10^3, \quad 737500 \text{ x } 10^{-5}$$

The term "floating point number" is used to describe numbers such as these because the decimal point can be made to "float along" the line of digits by multiplying by different powers of ten.

In PASCAL numbers that contain either a fractional part or an exponent part are called REAL numbers. The three values above for example, written as REAL numbers, are:

$$7.375, \quad +0.007375E3, \quad 737500E-5$$

The syntax of a REAL number is shown in the diagram below.

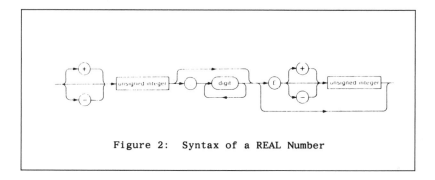

Figure 2:   Syntax of a REAL Number

Observe that an INTEGER number satisfies the syntax rules of REAL numbers. Hence, every INTEGER is also a REAL number. In this section however, we are concerned only with numbers having a fractional and/or an exponent part.

Some examples of invalid REAL numbers are:

```
2,457.21    (commas not allowed)
-7.         (fractional part must have one or more digits)
584E -20    (imbedded blanks not allowed)
.735        (no whole number part)
92.4E-3.8   (exponent must be an INTEGER)
```

Any number containing a decimal point or exponent is stored in the memory as though the decimal point preceded the first significant digit. Some examples follow.

Value in Pascal Program	Value Stored in Computer
7.375	+0.7375000E+01
-0.00621E-3	-0.6210000E-05
897524.0E27	+0.8975240E+33
+0.0	+0.0000000E+00

Given this information, we can now answer the question "What is the range of REAL numbers which can be used in a Pascal program?" There are two limits to consider. Each depends on the computer system used to run the program. First is the number of significant digits stored for each REAL value. On many computers this is 15. On a micro computer, sometimes as few as 4 significant digits are used. Second, the exponent range is also computer dependent with a range -75 to +75 being typical on many large computers.

The number line below shows the range of REAL numbers implied by the limits of the exponent value.

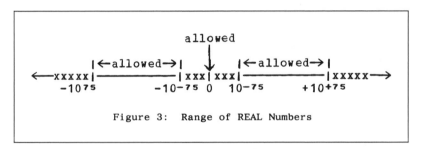

Figure 3:   Range of REAL Numbers

An attempt to write a REAL value in which the number of significant digits exceeds the maximum permitted will cause an error. Similarly, if a REAL number is written or generated with an exponent outside the permitted limits, an exponent underflow (too small) or exponent overflow (too large) occurs. Both of these are errors and execution terminates.

2.4.1 Operations with REAL Numbers

The operations of addition, subtraction, multiplication and division of REAL values have the same priorities as for INTEGER arithmetic. Some examples are:

Pascal Expression	Value	Stored in Memory
10.0/5+3.46	5.46	+0.5460000E+01
-30.0/8/100.0	-0.0375	-0.3750000E-01
4000.0+2.0*3000.0	10000.0	+0.1000000E+05
4.0 DIV 3.0	error	(DIV operates on INTEGER)
PRED (-10.2)	error	(PRED cannot be used with a REAL parameter)

The operators DIV and MOD and the standard functions PRED and SUCC cannot be used with REAL parameters.

There are two very important implications arising from the fact that only a fixed number of significant digits are stored for each REAL value.

First, consider the pair of expressions

a) 5.0E+20 - 5.0E+20 +1.0

b) 5.0E+20 +1.0 - 5.0E+20

The value of the first is 1.0 and that of the second is 0.0! Why? Assuming 15 significant digits are kept for each REAL value, the steps in the evaluation of each expression are shown below:

```
a)  500000000000000000000.0        b)500000000000000000000.0
   -500000000000000000000.0                            +1.0
   _____           _____
                       0.0                           5.0E20
                      +1.0                          -5.0E20
   _____           _____
                       1.0                              0.0
```

Note that in (b) the addition of 1 has no effect because only fifteen significant digits are kept in the sum.

Second, numbers in the computer's memory are stored using the binary number system. Recall that many functions cannot be represented exactly in the decimal number system using a finite number of digits. For example

1/3 = .33333333...

It is also true that many fractional values cannot be represented exactly in the binary system. For example

1/5 = .001100110011...

That is, there is often a small round-off error present when fractional values are stored in a computer. This leads to results such as

```
1/5 +1/5 +1/5 +1/5 +1/5 = .999999
```

The point to remember is that if one is working with fractional values the result may contain a round-off error. For example, how many times is the following WHILE loop executed?

```
X := 0.2;
WHILE X <> 1.0 DO
   X := X +  0.2
```

Because the value stored for 0.2 is only a very good approximation to one-fifth, the value of X *never exactly equals* 1. Therefore this loop does not terminate after five repetitions. To circumvent this problem you should test that the difference between the actual value and the exact value is acceptably small. This can be done as shown below:

```
X := 0.2;
WHILE ABS(X-1.0) > 0.00001 DO
   X := X + 0.2
```

The expression "ABS(X -1.0)" is the absolute value of the difference between the value of X and 1. The function value has the same type as its parameter. In this example as long as the ABS value is greater than some very small REAL value, we want to repeat the addition.

Since all INTEGER values are also REAL values, an INTEGER value may be used any place a REAL value can be used. If an operation involves both a REAL and an INTEGER value, the result is REAL. Examples are:

```
  i) 2 + 3.0 → 5.0 (result is REAL)

 ii) 1/4 → 0.25 (slash always produces a REAL result)

iii) 5 DIV 2 - 1.0 → 2 - 1.0
                   → 1.0

 iv) 5 DIV (2 - 1.0)→ 5 DIV 1.0
                    → error (DIV requires INTEGER arguments)
```

2.4.2 Standard Functions Involving REAL Values

The table below lists the standard functions available in Pascal for processing REAL values. In the table below;

r denotes a REAL value
i denotes an INTEGER value
x denotes either a REAL or INTEGER value

Purpose	Function Form	Type of Result	Examples
Absolute Value	ABS(r)	REAL	ABS(-4.0)→4.0
	ABS(i)	INTEGER	ABS(8)→8
Square	SQR(x)	INTEGER	SQR(-5.0)→25.0
Square Root	SQRT(x)	REAL	SQRT(25.0)→5.0
			SQRT(25)→5.0
Trigonometric	SIN(x)	REAL	SIN(2)→.9093
Functions	COS(x)	REAL	COS(2)→-.4161
(Angles in	ARCTAN(x)	REAL	ARCTAN(2)→1.107
Radians)			
Exponential	EXP(x)	REAL	EXP(2.3)→9.974
Natural Logarithm	LN(x)	REAL	LN(10)→2.303
Truncation	TRUNC(x)	INTEGER	TRUNC(7.8)→7
			TRUNC(-7.8)→-7
Round off	ROUND(x)	INTEGER	ROUND(7.8)→8
			ROUND(-7.8)→-8

2.4.3 Output of REAL Values

When WRITELN is used to display a REAL value, twenty positions are used to show the sign of the number, the fifteen significant digits and the exponent value. The value is right justified in the field.

Format specifiers can be used to control both the space (field width) and the appearance of the value within the output field. The format specifier has one of the following two forms:

    :integer   or   :integer:integer

The first integer is the number of positions used to display the value. If present, the second integer means display the value without an exponent and with the given number of digits to the right of the decimal point. Some examples follow.('b' denotes a blank)

```
WRITELN(-78.25)      →b-7.8250000000E+01
WRITELN(-78.25:10)   →b-7.825E+01
```

```
WRITELN(-78.25:10:3)→bbb-78.250
WRITELN(-78.25:10:1)→bbbbb-78.3
WRITELN(-78.25:6)   →b-7.8E+01
```

Observe that the value is rounded to the number of decimal places specified.

2.5 Constant Declarations

Any number in Pascal can be given a name. Once this is done, the identifier can be used any place the number can be used. Why would you want to do this? The most important reason is that it often makes a program more readable if names are used in place of numbers. For example: PI instead of 3.14159, SPEED_OF_LIGHT instead of 186000, etc.

Shown below is a partial program that declares PI, WORKING_DAYS and YEAR to be constants.

```
PROGRAM EXAMPLE (OUTPUT);

CONST
    PI            = 3.14159;
    WORKING_DAYS = 22;
    YEAR          = 1985;

BEGIN (*EXAMPLE*)
    .
    .
    .
END.(*EXAMPLE*)
```

In the fragment, the four lines following the program header constitute a *constant declaration*. A CONST declaration, if present must immediately follow the program header and consists of "CONST" followed by one or more constant definitions separated from each other by semicolons. Each constant definition consists of an identifier followed by an equal sign followed by a value. If the value is an INTEGER number, the associated name is of type INTEGER; if the value is REAL, the identifier is of type REAL. The rules for valid names are found in the next section and a syntax diagram of a constant declaration can be found in Appendix B. In the programs found in the remainder of the book, there are many examples of constant declarations. From now on, when the word "constant" is used it means either an actual value or a constant identifier defined in a CONST declaration.

2.6 Variables

So far we have only considered specific numbers or constants. If we simply want to use the computer as a hand calculator, we could stop right here. In many problems however, we are doing such things as adding to totals, counting, making approximations, etc. In such cases, the value of the total, the count, or the approximation changes during the course of execution of the program. Quantities whose values may change are called variables. This section provides rules for naming variables and for assigning values to them. For each variable used in a program, the Pascal compiler reserves an area of memory to store the value of the variable.

2.6.1 Variable Names

Each variable used in a Pascal program has a name. The rules for naming variables are the same as those for naming constants, procedures and programs. The word identifier is synonymous with name. Certain names are not allowed because they are reserved for a special purpose. In fact, there are thirty-five reserved names in Pascal. In alphabetical order they are:

AND	DO	IF	OR	THEN
ARRAY	ELSE	IN	PACKED	TO
BEGIN	END	LABEL	PROCEDURE	TYPE
CASE	FILE	MOD	PROGRAM	UNTIL
CONST	FOR	NIL	RECORD	VAR
DIV	FUNCTION	NOT	REPEAT	WHILE
DOWNTO	GOTO	OF	SET	WITH

You may have noticed that this list does not include words such as INTEGER, MAXINT or WRITELN. These are examples of *predefined* or *standard identifiers* in Pascal. This means they have a specific meaning and purpose *unless* you define them to be something else in your program. Generally speaking, this is not a good idea. A complete list of predefined identifiers is found in Appendix A. Aside from the thirty-five reserved words, any name may be used which satisfies the following syntax requirements.

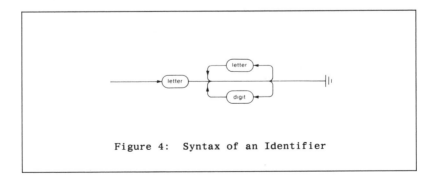

Figure 4:   Syntax of an Identifier

That is, an identifier must begin with a letter and may be followed by a sequence of letters and/or digits.

Many Pascal compilers permit the underscore character "_" to be used as a letter. This allows names which are more readable to be used. Examples are: "NET_PAY", "LAST_TIME" and "CURRENT_VALUE".

In theory there is no limit on the number of characters in an identifier; In practice, maximum lengths of 8, 16, 32 or 80 are often used. Check with your computing center or language reference manual if in doubt.

Upper and lower case letters in identifiers are considered equivalent. The identifiers SUM, Sum, sUm, SuM etc., are completely interchangeable. Because most output devices print in upper-case, we will use upper case letters in identifiers throughout the book so that the example programs will more closely resemble what you see in the program listings produced by your computer.

Examples of invalid identifiers are:

```
TAX%                  (percent sign not allowed)
9MAY                  (must start with a letter)
THIS_MAY_BE_TOO_LONG (may exceed maximum length)
DOWNTO                (DOWNTO is a reserved word)
```

2.6.2 Type of a Variable

As well as having a name, each variable has a type. A type defines the possible values which may be assigned to a variable. This is necessary so that the compiler knows how much memory to reserve to store the value of a variable. In Pascal there are five predefined types of which we have so far considered only INTEGER and REAL. The five are:

```
INTEGER     (whole numbers)
REAL        (whole numbers and numbers with a fractional
               part and/or an exponent part)
BOOLEAN     (true-false values; described in Chapter 3)
CHAR        (characters; described in Chapter 5)
TEXT        (a file of characters; described in Chapter 5
               and Chapter 12)
```

You can define your own types as well. How to do this is described in Chapter 6.

The name and type of each variable used in a Pascal program is defined in the *VAR declaration*. It has the form

```
VAR declaration; declaration; ... ; declaration
```

The VAR declaration follows any CONST declarations. Each declaration has the following syntax.

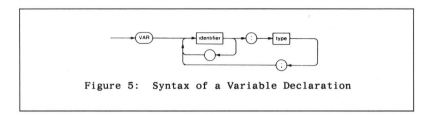

Figure 5:   Syntax of a Variable Declaration

Examples of valid VAR declarations are:

    i)   VAR   X : INTEGER

   ii)   VAR   X,Y,Z : REAL

  iii)   VAR   X : INTEGER;
                Y : REAL;
                Z : INTEGER

The third example points out that variables of the same type may appear in different lists.

Each of the following violates one or more of the syntax rules.

    i)   VAR X : INTEGER;
         VAR Y : REAL   (VAR must appear only once)

   ii)   VAR X : INTEGER;
             X : REAL   (X cannot be both REAL and INTEGER

  iii)   VAR X,Y : REAL
             Z   : REAL   (missing semicolon after first REAL)

2.7 Exercise 2.2

1.   What is the type and value of each of the following expressions?
          a) -2.0 + 3/5
          b) 9 DIV (14 MOD 3) /4
          c) TRUNC (ROUND (-3.25*2))
          d) SQR (SQRT(36))

2. What is the error in each of the following?
    a) 747.
    b) 22 + PRED(-21.) (two errors)
    c) 50/ 12MOD 5
    d) VAR
            X;Y:INTEGER

2.8 The Assignment Statement

There are two ways to assign a value to a variable: by using an assignment statement and by "reading" the value from an external file of values. The general form of an assignment statement is

```
variable := expression
```

The statement means "Determine the value of the expression on the right and assign this value to the variable on the left". Examples are

```
ABC := 427.2
X   := X + 1
```

Any value can be assigned to a variable provided it is "assignment compatible". Assignment compatibility for REAL and INTEGER values means that the variable and the value are of the same type or the variable is of type REAL and the value is of type INTEGER. at is The first three of the following are valid.

```
REAL variable    := REAL value
INTEGER variable := INTEGER value
REAL variable    := INTEGER value

INTEGER variable := REAL value (not allowed)
```

To assign the whole number part of a REAL value to an INTEGER variable, the TRUNC function can be used as in NUMBER := TRUNC(2.54). Because the ROUND function produces an INTEGER result, it can also be used to assign a value to an INTEGER variable as in "CLOSEST:=ROUND(-1.75)".

2.9 READing Values from the INPUT File

The second method of assigning a value to a variable is to obtain the value *at execution time* from an external (outside the program) source of values such as the keyboard. The Pascal procedures to obtain external values are READLN (read-line) which reads an entire line of values, and READ, which often is used to read only one value.

Using READLN

An example. Suppose we want to write a program to compute the square root of any positive number. A Pascal program to find the square root of 29.43 is the following:

```
PROGRAM ROOT1(OUTPUT);

(* THIS PROGRAM FINDS THE SQUARE ROOT OF 29.43 *)

VAR
  X : REAL;

BEGIN (* ROOT1 *)
  X := 29.43;
  WRITELN('THE SQUARE ROOT OF', X, '=', SQRT(X))
END. (* ROOT1 *)
```

This is fine for the value 29.43. To make it work with some other value, we would need to replace the assignment statement "X:=29.43" with one having a different value on the right side. If we were to tell a non-programmer how to do this, we would need to tell him where to find the assignment statement and how to change it. Wouldn't it be be nice if we could simply run the program and have the program ask for the value to be processed.

Shown below is a program which does exactly this. It makes use of the predefined procedure called READLN to assign a value to X.

```
PROGRAM ROOT2(INPUT,OUTPUT);

(* THIS PROGRAM FINDS THE SQUARE ROOT OF 29.43
   THE VALUE IS READ FROM THE INPUT FILE         *)

VAR
  X : REAL;

BEGIN (* ROOT2 *)
  WRITELN('ENTER A NUMBER');
  READLN(X);
  WRITELN('THE SQUARE ROOT OF', X, '=', SQRT(X))
END. (* ROOT2 *)
```

There are three differences between the programs.

First, the program header contains the identifier "INPUT" as well as "OUTPUT". "INPUT" is the name of the standard input file in Pascal. It is included in the program header because we want to obtain a value from the INPUT file at execution time. For most implementations of Pascal, the standard INPUT file is the keyboard. The value or values being processed are simply typed one line at a time.

Second, the first statement in the body of the program is

```
WRITELN( 'ENTER A NUMBER' )
```

This is called an *input prompt*. It is always a good idea to display a message on the screen which tells the user what data is wanted. If the input values are obtained from a source other than the keyboard, input prompts are not normally used.

Third, the assignment statement "X=29.43" has been replaced by:

```
READLN(X)
```

"READLN" is the name of a predefined procedure in Pascal. It is used to get one or more values from a file and assign them in sequence to the variables in the *parameter list*. In the example the parameter list has only one parameter, the REAL variable X.

When "READLN(X)" is executed, processing stops until a line of characters is entered from the keyboard. Depending on the terminal used, each line of data entered from the keyboard is terminated by pressing the 'RETURN' or 'ENTER' key. Pressing this *end-of-line key* sends an *'end-of-line character'* to the computer memory. In the example, if a value of 29.43 is entered, the five characters two-nine-point-four-three preceding the end-of-line character constitute a valid REAL value. Consequently the value 29.43 is assigned to the parameter X and processing continues. If an invalid REAL value such as 'A25P' is entered, an error message is displayed and execution stops. The main advantage of reading values is that only the contents of the INPUT file need to be changed to solve a different problem; the program can be left intact. In the example this means the program will work with whatever value is typed from the keyboard rather than just 29.43. Put another way, the program and data exist independently of each other. Separation of logic and data is almost always desirable.

Although used with a single parameter "X" in the example, READLN can have zero, one or several parameters. READLN with no parameters causes all characters in the remainder of the current INPUT line to be skipped. If used with more than one parameter as in

```
READLN (X,Y,Z)
```

the next three values (which must be separated by one or more blanks) are assigned to the variables X, Y and Z. Then, if the end-of-line character did not immediately follow the last digit of the Z value, all characters up to and including the end-of-line character are skipped. Thus if four or more values are present when there are three parameters, the extra values are skipped by READLN. If insufficient values are found, the next line of data entered is used to obtain the value(s). This means that if the keyboard is the INPUT file, the program waits for a data line to be entered. A summary of the operation of READLN is found at the end of this section.

READ, WRITE and EOLN (End-Of-Line)

The problem. Count the number of values in a single line of INPUT data. The algorithm is straightforward.

1. Initialize
   .1 Set Count = 0
   .2 Prompt for an input line
2. While not at the end of the line
   .1 Read and display the next value
   .2 Add one to Count
3. Display Count

There are two new challenges when translating this algorithm into Pascal. The first is "How do we know when we have read the last value?" Since the person entering the values must press the end-of-line key on the keyboard after entering the last value we might paraphrase the question as "How do we know when the next character in the input line is the end-of-line character?" Pascal includes a predefined function called EOLN (end-of-line) for this purpose. The EOLN function has a value of true if the next character in the input is the end-of-line character and is false otherwise.

The second challenge concerns the translation of "Read the next value". Remember that READLN *always reads all the remaining characters in an input line*. It skips to the end-of-line character after assinging a value to each parameter. However, because we want to read one number at a time, we want only one parameter. But READLN(X) for example would not do because it would read the first value and skip any remaining values in the INPUT line. Fortunately, the Pascal procedure READ operates just like READLN but does not skip to the end-of-line character after making the assignments of values to parameters. This is exactly what we want -- READ with a single parameter. Shown below is a program which also illustrates the use of the WRITE procedure. WRITE is used to build a line of output without displaying it. Further comments follow the program.

```
PROGRAM NUMBER_COUNT (INPUT, OUTPUT);

(* THIS PROGRAM COUNTS THE NUMBER OF VALUES IN A SINGLE
   LINE OF INPUT                                        *)

VAR
   COUNT  : INTEGER;
   NUMBER : REAL;

BEGIN (* NUMBER_COUNT *)
   COUNT := 0;
   WRITELN ('ENTER ZERO OR MORE VALUES ');
   WHILE NOT EOLN DO
     BEGIN
       READ (NUMBER);
       WRITE (NUMBER:8:2);
       COUNT := COUNT + 1
     END;
   WRITELN; (* DISPLAY THE OUTPUT LINE *)
   WRITELN ('THERE ARE', COUNT:3, ' VALUES')
END. (* NUMBER_COUNT *)
```

Some comments. First note that the test for continuing the WHILE-loop is "NOT EOLN". That is, while the value of the EOLN function is false or equivalently, while we have not reached the end-of-line character. NOT is one of the three Boolean (true-false) operators. They are discussed in detail in Chapter 3.

Second, the statement "WRITE(NUMBER:8:2)" causes the value of NUMBER to be appended to the current output line but the line is not displayed. Eight spaces are reserved for the value; two digits appear to the right of the decimal point. The WRITELN with no parameters following the loop triggers the printing of the output line. In general, the following are equivalent.

```
WRITELN ( x, y, z, ... )        and        WRITE ( x, y, z, ... );
                                           WRITELN
```

The third new feature is the use of the READ procedure. The correspondence between READLN and READ and their rules of operation are summarized below.

READ and READLN

General Form

```
READ( x, y, z, ... )                    READLN
                                          or
                                        READLN( x, y, z, ... )
```

Notes

1. READ must have at least one parameter.

2. READ(x,y,z,...) is equivalent to READ(x), READ(y), READ(z), ...

3. Operation of READ(x). The next value in the input line is obtained and assigned to the parameter x. If the end-of-line character is encountered before a value is found, the next line of data is obtained from the input file (the keyboard unlocks and the program waits for an input line). The value must be assignment compatible with the parameter.

4. READLN if used without any parameters causes any unread values in the current input line to be skipped.

5. READLN (x, y, z, ...) is equivalent to

    ```
    READ (x, y, z, ... );
    READLN
    ```

Reading Unknown Amounts of Data

Suppose a program is required to process an unspecified number of lines of input data. How would you know when the last line of values had been entered? There are three commonly used methods.

First, the program can request that the user enter the number of lines of input or number of values which will subsequently be entered. This value can be used to control the number of executions of a loop. The disadvantage of this approach is that the user must know in advance how many data items will be entered. This is not always possible especially if the decision to continue processing depends on the output from previously entered values.

A second approach is to use a *sentinel value*. A sentinel value is a special value such as 9999 which the program recognizes as signalling the end of input. As each value is read, it is compared with the sentinel value. If equal, the processing loop is terminated. Checking for a sentinel value is easy to program but means that a special value must be remembered and appended to the data. Sometimes this is a disadvantage. Files of input data which are stored on external devices such as tape or disk drives rather than entered from the keyboard have a special sentinel value called an *end-of-file mark* The presence of this end-of-file mark can be tested for using the EOF (end-of-file) function. Examples of its use are given in Chapter 5 which discusses non-keyboard files.

When the INPUT file is the keyboard, the third method is to recognize an empty line of input (containing just the end-of-line character) as indicating the end of data. Although this requires careful programming, it is the most natural from a user's point of view. Examples are found in Chapter 5.

2.10 Exercise 2.3

1. What is the error in each of the following?

    ```
    a) VAR I : INTEGER;
       BEGIN
           I:= ROUND(7/2) +1.0
       END
    b) X1 = 7
    c) MOM + DAD:=29
    d) A:=B:=C:=0.0
    ```

2. For each of (a) thru (f), assume the following declarations have been made.

    ```
        VAR
            I,J,K : INTEGER;
            X,Y,Z : REAL
    ```

    In each case, one or more READ statements and some INPUT data is given. Determine the values assigned to each variable or why the combination of READ procedures and data is invalid.

    a) READLN(I,X) with the data line 25 -0.034E-1 27

    b) READ(I,J,K,L) with the following two data lines:
         2 28 -MAXINT
         MAXINT

    c) READLN(X,Y,I,J) with the following line of data
         0.0 1.1 2.2 3.3

    d) READ(I,J,K); READ(X,Y,K)
                with the three lines of data below
       1 2 3 4
       -6E5
       27

    e) READ with the following input value
       17

    f) READ(K,K) with the following single input value
       10

3. Modify the program NUMBER_COUNT in the previous section so that it will process an unspecified number of values. Do this by using a sentinel value of your choice.

2.11 Summary

1. Numbers in Pascal contain three parts: a whole-number part(required), a fractional part (optional), an exponent part (optional). Numbers containing only the whole number part are of the type INTEGER; those with either of the optional parts are REAL numbers. The operators DIV and MOD can only be used with INTEGER values.

2. There are a number of predefined functions for processing numbers in Pascal. Some such as PRED (predecessor) and SUCC(successor) may only be used with INTEGERs.

3. Names may be given to constants by means of a constant declaration. If present, it immediately follows the program header unless a LABEL declaration (Chapter 4) is present.

4. Almost all programs contain one or more variables. Each variable has a name and a type. The type determines the range of values which the variable may have.
    Values can be assigned to variables using an assignment statement or by reading the values from the INPUT file.

5. The standard procedures READ and READLN can be used to read numeric values from the INPUT file. READ stops getting characters after a value has been obtained for each parameter. READLN is similar to READ but after making the assignments to the parameters, all characters up to the end-of-line character are skipped.

6. EOLN is a standard Pascal function which has a value of false unless the next character in the input file is the end-of-line character.

7. <u>WRITE</u> is a standard procedure which can be used to build up a line of
    output without displaying it. WRITELN with no parameters displays the
    current contents of the output line.

2.12 Programming Problems

2.1   Write a program to calculate the value of $12-(6-i)^2$ for values of i of 1,
      2, 3, ..., 12. Twelve lines of output should be produced. The first value
      on each line should be the value of i, the second, the value of the
      expression.

2.2   Tabulate (calculate and display) values of x and y given by the formula

$$y = \frac{x^3 - 4x^2 + x - 3}{|x + 2|}$$

      for a) x = 0., .25., .5, .75, ..., 1.75, 2.0
           b) x = -1, -3, -5, ..., -11, -13
           c) x = 10, 9, 8, ..., -9, -10.

2.3   Read values of X and N. Print the values of X, X/2, X/4, ..., $X/2^N$.

2.4   The sum of successive powers of the INTEGER values one thru N are
      given by the following formulae.

      a) Sum of values $\dfrac{N(N+1)}{2}$

      b) Sum of squares $\dfrac{N(N+1)(2N+1)}{6}$

      c) Sum of Cubes $\dfrac{N^2(N+1)^2}{4}$

      d) Sum of Fourth Powers $\dfrac{N(N+1)(2N+1)(3N^2+3N-1)}{30}$

      e) Sum of Fifth Powers $\dfrac{N^2(N+1)^2(2N^2+2N-1)}{12}$

      Write a program to calculate the sum of the first, second, third, fourth
      and fifth powers of the numbers one thru eight. That is, calculate the
      value of the five expressions above with N=8.

2.5   Write a program which reads in ten pairs of numbers, each pair
        representing a distance in millimeters and centimeters. After each pair
        of values is read, convert the distance to an equivalent distance in
        meters.

2.6   Write a program which reads six values, each representing a weight in
        kilograms. After each value is read, convert it to an equivalent weight
        in grams and milligrams. For example, a weight of 3.56789 kilograms
        becomes 3567 grams and 890 milligrams. The results of this program
        will clearly demonstrate the errors which may result when working with
        fractional REAL values.

2.7   Read twelve values each of which represents a number of hours.
        Express each value as the sum of weeks, days and hours. For example,
        193 hours becomes 1 week + 1 day + 1 hour.

2.8   For integer values in the range 11 thru 77 print the number and the
        remainder when the number is divided by the number obtained by
        leaving off the last digit. For example, for 36, 12 0 would be printed
        since 36 divided by 3 is 12 with 0 remainder.

2.9   An approximate value of the square root of x for x in the range 0.1
        thru 10 is given by the formula $(1+4x)/(4+x)$. Write a program which
        calculates the value of the square root of 0.5, 1.0, 1.5, ..., 9.5, 10, using
        both the formula and the SQRT function. Print the value of each result
        and the percentage error resulting from using the formula.

2.10   For values of x in the range .1 thru 1 an approximate value of the
        logarithm of x is given by the formula

$$\log x = -.076 + .281x - \frac{.238}{x + .15}$$

        Write a program which displays the values of log x using the formula
        and the built-in function LN. Use values of x of .2, .4, .6, .8, and 1.
        For each print the absolute value of the difference of the two log
        values.

2.11   Write a program which reads values of A, B and C representing the
        lengths of three sides of a triangle. Calculate the area of the triangle
        using the formula

$$Area^2 = S(S-A)(S-B)(S-C)$$

where S is one-half the perimeter of the triangle. Calculate the radius of the
inscribed circle (given by Area/S).

2.12   A series circuit consists of a resistor of R ohms, an inductance of L
henries and a capacitor of C farads. If the voltage across the circuit is
E volts at F cycles per second, the current in amperes flowing thru the
circuit is given by the formula

$$i = \cfrac{E}{R^2 + \left(\cfrac{2\ FL\ -\ 1}{2\ FC}\right)^2}$$

Write a program which reads values of R, L and C and computes the
current thru the circuit at 60 cycles per second for values of E of 100,
200, 300, ..., 900 volts.

2.13   Suppose you borrow $X for a period of N months at a monthly
interest rate of i (e.g. 0.01). The size of your monthly payment is given
by the formula

$$iX \frac{(1+i)^N}{(1+i)^N - 1}$$

Write a program which reads values of X, i and N and calculates the
size of the monthly payment.

2.14   Tabulate the values of the sine, cosine and tangent of angles of 0 , 5 ,
10 , ..., 60 (degrees). Note that the angles must be converted to radians
before the built-in functions can be used.

2.15   You are required to determine the smallest total number of bills
required to pay a sum of $1579.00 using only fifties, tens and one
dollar bills. Write a program to do this. No loop is required.

2.16   If an equation can be written in the form x-F(x)=0, then, subject to
certain conditions, a root of the equation can be found by obtaining
increasingly accurate approximations of the root. If x_1 is some initial
estimate of the root, then x_2, x_3, ... will be better estimates where
$x_n=F(x_{n-1})$. Suppose F(x) has the form A/(x+B) and the initial
estimate is called C. Write a program which reads values of A, B and
C. Calculate increasingly accurate estimates of the root until the
change in two estimates is less than 0.0001. Print every tenth estimate
as well as the final estimate. Test your program using first the function
12.3/(x+5.4) and second the function 3.99/(x-4). In each case use 2.0
as your initial estimate of the root.

2.17   A fraction of the form

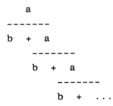

is called a continued fraction. Its value may be approximated to any desired accuracy by evaluating

A_0/B_0, A_1/B_1, A_2/B_2, ... where
$A_0 = 0$, $A_1 = a$, and $A_n = aA_{n-2} + bA_{n-1}$ for $n = 2, 3, \ldots$
$B_0 = 1$, $B_1 = b$, and $B_n = aB_{n-2} + bB_{n-1}$ for $n = 2, 3, \ldots$

Write a program which reads several pairs of values of "a" and "b" and for each, calculates A_{10}/B_{10}. Test your program on at least the following two cases. (i) a=1, b=1; (ii) a=1, b=2.

2.18   Find the roots of the equation $x^2-325678x-0.02=0$. Check the results by substituting the values found in the original equation. (You may get something far from zero, illustrating the potential problems of round off errors!)

2.19   Suppose a cyclist takes 15 seconds to uniformly reduce his speed from 35 kph (kilometers per hour) to 10 kph. Write a program which can be used to determine how long it would take him to stop at this rate of deceleration for various initial speeds. Read the speeds one-at-a-time from the keyboard. Use a negative number as a sentinel to terminate processing. Recall that acceleration equals the difference between the initial and final velocities divided by the time to effect the change.

CHAPTER 3: DECISION AND CONTROL

Questions Answered in this Chapter:

1. What are BOOLEAN values? How are they defined and used?

2. How can we execute a statement only when a particular condition is true?

This is one of the most important chapters in the book. It describes how to control the order of execution of statements in a program based on the truth of a given condition.

We begin with a study of true-false values, then study selective statement execution using the IF statement and the CASE statement.

3.1 BOOLEAN Values

A BOOLEAN value is one which is true or false. There are only two BOOLEAN constants, namely TRUE and FALSE. Each is a predefined identifier like MAXINT, and not a reserved word.

What operations can be performed with TRUE and FALSE?

First, because FALSE is considered to be less than TRUE, the six relational operators $<$, $<=$, $>$, $>=$, $=$, and $<>$ are well-defined. For example:

```
FALSE <= TRUE is true
TRUE  <= FALSE is false
```

The relational operators are seldom used with BOOLEAN values.

3.1.1 Operators AND, OR and NOT

The most important BOOLEAN operators are NOT, AND and OR.

NOT reverses the BOOLEAN value. Therefore NOT TRUE is FALSE and NOT FALSE is TRUE.

AND operates on a pair of BOOLEAN values. The four possible pairs and the results in each case are

```
TRUE  AND  TRUE    →  TRUE
TRUE  AND  FALSE   →  FALSE
FALSE  AND  TRUE   →  FALSE
FALSE  AND  FALSE  →  FALSE
```

That is X AND Y is TRUE if and only if X AND Y are individually TRUE. Another way of showing the truth value of the expression X AND Y is to use a truth table. Here is the truth table for the expression X AND Y.

X	Y	X AND Y
TRUE	TRUE	TRUE
TRUE	FALSE	FALSE
FALSE	TRUE	FALSE
FALSE	FALSE	FALSE

Each row in the table shows a different combination of values of the arguments. The rightmost column shows the value of the expression for the given combination of X and Y values.

The BOOLEAN operator OR produces a value of TRUE if either or both of the operator arguments are TRUE. The truth table for the expression X OR Y is shown below.

X	Y	X OR Y
TRUE	TRUE	TRUE
TRUE	FALSE	TRUE
FALSE	TRUE	TRUE
FALSE	FALSE	FALSE

In the same way that arithmetic operators have relative priorities, so the BOOLEAN operators NOT, AND and OR have relative priorities. In the absence of parentheses: NOT has the highest priority; AND has the next highest priority; OR has the lowest relative priority. In each case, operations are performed left to right. For example:

```
TRUE  AND  NOT  FALSE  OR  TRUE
```

has a value of TRUE arrived at in the following three steps.

```
TRUE AND NOT FALSE OR TRUE
    → TRUE AND TRUE OR TRUE
    → TRUE OR TRUE
    → TRUE
```

In other words, the expression is evaluated as if written with the following parentheses (TRUE AND (NOT FALSE)) OR TRUE.

How do we evaluate expressions that involve arithmetic and relational operators as well as the BOOLEAN operators? For example, what is the value of the following expression?

```
2 + 3 < 5 AND NOT 5 <> 7
```

To answer this we need to know the complete order of operator priorities. This is found in the table below.

```
                    Priority of Operators

    1. Functions
    2. NOT
    3. AND * / DIV MOD (equal priority)
    4. OR + - (equal priority)
    5. < <= = > >= <>, IN (equal priority)
       (IN is described in Chapter 13)
```

Parentheses are used to either change the order of operator priorities from that above or to help make clear the sequence of operations used in evaluating an expression.

If we put parentheses in the previous expression to show the order of evaluation the result is:

```
(2+3) < (5    AND   (NOT 5)) <> 7
```

Clearly this must produce an error because "NOT 5" has no meaning. A valid expression could be obtained by using parentheses in the following way:

```
((2+3) < 5) AND (NOT (5<>7))
```

This expression has a value of FALSE.

3.1.2 Predefined functions

The predecessor and successor functions PRED and SUCC are also allowed but there are only two valid possibilities. Because FALSE is less than TRUE, SUCC(FALSE) is TRUE and PRED(TRUE) is FALSE.

The ORD function can be used with BOOLEAN values but is seldom of use. Specifically ORD (FALSE) is 0; ORD (TRUE) is 1.

The predefined function ODD produces a BOOLEAN value. Its argument must be an INTEGER value. The result is TRUE if the value is odd and FALSE if it is an even INTEGER. For example

```
ODD (17 DIV 3 MOD 5) → FALSE
```

3.1.3 Input-Output

Either of the BOOLEAN values can be displayed on the OUTPUT file using the WRITELN procedure. It comes as no surprise that

```
WRITELN (TRUE, FALSE)
```

produces a line containing the character string 'TRUE FALSE'.

BOOLEAN values cannot be read from the INPUT file using the READ procedure. Instead the INTEGER values of 1 and 0 are often used to represent true and false respectively.

3.1.4 BOOLEAN Variables and Assignment Statements

There are many uses for BOOLEAN variables. In the partial program below the identifier LOOPING is a BOOLEAN variable used to control the number of repetitions of the WHILE loop.

```
VAR
  LOOPING : BOOLEAN;
BEGIN
  LOOPING := TRUE;
  WHILE LOOPING DO
    BEGIN
      .
      .     } body of the loop
      .
    END (* WHILE *)
```

An assignment statement of the form

```
BOOLEAN variable := BOOLEAN expression
```

is used to assign a value of TRUE or FALSE to a BOOLEAN variable. For example, consider the following declarations:

```
VAR
   X, OVERWEIGHT, DEFECTIVE, NOT_EQUAL,
   LAST_YEAR, THIS_YEAR                  : BOOLEAN;
   HEIGHT, WEIGHT, STRENGTH : REAL
```

Shown below are five examples of assignment statements involving BOOLEAN variables.

```
  i) DEFECTIVE := STRENGTH < 1000
 ii) LAST_YEAR := NOT THIS_YEAR
iii) OVERWEIGHT := (HEIGHT * 3 -160)< WEIGHT
 iv) NOT_EQUAL := X=X+1
  v) X := X = TRUE
```

The fourth example points out the very important distinction between the assignment operator ':=' and the relational operator '='.

Example (v) is "X:= X=TRUE". Consider the right hand side. It will be TRUE if X is TRUE and FALSE if X is FALSE. In other words the expression has the same value as X and therefore the statement is equivalent to X:=X which does nothing! This example illustrates that expressions in which relational operators are used to compare BOOLEAN values can often be replaced by simpler expressions. One of the exercise questions below asks you to do exactly this.

3.2 Exercise 3.1

1.   What is the value of each of the following expressions?
     a) NOT FALSE AND NOT TRUE
     b) (2 < 3) OR (2 <> 3)
     c) (5+(7 DIV 3) > 2 MOD 6) OR FALSE
     d) ORD(FALSE) + ORD(PRED(TRUE)) <> 0

2.   Write declarations to declare
     a)   GO and NOGO as constants with values of TRUE and FALSE
          respectively.
     b)   LOG1,LOG2, and LOG3 as BOOLEAN variables, X and Y as
          REAL variables and I and J as INTEGER variables.

3.   Explain the error in each of the following
     a) X < Y < Z
     b) X < 2 OR X > 5 (assume X is REAL)
     c) SUCC (7= SQRT(49))

4. The expression below is invalid because of operator priorities.

    NOT 3 < 5 OR 7-2 MOD 2   <= 6 AND TRUE

    a) Insert the minimum number of pairs of parentheses to make it an
        expression which can be evaluated.
    b) Add one additional pair of parentheses which will reverse the
        truth value from that in (a).

5. Replace each of the following with a simpler expression which does not
    have a relational operator. (Assume X is a BOOLEAN variable.)
    a) X < TRUE
    b) X <= FALSE
    c) X = FALSE
    d) X >= FALSE
    e) X > TRUE
    f) X <> FALSE
    g) X AND NOT(NOT (X))

6. Develop a truth table for each of the following expressions (Assume X and
    Y are BOOLEAN variables.)
    a) NOT X AND NOT Y
    b) NOT (X OR Y)
    c) NOT X OR NOT Y
    d) NOT (X AND Y)

7. For each of the following, write an expression which when evaluated will
    produce the values in the truth table. Assume X,Y and Z are BOOLEAN
    variables and that 'T' denotes TRUE, 'F' denotes FALSE.

a)

X	Y	RESULT
T	T	F
T	F	T
F	T	T
F	F	F

b)

X	Y	RESULT
T	T	F
T	F	T
F	T	T
F	F	T

c)

X	Y	Z	RESULT
T	T	T	F
T	T	F	F
T	F	T	F
T	F	F	T
F	T	T	F
F	T	F	T
F	F	T	T
F	F	F	F

8. Consider the following program.

```
PROGRAM EXER31(INPUT,OUTPUT);
CONST
   T = TRUE;
   F = FALSE;
VAR
   NUM1, NUM2 : REAL;
   BIG1, BIG2, EVEN : BOOLEAN;
BEGIN (* EXER31 *)
   READ(NUM1, NUM2);
   WRITELN('THE VALUES ARE', NUM1,' AND',NUM2);
   BIG1 := NUM1 > NUM2;
   BIG2 := NOT BIG1 AND (NUM1 <> NUM2);
   EVEN :<> NOT (BIG1 = BIG2);
   WRITELN('NUM1 > NUM2 IS', BIG1);
   WRITELN('NUM2 > NUM1 IS', BIG2);
   WRITELN('NUM1 = NUM2 IS', EVEN)
END. (* EXER31 *)
```

What is the output when used with each of the following lines of input
data?
   a) 20.2 -17   b) 5E-4 0.005E-1   c) 14 8

3.3 Conditional Execution (The IF Statement)

Consider the following problem. Read a pair of numbers having different values and print the value of the larger one. The algorithm is quite straightforward, namely:

1. Get values for X and Y
2. If X > Y then
   .1 write down the value of X
   Otherwise
   .1 write down the value of Y
3. Stop

The algorithm contains three steps. Within Step 2 however there is something new. Specifically, we want to *either* write down the value of X *or* write down the value of Y *depending* on whether or not X is less than Y. That is, we want to do one or the other but not both. Shown below is a Pascal program which is a translation of this algorithm.

```
PROGRAM BIGGER(INPUT, OUTPUT);

(* THIS PROGRAM READS A PAIR OF VALUES AND PRINTS
   THE VALUE OF THE LARGER ONE                    *)

VAR
  X, Y : REAL;

BEGIN (* BIGGER *)
  WRITELN ('ENTER A PAIR OF NUMBERS');
  READLN(X, Y);
  IF X > Y THEN
    WRITELN(X, ' IS LARGER THAN', Y)
  ELSE
    WRITELN(Y, ' IS LARGER THAN', X)
  END. (* BIGGER *)
```

This is the first example program which contains an IF Statement. The IF statement is one of the most powerful statements in any programming language. It is usually written in the following way.

```
IF boolean expression THEN
   statement1
ELSE
   statement2
```

Its effect is the following. The BOOLEAN expression following the reserved word IF is evaluated; if the expression is true, statement1 (called the "then-statement") is executed before proceeding. If the expression is false, statement2 (the "else-statement") is executed before proceeding. The word "THEN" is a reserved word in PASCAL which separates the BOOLEAN expression from the then-statement. "ELSE" is a reserved word which separates the then-statement from the else-statement. The then-statement and the else-statement are often compound statements as is illustrated in the program for the following problem.

Problem.   Calculate the value of $(5x-2)/(2x^2 + x - 21)$ for $x=0,1,2,...,10$. If the division is undefined (the denominator equals 0) for any value of x, print a message to indicate this. Here is a program to solve the problem.

```
PROGRAM CALCULATE(OUTPUT);

(* THIS PROGRAM CALCULATES THE VALUE OF
   (5X - 2) / (2SQR(X)+X-21) FOR X = 0 .. 10 *)

VAR
   X, VALUE, DENOM : REAL;

BEGIN (* CALCULATE *)
  X := 0;
  WHILE X <= 10 DO
    BEGIN
      DENOM := 2 * SQR(X) + X - 21;
      IF DENOM <> 0 THEN
        BEGIN (* CALCULATE AND PRINT *)
          VALUE := (5 * X - 2) / DENOM;
          WRITELN('FOR X=', X, ' THE VALUE IS', VALUE)
        END
      ELSE (* DENOM = 0 *)
        WRITELN('DIVISION IS UNDEFINED FOR X=',X);
      X := X + 1
    END (* WHILE *)
END. (* CALCULATE *)
```

In this example, two statements are executed if the condition is true and one if it is false. Note carefully the indentation used with the IF statement. In particular, 'IF' and 'ELSE' are aligned vertically with statements before and after the IF statement. The then-statement and the else-statement are indented. This helps to make the logic clear.

Suppose in this problem we decide to do nothing if the denominator is zero. That is, just skip over values of x which make the division undefined. In the program, this means the else-statement should be eliminated. Shown below are two equivalent methods.

Preferred	*Acceptable*
If DENOM <> 0 THEN	IF DENOM <>0 THEN
BEGIN	BEGIN
.	.
.	.
END;	END
X := X + 1	ELSE;
	X:= X+1

In the preferred method, the word ELSE and the else-statement are simply left out. The semicolon following the "END" separates the IF statement from the assignment statement which follows. In the second method the word ELSE separates the then-statement from the else-statement. In this case however, there is no statement between the ELSE and the semicolon which separates the IF statement from the assignment statement. In other words, the else-statement is null. A null statement is one which has nothing in it. You can create a null statement anywhere by placing two semicolons in succession.

Either or both of the then-statement and the else-statement may be null. The four possible forms are listed below.

a) IF expression THEN statement ELSE statement (both present)

b) IF expression THEN statement (null else-statement)

c) IF expression THEN ELSE statement (null then-statement)

d) IF expression THEN (both conditional statements omitted)

Note that case (c) (null then-statement) can be made equivalent to (b) simply by putting a NOT ahead of the BOOLEAN expression.

The fourth case points out a completely useless but valid form of the IF statement. Regardless of the expression value nothing is done. Problem. Suppose the real number line is partitioned into the four intervals shown below.

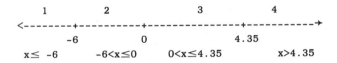

Write a program which reads a value and prints the number of the interval in which it lies. For example, if x is 2.1 then '3' should be printed because 2.1 is in interval 3. We shall analyze two simple algorithms.

Method A - Divide and Conquer

```
1. Read a value for x
2. If x ≤ 0 then (* interval 1 or 2 *)
      .1 If x ≤ -6 then
                  interval = 1
            else
                  interval = 2
   else (* interval 3 or 4 *)
      .1 If x ≤ 4.35 then
                  interval = 3
            else
                  interval = 4
3. Print value of x and interval
```

This method uses nested IF statements. That is, the then-statement and else-statement are also IF statements. Using this method, exactly two BOOLEAN expressions must be evaluated to determine the interval.

Method B - Sequential Search

```
1. If x ≤ -6 then
         interval = 1
   else
      if x ≤ 0 then
         interval = 2
      else
         if x ≤ 4.35 then
            interval = 3
         else
            interval = 4
2. Print the value of x and interval
```

Using this algorithm determine first if x is in interval 1; if not, try interval 2; if not, try interval 3; if not, x must be in interval 4.

There are two points to observe. First, the number of expressions which must be evaluated to locate the interval is one, two or three depending on the value of x. Using the first method, two were required regardless of the value of x. Second, notice the staircase-like structure of step 2 resulting from the usual way of indenting IF statements. When the program logic requires that a number of alternatives be examined, it is common to use the vertical alignment of statements shown in the program below which is a translation of the second algorithm.

```
PROGRAM SEQUENTIAL_SEARCH(INPUT,OUTPUT);

(* THIS PROGRAM SELECTS THE INTERVAL CONTAINING
   A GIVEN VALUE OF X                              *)

VAR
  INTERVAL : INTEGER;
  X         : REAL    ;

BEGIN (* SEQUENTIAL_SEARCH *)
  WRITELN ('ENTER A NUMBER');
  READLN(X);
  IF X <= -6.0 THEN
    INTERVAL := 1
  ELSE IF X <= 0 THEN
    INTERVAL := 2
  ELSE IF X <= 4.35 THEN
    INTERVAL := 3
  ELSE
    INTERVAL := 4;
  WRITELN(X, ' IS IN INTERVAL', INTERVAL)
END. (* SEQUENTIAL_SEARCH *)
```

Naturally, it can be written using the normal indentation rules without changing the meaning whatsoever.

Consider the following structure.

```
IF ... THEN IF ... THEN IF ... THEN ... ELSE
```

To which "IF" does the "ELSE" belong? The rule in Pascal is that ELSE is associated with the last IF preceeding it.

One additional example should make the rule clear. The logic required is the following. If $x \leq 10$ then if $x > 0$ then print 'HELLO'. However if $x > 10$ then print "GOODBYE". Does the program fragment below contain this logic?

```
IF X <= 10 THEN
  IF X>0 THEN
    WRITELN('HELLO')
ELSE
  WRITELN('GOODBYE')
```

Careful! To which IF does the ELSE belong? The last one, right? Therefore, the only way 'GOODBYE' gets written is if x is $\leq$ 10 and x$\leq$ 0 (more simply if x$\leq$ 0). This is not what was asked. Remember that the indentation of statements can be used to advantage to make the program structure visible but indentation has no effect on program logic. In this example, indentation conceals the logic. To force the else-statement to belong to the first IF we need to complete the inner IF before encountering the ELSE. Two methods are shown below.

Preferable	*Acceptable*

```
    IF X <= 10 THEN              IF X <= 10 THEN
       BEGIN                        IF X > 0 THEN
          IF X > 0 THEN                WRITELN('HELLO')
             WRITELN('HELLO')      ELSE
       END                      ELSE
    ELSE                           WRITELN('GOODBYE')
       WRITELN('GOODBYE')
```

However, there are even better ways to define the same logic. The method on the left below uses a compound condition; that on the right reverses the test in the first condition.

Compound	*Reversed Condition*

```
    IF (X<=10) AND (X>0)THEN     IF X>10 THEN
       WRITELN('HELLO')             WRITELN('GOODBYE')
    ELSE                         ELSE IF X>0 THEN
       WRITELN('GOODBYE')           WRITELN('HELLO')
```

3.4 Selecting One of Several Cases

Frequently we need to do something different for each of several values of a variable. For example, suppose each of one-hundred lines in the INPUT file contains two values, the first being an integer representing a student's identification number and the second a value of 1, 2 or 3 having the following meanings:

> 1 - FAIL
> 2 - PASS
> 3 - HONOURS

The task is to read the input data and print a list showing the identification number followed by 'FAIL', 'PASS' or 'HONOURS'. In the program below a CASE statement is used to specify the action to be taken in each of the three cases.

```
PROGRAM CLASS_LIST(INPUT,OUTPUT);

(* THIS PROGRAM PRINTS THE PERFORMANCE INDICATOR
   OF EACH STUDENT IN A CLASS                       *)

VAR
   CLASS_SIZE, COUNT, IDENT, PERFORMANCE : INTEGER;

BEGIN (* CLASS_LIST *)
   WRITELN('ENTER THE NUMBER OF STUDENTS IN THE CLASS');
   READLN(CLASS_SIZE);
   WRITELN('ENTER THE ID# AND PERFORMANCE CODE OF EACH');
   COUNT := 1;
   WHILE COUNT <= CLASS_SIZE DO
     BEGIN
        READLN(IDENT, PERFORMANCE);
        CASE PERFORMANCE OF
          1: WRITELN(IDENT, ' FAIL');
          2: WRITELN(IDENT, ' PASS');
          3: WRITELN(IDENT, ' HONORS')
        END; (* CASE *)
        COUNT := COUNT + 1
     END (* WHILE *)
END. (* CLASS_LIST *)
```

In this example the CASE statement specifies the actions to be taken in each of the three possible values or cases of the variable PERFORMANCE. Each case has the form below.

```
list of constants : statement
```

In the example above each list of constants has a single value. Cases are separated by semicolons.

The other important features of the CASE statement are illustrated in the following example.

Given a value of x, calculate y as follows

$$y = \begin{cases} 0 \text{ if } x < 0 \\ 3x + 2.5 \text{ if } 0 \le x < 5 \\ 4x^2 - 8 \text{ if } 5 \le x < 15 \\ 7(x-14) \text{ if } 15 \le X < 20 \\ 0 \text{ if } X \ge 20 \end{cases}$$

Although we can define the required logic using a sequence of IF statements, a CASE statement will be used in order to learn more about it. First, assume that x is a REAL value. Because the constants which separate the cases must have discrete integer values, we need to convert the value of x into an INTEGER value which indicates which of the five cases is to be used. If we

truncate the fractional part of x and DIV by 5 we get an INTEGER value
with the following meanings.

Range of x	Value of TRUNC(x) DIV 5
x < 0	negative
0 ≤ x < 5	0
5 ≤ x < 15	1,2
15 ≤ x < 20	3
x ≥ 20	4,5,6,...

Shown below is a partial program containing the logic.

```
VAR
  X, Y : REAL;
  CHOPPED : INTEGER;

BEGIN
  .
  .
  CHOPPED := TRUNC(X) DIV 5;
  IF (CHOPPED < 0) OR (CHOPPED > 3) THEN
    Y := 0
  ELSE
    CASE CHOPPED OF
        0 : Y := 3*X + 2.5;
      1,2 : Y := 4*SQR(X) - 8;
        3 : Y := 7 * (X-14)
    END (* CASE *)
  .
  .
```

It is necessary to determine if CHOPPED is negative or greater than three
before entering the CASE statement because the value of the "case-expression"
(CHOPPED in the example) must match one of the constants which separate
the cases. If not, an error occurs. Some Pascal compilers provide an
"OTHERWISE" case - which is executed if the value of the case expression
does not match any of the case selector constants. Note that the constants 1
and 2 are associated with the second case.

One last point. The statement to be executed in a case can of course be a
compound statement or an empty statement. Shown below is an example of a
valid but useless CASE statement. Assume DUMB is a BOOLEAN variable.

```
CASE DUMB OF
  TRUE  : ; (* empty case - do nothing *)
  FALSE : BEGIN
            END (* empty compound case *)
END (* DUMB CASE *)
```

The general form and rules of the CASE statement are:

The CASE Statement

General Form

> CASE case-expression OF
>   list1 : statement;
>   list2 : statement;
>   .
>   .
>   listN : statement
> END

Notes

1. The case expression must be an ordinal type (The only ordinal type we have studied so far is INTEGER)

2. The lists must consist of unique constants separated by commas compatible with the type of the case expression. A constant cannot appear in more than one list.

3. When executed, the value of the case-expression must match a constant in one of the lists.

3.5 Exercise 3.2

1. Explain why a semi-colon *never* precedes the word "ELSE".

2. For each of the following partial programs, state the output.

```
a) IF 2 <> 5 DIV 2 THEN
       WRITELN ('NOPE')
   ELSE
       WRITELN ('YEP')


b) IF ROUND(SQRT(17.0))>4.0 THEN
       WRITELN('GREATER')
   ELSE
       WRITELN('LESSER')
```

```
c) IF SUCC(3) = PRED(2) THEN
       WRITELN('WHAT?')
   ELSE IF PRED(3) = SUCC(2) THEN
       WRITELN('WELL MAYBE')

d) IF TRUE <> FALSE AND NOT FALSE THEN
       IF 6/2 = 4DIV2 THEN
           WRITELN ('HI THERE')
   ELSE
       WRITELN ('SO LONG')

e) X:=2.0
   IF X>0 THEN;
       WRITELN (X)
```

3. What is the error in each of the following?

```
a) IF 2 THEN
       X:=4

b) IF A>B THEN
       A:=B;
   ELSE
       B:=A

c) IF X <> Y THEN
       X:=X+1;
       Y:=Y-1
   ELSE
       X:=4

d) IF P=Q THEN
       P:=SQR(P);
   ELSE
```

4. Suppose three ranges of INTEGER values are called A,B and C. Suppose also that a value for an INTEGER variable N has been obtained. For each of the following ranges of A,B,C write one or more IF statements to determine the interval or intervals in which N lies. If it does not appear in any, write 'NONE'.

	A	B	C
a)	0 to 15	16 to 25	26 to 50
b)	0 to 15	16 to 25	0 to 25
c)	0 to 15	5 to 20	10 to 25
d)	less than 0	<>4	<>2
e)	1 to 100	20 to 80	50 to 60

5. Repeat question 4a and 4b above without using any ELSEs in the IF statements.

6. Rewrite the following line using proper indentation to show the logic structure.

    IF a THEN b ELSE IF c THEN d ELSE e

7. Given the following sequences of IFs and ELSEs (every IF of course must have an associated 'THEN'), insert BEGIN-END pairs where necessary to achieve the objective stated. Use proper vertical alignment.

    a) IF IF ELSE ;Match the ELSE with the first IF.

    b) IF   IF   ELSE   IF   ELSE   ; Match the first ELSE to the second IF and the second ELSE to the first IF.

    c) IF   IF   IF   IF   ELSE   ELSE   ; Match the first ELSE with the third IF and the second ELSE with the second IF.

8. Consider the following program.

```
PROGRAM TESTCASE(INPUT,OUTPUT);
VAR
   X : INTEGER;
BEGIN (* TESTCASE *)
   WRITELN('ENTER AND INTEGER');
   READLN(X);
   CASE X DIV 2 DIV 3 OF
         0 : WRITELN('VALUE OF ZERO');
      1,2,3 : BEGIN
                 IF X DIV 2 DIV 3 = 1 THEN
                    WRITELN('ONE')
                 ELSE IF X DIV 2 DIV 3 = 2 THEN
                       ELSE WRITELN('THREE?')
              END;
          4 :
   END (* CASE *)
END. (* TESTCASE *)
```

    What is the output for each of the following values of X?
        a) X = 5
        b) X = 17
        c) X = 29
        d) X = 18
        e) X = 6

9. In each of the following, you are given a sequence of possible values of an INTEGER variable N and a partitioning of these values into cases. Write one or more CASE statements, using an IF statement where necessary so that the statement(s) could be used to define the actions associated with each case. For example, given that N is one of 1,2,3...100 and that case 1 is the odd numbers, case 2 is the even numbers, then either of the following could be used.

CASE N MOD 2 OF   CASE ODD (N) OF
    0: (*even*)   TRUE: (*odd*)
    1: (*odd*)   FALSE: (*even*)
END   END

a) N is one of 1,2,3,101,102,103. Case1=1,101; Case2=2,102; Case3=3,103

b) N is one of 10, 20, 30, 40, 100, 200, 300, 400. Case1=10,100; Case2=20,200; Case3=30,300; Case4=40,400

c) N is limited to the values defined by the following cases. Case1=1,99; Case2=2,98; Case3=3,97

d) N is any INTEGER. Case1= MAXINT; Case2 is $N<0$; Case3=0; Case4 is $N>0$.

e) N is any INTEGER. Case1 is $N<0$ or $N>40$; Case2 N is 3,9,15,21,27 or 33; Case3 N is 2,6,12,18,24,30,or 36; Case4 other values of N.

3.6 Summary

1. The BOOLEAN values are TRUE and FALSE. The most useful operators for manipulating BOOLEAN expressions are NOT, AND and OR which have decreasing priorities.

2. The IF statement is used to specify both the action to be taken when a BOOLEAN expression is TRUE and the action to be taken when the expression is FALSE. Either action may be a null statement.

3. A CASE statement is frequently a convenience when the selection of an action depends on the value of an INTEGER or other ordinal variable.

3.7 Programming Problems

3.1 Write a program which reads an INTEGER value and determines the number of non-zero digits in the number. Hint: Divide the number by 10, 100, 1000, etc. and add one to a counter if the quotient is non-zero.

3.2 Read a pair of INTEGER values M and N. Read a value of K. Determine if the last K digits in each number are the same. The output should appear as "LAST __ DIGITS OF ___ AND ___ ARE EQUAL (UNEQUAL)".

3.3 Read the lengths of the sides of a triangle. Print "0" if the lengths do not form a triangle; "1" if the sides are all unequal; "2" if the triangle is isosceles; "3" if the triangle is equilateral.

3.4 Read an unknown number of INTEGER values recorded one value per line. Print the largest and smallest value of those that are read as well as each value which is read.

3.5 Temperatures in Fahrenheit (F) may be converted to Celcius (C) and vice-versa using the formulas:

$$F = \frac{9}{5} C + 32 \qquad\qquad C = \frac{5}{9} (F - 32)$$

Write a program which reads ten pairs of values. The second value of each pair is a temperature in degrees. The first value is a "1" if conversion from Centigrade to Fahrenheit is required, a "2" if conversion from Fahrenheit to Centigrade is required. Print ten lines of the form "___ DEGREES F (C) EQUALS ___ DEGREES C (F)".

3.6 The value of the cube root of a number may be calculated by starting with two estimates -- one high (H) and one low (L). A better estimate is then (H+L)/2. A check can be made of the new estimate to see if it is high or low. If high, it can be used as the new H value, if low, as the new L value. The process can then be repeated until any desired accuracy is obtained. Write a program which uses 3 and 4 as initial estimates of the cube root of 50. Use the procedure above until the estimate differs from previous value by less than 0.01. Print the high and low estimates before each new estimate is calculated.

3.7   Read any four non-negative INTEGER values. Call them I1, I2, I3, and I4. Replace them with the four values |I1-I2|, |I2-I3|, |I3-I4|, and |I4-I1|. If they are all equal, print the four values. If at least two of them are different, continue the process using the replacement values as the starting values. Continue until all four differences are equal. Print the values of I1, I2, I3 and I4 at each stage of the calculations.

3.8   The day of the week for any date consisting of a year (Y), a month (M) and day (D) can be found using the following formula.

$$weekday = K \bmod 7 + 1 \quad where$$

$$K = D + 2M + \frac{3M+3}{5} + Y + \frac{Y}{4} + \frac{Y}{100} + 1$$

All divisions in the formula are INTEGER (DIV) divisions. When using the formula, January and February of a year are considered as months 13 and 14 of the previous year. For example, Jan. 26, 1985 should be considered as the 26th day of the 13th month of 1984. In the formula, a value of 1 for the weekday represents Monday, 2 a Tuesday, etc. Read several dates including your own birthday and print the day of the week for each. Stop when the year has a negative value.

3.9   Read the X-Y coordinates of three points. Determine if the third point and the origin lie on the same side of the line which goes thru the first two points. Print "YES" if they do and "NO" if they don't. Print the coordinates of the three points.

3.10   Modify problem 2.13 in the following way. Read values of X, n, i, and PER where: X is the amount of the loan; n is the number of payments; i is the *annual* interest rate; PER is the number of months between payments. Calculate the size of the payment made in each period using the given formula. Note that the interest rate for a period is related to the annual interest rate in the following way: (period rate + 1)^m = (annual rate +1) where "m" is the number of periods in a year.

3.11   For any twelve hour period, determine the times to the nearest minute when the minute hand is as far past six as the hour hand is away from six.

3.12   Consider any four digit number. Let K1, K2, K3 and K4 be the values of the four digits in the number. Form a new number by adding the squares of the digit values. Repeat the process (find the digits, square and add) each time obtaining a new number. Write a program which reads a four digit number and generates new numbers until either a value of one is found or until a value of twenty is found for the second time. One of these events will occur regardless of the number you start with!

3.13   Find the x which produces the largest value of y using the formula y=Ax+B when x is in the interval beween C and D. Read the values of A, B, C and D from the input file.

3.14   Find the value of x which produces the largest value of y using the formula $y=Ax^2+Bx+C$ when x is in the interval between D and E. Read the values of A, B, C, D and E from the input file. Test your program using at least the following three sets of values.
       a) A=-1, B=0, C=9, D=-4, E=4
       b) A=+1, B=-4, C=1, D=2, E=8
       c) A=-1, B=6, C=-2, D=-1, E=2

3.15   The greatest common divisor (GCD) of two numbers M and N can be calculated in the following way (Euclid's Algorithm). Divide the larger by the smaller. If the remainder is zero, the GCD is the smaller. If not, divide the smaller by the remainder. If zero, the remainder is the GCD. If not, continue dividing the remainder into the previous remainder until a remainder of zero is obtained. The GCD is the value of the last non-zero remainder. Write a program to find the GCD of any two INTEGER values. Test your program by reading a pair of data values. Stop when a pair of zeros is read.

3.16   A rectangular room has a length, width and height of L, W, and H respectively. The length of the room runs in an East-West direction. An ant is located on the East wall a distance AH above the floor and AN North of the South wall. The ant's food is stuck on the West wall a distance FB below the ceiling and FS south of the North wall. Write a program which reads values of L, W, H, AH, AN, FB and FS and calculates the shortest distance the ant must travel to reach its food. Hints: The shortest distance is a straight line which will include travel along *one* of the ceiling, floor, South wall or North wall. (Naturally parts of the East and West walls will have to be covered as well.) To evaluate the lengths of the four paths, pretend the room is made of cardboard and "unfold" it in four different ways to see the four paths. The length of each path can be calculated easily using the Pythagorus Theorem.

3.17   A corridor three feet wide and seven feet high makes a right-angled
turn into another corridor having the same dimensions (The corner is
"L" shaped.). A plumber has a long thin rigid pipe which he wants to
take around the corner. a) What is the longest length of pipe which will
go around the corner? b) What is the narrowest width of corridor which
will permit an eight foot pipe to go around? c) Do your answers to (a)
and (b) change if the corner is "T" shaped? Write a program to answer
these questions.

3.18   Modify your program for the previous question so that it will work if
the corridors intersect at an angle of x degrees. Assume x is the acute
angle at the intersection. Answer questions (a) and (b) of the previous
problem for values of x of 15, 30, 45, 60 and 75 degrees.

3.19   Brownsville, Jonesville and Smithville are located on the same
highway. The distances are shown in the following diagram.

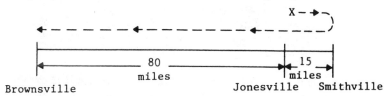

Assume that cars travelling from Smithville to Brownsville leave
Smithville at one minute intervals and travel at a constant rate of 45
miles per hour. Suppose you leave Jonesville heading for Smithville just
as a Ford is leaving Smithville heading for Brownsville. When you
reach Smithville, you immediately turn around and head for
Brownsville. a) At what constant rate must you drive to reach
Brownsville at the same time as the Ford? b) How many cars do you
pass on your trip? Include both the cars you encounter on your trip to
Smithville and the cars you pass on you trip to Brownsville.

3.20   An airline operates planes which have first-class and economy seats. If
a customer approaches a ticket clerk, the clerk asks which type of seat
is wanted. If that type is available, a ticket is issued for that type. If
not available, the customer is asked if the alternate type of seat would
be acceptable (provided one is available). If it is acceptable, a ticket of
the alternate type is issued. If it is not acceptable, no ticket is issued.
Write a program which will print one of the messages "ISSUE FIRST
CLASS", "ISSUE ECONOMY", or "DONT ISSUE TICKET" based
on the rules above. Input to the program consists of four INTEGER
values. The variables to which these four values will be assigned have
(respectively) the following meanings.

$$WANT = \begin{cases} 1 \text{ if customer wants first-class} \\ 2 \text{ if customer wants economy} \end{cases}$$

$$ALTNAT = \begin{cases} 1 \text{ if customer will take alternate type} \\ 0 \text{ if customer won't take alternate type} \end{cases}$$

$$FAVAIL = \begin{cases} 1 \text{ if first-class seat is available} \\ 0 \text{ if first-class seat is not available} \end{cases}$$

$$EAVAIL = \begin{cases} 1 \text{ if economy seat is available} \\ 0 \text{ if economy seat is not available} \end{cases}$$

For example, a data record containing "2 1 0 1" means: the customer wants an economy seat; he will take the alternate type; no first class seat is available; an economy seat is available. Therefore the message "ISSUE ECONOMY TICKET" should be printed.

Test your program by reading sixteen different lines of data -- one for each of the sixteen possible combinations of the four values. Print an appropriate message after each line of data.

3.21   Write a program to print all integers in the range 100 to 500 which have the property that the digits in the number are different. Print the results 4 numbers per line.

3.22   A decision table is a method of describing rules for making decisions in a tabular form. Shown below is a simple decision table for deciding whether or not to get up in the morning.

| | | RULES | | | | |
		1	2	3	4	5
Conditions	Went to bed late	Y	Y	N	N	N
	Have a morning class			Y		N
	Test today	Y	N		Y	N
Actions	Get up	X		X	X	
	Stay in bed		X			X

The five decision rules in the table show which of two actions to take
depending on three yes-no conditions. The yes-no conditions are: Did
you go to bed late?; Do you have a morning class?; Do you have a test
today?. The five decision rules are defined by the entries in the five
columns of the table. Consider Rule (column) 1. It says that if you
went to bed late and if you have a test today, then you should get up.
In this rule, the action you take is independent of whether or not you
have a morning class (There is no entry in Rule 1 for the second
condition). Rule 5 says for example that if all three conditions are
negative, then sleep in.

Suppose 5 data records have been prepared each of which contains
three numbers. The first value is a 1 (meaning went to bed early) or a
0 (did not go to bed early); The second is a 1 (morning class) or a 0
(no morning class); the third is 1 (test today) or 0 (no test today).
Write a program which reads the data and for each set prints messages
describing the conditions which are represented and the action to be
taken.

3.23   Write a program to reflect the logic described by the decision table
below. Choose a suitable form for representing the conditions as data
values. After reading each data record and echoing the conditions,
output a line of the form 'COMMISSION RATE IS __ PERCENT'
or 'CASE SHOULD BE INVESTIGATED'.

| | | R U L E S | | | |
Sales Commission Table	1	2	3	4	5
Units sold < 100	Y		N	N	E
Units sold 100-199		Y	N	N	L
Units sold 200-299			Y	Y	S
With company more than 2 yrs			Y	N	E
Commission is 2% sales	X				
Commission is 3% of sales		X			
Commission is 4% of sales				X	
Commission is 5% of sales			X		
Investigate					X

3.24   Consider the two circles defined by the pair of equations $x^2+y^2=9$
and $(x-2)^2+(y-4)^2=16$. Write a program which reads values of x and y
and prints a TRUE if the point (x,y) lies inside both circles and
FALSE otherwise. Test the program on the following points: (1,1),
(1,-1), (2,-.5), (0,1), (0,-2.5).

3.25   On the island of Ho, there are two races -- the Good Guys who always
tell the truth, and the Bad Guys who always lie. On my last visit to the
island, I met three villagers named Tom, Dick and Zack. I asked each
of them one question. Their answers are shown in parentheses.

```
Q: Tell me Tom, is Dick a Good Guy?  (yes)
Q: Dick, do Tom and Zack belong to the same race? (no)
Q: Zack, what about Dick, is he a Good Guy? (yes)
```

Write a program to determine the races of the three villagers. To solve
this problem, generate the eight possible combinations of race-to-people
assignments using three FOR-loops. Check each combination to see if
they would answer the questions in the manner described. This can be
done using as few as three IF statements. Remember that the computer
cannot think or reason and *you* must find the implications of each
answer under the assumption that the speaker was first of all, a Good
Guy, and secondly, a Bad Guy. The results of this analysis will permit
you construct the appropriate IF statements.

3.26   There are three bags labelled "cookies", "brownies" and "cookies and
brownies". Although one bag contains cookies; one contains brownies
and one contains a mixture, none of the labels are correct. Write a
program which selects one item from one of the bags and determines
the correct matchup of labels and contents. The program should output
a line of the form "By sampling one item from the _____ bag, it can
be determined that:" followed by three lines of the form: "The _____
bag contains _____".

CHAPTER 4: LOOP CONTROL

Questions Answered in this Chapter:

1. What three Pascal statements are available for controlling the number of repetitions of a statement? What are the advantages and disadvantages of each?

2. How is the GOTO statement used to explicitly control the order of statement execution? Under what circumstances should it be used?

This chapter describes ways of controlling loops in a Pascal program. Until now we have only used a WHILE statement. Pascal also provides a REPEAT-UNTIL statement and a FOR statement. Each is appropriate in certain circumstances.

The final section in the chapter describes the GOTO statement which, when used with statement labels, allows you to explicitly control the order of statement execution.

4.1 Loops And Loop Control

Almost all computer programs contain one or more program loops. A loop contains a sequence of one or more statements which is executed repeatedly. Loop control refers to the mechanism for controlling the number of repetitions of the sequence. There are two forms of loop control - external and internal. External control refers to events beyond the control of the program. Examples are computer breakdowns, intervention by the computer operator, or exceeding the time allowed for the program to compile and execute. We are not concerned here with factors outside of the control of a program which cause a loop to terminate. Internal loop control means the decision to stop further repetitions is made by the program.

4.2 The WHILE Statement: A Summary

Each of the example programs used so far has used a WHILE statement to control a loop. The WHILE statement is the most general and flexible method of loop control. The general form and rules are as follows.

The WHILE Statement

General Form

> WHILE Boolean expression DO
> statement (body of the loop)

Notes

1. DO separates the expression from the body of the loop.

2. GOTO (see Section 4.5) can direct control to a statement within the body of a WHILE loop from a statement outside the loop.

3. The expression is evaluated. If true, the statement is executed and the expression is evaluated again; If false, execution continues with the statement following the WHILE statement.

A simple but dumb example of a WHILE loop is the following: *

```
COUNT := 0;
WHILE COUNT <= 10 DO
     COUNT := COUNT + 1
```

This simple example illustrates the three key ideas associated with every WHILE loop. First, a statement preceding the WHILE statement must be used to initialize the condition tested in the WHILE statement. This is performed by the statement "COUNT:=0". Second, something must happen during some iteration of the loop to cause the condition to become false. This occurs after COUNT is assigned a value of 11. Third, if the condition is initially false the body of the loop is not executed.

The example fragment below illustrates nested WHILE statements. What values are written by the following program fragment?

```
I:= 1; (* INITIALIZE I-LOOP *)
WHILE I <> 5 DO
  BEGIN
    J := 0; (* INITIALIZE J-LOOP *)
    WHILE J <= I DO
      BEGIN
        WRITELN(J);
        J := J + 1
      END; (* J-LOOP *)
    I := I + 1
  END (* I-LOOP *)
```

The recommended style guidelnines for the WHILE statement are:

Style Guidelines for WHILE

- Where possible, the statement(s) initializing the list condition should immediately precede the WHILE statement.

- If more than one initializing statement is needed, either use a compound statement or indent the initializing statement following an appropriate comment.

- The statement constituting the body of the loop is indented. If it is a compound statement, the END should be followed by a comment indicating the WHILE statement being terminated.

4.3 REPEAT-UNTIL

In many circumstances it is known in advance that the body of the loop will be executed at least once. In this case, the decision to continue repetitions can be made *after* the first execution of the body statements. That is, the body of the loop is repeated until a condition is satisfied. This is precisely the purpose of the REPEAT-UNTIL statement. As an example consider the following simple problem. Read a sequence of INTEGER values. Print each value and the cumulative sum of the values after each value has been read. Stop when a negative value is read but include the value in the total. Here is a program to solve the problem.

```
PROGRAM INTEGER_SUM(INPUT,OUTPUT);

(* THIS PROGRAM PRINTS THE CUMULATIVE SUMS OF AN
   UNSPECIFIED NUMBER OF INTEGER VALUES, STOPPING
   AFTER ADDING A NEGATIVE VALUE              *)

VAR
  NUMBER, SUM : INTEGER;

BEGIN (* INTEGER_SUM *)
  SUM := 0;
  REPEAT
    WRITELN('ENTER A NUMBER');
    READLN(NUMBER);
    SUM := SUM + NUMBER;
    WRITELN(NUMBER:5, 'SUM IS NOW', SUM:8);
  UNTIL NUMBER < 0
END. (* INTEGER_SUM *)
```

There are three differences between the WHILE and REPEAT-UNTIL methods of loop control. First, with a REPEAT-UNTIL the decision to continue repetitions follows the body of the loop. This means the body is executed at least once. Second, the statement which sets the value of the test condition may be part of the loop body. Third, because REPEAT and UNTIL are reserved words, there is no need to use a compound statement even if the body of the loop contains more than one statement. That is "REPEAT" and "UNTIL" act as delimiters of the loop body.

Which should you use, WHILE or REPEAT-UNTIL? In many cases it is largely a matter of personal preference. A WHILE statement must be used however if the program logic and/or data is such that the loop body may not be executed. For example, if the problem above were changed so that a negative value simply indicated stop, a WHILE would be a much better choice for the loop control statement.

The rules of the REPEAT-UNTIL statement are summarized below.

The REPEAT-UNTIL Statement

General Form

        REPEAT
            statement(s)
        UNTIL Boolean expression

Notes

1. The statements forming the body of the loop are contained between the reserved words REPEAT and UNTIL.

2. GOTO (See Section 4.5) can direct control to a statement within the body of a REPEAT-UNTIL loop from a statement outside the loop.

3. Logic. The statements between REPEAT and UNTIL are executed; the Boolean expression is evaluated; if false the statements are executed again; if true, execution continues with the next statement.

4. The REPEAT and UNTIL should be vertically aligned. The statements in the body of the loop are indented.

4.4 The FOR Statement

Many loops are executed either a fixed number of times or once for each value in a consecutive sequence of integers. The FOR statement is a convenient method of loop control in either of these situations. Consider the following problem. Read a value of X and a positive integer value of N. Calculate the value of X-to-the-Nth.

```
PROGRAM POWER_OF_X(INPUT,OUTPUT);

(* THIS PROGRAM CALCULATES X-TO-THE-NTH WHEN
   N IS A POSITIVE INTEGER VALUE              *)

VAR
  X, ANSWER : REAL;
  N, INDEX  : INTEGER;

BEGIN (* POWER_OF_X *)
  WRITELN('ENTER A NUMBER AND AN EXPONENT');
  READLN(X, N);
  ANSWER := X;
  FOR INDEX := 2 TO N DO
    ANSWER := ANSWER * X;
  WRITELN(X,' TO THE', N, ' =', ANSWER)
END. (* POWER_OF_X *)
```

The FOR statement in the example means: Assign each of the consecutive integers from two thru N inclusive to INDEX . After each assignment, execute the statement "ANSWER:=ANSWER*X". You may ask "What happens if N is 1? Is the body of the loop executed?" The answer is no. The initial value must be less than or equal to the final value.

The FOR statement is convenient in that all the information necessary to control the loop is contained in a single line. The disadvantage is that its use is limited to loops which are executed a fixed number of times (once for each value in a consecutive range of integers).

Consider a second problem. Calculate the value of $3x^2/(x+2)$ for x=10, 9.5, 9.0, ..., 5.0, 4.5 Use a FOR statement to define and control the loop. Note that there are 12 values of x and that they differ by one-half. This suggests how a FOR-loop can be used in the program. The FOR statement contains the reserved word DOWNTO to define a decreasing sequence of INTEGER values which are assigned to the index variable LOOPVAR.

```
PROGRAM FOR_AGAIN(OUTPUT);

(* THIS PROGRAM CALCULATES 3 * SQR(X) / (X+2) FOR
   X = 10, 9.5, 9, .. , 4.5                     *)

VAR
  LOOPVAR : INTEGER;
  X       : REAL;

BEGIN (* FOR_AGAIN *)
  FOR LOOPVAR := 20 DOWNTO 9 DO
    BEGIN
      X := LOOPVAR/2;
      WRITELN(X:5, 3*SQR(X)/(X+2):8)
    END (* FOR *)
END. (* FOR_AGAIN *)
```

Questions such as "What happens if the initial value is "beyond" the final value?" or "Can the value of index variable be changed within the body of the loop?" are answered in the following rules.

The FOR Statement

General Form

   FOR control variable := initial value TO final value DO
      body statement

Notes

1. The control variable must be a locally-defined INTEGER or other ordinal variable. (Ordinal and local variables are described in Chapters 7 and 8 respectively.) It cannot be a component of a structured variable or "pointed at" by another variable. (Structured variables and pointer variables are described in Part II.)

2. The initial value and final value may be created using any expression having a type which is compatible with the control variable.

3. The expressions defining the initial value and final value are evaluated prior to the first execution of the loop body. Subsequent changes in any variables used in these expressions have no effect on the number of times the body is executed.

4. The control variable may be used in the body statement but its value must not be changed.

5. If TO is used then:
   a) Following each execution of the body statement, the control variable is set equal to SUCC(control variable)
   b) If the initial value is greater than the final value, the body statement is not executed.

6. TO may be replaced by DOWNTO. In this case:
   a) Following each execution of the body statement, the control variable is set equal to PRED(control variable).
   b) If the initial value is less than the final value, the body statement is not executed.

7. After the specified number of repetitions of the body-statement, the value of the control variable is indeterminate (cannot be predicted with certainty).

8. GOTO (Section 4.5) can direct control to a statement inside a FOR-loop from a statement outside the loop but an error will occur unless control is redirected outside the loop prior to the next test of the control variable.

4.5 Exercise 4.1

1. State the output produced by executing each of the following fragments. Assume that the following variable declarations have been made:

```
VAR
    I, J, K : INTEGER;
    X, Y, Z : REAL

a) I := 5;
   WHILE I > 5*I DO
     BEGIN
       WRITELN(I);
       I := I - 3
     END
```

```
b) READ(X);
   WHILE X <> SQRT(X) DO
     BEGIN
       WRITELN(X,SQR(X));
       READ(X)
     END
       .
       .
       .

   (with the input data below)
       5.0   14   21 1.0   100    0

c) I := 1;
   WHILE NOT(SUCC(I) > 8) DO
     BEGIN
       J := PRED(I);
       WHILE J < 2 * I DO
         J := J + 3;
       WRITELN(I,J);
       I := I + 1
     END

d) REPEAT
     READLN(I,J,K);
     WRITELN(I,J,K)
   UNTIL I DIV J MOD K = 0
       .
   (with the input data below)
      25  10  15
      18   6   2
       4  -4   4
      27   3   9
     100  10  10

e) I := 10;
   WHILE I <= 30 DO
     REPEAT
       I := I + 10;
       J := I;
       FOR I := 1 TO 3 DO
           WRITELN(I);
       I := J
     UNTIL I > 20

f) FOR I := 5 TO 10 DO
     FOR J := 10 DOWNTO I DO
       WRITELN(I+J)
```

g) What is the error in the following?

```
FOR K := -3 TO +3 DO
    WHILE K <> 0 DO
        K := K + 1
```

2. Rewrite the example program fragment in Section 4.2 using an equivalent REPEAT-UNTIL statement instead of the WHILE statement.

3. Consider the problem solved by the example program INTEGER_SUM in Section 4.3.

    a) Replace the REPEAT-UNTIL statement with equivalent logic using a WHILE statement.

    b) Suppose a negative value is not to be added to the sum but simply means stop reading more values. Modify the program to do this using:

        1. a REPEAT-UNTIL statement

        2. a WHILE statement

4. Assuming N to be an INTEGER variable the program fragment below prints the values 2,4,6,...,10 using a FOR-loop.

```
FOR N:=1 TO 5 DO
    WRITELN ( 2 • N )
```

    Use a similar approach in a FOR loop to generate the following sequences of values:
    a) -21, -18, -15, ..., 0
    b) 1,8,27,64,125
    c) 1,0,1,0,1,0,1,0 (use the MOD Operator)
    d) 9.25,9.00,8.75,8.5,...,6.75
    e) 14,5,0,5,14

5. Nested FOR-loops can be used to generate particular sequences of values. For example, assuming M and N to be INTEGER variables the output of

```
FOR M := 1 TO 3 DO
    FOR N := 3 DOWNTO M DO
        WRITELN(N)
```

    is the sequence 3,2,1,3,2,3. For each of the following, write a pair of nested FOR-loops to produce the sequence of values shown.
    a) 0,1,2,0,1,2,0,1,2,0,1,2
    b) 400,300,200,100,40,30,20,10,4,3,2,1
    c) 1,2,3,4,5,6,7,1,3,5,7,1,4,7
    d) 90;81,80;72,71,70;...;9,8,7,...,1,0

6. Answer the following questions:

a) Can a WHILE loop always be used to produce the equivalent logic of a FOR loop even if the body of the loop changes the values of variables used to define the initial and final values?

b) Can a REPEAT-UNTIL loop always be written which will duplicate the logic of a FOR loop?

4.6 Labels and The GOTO Statement

This section may be omitted on first reading.

In the early days of programming, there were no WHILE, REPEAT or FOR statements. Instead, all loop control (and IF-THEN-ELSE logic for that matter) was accomplished using GOTO statements. GOTO statements are available in the Pascal language but except in specific circumstances, their use is not encouraged. They provide no capabilities which are not available thru the WHILE and IF-THEN-ELSE constructs.

Shown below is a simple program to read and count the number of non-negative values in a data stream of ten real numbers. If a negative value is encountered, no further values are read. See if you can determine how many new features the program contains.

```
PROGRAM GOTO_USAGE(INPUT,OUTPUT);

(* THIS PROGRAM COUNTS THE NUMBER OF NON-NEGATIVE
   VALUES IN A SEQUENCE OF AT MOST TEN NUMBERS   *)

LABEL
  99;
VAR
  X     : REAL;
  COUNT : INTEGER;

BEGIN (* GOTO_USAGE *)
    COUNT := 0;
    WHILE COUNT <= 9 DO
      BEGIN
        WRITELN('ENTER A NUMBER, (NEGATIVE TO EXIT)');
        READLN(X);
        IF X < 0 THEN
          GOTO 99;
        WRITELN(X);
        COUNT := COUNT + 1
      END;
  99 : WRITELN(COUNT, ' NON-NEGATIVE VALUES WERE READ')
END. (* GOTO_USAGE *)
```

First, let's look at the mechanics of GOTOs and labels. A GOTO statement has the form

```
GOTO label
```

A label is an integer value which has been declared as a label in a LABEL declaration. A LABEL declaration has the form

```
LABEL integer, integer,...,integer;
```

A LABEL declaration (there can only be one in a block) must immediately follow the block header and precede all other declarations. A statement which is preceded by a label and a colon becomes a "labelled statement". Execution of "GOTO n" where n is declared as a label means the next statement executed will be the one having the label n.

This example illustrates one of the situations where GOTOs are considered acceptable.

In this problem we may want to exit from the loop without satisfying the WHILE condition. That is, if a non-negative value is read, jump out of the loop immediately. When this condition occurs the statement "GOTO 99" is executed and control is transferred to the labelled statement:

```
99: WRITELN(COUNT,' NON-NEGATIVE VALUES WERE READ')
```

If the data contains no negative values the WHILE loop is executed ten times before printing the results.

Shown below is a program body which accomplishes the same thing without using a GOTO. Compare the two loops carefully.

```
BEGIN (* NO GOTO *)
  COUNT := 0;
  WRITELN('ENTER A NUMBER (NEGATIVE TO EXIT)');
  READLN(X);
  WHILE (COUNT < 10) AND (X >= 0) DO
    BEGIN
      COUNT := COUNT + 1;
      WRITELN(X);
      WRITELN('ENTER A NUMBER (NEGATIVE TO EXIT)');
      READLN(X)
    END;
  WRITELN(COUNT, 'VALUES HAVE BEEN READ')
END. (* NO GOTO *)
```

The rules for the GOTO statement follow.

GOTO Statement

General Form

> GOTO label

Notes

1. All labels referenced in a GOTO statement must be declared as labels in a LABEL declaration in the block containing the GOTO.

2. The "value" of a label cannot be created using an expression. For example: "I:=99; GOTO I' and "GOTO 9*11" are invalid.

3. It is considered an error by some compilers to go to a statement which is within a compound statement or within the body of a WHILE, REPEAT or FOR loop.

4. Labelled statements in the same block must have different labels.

When using GOTOs and LABELs, the guidelines below should be followed.

Style Guidelines for GOTO

● GOTOs and labels *may* be appropriate when the decision to terminate repetitions is more naturally made in the middle of the loop rather than at the beginning or end of the loop.

● If a GOTO is used to exit from a loop the labelled statement should be placed immediately following the end of the loop.

● It is often a good idea to label a null statement to emphasize that it is simply an entry point to further processing. For example:

```
        WHILE TRUE DO
          BEGIN
              .
          GOTO 99
              .
          END;
    99: (* LOOP EXIT *)
```

● Values such as 99, 999, 9999, etc. should be chosen as labels, used consistently and supplemented with comments.

4.7 Exercise 4.2

1. Replace each of the following with a statement or statements which do not use GOTOs. Assume all necessary declarations have been made.

   a)
   ```
          IF X < Y THEN
             GOTO 10;
          Z := Y;
          GOTO 20;
      10: Z := X;
      20: (* CONTINUE *)
   ```

   b)
   ```
          REPEAT
             .
             .
          IF A OR B THEN GOTO 99
          UNTIL FALSE;
      99: (* CONTINUE *)
   ```

2. Suppose ELSE was not available in an IF statement. Show how a GOTO could be used to produce the same logic.

3. For the logic present in a WHILE, REPEAT and FOR loop, show an equivalent program structure using IF and GOTO statements.

4.8 Summary

1. Almost all programs contain one or more program loops -- sequences of statements which are executed more than once. Pascal provides three powerful methods of controlling the number of repetitions of a loop. They are the:

   WHILE loop: The most general and flexible; the test to execute is made at the beginning of the loop.

   REPEAT-UNTIL loop: The test is made at the end of each repetition; the body is executed at least once.

   FOR-loop: Useful when a loop is to be executed once for each value in a range of consecutive values.

2. When used in conjunction with statement labels, GOTO statements provide a means of explicit control of the order of statement execution. They make it easier to exit from a loop when special conditions exist. Logic involving GOTOs can always be written using other statements and almost without exception, this is desirable.

4.9 Programming Problems

4.1 Tabulate values of the function $(x^2-x+7)/(x^2+2)$ for the values of x below. Use FOR-loops to generate the x-values.

      a) 1, 2, 3, ..., 20
      b) 3, 6, 9, ..., 24
      c) 0, -1, -2, ..., -8
      d) 12, 10, 8, ..., -10

4.2 Tabulate values of the function

$$y = \frac{3\sin^3 x + 4\cos^3 x}{16x^2+8x-3}$$

for x = -1, -3/4, -1/2, ... 3/4,1. Skip over values of x which make the division undefined.

4.3 If x_0 is an initial estimate of the value of $1/\sqrt{z}$, successively better estimates are given by x_1, x_2, etc. where $x_n=0.5x_{n-1}(3-zx^2_{n-1})$, n=1,2,.... . Use this procedure in a program to calculate the fifth estimate of $1/\sqrt{2}$. Use 0.4 as your initial estimate. Print each estimate.

4.4 Suppose division could not be done on a computer. One method of obtaining increasingly accurate approximations to a value of 1/A is to calculate $x_0,x_1,x_2,$ etc. where x_0 is some initial estimate of the reciprocal and the value $x_n=x_{n-1}$ $(2-Ax_{n-1})$, n=1,2,3,.... Write a program which calculates the tenth approximation to a value of 1/3 (i.e: A=3) using the method described above. Use 0.3 as your initial estimate.

4.5 The sum of cubes of the numbers one thru N is equal to the square of the sum of the numbers one thru N. For example, $1^3+2^3+3^3=(1+2+3)^2$. Suppose you want to use this fact to find an approximate value of the square root of the number K. This could be done in the following way. Find M such that the sum of cubes of the numbers one thru M is less than K and the sum of cubes of the numbers 1 thru (M+1) is greater than K. (If by chance the sum of cubes equals K, the square root is exactly 1+2+3+...+M.) Conclude that the square root of K lies somewhere between the sum of the values 1 thru M and the sum of the values 1 thru M+1. Write a program which reads a value of K and computes an approximate square root using this method. Accuracy can be improved by multiplying K by an even power of ten and dividing the result by one-half the power of ten used. For example, to find the square root of 12.357, use 123570 as the value of K and divide the result by 100.

4.6   The sequence of numbers 1, 1, 2, 3, 5, 8, 13, ... is called the Fibonacci sequence. Each term in the sequence except the first two (which are each equal to one) is obtained by adding the previous two terms. Write a program which reads a value of N and prints the first N terms of the sequence on separate lines. Between each value printed, print the ratio of the current term to the previous term. What is apparently true about these ratios as the terms become larger?

4.7   The probability that no two people in a group of N people have the same birthday is given by the formula

$$P_n = P_{n-1}\left(1 - \frac{n-1}{365}\right) \qquad \text{where } P_0 = 1$$

Use this formula in a program which determines the smallest number of people such that the probability of no matching birthdays is less than one-half. Assume the result occurs for N less than fifty. Use a FOR statement in generating the values of P_1, P_2, ... Compare each value to one-half to determine if it is necessary to exit from the FOR-loop.

4.8   At a party of N couples, the men pull a woman's name out of a hat to see who their partner will be for the next activity. The chance that no man draws his partner's name can be obtained from the following relationship.

$$P_n = \frac{n-1}{n} P_{n-1} + \frac{1}{n} P_{n-1} \qquad \text{where } P_1 = 0, \text{ and } P_2 = 0.5$$

Read a value of N and calculate the probability that no man draws his wife's name for groups of people of 1, 2, 3, ..., N.

4.9   A family of functions: $F_1(x)$, $F_2(x)$, $F_3(x)$, ... is defined by the following relationships.

$$F_1(x)=1, \quad F_2(x)=x, \quad F_n(x) = \frac{2n-1}{n} F_{n-1}(x) - \frac{n-1}{n} F_{n-2}(x)$$
$$\text{where } n = 2, 3, 4, \ldots$$

Write a program which reads a value of x and calculates the first ten functions of x as defined above.

4.10   Read a value of N. Assume N is ten or less. Print out all triples of positive integer values which add up to N. Print out all triples of non-negative integer values which add up to N.

4.11   Tabulate values of the function

$$z = \frac{x^2 - 2xy + 3y^2}{xy + 3x + 2y + 4}$$

using all pairs of x and y values in the ranges x=1,2,3,...,6; y=1,2,3,4,5. Use a pair of nested FOR-loops to generate the x and y values.

4.12   Read a value of K. Assume K is six or less. Print the values of K MOD (M+N), K MOD (M*N) and K MOD M^N where M and N can take any values in the set 1,2,3,...,(K-1).

4.13   Suppose computers could only multiply and divide by two. (In fact, this isn't far from the truth!) The product of any two numbers M and N can still be done using the "Russian" method of multiplication. It consists of successively dividing the smaller number by two (ignoring any remainder) and successively multiplying the larger value by two. As this process is being carried out, add to a total only those multiples of the larger value for which the division of the smaller produced an odd quotient. For example, to multiply 37 by 65 the following results would be obtained.

```
37              65
18             130 (not added to total)
 9             260
 4             520 (not added to total)
 2            1040 (not added to total)
 1            2080
               ----
              2405 (the total)
```

If you don't believe it, what is 37 times 65? Write a program which reads a pair of values and calculates their product using the above technique.

4.14   Suppose the sales tax is seven percent rounded to the nearest cent. A restaurant owner serving meals costing him between one and nine dollars (without tax) wants to price his items so that with the tax added, the total is a multiple of five cents. Print a table with two items per line showing for each the item price, tax and total which satisfy this criterion.

CHAPTER 5: CHARACTERS AND TEXT PROCESSING

Questions Answered in this Chapter:

1. What facilities exist in Pascal for processing characters and words?

2. What is meant by the type TEXT?

To this point, we have described the nature of, and the processing which can be done with three of the predefined types of values in Pascal, namely: INTEGER, REAL and BOOLEAN. In this chapter we consider the two remaining predefined types -- CHAR and TEXT. Knowledge of how to process characters and text data will greatly increase the scope of problems which you can solve. Character and text processing applications are the cornerstones of office automation and almost all other non-numeric processing done by computers.

5.1 Character Values

A character is represented by a single printed symbol enclosed in single quotes. 'x', '?', ':', '9' are four constants of the type CHAR. Sequences of more than one character such as 'JOHN', 'SEPT.1985', etc., are called literals or strings and are dealt with more completely in Chapter 10 which describes arrays. A value of type CHAR is similar to a literal or string of length one since it contains only one character.

How many characters can be used in Pascal? That depends on the computer system used to run your Pascal program. Character sets of 64, 96, 128 and 256 characters are commonly found. The two most common sets are called the ASCII (ask-ee) and the EBCDIC (ebb-c-dic) sets. They are described in Appendix A.

5.1.1 An Example

Consider the following problem. Read a sentence from the INPUT file and count the number of words in the sentence. Sounds easy, doesn't it? Before rushing into writing a program, ask yourself this question: "When is a word a word?" For example, are hyphenated words one word or two? Is a number like 3.14 considered to be a word? How will we know when we reach the end of the sentence? To make the program logic simple, let us make the following four assumptions: 1) Exactly one blank separates each pair of words; 2) The first character in the INPUT file is non-blank (starts the first word); 3) Any contiguous sequence of non-blank characters is a word; 4) The end-of-line character immediately follows the last character in the sentence.

With these assumptions the algorithm is simple. Starting with a count of 1, we simply add one to the word count each time a blank is encountered. Here is the program.

```
PROGRAM WORD_COUNT (INPUT,OUTPUT);

(* THIS PROGRAM COUNTS THE NUMBER OF WORDS IN
   A SENTENCE CONTAINED IN A SINGLE LINE OF
   THE INPUT FILE                                  *)

CONST
   BLANK  = ' ';
VAR
   NEXTCHAR : CHAR;
   COUNT    : INTEGER;

BEGIN (* WORD_COUNT *)
   COUNT := 1;
   WRITELN('ENTER A SENTENCE');
   WHILE NOT EOLN DO
     BEGIN
       READ(NEXTCHAR);
       WRITE(NEXTCHAR);
       IF NEXTCHAR = BLANK THEN
           COUNT := COUNT + 1
     END;
   WRITELN; (* OUTPUT THE SENTENCE *)
   WRITELN('THE NUMBER OF WORDS IS', COUNT:3)
END. (* WORD_COUNT *)
```

Comments.

1. CHAR constants and variables are declared in the same way as other types of constants and variables.

2. When used with a CHAR value, the WRITE procedure appends the character to the end of the line but does not display the line. The actual printing is accomplished by the WRITELN following the loop. Had we used WRITELN (NEXTCHAR), within the loop, each character of the input would have appeared on a separate line.

3. Two characters can be compared for equality as in "NEXTCHAR=BLANK". In fact, the only operators which can be used with values of type CHAR are the relational operators. More will be said about this in the next section.

4.   What triggers the pause that allows a line of input to be entered? In this
     example it is the first evaluation of EOLN. The procedures READ and
     READLN and the EOLN function all unlock the keyboard and wait for a
     line of data to be entered whenever all previously entered characters have
     been read.

5.2 Operations With CHAR Values

Only the six relational operators can be used with CHAR values. Clearly
equal-to and not-equal-to are meaningful when comparing two characters but
how is less-than or greater-than evaluated? On computers which processes
Pascal programs, there is a dictionary order of characters called the *collating
sequence*. The collating sequence is such that

1.   The digits '0' thru '9' are consecutive and increasing.

2.   The letter ranges 'a' thru 'z' and 'A' thru 'Z' are each in dictionary order
     but not necessarily consecutive. (In the EBCDIC set for example, there
     are seven characters between 'i' and 'j'.)

3.   The relative positions of other characters are dependent on the computer
     system used.

The collating sequences of the ASCII and EBCDIC character sets are found
in Appendix A. A certain degree of independence of program logic from
specific computer system peculiarities can be obtained by using the standard
functions ORD and CHR which are now described.

For a character x, ORD(x) gives the position of the character in the
collating sequence. For example, on the computer system used by the author,
ORD('A') is 193, ORD('B') is 194, and ORD('$') is 91. The function ORD
produces an INTEGER value.

The function CHR is the inverse of ORD. That is, given an INTEGER
argument, it produces the character having that ORD value in the collating
sequence. For example: CHR(193) is 'A'; CHR(91) is '$'; CHR(249) is '9'.

Because ORD and CHR are inverse functions it follows that for an
INTEGER value i and a character x that:

```
ORD(CHR(i)) = i      and      CHR(ORD(x)) = x
```

When comparing two characters using one of the relational operators, it is
their order in the collating sequence which is compared. That is, for a pair of
characters x and y

```
x < y  if and only if  ORD(x) < ORD(y)
```

Character values may also be used as arguments of the standard functions PRED (predecessor) and SUCC (successor). The result is the character immediately before or after the given character in the collating sequence. To print the digits '0' thru '9', one could write:

```
X:= '0';
WHILE X <= '9' DO
  BEGIN
    WRITELN(X);
    X:=SUCC(X)
  END
```

A much better approach would be the following

```
FOR X:= '0' TO '9' DO
   WRITELN (X)
```

This emphasizes the point that the control variable in a FOR statement can have any ordinal type.

When a CHAR value is written without any format specification, it occupies a single print position. If a field width is provided, the character appears in the rightmost position reserved for the value. For example

```
WRITELN('A':3, '$':2)
```

produces blank-blank-A-blank-$.

5.3 Text File Input and Output

Before looking a the type TEXT in general, we discuss briefly the processing of data obtained from non-keyboard INPUT files.

5.3.1 Non-keyboard INPUT Files

Thus far we have assumed the standard INPUT file is the keyboard. Depending on what Pascal processor you are using, the location of the INPUT file may be other than the keyboard. A common approach assumes the INPUT lines follow the program and are separated from the it by a special line of "job control" information. On the system used by the author, a $ENTRY line separates the source program from the INPUT file. With the Waterloo Pascal processors for example, the organization is as follows.

```
PROGRAM  x (...);   ⎫
   .                ⎪
   .                ⎬  source program
   .                ⎪
END.                ⎪
$ENTRY              ⎭
line 1 of data•     ⎫
line 2 of data•     ⎪
   .                ⎬  the INPUT file
   .                ⎪
last line of data•■ ⎭
```

In the above '●' represents the end-of-line character. The 'lozenge symbol '■'
represents a special marker called the *end-of-file marker* which follows the
end-of-line character after the last line of the file. An end-of-file marker is
necessary to indicate the end of the file. It is not a character which can be
read but its presence can be detected using the built-in EOF (end-of-file)
function. Specifically EOF is true if the next read would attempt to read the
end-of-file marker; it is false otherwise. An example. Suppose the INPUT data
follows the program and is separated from it by $ENTRY. The problem is to
read and echo the characters in each line. Because input is interactive and not
"batched", a prompt for input is unnecessary. A suitable program follows.

```
PROGRAM FILE_ECHO(INPUT,OUTPUT);

(* THIS PROGRAM READS EACH CHARACTER IN THE
   INPUT FILE AND WRITES IT ON THE OUTPUT FILE
   THE INPUT DATA FOLLOWS THE $ENTRY LINE      *)

VAR
   X: CHAR;

BEGIN (* FILE_ECHO *)
   WHILE NOT EOF(INPUT) DO
     BEGIN
       WHILE NOT EOLN(INPUT) DO
         BEGIN
           READ(X);
           WRITE(X)
         END; (* A LINE OF INPUT *)
       WRITELN; (* PRINT THE LINE *)
       READLN (* SKIP THE EOL CHARACTER *)
     END
END.(* FILE_ECHO *)
$ENTRY
THIS IS LINE ONE OF THE INPUT FILE
RIGHT NOW THE BROWNS ARE BEATING THE CHARGERS
```

Comments.

1. Two loops are required. The body of the outer loop is executed once for each line of input. The body of the inner loop is executed once for each character in a line.

2. The WRITELN is necessary to display the characters accumulated by the WRITEs in the inner loop. The READLN is necessary to skip the end-of-line character so that the next line can be read. (Without the READLN, the program would stop after processing the first line. Make sure you understand why.)

5.3.2 The Type TEXT

The predefined identifiers INPUT and OUTPUT have the type TEXT. An identifier with the type TEXT has a "value" which is a sequence of one or more characters. This sequence may be partitioned into one or more *lines* where a line is a sequence of zero or more characters followed by the end-of-line character. When obtaining data from a TEXT source such as the keyboard, the data is read one line at a time and stored in the computer's memory.

When performing output operations, each WRITE appends one or more characters to the sequence created to that point. WRITELN appends the end-of-line character to the sequence after writing any parameter values. It is the end-of-line character which causes the sequence to be sent to the actual device.

Although INPUT and OUTPUT are predefined variables of the type TEXT, other identifiers can be declared as having that type as in:

```
VAR
    A, B, C : TEXT
```

For the time being however, we will limit our use of TEXT variables to the standard files INPUT and OUTPUT. The type TEXT is a special kind of the type called FILE. FILE types are described in detail in Chapter 12. The procedures READ, READLN, WRITE, WRITELN, and the functions EOLN and EOF can be used with any TEXT file. The PAGE procedure can be used with TEXT files which are printed.

If a source of input data other than INPUT or if output is written on files other than OUTPUT, it is necessary to identify which file is being used in a READ, READLN, WRITE, WRITELN, EOF, EOLN, or PAGE procedure or function. This is done by making the file or TEXT identifier the first name in the parameter list of the corresponding procedure or function. Shown below are equivalent expressions using INPUT and OUTPUT as example files. If omitted, INPUT is assumed for READ, READLN, EOLN, and EOF; OUTPUT is assumed for WRITE, WRITELN and PAGE. These ideas are illustrated below.

Explicit Reference	Implicit Reference
READ(INPUT,...)	READ(...)
READLN(INPUT,...	READLN(...)
EOLN(INPUT)	EOLN
EOF(INPUT)	EOF
WRITE(OUTPUT,...)	WRITE(...)
WRITELN(OUTPUT,...)	WRITELN(...)
PAGE(OUTPUT)	PAGE

5.4 Exercise 5.1

1. What is the value of:

    a) CHR (ORD('8')-1)
    b) SUCC(CHR(1 + ORD('0')))
    c) ('A'<>'B')or('B' <= PRED('B'))

2. Suppose that it is known that

        ORD ('A') = ORD ('a') + 64

    What is it that you hope the value of the expressions ORD('b')+64, ORD('c')+64,etc., would be? Why might this not be the case?

3. Assuming variable X to be of type CHAR, what is the error in each of the following?

    a) X:=9
    b) '123' <=X
    c) ORD('X'+2)
    d) CHR(MAXINT)
    e) READ(X:5)
    f) X:= 'ABC'
    g) X=('A'or'E'or'I' or'O'or'U')

4. What is the output from the following FOR loop. Assume X is of type CHAR.

        FOR X:= 'A' TO 'Z' DO
           WRITELN(ORD(X):5,X)

5. Assume the file INPUT contains the following sequence of characters where '●' denotes end-of-line and "■" denotes end-of-file.

    ABC●D●●EF●■

    What is the output produced by each of the following? Assume X has the type CHAR.

    a)   ```
         READ (X);
         WRITELN(X);
         IF NOT EOLN THEN
             READLN;
         WRITE(X);
         READLN;
         IF NOT EOLN THEN
             WRITELN(X);
         ```

    b)   ```
         WHILE NOT EOLN DO
             READ(X);
         WRITE(X);
         READLN(X);
         WRITELN;
         REPEAT
           READLN(X);
           WRITELN(X)
         UNTIL EOF
         ```

6. Write a program to count the number of lines of data in a non-keyboard input file.

7. Write a program to print the characters in the odd numbered lines of an INPUT file which contain either an even or an odd number of lines.

5.5 Numeric INPUT and OUTPUT

As we already know, READ and READLN can be used obtain INTEGER and REAL values from the INPUT file. Since INPUT has the type TEXT -- a sequence of characters -- how are numeric values created and assigned to INTEGER and REAL variables? The answer is that the READ and READLN procedures actually read characters one at a time from the INPUT file and construct a numeric value from the signs, digits and exponents present. For INTEGER and REAL variables the algorithm is:

1. Skip (read and ignore) blanks and end-of-line characters until the first digit is found. If the first non-blank, non end-of-line character is not a digit, an error occurs.
2. Read characters one at a time and create the numeric value stopping when the first non-digit (other than 'E' -- the exponent indicator) is found.

The WRITE procedure does the opposite. Given a number and an optional format specifier, WRITE appends an appropriate sequence of characters to the end of the output file.

We could do these conversions ourselves. Consider a simple case. Read the digits in an unsigned integer character-by-character; convert it to an INTEGER value; write it on the OUTPUT file as a string of characters. A suitable program follows.

```
PROGRAM NUMBER_CONVERSION(INPUT,OUTPUT);

(* THIS PROGRAM READS A SEQUENCE OF CHARACTERS FORMING
   AN INTEGER, CONVERTS IT TO AN INTEGER AND OUTPUTS
   THE NUMERIC VALUE AS A CHARACTER STRING              *)

VAR
  NUMBER, DIGIT_VALUE, DIVISOR : INTEGER;
  X                            : CHAR;

BEGIN (* NUMBER_CONVERSION *)
  (* 1 - INITIALIZE                    *)
     WRITELN('ENTER AN UNSIGNED INTEGER');
     NUMBER := 0;
  (* 2 - PERFORM CHARACTER TO INTEGER CONVERSION *)
     WHILE NOT EOLN DO
       BEGIN (* READ DIGITS AND BUILD VALUE *)
         READ(X);
         DIGIT_VALUE := ORD(X) - ORD('0');
         NUMBER := 10 * NUMBER + DIGIT_VALUE
       END;
     WRITELN('THE NUMBER IS',NUMBER:6);
  (* 3 - PERFORM INTEGER TO CHARACTER CONVERSION *)
     DIVISOR := 10000; (* ASSUME VALUE IS <= 99999 *)
     WHILE DIVISOR >= 10 DO (* EXTRACT DIGITS *)
       BEGIN
         DIGIT_VALUE := NUMBER DIV DIVISOR;
         WRITE(CHR(ORD('0') + DIGIT_VALUE));
         NUMBER := NUMBER MOD DIVISOR;
         DIVISOR := DIVISOR DIV 10
       END; (* DIGIT EXTRACTION *)
     WRITE(CHR(ORD('0') + NUMBER)); (* LAST DIGIT *)
     WRITELN (* OUTPUT THE DIGITS *)
END. (* NUMBER_CONVERSION *)
```

Comments.

1. Note the assignment statement

```
DIGIT_VALUE := ORD(X) - ORD('0')
```

This line converts a digit in the form of a character to its equivalent numeric value. It works because the positions of the characters '0', '1', ... ,'9' in the collating sequence are consecutive. Therefore ORD('8') is 8 more than ORD('0').

2. Observe that NUMBER is calculated by:

```
NUMBER := 10 * NUMBER + DIGIT_VALUE
```

After each digit is read, the new value is obtained by multiplying the old value by ten and adding the new digit value.

3. The conversion from INTEGER to characters is straightforward. The number is successively divided by decreasing powers of ten and the quotient in the DIV operation is converted to a CHAR value using the CHR function. The MOD operation removes the most significant digit from the number it preparation for the next iteration of the loop.

4. This algorithm will always print five digits for every value entered. Logic can be included to suppress non-significant leading zeros.

The READ and READLN procedures use the basic approach illustrated in the foregoing program. When these procedures terminate, the next character available for reading is the first character following the last digit of the number.

5.5.1 Mixed CHAR and Numeric INPUT

The following problem illustrates how a mixture of characters and numbers can be input using READ and READLN. Suppose the INPUT file contains payroll data with one employee's data in each line. An end-of-file marker follows the last line of input. The location and meaning of the values in each line are as follows:

positions	data	type of data
1-15	employee name	characters
16-19	hours worked	real
20-24	pay rate	real
25-35	department	character
36-EOL	other data	doesn't matter

A sample four-line file follows.

```
position → 123456789 123456789 12345689 123456
```

```
JIM DODD          40.0 8.75 COMPUTING
KAY HARRISON      48.0 8.75 COMPUTING
MIKE RUWALD       42.5 9.25 OPERATIONS
MURRAY SHAKER     37.5 5.00 PERSONNEL
```

The problem is to read the data and print a payroll register showing the name, department and pay received for each employee.

```
PROGRAM PAYROLL_1(INPUT,OUTPUT);

(* THIS PROGRAM CALCULATES THE PAY FOR EACH
   EMPLOYEE IN THE INPUT FILE                *)

CONST
   NAME_LENGTH = 15;
   DEPT_LENGTH = 10;
VAR
   HOURS, RATE, PAY, TOTAL_PAY : REAL;
   NEXTCHAR                    : CHAR;
   I                           : INTEGER;

BEGIN (* PAYROLL_1 *)
   TOTAL_PAY := 0;
   WHILE NOT EOF DO
      BEGIN
         (* 1 - READ THE NAME *)
            FOR I:= 1 TO NAME_LENGTH DO
               BEGIN
                  READ(NEXTCHAR);
                  WRITE(NEXTCHAR)
               END; (* FOR *)
         (* 2 - CALCULATE PAY *)
            READ(HOURS,RATE);
            PAY := HOURS * RATE;
            TOTAL_PAY := TOTAL_PAY + PAY;
         (* 3 - READ AND PRINT THE DEPT *)
            FOR I:= 1 TO DEPT_LENGTH DO
               BEGIN
                  READ(NEXTCHAR);
                  WRITE(NEXTCHAR)
               END;
         (* 4 - PRINT THE LINE *)
            WRITELN(PAY:8:2);
            READLN (* GET READY FOR NEXT LINE *)
      END; (* WHILE *)
   WRITELN('THE TOTAL PAY IS', TOTAL_PAY:9:2)
END. (* PAYROLL_1 *)
```

This example illustrates that a mixture of character and numeric data can be read properly. The main differences are:

1.   A character READ reads only one character.

2.   A numeric READ skips leading blanks, ignoring end-of-line characters looking for a digit or sign. It terminates having read the last digit in the number.

5.6 Exercise 5.2

1.   Suppose the input file contains the following four lines where ● denotes the end-of-line character.

    2 25●   -17.5   19   -0.0● 5 50 17● 10.0●

Suppose that X,Y,Z are REAL variables. For each of the following, determine the values assigned to the variables by executing each of the following sequences of statements.

a)   READ (X,Y);
     READLN(Z)

b)   READLN(X,Y);
     READ(Z)

c)   READLN(X);
     READLN(Y);
     READLN(Z)

d)   READLN;
     READLN(X,X,X,X);
     READLN(Y,Y,Y,Z)

2.   You are given the following declarations:

         VAR
           C1,C2,C3:CHAR;
           R1,R2   :REAL;
           I1,I2   :INTEGER

Suppose the INPUT file contains the following three input lines ('b' denotes a blank, '●' denotes the end-of-line character).

```
bbXY24.5b●b17Z●-8PQ90b●
```

For each of the following write a sequence of READ and/or READLN statements using as few READs as possible which cause the variables to be assigned the values shown.

a) C1='X', R1=24.5, I1=17
b) C3=blank, R2=17.0, C1='Z', C2='-'
c) I1=17, I2=-8, C2=blank

5.7 Summary

1. A value of type CHAR is a single character. Depending on the computer system used there may be as many as 256 different characters defined. Characters have an order assigned to them called the collating sequence which allows the relational operators to be used when comparing two characters.

2. Four standard functions are available for processing character values. They are:

   ● ORD(X) returns the position of the argument character in the collating sequence

   ● CHR(i) returns the character with the ORD value of i in the collating sequence

   ● PRED(X) returns the character preceding X in the collating sequence

   ● SUCC(X) returns the character following X in the collating sequence

3. When writing CHAR values without a format specifier, each character occupies one output position. If a field width is present, the character is placed in the rightmost position of those reserved for the value.

4. INPUT has the type TEXT meaning a file or sequence of characters consisting of one or more lines each of which is terminated by an end-of-line character. The end-of-line character normally prints as a blank. An end-of-file marker follows the last line on non-keyboard input files.

5. The standard procedures READ and READLN can be used to obtain the next CHAR, INTEGER or REAL value from a TEXT sequence. READ and READLN cannot be used to read BOOLEAN values.

6. EOLN is true when the next character to be read is the end-of-line character. EOF is true if the next READ would attempt to read the end-of-file marker.

7. When reading a number, the READ procedure does much more than return a single character. It skips leading blanks and end-of-line characters until a digit or sign is found. Then the characters defining the number are read sequentially and the value of the number is computed. A subsequent read begins with the first character following the number.

8. READLN operates like READ except that once a value has been assigned to each variable in the parameter list, all characters up to and including the next end-of-line character are read and ignored. A subsequent read begins with the first character in the next line.

5.8 Programming Problems

5.1 Write a program to eliminate the vowels in an input file containing several lines of characters. That is, echo the input, ignoring vowels. Start a new line of output when an end-of-line character is detected.

5.2 For security purposes it is occasionally necessary to "star out" dollar amounts. For example to replace "$19475.52" with "$*****.**". Develop an algorithm and write a program to replace the digits in dollar amounts with a '*'. Test your program on the following passage.

> In a company of 75 employees, salaries of $20000 or more are not uncommon. The president makes over $45000.00 while the mail clerk has an hourly rate of $5.25.

5.3 The input consists of a single line of text. Count the number of letters, digits and other characters in the line.

5.4   Write a program which reads a single line of input, echoing each
       character as it is read, and prints a count of:
       a) the number of non-blank characters
       b) the number of vowels
       c) the number of digits (characters between '0' and '9')
       d) the number of times two successive letters are the same

       Test your program on the following line of input.

            bookkeeping is 99 percent routine

5.5   Assume that a word is any successive sequence of non-blank characters
       and that a single blank separates each pair of words. Write a program
       which reads several lines of text, echoing each character as it is read
       and which prints a count of:

       - the number of words
       - the length of the longest word
       - the length of the shortest word
       - the number of words ending in 's'
       - the average length of the words

       Improve the generality of the program by recognizing the common
       punctuation marks as denoting the end of a word.

5.6   Suppose you only have the ability to read characters from the input
       file. To create REAL values it would be necessary to read the
       characters comprising the value and build the numeric value using
       Pascal statements. Write a program which reads an input file
       containing one REAL value per line. Assume that blanks may precede
       the first digit and that the end-of-line character immediately follows the
       last digit. For each line read, write a single output line of the form "X
       is a value of Y" where X and Y denote the characters and the REAL
       value respectively. If the input contains an exponent (e.g., 2.45E-03),
       use the exponent style of formatting when displaying the REAL value.
       Test your program on the following lines of input (• denotes
       end-of-line).

            2.0 •-5•nn+98E-2•47500.0E3•-21.005E-12•

5.7   The program reads one or more lines of characters from the INPUT
       file representing a statement, question or exclamation. Assume that the
       first occurrence of a period, question mark or exclamation mark
       denotes the end of the input. Echo each "sentence" read and print one
       of "statement", "question" or "exclamation" on the line following.

5.8   The input file contains the names of several cities having one-word
        names of not more than ten characters. More than one name may
        appear in a line. Read the data and print the names, one city per line
        so that the *last* character of each name appears in print position 12.
        Test your program using the data

        CHICAGO•DENVER PARIS•LONDON WATERLOO MOSCOW•
        BOMBAY   TEHRAN TOKYO•

5.9   Write a program which will echo an input file and which translates all
        lower case letters to upper case.

5.10   Write a program which counts the number of times the word "THE"
        appears in an INPUT file. Test your program using the lines below.

        THE PROBLEM OF FAT THEODORE GOETHE IS THE•
        ACCURATE PRONUNCIATION OF THE WORD 'THE'•

5.11   The input file contains the names of several individuals, one individual
        per line each having two given names or initials preceding the surname.
        Extra blanks may precede the first name or separate any pair of names.
        Read the data and output the names one per line replacing each given
        name with the initial. Some sample input and output is shown below.

        JOHN BRUCE MOORE   ➜ J. B. MOORE
        JULIAN P. HUXLEY   ➜ J. P. HUXLEY
        R. R. REAGAN   ➜ R. R. REAGAN
        Z. ADOLPH SHICKELGRUBER   ➜ Z. A. SHICKELGRUBER

5.12   Write a program that reads a sequence of words separated by blanks
        and determines how many of them are valid Pascal identifiers. Echo
        each word read and print a line of form "THERE ARE x VALID
        IDENTIFIERS".

5.13   Input to the program consists of several lines of characters, each
        containing an arithmetic expression. For each expression determine if
        the number of left and right parentheses match and that at no time in
        the left-to-right scan does the number of right parentheses exceed the
        number of left parentheses. After echoing each input line, output one of
        the following messages: "VALID", "INVALID - TOO FEW RIGHT
        PARENTHESES", or "INVALID - TOO MANY RIGHT
        PARENTHESES".

5.14   Suppose an input file contains several names and ages of people as in
the following sample INPUT file.

```
RUTH 25, JEREMIAH 17, ARCHIE 20, •
VERONICA 14, TOM 28•
```

A comma immediately follows each age except that of the last person.
Write a program to read the input and print a table as shown below
following which the average age of the people is displayed.

```
RUTH              25
JEREMIAH          17
ARCHIE            20
VERONICA          14
TOM               28
        AVERAGE   20.8
```

5.15   Assume that a program comment begins and ends on the same line.
Write a program which reads a Pascal source program as input, and
prints the comments it contains, one output line per comment.

5.16   An input file contains several lines of text. Assume that a word begins
with the first character after a blank and terminates with the first
blank character thereafter. Write a program which reads the input file
and reformats it so that no word starts to print after position 30 in an
output line. Replace instances of multiple blanks in the input with a
single blank in the output.

5.17   The product of (x-a)(x-b)(x-c)(x-d) is a fourth degree polynomial of
the form $px^4+qx^3+rx^2+sx+t$. Write a program which reads values of
"a", "b", "c", and "d" and calculates the values of p, q, r, s, t. Print a
line of the following form.

(___)X**4+(___)X**3+(___)X**2+(___)X+(___)

where the dashes represent the values calculated.

5.18   Write a program to determine
   a) how many characters can be printed on a line in the standard
       OUTPUT file.
   b) how many INTEGERs can be printed on a line if no format code
       is specified.
   c) how many REAL values can be printed on a line if no format
       codes are specified.

5.19   Write a program which prints a table showing the ORD value, hexadecimal value and binary value for the upper case letters and digits. Note: if $h_1h_2h_3$ is the hexadecimal form of a number, it represents the following value

$$h_1 \times 16^2 + h_2 \times 16^1 + h_3 \times 16^0$$

The hexadecimal characters are '0' thru '9' and 'A' thru 'F' where A = 10, B = 11, C = 12, D = 13, E = 14, F = 15

CHAPTER 6: TYPES OF VALUES

Questions Answered in this Chapter:

1. How are types of values classified in Pascal?

2. What is an enumerated type? How is it defined and used?

3. What are subrange types? What are the advantages and disadvantages of using subranges?

6.1 Types of Values

One of the strengths of the Pascal language is the requirement that each variable used in a program must be declared as having a certain type. This type dictates the acceptable set of values which can be assigned to a variable. For example, the type INTEGER consists of the values -MAXINT, -MAXINT+1, -MAXINT +2, ...,0, ..., +MAXINT-1, +MAXINT; BOOLEAN consists of the two values FALSE and TRUE; CHAR consists of single characters such as 'A', '#', '9'. The type REAL in theory at least encompasses all numbers between some positive and negative limits but because only a fixed number of bits (often 32) is used to store each REAL value, there are only a finite number of bit patterns and hence a finite number of REAL values which can be used in a Pascal program. Section 2.3 discusses these limits in detail.

The diagram below shows the types which can be used in a Pascal program.

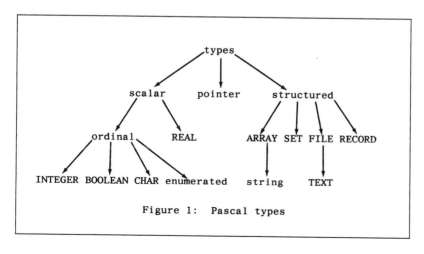

Figure 1: Pascal types

This tree-diagram shows that types are classified into three groups --
scalar, pointer and structured. Scalar types are those whose members are
single values (a single number, character or boolean value). A pointer value is
a memory address or location of some other value. The existence of pointer
variables in Pascal gives great flexibility and power for creating unique,
dynamic data structures. Pointers are discussed in Chapter 14. The third group
of types --- structured types, refers to collections or aggregations of scalar
types. We have already discussed and used one of these, namely TEXT which
is a sequence of characters. The discussion of composite data types forms the
basis of Part II of this book.

This chapter contains a detailed discussion of scalar types in Pascal. In
particular Section 2 describes the why and how of creating new enumerated
types. Section 3 describes the purpose and method of defining subranges of
ordinal types.

6.2 The Standard Ordinal types - A Summary

Pascal provides four standard, predefined, scalar types namely:
INTEGER, BOOLEAN, CHAR and REAL. The first three are called ordinal
types because the values belonging to each are assigned an integer ordering. In
the case of INTEGER the ordering is natural, from -MAXINT to
+MAXINT. For the BOOLEAN type, it was arbitrarily decided that FALSE
precedes TRUE and that ORD(FALSE)=0. For the type CHAR, the ordering
agrees with that of normal dictionary ordering for the most part since: the
lower case letters are in alphabetical order; the upper case letters are in
alphabetical order; and the digits are in order of ascending value. Special
programming is necessary to cause a sort of upper and lower case letters to
appear in correct sequence. Usually this is done by temporarily converting
lower case to upper case; performing the sort; and re-converting to lower case
where necessary.

The type REAL is not considered ordinal even though there are only
finitely many REAL values which can be represented on a computer.

For all ordinal types, the standard functions ORD, PRED and SUCC are
well-defined as summarized in the table which follows.

Type of Parameter	Function		
	ORD	PRED	SUCC
INTEGER	ORD(i)=i	PRED(i)=i-1	SUCC(i)=i+1
BOOLEAN	ORD(FALSE)=0	PRED(TRUE)=	SUCC(FALSE)=
	ORD(TRUE)=1	FALSE	TRUE
CHAR	ORD(x)=pos'n	PRED(x)=char	SUCC(x)=char
	in coll. seq	preceding	following
12			

The relational operators $<$, $=$, $>$, etc., are also well-defined for every ordinal type. For any pair of values x and y, say, belonging to an ordinal type it is true that

```
x < y if, and only if ORD(x) < ORD(y)
```

Similar definitions can be given for the other five relational operators.

The function PRED is well-defined for all values of a given type except that having the minimum ORD value. Similarly SUCC is well-defined for all parameters of an ordinal type except the value having the largest ORD value.

6.3 Enumerated types

Most programmers would be quite happy to go through life using only the four standard scalar types. Pascal however, allows you to define new ordinal types. To do this you must provide three pieces of information.

1. The name of the type (a type identifier)
2. The names of the values belonging to the type
3. The order of the values in the type

6.3.1 An Example

Consider the following example. Shown below is a type declaration which defines an enumerated type called DAY_TYPE. It is called enumerated because you must enumerate (provide an exhaustive list of all the values in) the type.

```
TYPE
    DAY_TYPE = (SUNDAY,MONDAY,TUESDAY,WEDNESDAY,
                THURSDAY,FRIDAY,SATURDAY)
```

A TYPE declaration is placed between the CONST and the VAR declarations in a program. The name of the type is DAY_TYPE. The suffix "_TYPE" is appended to "DAY" to help remember that it is a type identifier. It also permits "DAY" to be used as the name of a variable of type DAY_TYPE. The seven values in the type are SUNDAY, MONDAY, ... , SATURDAY. The values in an enumerated type must be identifiers which are not used for any other purpose in the program. The ordering of the values is implied by the order in which the values are listed. By definition, the first value has an ORD value of 0, the second 1, etc. That is ORD(SUNDAY)=0, ORD(MONDAY)=1,..., ORD(SATURDAY)=6. Values of an enumerated type may be used as parameters of the PRED and SUCC functions. Relational operators can be used to compare two values of an enumerated type.

```
PRED(MONDAY)              →  SUNDAY
SUCC(SUCC(THURSDAY))      →  SATURDAY
WEDNESDAY > TUESDAY       →  TRUE
    because ORD(WEDNESDAY) > ORD(TUESDAY)
```

For an enumerated type there is no standard function which, given an ORD value, returns the value at that position. To do this, a program loop or CASE statement is normally used. The general form and rules for the definition of an enumerated type are given below.

Enumerated Types

General Form

      TYPE name = (value, value, .. , value)

1. The values in the type must be identifiers and may not be used for any other purpose.

2. The list of values is enclosed in parentheses.

3. The ORD value is implied by the sequence in which the identifiers are listed. The ORD value of the first item is 0.

4. If more than one enumerated type is declared, the following form is used.

      ... (continued on the next page)

```
TYPE
  name1 = (value list);
  name2 = (value list);
     .

     .
  nameN= (value list)
```

6.3.2 Using Enumerated Types

Once an enumerated type has been declared, how can it be used?

Variables having an enumerated type can be assigned values of that type. For example, given the definition of the DAY_TYPE above, we can declare

```
VAR
  START_DAY, END_DAY : DAY_TYPE
```

and then use assignment statements such as:

```
START_DAY := MONDAY;
END_DAY := FRIDAY
```

Another useful way of using ordinal-valued variables in general and enumerated variables in particular is as the control variable in a FOR loop. For example, with respect to DAY_TYPE above the following statement can be used:

```
FOR DAY := SUNDAY TO SATURDAY DO
    statement
```

There is one significant limitation when processing variables having an enumerated type. You cannot use READ or READLN to get their values from the INPUT file nor can you use WRITE or WRITELN to write their values on the OUTPUT file.

This means that a coding scheme using values of a READable type (INTEGER, REAL or CHAR) must be used to simulate the input of enumerated values. For example, we could let 0 represent SUNDAY, 1 denote MONDAY, etc. Shown below is a program which causes the variable DAY to be assigned one of the values in DAY_TYPE.

```
PROGRAM READ_DAY_VALUE(INPUT,OUTPUT);

(* THIS PROGRAM READS THE DAY-OF-THE-WEEK AS AN
   INTEGER AND CONVERTS IT TO THE CORRESPONDING
   INTERNAL CONSTANT                                 *)

TYPE
   DAY_TYPE = (SUNDAY, MONDAY, TUESDAY, WEDNESDAY,
                THURSDAY, FRIDAY, SATURDAY);
VAR
   DAY      : DAY_TYPE;
   DAY_CODE : INTEGER;

BEGIN (* READ_DAY_VALUE *)
   WRITELN('ENTER DAY NUMBER (0 TO 6)');
   READLN(DAY_CODE);
   IF (DAY_CODE < 0) OR (DAY_CODE > 6) THEN
     WRITELN(DAY_CODE, ' IS INVALID')
   ELSE (* CONVERT TO DAY_TYPE *)
     CASE DAY_CODE OF
        0: DAY := SUNDAY;
        1: DAY := MONDAY;
        2: DAY := TUESDAY;
        3: DAY := WEDNESDAY;
        4: DAY := THURSDAY;
        5: DAY := FRIDAY;
        6: DAY := SATURDAY
     END (* CASE *)

   (* REST OF PROGRAM HERE *)

END. (* READ_DAY_VALUE *)
```

Because values of an enumerated type cannot be written directly on the
OUTPUT file, a CASE statement is normally used to achieve the desired
result as in the following:

```
DO CASE DAY OF
   SUNDAY: WRITE('SUNDAY');
   MONDAY: WRITE('MONDAY');

      .

   SATURDAY: WRITE('SATURDAY')
END (*CASE*)
```

Having seen that input-output of values of enumerated types is somewhat awkward, it is natural to ask the question "Where does it make sense to use them?"

There are several appropriate situations, but the primary motivation is that their use improves program documentation. That is, a program is more readable and hence understandable if meaningful names are given to the objects being manipulated in a program. If a coding scheme such as 0 for Sunday, 1 for Monday and so on is used, you must remember what the codes mean. It is preferable to use names representing the concept, idea or item involved.

Secondly, even though one can use a constant declaration such as

```
CONST
    SUNDAY=0;MONDAY=1; etc.
```

and then use the names SUNDAY, MONDAY and so on, there is a certain amount of automatic error-checking associated with an enumerated variable. For example, using the approach above, there is nothing illegal about an expression such as

```
SATURDAY + 1
```

even though it would give a value beyond the end of the week. On the other hand, the expression

```
SUCC(SATURDAY)
```

will automatically be reported as an error.

Enumerated variables are often used internally within a program to give a name to one of several cases. Two simple examples follow.

Example 1.

First suppose a person may be classified as SKINNY, NORMAL or FAT depending on the relationship of his or her height to weight. In particular suppose, given a weight W in pounds and a height H in inches the rule is

```
SKINNY if W < 3.8H - 118
FAT    if W > 4.2H - 132
NORMAL   otherwise
```

The program skeleton below uses an enumerated type called WEIGHT_TYPE. The program reads several pairs of weight and height values and prints the weight class of each.

```
PROGRAM FAT_SKINNY(INPUT,OUTPUT);

(* THIS PROGRAM CLASSIFIES A PERSON BASED
   ON THE RELATIONSHIP OF HEIGHT AND WEIGHT *)

TYPE
  WEIGHT_TYPE = (SKINNY, NORMAL, FAT);

VAR
  HEIGHT, WEIGHT : REAL;
  CLASS          : WEIGHT_TYPE;

BEGIN (* FAT_SKINNY *)
  WRITELN('ENTER WEIGHT (POUNDS) AND HEIGHT (INCHES)');
  READLN(WEIGHT, HEIGHT);
  IF WEIGHT < (3.8 * HEIGHT - 118) THEN
    CLASS := SKINNY
  ELSE IF WEIGHT > (4.2*HEIGHT - 132) THEN
    CLASS := FAT
  ELSE
    CLASS := NORMAL;
  CASE CLASS OF
    SKINNY : (* PROCESS SKINNY PEOPLE *);
    NORMAL : (* PROCESS NORMAL PEOPLE *);
    FAT    : (* PROCESS FAT PEOPLE *);
  END (* CASE *)
END. (* FAT_SKINNY *)
```

Example 2.

A second common application uses the values of an enumerated type to represent different conditions for terminating a loop. When a particular condition arises, the value of the "loop variable" is set to reflect the situation. The program skeleton below illustrates these ideas.

```
TYPE
  CONDITION_TYPE = (GO, WARNING, FATAL_ERROR);

VAR
  CONDITION : CONDITION_TYPE;

BEGIN

  CONDITION := GO;
  WHILE CONDITION = GO DO
    BEGIN
      IF ... THEN CONDITION := WARNING
        .
      IF ... THEN CONDITION := FATAL_ERROR
        .
    END
```

END.

Following the loop a test is made (often using a CASE statement) to determine the reason for loop termination and take appropriate action.

Enumerated type names. Frequently, it is natural to want to give an enumerated variable the same name as its type. This is illegal since each identifier in a program may have one and only one use. To overcome this problem it is a good idea to append the word "TYPE" to the type name as has been done in the examples. Further illustration of this idea appears in the following type declarations and complementary variable declarations.

```
TYPE
   STOPLITE_TYPE        =      (RED,ORANGE,GREEN);
   MONTH_TYPE           =      (JAN,FEB,MAR,APR,MAY,JUN,JULY,
                                AUG,SEPT,OCT,NOV,DEC);
   SUIT_TYPE            =      (CLUBS,DIAMONDS,HEARTS,SPADES);
   CAUSE_OF_DEATH_TYPE  =  (ACCIDENT,CORONARY,CANCER,OTHER);
   CHORD_TYPE           =      (MAJOR,MINOR,HARMONIC);
   LAUGH_TYPE           =      (SNICKER, CHUCKLE, GUFFAW, BELLY);

VAR
   STOPLITE             : STOPLITE_TYPE;
   MONTH                : MONTH_TYPE;
   SUIT                 : SUIT_TYPE;
   CAUSE_OF_DEATH       : CAUSE_OF_DEATH_TYPE;
   CHORD                : CHORD_TYPE;
   LAUGH                : LAUGH_TYPE
```

6.4 Subranges

For any ordinal type (INTEGER, CHAR, BOOLEAN or enumerated) a subrange of consecutive values is defined by:

```
lower value  .. higher value
```

The double period is read as "through". It is not necessary to surround the ".."
with blanks but it is good programming style. An example subrange is 1 .. 20
representing the range of INTEGER values 1 through 20 inclusive. Subranges
may be defined as types as in:

```
TYPE
   UPPER_CASE_RANGE    = 'A' .. 'Z' ;
   DIGIT_RANGE         = 0 .. 9 ;
   CHAR_DIGIT_RANGE    = '0' .. '9' ;
   MONTH_NUMBER_RANGE  = 1 .. 12
```

By appending "_RANGE" to a subrange identifier, the purpose becomes clear.
Subranges of enumerated types are permitted. Using the previous definition of
DAY_TYPE, the following subrange can be defined.

```
TYPE
   WEEKDAY_RANGE = MONDAY .. FRIDAY
```

The rules of subrange definition and use are as follows:

Subrange Declarations

General Form

      value 1 .. value 2

Notes

1.   Value 1 and value 2 must belong to the same ordinal type (called
     the base type) and value 1 must be less than or equal to value 2.
     If value 1 equals value 2, the range has only one value.

2.   Any operation which is well-defined for the base type is
     well-defined for the subrange type.

3.   Variables having types which are different ranges of the same
     base type are assignment compatible.

Why use subranges? Good Pascal programmers use subrange types to provide
automatic error checking of values assigned to variables. Suppose for example,
a program contains the assignment statement

```
HOURS_WORKED:= REG_HOURS + OVERTIME_HOURS
```

Since it is somewhat difficult to conceive of a person working a negative number of hours or more than 100 hours in a week, it makes sense to use the following declarations.

```
TYPE
    HOURS_RANGE = 0 .. 100;

VAR
    HOURS_WORKED : HOURS_RANGE
```

Any attempt to assign a value outside the range 0 through 100 to the variable HOURS_WORKED will result in an error message such as

```
***ERROR*** THE VALUE ASSIGNED TO "HOURS_WORKED"
            IS OUT OF RANGE
```

Most PASCAL compilers do *not* provide subrange checking on values obtained from the INPUT file. To do so would mean the program would grind to a halt every time an invalid data value was read. You the programmer should include logic in your program to validate all input data. In the example above for instance, assuming the values of REG_HOURS and OVERTIME_HOURS are obtained from the INPUT file, it would make sense to include the following statements in the program.

```
READ ( REG_HOURS, OVERTIME_HOURS);
WRITELN( REG_HOURS, OVERTIME_HOURS);
IF(REG_HOURS < 0) OR (REG_HOURS > 100) THEN
    WRITELN('VALUE OF REG_HOURS OUT OF RANGE');
IF(OVERTIME_HOURS < 0) OR (OVERTIME_HOURS > 100)THEN
    WRITELN('VALUE OF OVERTIME_HOURS OUT OF RANGE')
```

The first WRITELN statement simply echos the input data. This is always a good practice to follow when debugging. The two IF statements are used to validate the values of regular hours and overtime hours. Without proper editing of input values, you may end up processing "garbage values" in your programming. There is a well known maxim among computer people called the GIGO (guy-go) rule - "garbage in, garbage out".

6.5 Type Declarations

6.5.1 Summary

We have seen that types other than the standard, predefined types can be declared and used in Pascal. To create a new type, a type declaration of the form below is used.

```
TYPE
  name = type specification;
  name = type specification;
       .
       .

  name = type specification
```

In the case of scalar types, (structured and pointer types are described in Part II), each TYPE specification has one of the forms:

name = (list of value names) (* enumerated type *)

name = value 1 .. value 2 (* subrange type *)

name = typename (* makes two types equivalent *)

The third case can be used to define synonyms for types. For example, if you would rather use WHOLE_NUMBER instead of INTEGER, simply declare

```
TYPE
  WHOLE_NUMBER = INTEGER
```

If type declarations are present, they must appear after any constant declarations and before all variable declarations. The order of declarations is fixed and is as follows.

```
LABEL      - labels (described in Chapter 4 - infrequently used)
CONST      - constants
TYPE       - types
VAR        - variables
FUNCTION   - functions (described in Chapter 7)
PROCEDURE  - procedures (described in Chapter 8)
```

There is a reason for the ordering. In Pascal no identifier may be used in any expression unless it has been previously declared or is one of the predefined identifiers. Thus, aside from LABELs (described in Chapter 4) which are independent of other entities this means that: constant declarations must precede type declarations since constants may be used in type definitions; type declarations must precede variable declarations because each variable must have a type. Finally, functions and procedures may reference constants, types and variables and thus must follow these three.

For variables which may be assigned a value in an enumerated type or a subrange type, it is not necessary to define the type separately using a TYPE declaration. Instead, the type specification may follow the list of variables having that type in a VAR declaration. For example the following declaration specifies that X, Y, and Z are to be positive INTEGERs.

```
VAR X,Y,Z : 1 .. MAXINT
```

That is, it is permissible to put the type specification in a variable declaration rather than defining the type separately and giving it a name. The advantage of this is simplicity. If done, the type specification should appear only once as in the example above rather than

```
VAR
    X : 1 .. MAXINT;
    Y : 1 .. MAXINT;
    Z : 1 .. MAXINT
```

If an enumerated type is not declared in a TYPE declaration, then all variables having that type must appear in the same VAR declaration. For example, the following is an error because the values RED, GREEN, BLUE appear in two type definitions. An enumerated value can only appear in one declaration.

```
VAR
    COLOR1 : (RED,GREEN,BLUE);
    COLOR2 : (RED,GREEN,BLUE)
```

6.5.2 Type Compatibility

When a scalar value is assigned to a variable, the value and variable must be type compatible. Similarly when two scalar values are compared using one of the relational operators, they must be type compatible. This means the types of the variable and the value being assigned or the types of the two values being compared must be one of the following:

- the same type
- one type is a subrange of the other type
- each type is a subrange of a common base type
- one is INTEGER or a subrange of INTEGER and the other is REAL

The one exception (described in Chapter 2) is that a REAL value cannot be assigned to an INTEGER or INTEGER-compatible variable. For example the value 17.3 cannot be assigned to an INTEGER variable.

6.6 Exercise 6.1

1. Write enumerated type declarations to define each of the following

    a)   PITCH_TYPE having the values STRIKE and BALL

    b)   SPECTRUM_TYPE having the values RED, ORANGE, YELLOW, GREEN, BLUE, INDIGO and VIOLET.

    c)   GRADE_TYPE having the values PASS, FAIL, DID_NOT_WRITE, AUDIT, CREDIT.

2. Write subrange declarations to declare the following types

    a) POSINT_RANGE - the set of positive integers
    b) LOW_LETTERS_RANGE - the set of lower case letters
    c) MONTH_LENGTH_RANGE - the range of INTEGERS 1 thru 31

3. Given the declaration

    TYPE   DAY_TYPE = (MON, TUES, WED, THURS, FRI, SAT, SUN)

    define subrange types WEEKDAY_RANGE and WEEKEND_RANGE appropriately. Explain why this couldn't be done if SUN was listed as the first day of the week.

4. Explain the error in each of the following type declarations.
    a) ALERTNESS_TYPE = ALERT,SLEEPY,DRUGGED,EXCITED
    b) NON_NEG_RANGE = (0..MAXINT)
    c) LETTER_RANGE = 'a'..'z' OR 'A'..'Z'
    d) PUNC_TYPE = (',','.',';',':')
    e) NEG_RANGE = -1..MAXINT

5. Can you think of any good reason for declaring a subrange type consisting of a single value as in

    TYPE
       TEN_RANGE = 10 .. 10

6. Given that DAY_TYPE consists of the values MON thru SUN as defined in question 3 above and given two variables called TODAY and TOMORROW of type DAY_TYPE, write a statement or statements which will assign TOMORROW the next day of the week following the value of TODAY.

6.7 Summary

1. Each constant and variable used in a Pascal program has a type. The family of scalar (single-value) types in Pascal includes the standard types INTEGER, BOOLEAN, CHAR and REAL. The first three are ordinal types meaning that the functions ORD, PRED and SUCC can be used.

2. Enumerated types may be created by providing a list of identifiers defining the values of the type. Although input and output of enumerated values is awkward, their use improves program readability and they are often handy for identifying and distinguishing cases.

3. Subrange types are contiguous sequences of values of an ordinal type. Subranges should be used to provide automatic error checking of values being assigned to variables.

4. TYPE declarations are used to associate names with a particular type. If present they must appear immediately before the VAR declaration. Specifications of enumerated and subrange types may alternatively be part of a VAR declaration.

6.8 Programming Problems

In all of the following, make use of enumerated types and/or subrange types where appropriate.

6.1　Write a program to make change for the purchase of items under one dollar. Input to the program consists of pairs of REAL numbers, the first being the cost of the purchase and the second the amount of money given to the cashier. Use the minimum number of coins chosen from pennies, nickels, dimes and quarters to make up the change. Print the amount of the purchase, the money given, and the number of coins of each type in the change. Test your program using the values below.

Cost(¢)	Paid($)
50	1.00
47	.50
25	.25
17	1.00
71	.75

6.2   Prepare a number of lines of data, each containing a different person's
        height in inches and weight in pounds. Write a program which reads
        the lines one at a time and prints a table of the form shown below.

```
HEIGHT              WEIGHT

   XXX                 XXX
   XXX                 XXX
   etc.                etc.


AVERAGE HEIGHT IS XXX.X INCHES
AVERAGE WEIGHT IS XXX.X POUNDS
```

6.3   Two ladders of lengths twenty feet and thirty feet respectively are
        positioned across a laneway between two buildings as shown in the
        following diagram. They cross at a point eight feet above the ground.
        How wide is the laneway?

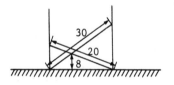

        Print your answer as "THE LANE IS XX.XXX FEET WIDE". Obtain
        your answer by starting with two estimates -- one high say 21, and one
        low, say 3. Use the average of the high and low estimates as a better
        estimate. Calculate where the ladders would cross if the lane had a
        width equal to the new estimate. Based on this result, use the new
        estimate to replace either the previous high estimate or the previous
        low estimate. Repeat the procedure. Continue repetitions until the
        difference in two successive estimates is less than 0.001. Can you find
        an equation which, when solved, would give the exact value of the
        width? (This is not easy.)

6.4   Check balancing. The input file contains a deposit-withdrawal code in
        position one and a dollar amount of the form XXX.XX in positions
        three thru eight. A "1" in position one indicates a deposit and a "2"
        indicates a withdrawal. The dollar amount indicates the size of the
        deposit or withdrawal. Write a program which reads an unknown
        number of lines of data and for each prints either

```
$XXX.XX DEPOSIT, BALANCE IS NOW $XXXX.XX
                    or
$XXX.XX WITHDRAWAL, BALANCE IS NOW $XXX.XX
```

Assume the starting balance is zero. If the attempted withdrawal is larger than the balance, print the line "WITHDRAWAL OF $XXX.XX WOULD EXCEED BALANCE, NOT PROCESSED".

6.5   Read an unknown number of lines of data each of which contains two INTEGER values. Each of the values is either a 1, a 2, or a 3. Count the total number of ones, twos and threes and print a line of the form "MORE 2'S THAN 1'S OR 3'S" based on the counts obtained.

6.6   Write a program which reads in an INTEGER value representing a number of cents. Calculate the smallest number of coins required to pay this amount using quarters, dimes, nickels and cents. Display the output as shown in the following example.

46 CENTS REQUIRES 1 QUARTER, 2 DIMES, 0 NICKELS, 1 CENT

The program should use the plural or singular (e.g. DIMES or DIME) depending on the number of coins required.

6.7   Modify the program for the previous problem so that zero values are suppressed. For example, the output for 46 cents would appear as

46 CENTS REQUIRES 1 QUARTER, 2 DIMES, 1 CENT

6.8   Write a program which reads a set of twenty-five INTEGER values of varying magnitudes and prints them using as few lines as possible. Do not print any symbols to the right of print position thirty.

6.9   Write a program which reads a value of N and then N more INTEGER values. Print the N values as shown below.

$$X(1) = \underline{\quad} \quad X(2) = \underline{\quad} \quad \ldots \quad X(n) = \underline{\quad}$$

6.10   The digital sum of a number is obtained by summing the values of the digits to get a new number. The process (sum of digits) is repeated until the sum has only one digit. The result is called the sum of the digits of the original value. For example:

123456789 → 45 → 9

Write a program to calculate the sum of the digits for several values in the input file.

6.11   A room has a length, width and height of 3, 4 and 2.5 meters respectively. A second room has corresponding dimensions of 3.5, 3.5 and 3 meters. Write a program to determine which room has the longer diagonal from the bottom left corner at one end to the diagonally opposite corner at the ceiling at the other end.

6.12   An Armstrong number of N digits is one for which the sum of the

Nth powers of the digits equals the original number. For example, 153 is an Armstrong number because $1^3 + 5^3 + 3^3 = 153$. Write a program to find all two and three digit Armstrong numbers.

6.13   A number is balanced if the largest digit in the number equals one-half the sum of the digits in the number. For example, 123 is balanced because $(1+2+3)/2 = 3$. Find all balanced numbers between 1 and 1000.

6.14   The economic order quantity (EOQ) for a product is the optimal number of units of the product to order based on the ordering cost, the demand and the cost of holding the product in inventory. In the simplest case, the EOQ is given by the formula

```
Q =  sqrt(2KD/h)
where: K is cost of placing an order
       D is the demand (products/unit of time)
       h is the holding cost ($/product/unit of time)
```

For example, if it costs $100 to place an order; the demand is $1600 widgets/month and the holding cost is $2.00 per widget per month, then the optimal order quantity is the square root of 2*100*1600/2 or 400. The order should be placed each D/Q units of time which, for the example above means every 1600/400 or 4 months.

Write a program which reads values for K, D and h from the input file and prints a table showing the order quantity and ordering frequency for values of the demand of D, 2D, 3D, ..., 10D.

CHAPTER 7: FUNCTIONS

Questions Answered in this Chapter:

1. How can functions other than the standard functions be defined and used in Pascal programs?

2. What is meant by the block structure of a program?

3. What are global and local variables?

7.1 Introduction

The standard Pascal language contains many predefined functions. A complete list can be found in Appendix A. They can be classified in many ways. For instance, there are mathematical functions such as SQRT, ABS, ROUND; there are functions related to the order of values such as ORD, PRED and SUCC; functions EOLN and EOF are associated with input files. Others are described in Part II.

To make use of any of these functions, an expression of the form below is used.

```
name (actual parameter list)
```

Until now we have simply used the term "parameter" rather than "actual parameter". As we will soon see it is necessary to distinguish between actual parameters and formal parameters. Actual parameters are actual values used in the calculation of a function value; formal parameters are identifiers used in the *definition* of a function.

A function invocation consists of a function name followed by a list of parameters enclosed in parentheses. At execution-time, this causes the following events to occur:

1. The value of each parameter is "passed to" the function.

2. Control is transferred to the function routine so the function value can be calculated.

3. The expression is replaced by the value of the function.

Although Pascal provides numerous useful functions, there are many others which would be nice to have. For example, the following more or less general purpose functions would be used if available.

- the parameter is a non-negative INTEGER value; the result is the factorial value of the parameter (Factorial N is 1x2x3x...xN)

- the parameter is a lower case letter and the function value is the matching upper case letter (and vice-versa)

- the parameter is a digit as a CHAR value and the function value is the corresponding INTEGER value

- the parameters are a pair of values and the function value is the larger of the two

- the parameter is a value of an ordinal type and the function value is the next value in the type where the next value after the maximum value is the minimum value (i.e., the values "wrap around")

- the parameter is an INTEGER; the result is the value within a given type having that ORD value. (A separate function is required for each type.)

- the parameter is a pair of values from a given type; the result of the function is the number of values between them

The purpose of this chapter is to explain how you can write and use functions such as these in a Pascal program.

7.2 An Example FUNCTION

Suppose a function called BIGGER is required which is passed two REAL values and returns the value of the larger as the function value. That is, we want the expression

```
BIGGER (28.3,-17)
```

to have the value 28.3. Let's suppose BIGGER is to be used in a program which reads ten pairs of REAL values and prints the larger value in each pair. That is, the body of the program includes the following statements:

```
      FOR COUNT := 1 TO 10 DO
        BEGIN
          WRITELN('ENTER TWO NUMBERS');
          READLN(X,Y);
          WRITELN('THE LARGER IS',BIGGER(X,Y))
        END
```

Shown below is a complete program. It includes a FUNCTION declaration for BIGGER.

```
PROGRAM BIG10(INPUT,OUTPUT);

(* THIS PROGRAM PRINTS THE LARGER OF EACH OF
   TEN PAIRS OF VALUES READ FROM THE INPUT FILE *)

VAR
  X, Y : REAL;
  COUNT: INTEGER;

FUNCTION BIGGER(NUM1:REAL; NUM2:REAL) : REAL;

  (* RETURNS THE LARGER OF NUM1 AND NUM2 *)

  BEGIN (* BIGGER *)
    IF NUM1 > NUM2 THEN
      BIGGER := NUM1
    ELSE
      BIGGER := NUM2
  END; (* BIGGER *)

BEGIN (* BIG10 *)
  FOR COUNT := 1 TO 10 DO
    BEGIN
      WRITELN('ENTER TWO NUMBERS');
      READLN(X,Y);
      WRITELN(X, Y, BIGGER(X,Y))
    END
END. (* BIG10 *)
```

Comments

1. Aside from the function declaration, the rest of the program contains no new features.

2. FUNCTION declarations follow the VAR declaration. Each consists of a *function header* and a *block*. (Recall that a program consists of a program header and a block.)

3. The function header in the example is

    ```
    FUNCTION BIGGER(NUM1 : REAL; NUM2 : REAL) : REAL
    ```

    A function header contains four kinds of information, namely:

    *   the word "FUNCTION" which is a reserved word identifying a function header.

    *   the name of the function. It may be any valid identifier.

    *   a *formal parameter list* which consists of one or more variable declarations representing the values which will be passed to the function. These variables are declared in the same way as VAR declarations (e.g., "NUM1, NUM2 : REAL" can be used instead of "NUM1 : REAL; NUM2 : REAL"). The types of the formal parameters must match one-for-one with the types of the corresponding actual parameter expressions.

    *   the type of the function value (e.g. REAL)

4. The block of the function looks the same as the block of a complete program. It contains declarations and a body. Although not needed in this example, a function block can include CONST, TYPE and VAR declarations and in fact other FUNCTIONs can be declared within a function block. In the example, the body of the BIGGER block consists of a single IF statement enclosed within a BEGIN-END pair. Note that the END of the function block is followed by and separated from the body of the program by a *semicolon* not a *period*. A Pascal program contains only one period -- at the end of the program block.

5. The value of the function is assigned to the function name by an assignment statement in which the function name is the target. In the example there are two such statements.

    ```
    BIGGER:= NUM1   and   BIGGER:= NUM2
    ```

6.   The function BIGGER is invoked by the appearance of

     BIGGER (X,Y)

This is one of the expressions which appeared in the WRITELN statement. At execution time, the values of the actual parameters X and Y are calculated. These values are assigned to the corresponding formal parameters and control is then passed to the function BIGGER. BIGGER then "does its thing" and the value assigned to the function name replaces the expression "BIGGER (X,Y)".

The recommended style of indentation for function declarations is to indent the entire function block.

7.3 A Second Example

Functions may be defined and used within other functions. To illustrate how, consider the following problem. Read three numbers and determine if their values are such that they could represent the lengths of the sides of a triangle. If so, determine whether the largest angle in the triangle is greater than 90 degrees, equal to 90 degrees or less than 90 degrees.

Analysis. For three lengths to form the sides of a triangle there are two requirements which must be met. First, the lengths must be positive. Second, the length of the longest side must be less than the sum of the other two sides. (You can't make a triangle with sides of lengths 1,2 and 50). If the sides form a triangle, then the type of triangle (obtuse-angled, right-angled or acute-angled) can be determined by employing the Pythagorean Theorem which states that for a right-angled triangle, the square of the longest side must equal the sum of the squares on the other two sides. If greater, the triangle is obtuse-angled; if less, it is acute-angled. Having refreshed our memory of the geometry involved, the mainline algorithm is simply two steps, namely:

Mainline Algorithm

    1. Get the values of Side1, Side2 and Side3
    2. If they form a triangle then
        print the type of triangle
      Else
        print the message "not a triangle"

The data required by the mainline algorithm consists of three REAL values for the sides of the triangle and a variable which can take on one of the values "obtuse", "right-angled", or "acute". We can anticipate using an enumerated type to indicate the type of triangle.

Having completed an analysis of the logic and data of the mainline algorithm, we now refine step 2. This will lead us to two "sub-algorithms" each having particular data requirements.

How do we do step 2? Consider the phrase "they form a triangle". What is needed is a function which is passed the values of Side1, Side2 and Side3 and returns "true" if they do form a triangle and "false" otherwise. The logic for the triangle test is therefore:

Triangle Test Algorithm

    If Side1 or Side2 or Side3 is < 0 then
      .1 function is false (not a triangle)
    Else
      .1 If the longest side > sum of other two then
            function is false
         else
            function is true.

To get the value of the longest side we can use the BIGGER function since the largest of x,y,z is BIGGER (x, BIGGER(y,z))

The data requirements for the triangle test are simply the values of the three sides and a variable for the value of the longest side.

The remaining logic needed to complete the entire algorithm must produce the type of triangle. This can be written as follows:

Triangle Type Algorithm

    1. Determine lengths of longest, middle and smallest sides
    2. Calculate the value of
          longest ^{2} - (middle ^{2} + smallest ^{2})
    3. If this difference is
          negative : triangle type is acute
          zero   : triangle type is right-angled
          positive : triangle type is obtuse

To get the smallest value we can either use BIGGER or write a new function.

The data requirements for the Triangle Type Algorithm consist of: the lengths of the three sides and the values of the longest, middle and shortest sides.

This completes an analysis of the logic and data requirements of the problem. Although the algorithm can be programmed without the use of functions, the natural structure of the logic makes their use desirable as well as instructive in learning the mechanics of their use in Pascal programming.

The overall structure of the program is as follows. The mainline invokes two functions. The FUNCTION headers are:

A_TRIANGLE: BOOLEAN
    - having a value TRUE if the sides form a triangle; FALSE otherwise. It is shown with no formal parameters. The reason will be explained shortly.

KIND(S1, S2, S3 : REAL) : TRI_TYPE
    - where S1,S2,S3 are formal parameters representing the values of the sides; and TRI_TYPE has the values OBTUSE, RIGHT_ANGLED, and ACUTE

Both of the functions A_TRIANGLE and KIND will use the BIGGER function. Recall that this function header is

    BIGGER (X, Y : REAL) : REAL

After what may have seemed like a rather lengthy discussion of the solution to a fairly simple problem, we are ready to write the program. The analysis has demonstrated the application of the "what-how" approach to algorithm development and the parallel specification of the data requirements for each module of the algorithm. The program structure follows.

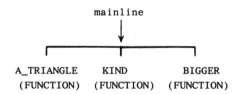

The program follows. Because no name can be used without previously having been declared, BIGGER must be declared before A_TRIANGLE and KIND and these in turn must appear ahead of the mainline.

```
PROGRAM TRIANGLE1(INPUT,OUTPUT);

(* THIS PROGRAM READS THREE NUMBERS AND DETERMINES
   IF THEY FORM A TRIANGLE AND IF SO, WHAT TYPE   *)

TYPE
  TRI_TYPE = (ACUTE, RIGHT_ANGLED, OBTUSE);
VAR
  SIDE1, SIDE2, SIDE3 : REAL;
(********************************************************)
FUNCTION BIGGER(X:REAL; Y:REAL) : REAL;
  BEGIN (* BIGGER *)
    IF X > Y THEN
      BIGGER := X
    ELSE
      BIGGER := Y
  END; (* BIGGER *)
(********************************************************)
FUNCTION A_TRIANGLE : BOOLEAN;
  VAR
    LONGEST : REAL;
  BEGIN
    IF (SIDE1 <= 0) OR (SIDE2 <= 0) OR (SIDE3 <= 0) THEN
      A_TRIANGLE := FALSE
    ELSE
      BEGIN
        LONGEST := BIGGER(SIDE1, BIGGER(SIDE2,SIDE3));
        IF LONGEST > 0.5 * (SIDE1 + SIDE2 + SIDE3) THEN
          A_TRIANGLE := FALSE
        ELSE
          A_TRIANGLE := TRUE
      END (* ELSE *)
  END; (* A_TRIANGLE *)
(********************************************************)
FUNCTION KIND(S1,S2,S3:REAL) : TRI_TYPE;

  (* THE FUNCTION VALUE IS ONE OF ACUTE,
     RIGHT_ANGLED OR OBTUSE DEPENDING ON THE
     THE TYPE OF TRIANGLE DEFINED BY THE SIDES *)

  CONST
    WEENY = 0.00001;
  VAR
    LONG, MEDIUM, SHORT, DIFFERENCE : REAL;
```

... (continued on the next page)

```
  BEGIN (* KIND *)
    LONG := BIGGER(S1, BIGGER(S2,S3));
    SHORT := -BIGGER(-S1, BIGGER(-S2,-S3));
    MEDIUM := (S1 + S2 + S3) - (LONG + SHORT);
    DIFFERENCE := SQR(LONG) - (SQR(MEDIUM) + SQR(SHORT));
    IF ABS(DIFFERENCE) < WEENY THEN
      KIND := RIGHT_ANGLED
    ELSE IF DIFFERENCE > 0 THEN
      KIND := OBTUSE
    ELSE
      KIND := ACUTE
  END; (* KIND *)
(*****************************************************)
BEGIN (* TRIANGLE MAINLINE *)
  WRITELN('ENTER LENGTHS OF THE SIDES');
  READLN(SIDE1, SIDE2, SIDE3);
  WRITELN('THE LENGTHS ARE', SIDE1:6:2, SIDE2:6:2, SIDE3:6:2);
  IF A_TRIANGLE THEN
    BEGIN (* INDICATE KIND OF TRIANGLE *)
      WRITE('  THEY FORM A TRIANGLE WHICH IS ');
      CASE KIND(SIDE1,SIDE2,SIDE3) OF
        RIGHT_ANGLED : WRITELN('RIGHT ANGLED');
        ACUTE        : WRITELN('ACUTE ANGLED');
        OBTUSE       : WRITELN('OBTUSE ANGLED')
      END (* CASE *)
    END (* IF *)
  ELSE
    WRITELN('  THEY DO NOT FORM A TRIANGLE.')
END. (* TRIANGLE *)
```

Comments:

There are several new ideas illustrated in the program. Complete rules about functions and their first cousins, procedures, are found in Chapter 8.

1. The overall structure of the program consists of the program header followed by the program block. The program block contains a TYPE declaration, a VAR declaration and three FUNCTION declarations. Constants, types and variables declared in the program block can be used within the functions.

2. Each function declaration has the same structure as a complete program -- a header followed by a block. The formal parameters in the header and the declarations made *within* a function block are *local* to the function block. This means they are not known outside the block. For example, the constant WEENY declared within KIND can only be used within the KIND block.

3.   Consider the BOOLEAN-valued function called A_TRIANGLE. It does not have any formal parameters to represent the values passed to the function. The values needed to determine the function value are those of the variables SIDE1, SIDE2, and SIDE3. Since these variables are declared in the program block, they can be used within the function. Although these "global" variables provide communication between the program body and a function, in general their use is *not recommended*. Communication should be via assignments of actual parameter values to formal parameters. Passing values via parameters avoids "side-effects" which are discussed further in Chapter 8. Side effects arise from careless programming and cannot occur if parameter lists are used to pass values.

4.   Consider the function KIND. It has three formal parameters S1, S2 and S3. These variables, as well as the constant WEENY and the variables LONG, MEDIUM and SHORT are local to KIND. Thus any change in the value of any of these local variables does not affect the value of any variable outside of KIND, even a global variable having the same name. That is, if a local identifier and a global identifier are the same, the local declaration has precedence.

5.   The use of BIGGER to get the value of SHORT (the minimum value) may be one of those things which is not obvious. Suppose the values of the sides are 7, 10 and 5. The assignment statement is evaluated as follows:

```
SHORT := -BIGGER(-7, BIGGER(-10,-5))
      →  -BIGGER(-7, -5)
      →  -(-5)
      →  5
```

It works because if $x > y$ then $-x < -y$. It points out that sometimes you can take advantage of existing logic. However, if by doing this, you confuse someone reading the program it is probably better to take a more straightforward approach such as creating a SMALLER function.

6.   The mainline logic is very simple. Note the readability of the line

```
IF A_TRIANGLE THEN
```

It is a good idea to use names which convey as much meaning as possible.

This concludes the discussion of the example. It illustrates many of the important concepts and application of Pascal functions.

7.4 Nested Function Declarations

In this section an example of nested function declarations is presented. Nested functions are functions declared within functions. In order to concentrate on the new ideas , we will use the same problem as before -- the type of triangle problem -- but make the assumption that the three lengths can be used as the sides of a triangle. That is, the mainline is simply:

  1. Read and print the lengths.
  2. Print the kind of triangle.

As before, we shall use a FUNCTION called KIND to determine the triangle type. Its header is:

    FUNCTION KIND (S1, S2, S3 : REAL) : TRI_TYPE

The function KIND invokes BIGGER to get the length of the longest side and a separate function called SMALLER will be used to get the length of the smallest side. BIGGER and SMALLER will be defined *within* KIND. Here is the complete program.

```
PROGRAM TRIANGLE2(INPUT,OUTPUT);

(* THIS PROGRAM READS THREE NUMBERS AND DETERMINES
   IF THEY FORM A TRIANGLE AND IF SO, WHAT TYPE    *)

TYPE
  TRI_TYPE = (ACUTE, RIGHT_ANGLED, OBTUSE);
VAR
  SIDE1, SIDE2, SIDE3 : REAL;
(***********************************************************)
FUNCTION KIND(S1,S2,S3:REAL) : TRI_TYPE;

  (* THE FUNCTION VALUE IS ONE OF ACUTE, RIGHT_ANGLED,
     OR OBTUSE DEPENDING ON THE LENGTHS OF THE SIDES *)

  CONST
    WEENY = 0.00001;
  VAR
    LONG, MEDIUM, SHORT, DIFFERENCE : REAL;
  (*****************************************************)
  FUNCTION BIGGER(X:REAL; Y:REAL) : REAL;
    BEGIN (* BIGGER *)
      IF X > Y THEN
        BIGGER := X
      ELSE
        BIGGER := Y
    END; (* BIGGER *)
```

          ... (continued on the next page)

```
(****************************************************)
FUNCTION SMALLER(X,Y:REAL) : REAL;
  BEGIN
    SMALLER := -BIGGER(-X, -Y)
  END; (* SMALLER *)
(****************************************************)
BEGIN (* KIND *)
  LONG := BIGGER(S1, BIGGER(S2,S3));
  SHORT := SMALLER(S1, SMALLER(S2,S3));
  MEDIUM := (S1 + S2 + S3) - (LONG + SHORT);
  DIFFERENCE := SQR(LONG) - (SQR(MEDIUM) + SQR(SHORT));
  IF ABS(DIFFERENCE) < WEENY THEN
    KIND := RIGHT_ANGLED
  ELSE IF DIFFERENCE > 0 THEN
    KIND := OBTUSE
  ELSE
    KIND := ACUTE
  END; (* KIND *)
(****************************************************)
BEGIN (* TRIANGLE MAINLINE *)
  WRITELN('ENTER THE LENGTHS OF THE SIDES');
  READLN(SIDE1, SIDE2, SIDE3);
  WRITELN('THE LENGTHS ARE', SIDE1:6:2, SIDE2:6:2, SIDE3:6:2);
  WRITE('THEY FORM A TRIANGLE WHICH IS ');
  CASE KIND(SIDE1,SIDE2,SIDE3) OF
    RIGHT_ANGLED : WRITELN('RIGHT ANGLED');
    ACUTE        : WRITELN('ACUTE ANGLED');
    OBTUSE       : WRITELN('OBTUSE ANGLED')
  END (* CASE *)
END. (* TRIANGLE2 *)
```

Comments

1. The structure of the program is shown in the tree-like diagram below.
    There are four blocks: the program block, the KIND block, and the
    BIGGER and SMALLER blocks.

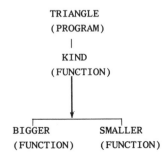

The diagram shows that the function KIND is declared within the program TRIANGLE and that the functions BIGGER and SMALLER are declared within the function KIND.

2.   The function KIND invokes the function BIGGER to get the value of LONG. To get the value of SHORT, SMALLER is invoked and it in turn invokes BIGGER using as actual parameters the negative of the values it received. BIGGER is declared before SMALLER because SMALLER contains a reference to BIGGER.

7.5 Rules of Scope

Each constant, type, variable, function or procedure name used in a Pascal program has a *scope*. The scope of an identifier is given by specifying the set of blocks in which the identifier is "known" and hence can be used. The rules of scope answer questions such as, if a variable is used in the mainline, can it be used in a FUNCTION? What if that FUNCTION also declares an object with the same name? Almost all rules of scope are embodied in the following simple statement.

> *Basic Scope Rule*
>
> "You can see out, but you can't see in"

To see what it means, let's put a box around the program and each of the function blocks in TRIANGLE2. This kind of box diagram is an alternate way of depicting the block structure of a program. (The other being a declaration tree such as that above.)

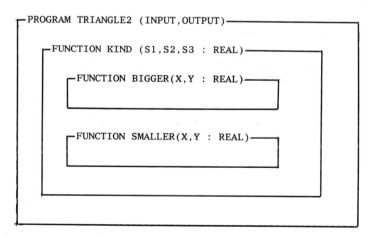

Now, no matter where you are in the program, you are inside at least one box or block. In the program mainline you are only in the PROGRAM block. Inside BIGGER you are inside three blocks: the BIGGER block, the KIND block and the PROGRAM block. The walls of each block are such that if you are inside a block *you can see out but you can't see in*. This means that:

- in the program body only the objects declared in the PROGRAM block can be used. Objects declared within KIND (including the functions BIGGER and SMALLER) cannot be used in the mainline because it would mean you have to penetrate the walls of KIND to see their declarations.

- in the function KIND, all objects declared outside its walls (those in the program block) are known. Objects declared *within* BIGGER and SMALLER are unknown.

- in the BIGGER block, objects declared in the KIND block and in the PROGRAM block are usable because they are outside the BIGGER block. Objects declared within SMALLER are unknown in BIGGER because this would necessitate seeing into the SMALLER block.

The words local and global are the technical terms used when describing the scope of an identifier. Local and global relate a particular identifier to a particular block. The identifier is either local to the block, global to the block or has no relationship to the block. There are three key ideas.

First, an identifier is local to a block if it is declared within the block or, if it is a formal parameter in the block header. Second, an identifier is global with respect to a block if it declared outside the block and can be "seen" according to the "you can see out but can't see in" rule. Third "globalness" is inherited by internally declared blocks. That is, if an identifier is global with resect to a particular block, it is global with respect to all blocks declared within that block. This statement is simply an explicit implication of the see-out rule.

Because local and global relate a particular identifier to a particular block. the statement "X is global" is incomplete. However, because identifiers declared in the program block are global with respect to all blocks in a Pascal program, we sometimes get careless and simply refer to these identifiers as being global.

The meaning of global can also be illustrated using a tree diagram to show the nesting of block declarations. Consider the example below.

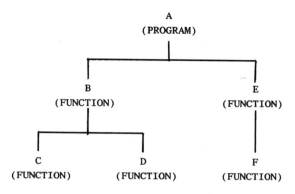

The tree indicates that C and D are declared withinin B which is declared within the PROGRAM block; further that F is declared within E which is declared within the program block. An identifier is global with respect to a block if it is declared in a block which can be reached by going up the tree. An identifier cannot be used if the path to the block in which it is declared includes any downward step. Therefore, identifiers in B are global to blocks C and D. Identifiers declared within C are unknown everywhere but within C. Identifier D can be used in C because it is declared in block B which is reached by going up the tree. Identifiers declared within E are local to E and global with respect to block F.

There are two recommendations for indentation style in programs with internally declared blocks. They are used in the examples throughout the book.

Indentation Guidelines for Block Declarations

- The reserved word FUNCTION or PROCEDURE (procedures are described in Chapter 8) is vertically aligned with the reserved words CONST, TYPE, VAR in the block containing the declaration.

- The declared block is indented.

7.6 Exercise 7.1

1. For each of the following programs or program fragments, state the output produced.

```
a) PROGRAM EX7_1A(OUTPUT);

   VAR
     I : INTEGER;
     X : REAL;

   FUNCTION ROUND(X:REAL) : REAL;
     BEGIN
       IF X < 0 THEN
         ROUND := TRUNC(X - 0.5)
       ELSE
         ROUND := TRUNC(X + 0.5)
     END;

   BEGIN
     FOR I := -5 TO 5 DO
       IF I <> 0 THEN
         WRITELN(I, ROUND(I+1/I))
   END.
```

```
b) PROGRAM EX7_1B(OUTPUT);
   VAR
     I, J, K : INTEGER;
   FUNCTION BUMP(J, I : INTEGER) : INTEGER;
     BEGIN
       J := I + 1; K := J + I; WRITELN(I, J, K);
       BUMP := I + J + K
     END;

   BEGIN
     I := 1; J := 2; K := 3;
     WRITELN(BUMP(J, K))
   END.
```

```
c) PROGRAM  EX71_1C(INPUT,OUTPUT);

   CONST
     BLANK = ' ';
   VAR
     ORDA, ORDZ : INTEGER;
     X          : CHAR;
```

... (continued on the next page)

```
          FUNCTION F1(X:CHAR) : CHAR;
            FUNCTION F2(Z:CHAR) : CHAR;
              BEGIN (* F2 *)
                          F2 := CHR(ORDZ -ORD(Z) + ORDA)
              END; (* F2 *)
            BEGIN (* F1 *)
              WHILE X = BLANK DO
                READ(X);
              F1 := F2(X)
            END; (* F1 *)
          BEGIN (* MAINLINE *)
            ORDA := ORD('A');
                    ORDZ := ORD('Z');
            REPEAT
              READ(X);
              WRITELN(F1(X))
            UNTIL EOLN
          END. (* EX71_1C *)
          $ENTRY
          HAPPY NEW YEAR
```

2. What errors are present in each of the following

```
        a) FUNCTION (A, B :REAL);
           BEGIN
             WRITELN('THERE ARE 4 ERRORS)
           END
```

```
        b) FUNCTION BUMP(NUM):INTEGER;
           BEGIN (* BUMP *)
             BUMP := NUM + 1
           END: (* BUMP *)
```

```
        c) FUNCTION POWER(BASE:REAL;EXPON:INTEGER):REAL:
           VAR
             I : INTEGER;
           BEGIN (* POWER *)
             POWER := BASE;
             I := 1;
             WHILE I <= EXPON DO
               BEGIN
                 POWER := POWER * BASE;
                 I := I + 1
               END
           END (* POWER *)
```

```
d) PROGRAM WRONG(INPUT, OUTPUT);
   VAR
     A, B : REAL;
     C : INTEGER;
   FUNCTION KELLY(X:REAL; Y:INTEGER; Z:REAL):REAL;
     BEGIN
       KELLY := X + Y + Z
     END;
   BEGIN
     READLN(A,B,C);
     WRITELN(KELLY(A,B,C))
   END. (* WRONG *)
```

7.7 Recursive Functions

In general, it is a mistake to define something in terms of itself. To tell someone unfamiliar with English for instance, that "awkwardness" means "being awkward" probably is of little help. In mathematics and programming however, there are many functions and problems where the value of a function can be stated in terms of another value of the same function. Here are three examples:

- the sum of (M,N,O,P) is M plus the sum of (N,O,P)

- the value of factorial N is N times the value of factorial (N-1)

- the largest value of (A,B,C,D) is the larger of A and the largest of (B,C,D)

In each of these cases the solution to the problem involves applying the same function ("sum", "factorial" or "largest") to a simpler problem. Thus as long as the value of the function is known for the limiting or simplest case the problem can be solved.

For the examples given above this means: we can find the sum of any sequence of numbers if we can find the sum of two numbers; we can calculate the factorial of any positive integer if we know the value of factorial zero; and we can determine the largest value in any set of values if we can determine the larger of a pair of values. A recursive function is one in which the function value can be obtained by successively applying the function rules until the problem reduces to a simple case.

The factorial function will be used as an example. Given a non-negative integer N we know

```
FACT(N) = N x FACT (N-1)  for N > 0
FACT(0) = 1 ( by definition)
```

Thus, we can calculate FACT(N) if we can calculate FACT(N-1); we can calculate FACT(N-1) if we can calculate FACT(N-2); etc. Since eventually, we get to FACT(0), for which the value is known, we can "substitute backwards" and hence obtain the value of FACT(N). The program below displays the value of the factorial of a number obtained from the INPUT file.

```
PROGRAM FACTORIALS (INPUT, OUTPUT);

(* THIS PROGRAM CALCULATES THE VALUE OF THE
   AN INTEGER ENTERED AT THE KEYBOARD        *)

VAR
  NUM, FACT_NUM : INTEGER;

FUNCTION FACT(N:INTEGER) : INTEGER;
  BEGIN (* FACT *)
    WRITELN('THE PARAMETER HAS THE VALUE', N:3);
    IF N = 0 THEN
      FACT := 1
    ELSE
      FACT := N * FACT(N-1)
  END; (* FACT *)

BEGIN (* MAINLINE *)
  WRITELN('ENTER A NON-NEGATIVE INTEGER');
  READLN(NUM);
  FACT_NUM := FACT(NUM);
  WRITELN('FACTORIAL(', NUM:3, ') IS', FACT_NUM:8)
END. (* FACTORIALS *)
```

The output when the program is executed using 3 is shown below.

```
ENTER A NON-NEGATIVE INTEGER
THE PARAMETER HAS THE VALUE   3
THE PARAMETER HAS THE VALUE   2
THE PARAMETER HAS THE VALUE   1
THE PARAMETER HAS THE VALUE   0
FACTORIAL(  3) IS         6
```

Consider what happens when FACT is passed a value of 3.

1. The value of 3 is assigned to the formal parameter N.

2. The body of the function is executed. Since N is not 0 the statement
    FACT:=3* FACT(2) is executed.

3. To obtain the value of FACT(2), the function FACT is again invoked this
    time with a parameter value of 2. This causes FACT := 2 * FACT(1) to
    be executed.

4. To obtain FACT(1), the function is invoked with a parameter value of 0.

5. On this fourth invocation of FACT the function value is set equal to 1
    and thus FACT(1) becomes 1*FACT(0) or 1.

6. Knowing FACT(1) means FACT(2) can then be calculated as 2*FACT(1)
    or 2.

7. Finally, the value of FACT(3) is obtained from 3*FACT(2) causing
    FACT_NUM to be replaced by 6 prior to the WRITELN statement.

All recursive functions work this way. That is, to obtain the function value
associated with the first invocation, one or more subsequent invocations of the
function are made, each one causing the immediately previous one to be held
pending or stacked. When a function value can be assigned without further
function invocations, the last function value is substituted in the expression for
the second last; the second last function value is then substituted in the
expression for the third last and so on.

A second example. Consider Euclid's algorithm for finding the Greatest
Common Divisor (GCD) of a pair of positive integers. The GCD of two
integers M and N (assume M is bigger than N) is given by:

$$GCD(M,N) = \begin{cases} GCD(N,M) & \text{if } M < N \\ M & \text{if } N = 0 \\ GCD(N, M \text{ MOD } N) & \text{otherwise} \end{cases}$$

For example:
```
     GCD (26,4)   →  GCD(4,26 MOD 4)
                  →  GCD(4,2)
                  →  GCD(2,4 MOD 2)
                  →  GCD(2, 0)
                  →  2
```

By looking at the definition of GCD(M,N), we see the function invokes itself
until the second parameter has a value of zero. When this happens, the
function value is the value of the first parameter. The program below reads a
pair of integer values and if both are positive, computes their GCD.

```
PROGRAM GCD_VALUE(INPUT,OUTPUT);

(* THIS PROGRAM DETERMINES THE GREATEST COMMON
   DIVISOR OF TWO POSITIVE INTEGER VALUES        *)

VAR
  X, Y : INTEGER;

FUNCTION GCD(M,N:INTEGER) : INTEGER;
  BEGIN (* GCD *)
    IF M < N THEN
      GCD := GCD(N,M)
    ELSE IF N = 0 THEN
      GCD := M
    ELSE
      GCD := GCD(N, M MOD N)
  END; (* GCD *)

BEGIN (* GCD_VALUE *)
  WRITELN('ENTER A PAIR OF INTEGERS');
  READLN(X,Y);
  IF (X > 0) AND (Y > 0 ) THEN
    WRITELN('THE GCD OF', X:5, ' AND', Y:5,
            ' IS', GCD(X,Y):5)
  ELSE
    WRITELN('** ERROR **, X AND Y MUST BE POSITIVE')
END. (* GCD_VALUE *)
```

Recursive functions have many useful applications. Many of these involve an array of values (see Chapter 10).

7.8 Exercise 7.2

1. What is the output of the following program?

```
PROGRAM EX72_1(OUTPUT);
VAR N:INTEGER; A:REAL;
FUNCTION F(MOM:INTEGER; DAD:REAL):REAL;
  BEGIN
    IF MOM=1 THEN
      F := DAD
    ELSE
      F := F(MOM-1,DAD+1)
  END; (* F *)
BEGIN (* MAINLINE *)
  A := 10.5;
  FOR N := 5 DOWNTO 1 DO
    WRITELN(N,A,F(N,A))
END. (* EX72_1 *)
```

2. What are the errors in the following program?

```
PROGRAM EX72_2(INPUT,OUTPUT);
VAR
  X, Y : CHAR;

FUNCTION FIRST(A,B:CHAR) : CHAR;
  BEGIN
    IF A < B THEN
      FIRST := A
    ELSE
      FIRST := LAST(A,B)
  END; (* FIRST *)

FUNCTION LAST(A,B:CHAR) : CHAR;
  BEGIN
    IF A > B THEN
      LAST := A
    ELSE
      LAST := FIRST(A,B)
  END; (* LAST *)

BEGIN (* MAINLINE *)
  READLN(X,Y);
  WRITELN(FIRST(A,B), LAST(A,B))
END. (* EX72_2 *)
$ENTRY
KP
```

3. Suppose the value of the function BIGGER(X,Y) is the larger of the two parameter values. Does the expression BIGGER(X, BIGGER (Y,Z)) involve recursion or not? Explain.

4. The definition of a Pascal program specifies that it contains a PROGRAM header followed by a block. Since a block can contain other blocks, is the definition of a Pascal program recursive? If so, what is the stopping rule?

7.9 Summary

1. A Pascal program consists of a PROGRAM header followed by a block followed by a period. The block contains declarations followed by a program body as shown below.

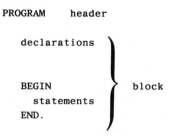

```
PROGRAM    header

   declarations

   BEGIN                          block
      statements
   END.
```

Block declarations may include functions. Theoretically blocks may be nested to any depth.

2. A Pascal function is used to calculate a value from one or more values passed to it. A function is declared within a block and consists of a function header followed by a block as shown below.

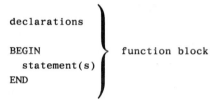

```
FUNCTION name (formal parameter list): function type;

   declarations

   BEGIN                          function block
      statement(s)
   END
```

3. A function is invoked by the appearance of

                    name (actual parameter list)

in an expression. The number and type of parameter expressions must correspond one-for-one with the number and type of the formal parameters in the FUNCTION header.

When a function is invoked, the values of the parameter expressions are assigned to the corresponding formal parameters. Then the local declarations are created and the function body is executed. The value assigned to the function name replaces the expression which invoked the function.

4. Identifiers declared in a block and the formal parameters in the header of a block are local to the block. Their declarations have precedence over any declarations of the same identifiers in an outer block.

5. An identifier is global with respect to blocks declared within the block containing the identifier declaration.

6. A function may invoke itself.

7.10 Programming Problems

7.1 One method of generating INTEGER "random" numbers is as follows. Pick a large integer value, say 1792534165. Square it and extract the middle 5 digits (those in the thousands thru the ten millions postions). Call this number N1. Square N1 and take the middle 5 digits calling the result N2. Continue the process of squaring and extracting. The sequence of numbers N1,N2,N3,... is often one which has no detectable or predictable pattern. Such a random sequence of numbers -- N1,N2, etc. -- can be converted to numbers which lie in the interval (I,J) by calculating I + N MOD (J-I+1) for each number in the sequence. Write a program to generate 30 random numbers in the range 7 thru 15. On each line print the value of N1 and the derived number in the (7,15) range. Use a function for the step in the algorithm which squares and extracts the 5 digit number.

7.2 Write a function called ANG which, for the triangle shown below, calculates the size of angle A in degrees.

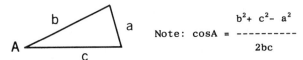

Note: $\cos A = \dfrac{b^2 + c^2 - a^2}{2bc}$

The lengths of the sides "a", "b" and "c" are passed to the function. Test the function by writing a mainline which reads the lengths of the sides and uses ANG to calculate the sizes of the three angles in the triangle.

7.3 The area of a regular polygon of N sides in which each side has a length "s" is equal to $Ns^2\cot(180/N)/4$. Write a function called POLAIR having parameters N and s to calculate the area. Test POLAIR by writing a mainline which uses the function to calculate the areas of regular polygons of *perimeter* one having 3, 4, 5, ..., 20 sides.

7.4 Write three functions called SIND, COSD and TAND to produce the sine, cosine and tangent values of an angle in degrees. Use the functions in a program which prints a table of the cosecant, secant and cotangents of angles of 10, 20, 30, ..., 80 degrees.

7.5 Write a function which will round off any REAL value greater than 0.1 correct to N decimal places. Assume N is positive. This can be done by adding $5*10^{-N}$ to the value; multiplying by 10^N; using the function TRUNC; dividing by 10^N.. Test your function by rounding the value of 12.73469 correct to 1, 2, 3, and 4 decimal places.

7.6 Write a function called LOGB having two parameters X and B. The value of the function is the logarithm of X using base B. Note that

$$\log_B X = \log_A X / \log_A B$$

Use LOGB to print a table of the logs of the values one thru ten using bases 2, 4, 6, 8, and 10. Make use of the built in LN function which calculates logarithms using base e.

7.7 Write a function called KRONIKER which has two INTEGER parameters M and N. The value of KRONIKER should be zero if M and N are unequal and one if M equals N. Make up your own program to test the function.

7.8 The value of the inverse sine of x radians (x must be between plus and minus pi/4) is given by the following expression.

$$\sin^{-1}x = x + \frac{1}{2 \cdot 3}x^3 + \frac{1 \cdot 3}{2 \cdot 4 \cdot 5}x^5 + \frac{1 \cdot 3 \cdot 5}{2 \cdot 4 \cdot 6 \cdot 7}x^7 + \ldots$$

Write a function which calculates the inverse sine of a value of 0.25. (What angle is such that its sine equals 0.25?) Obtain the result correct to three decimal places.

7.9 Large values of factorial N can be approximated using Stirling's formula which is

$$N! \text{ is approximately } e^{-N}N \sqrt[N]{2 N \pi}$$

Calculate the values of factorial 1, 2, 3, ..., 20 using the approximation formula.

7.10 An approximate value of PI can be calculated using one of several formulae. Two of these are:

$$\frac{\pi^2}{8} = 1 + \frac{1}{3^2} + \frac{1}{5^2} + \frac{1}{7^2} + \ldots$$

$$\pi = \sqrt{\frac{6}{1^2} + \frac{6}{2^2} + \frac{6}{3^2} + \frac{6}{4^2} + \ldots}$$

Write two different functions to calculate an approximate value of PI using the given formulae. Which formula requires the fewest terms to get a good approximation to PI?

7.11   In the Julian calendar, the days of the year are numbered sequentially from 1 to 365 (in non-leap years). Develop a function having two parameters called MONTH and DAY which returns the Julian day for any given month-day pair. Use the function in a program to print a Julian calendar having 12 columns, one for each month, and 31 rows. The entry in the Ith row and Jth column should be the Julian day for the Ith day in the Jth month.

7.12   (Recursion) The Fibonacci sequence of numbers is 0, 1, 1, 2, 3, 5, 8, ... where each number except the first two is the sum of its immediate two predecessors. Write a function with the header:

FUNCTION FIBONACCI(N:INTEGER):INTEGER

which produces the Nth number in the sequence. Use recursion to get the function value. Test your function by writing a program which uses FIBONACCI to generate the first ten Fibonacci numbers.

7.13   (Recursion) The Kth triangular number has the value 1 + 2 + 3 + ... + K. Its value is therefore K plus the (K-1)th triangular number. Write a function which calculates the Kth triangular number recursively. Test the program by printing the first twelve triangular numbers on four lines of three numbers each.

CHAPTER 8: PROCEDURES

Questions Answered in this Chapter:

1. What are Pascal procedures?

2. How do procedures differ from functions?

3. How should a large program be broken down into procedures and functions?

8.1 What are Pascal Procedures?

This chapter describes the third kind of block that is often part of a Pascal program. Recall that every program has one and only one program block; that is a program header followed by a block. Furthermore a block consists of declarations followed by a single compound statement called the body of the block. A block may contain declarations of one or more other blocks. Function blocks are described in the last chapter. Procedure blocks or simply procedures are described in this chapter.

The mechanics and rules of use of procedures are practically identical to those of functions. The real difference is in the purpose of a procedure as opposed to the purpose of a function. Whereas the purpose of a function is to determine a value from one or more values made available to it, the purpose of a procedure is primarily to group together a related set of statements that perform some well-defined step in an algorithm. The group of statements is given a name -- the procedure name and, like a function, values may be passed to it. Procedures often return one or more values.

The reasons for grouping a set of declarations and statements together by name include the following:

- the program is more readable

- procedures can be tested and debugged separately

- by isolating a logic step in a procedure, the parts of a program are more independent and the likelihood of logic errors is reduced

- the same procedure can be invoked from different places in a program; thus a commonly used chunk of logic needs to be written only once

Standard Pascal includes thirteen predefined procedures of which we have used five, namely: READ, READLN, WRITE, WRITELN and PAGE. The other eight are associated with data structures and file input-output. They are described in Part II.

The remainder of the chapter begins with an example illustrating the simplest use of procedures; then shows how they can be used to return multiple values; how procedures can call themselves; and summarizes the rules of function and procedure usage. The chapter concludes with some guidelines and suggestions for attacking complex programming tasks.

8.2 A First Example

We want to print a report showing the value of the square and the square root of numbers from one to fifty. The format of the report is to be as shown below.

```
┌──────────────────────────────────────────────────────┐
│                      DATE: XX–XX–XX                    │
│                                                        │
│       VALUE            SQUARE        SQUARE  ROOT       │
│                                                        │
│         X              XXXX          XX.XXX             │
│         X              XXXX          XX.XXX             │
│         .                .             .                │
│         .                .             .                │
│         X              XXXX          XX.XXX             │
└──────────────────────────────────────────────────────┘
```

The algorithm is very simple, namely:

1. Get the date
2. Print heading lines
3. For Num = 1 to 50 do
        .1 Print Num, Num^2, SQRT.(Num)

In the program which follows a PROCEDURE is used to perform step 2. This involves the following three substeps:

1. Go to the top of the page
2. Print the date line
3. Print the column headings

The complete program follows.

```
PROGRAM SQUARE_STUFF(INPUT,OUTPUT);

(* THIS PROGRAM  TABULATES THE SQUARE AND SQUARE
   ROOT OF NUMBERS FROM 1 TO 50                    *)

TYPE
  YEAR_RANGE = 1900..2000;
  MONTH_RANGE = 1..12;
  DAY_RANGE   = 1..31;

VAR
  YEAR   : YEAR_RANGE;
  MONTH  : MONTH_RANGE;
  DAY    : DAY_RANGE;
  NUMBER : INTEGER;

PROCEDURE PRINT_HEADING(YR:YEAR_RANGE; MON:MONTH_RANGE;
                        DAY:DAY_RANGE);

  (* THIS PROCEDURE PRINTS THE HEADING LINES *)

    CONST
      BLANK = ' ';
      PAGE_WIDTH = 60;
    VAR
      I : INTEGER;

    BEGIN (* PRINT_HEADING *)
      PAGE; (* GO TO TOP OF PAGE *)
      FOR I := 1 TO PAGE_WIDTH - 17 DO
        WRITE(BLANK);
      WRITELN('DATE:',YR:5, MON:3, DAY:3);
      WRITELN;
      WRITELN(' VALUE  SQUARE  SQUARE ROOT');
      WRITELN
    END; (* PRINT_HEADING *)

BEGIN (* SQUARE_STUFF *)
  WRITELN('ENTER YEAR, MONTH AND DAY');
  READLN(YEAR, MONTH, DAY);
  PRINT_HEADING(YEAR, MONTH, DAY);
  FOR NUMBER := 1 TO 50 DO
    WRITELN(NUMBER:6, SQR(NUMBER):8, SQRT(NUMBER):12:3)
END. (* SQUARE_STUFF *)
```

Comments

1. The program declarations include the declaration of a PROCEDURE having the form below.

    ```
    PROCEDURE heading
    ```

    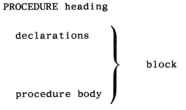

    ```
        declarations
                                      block
        procedure body
    ```

    Thus, aside from the procedure heading, a procedure is indistinguishable from a FUNCTION or a PROGRAM.

2. The procedure heading in the example consists of the line

    ```
    PROCEDURE PRINT HEADING(YR:YEAR_RANGE; MON:MONTH_RANGE;
                                     DAY:DAY_RANGE)
    ```

    It contains a formal parameter list having declarations for three formal parameters. Unlike standard procedures such as WRITE, EOF and PAGE which can be used with zero, one or several parameters, the number and type of formal parameters must match the number and type of the actual parameters passed to it when the procedure is executed. Furthermore, if the type of a formal parameter is other than one of the predefined types INTEGER, REAL, CHAR, BOOLEAN, TEXT, that type must be defined prior to the procedure heading. This is why YEAR_RANGE, MONTH_RANGE and DAY_RANGE were declared in the program block. It would be illegal, for instance, to use the header

    ```
    PROCEDURE PRINT_HEADING(YR:1900..2000;MON:1..12;DAY:1..31)
    ```

    because the formal parameter types are not previously declared type identifiers.

3. A procedure is invoked by a statement of the form:

    ```
    procedure name (actual parameter list)
    ```

    When a procedure call is executed, three actions occur:

    1. The values of the actual parameter expressions are calculated and assigned to the corresponding formal parameters.

2. The block of the procedure is executed. Identifiers declared within the procedure are created and the procedure body is executed.

3. Control returns to the statement following the procedure invocation.

The preceding program also illustrates why procedures are used. In the example, the program body contains three simple steps, namely:

1. Get the date
2. Print the heading
3. Perform the calculations

By making the seven statements required to print the heading into a separate procedure we achieve the following two objectives:

*   The program structure is more visible because the program body consists of three simple steps. If the seven statements in PRINT_HEADING were part of the mainline, they would overshadow the other two steps.

*   Debugging the program is easier because the statements used to print the heading are isolated in a procedure. Constants, types and variables needed to print the heading can be created and used knowing that their existence will not have any effect on other parts of the program.

8.3 Using Procedures to Return Values.
The preceding example demonstrates the use of procedures to isolate a part of the program logic and its associated declarations. By doing this the program structure becomes more visible and debugging time is reduced. A second use of procedures - often combined with the first - is to return one or more values to the calling block. Recall that a function assigns a single value to the function name. A procedure on the other hand is often used to return multiple values. This requires two things to be done. First, the variables whose values are to be calculated in the procedure are put in the actual parameter list. Second, the declarations of the corresponding formal parameters in the procedure header are preceded by "VAR".

A very simple problem will be used to illustrate the method. The problem is to print the numbers from one to ten. To do this we will employ a procedure called BUMP to generate the next value in the sequence. Here is the program.

```
PROGRAM ONE_TO_TEN(OUTPUT);

(* THIS PROGRAM PRINTS THE VALUES 1 THRU 10 *)

VAR
  NUMBER : INTEGER;

PROCEDURE BUMP( VAR NUM : INTEGER );
  BEGIN
    NUM := NUM + 1
  END; (* BUMP *)

BEGIN (* ONE_TO_TEN *)
  NUMBER := 1;
  WHILE NUMBER <= 10 DO
    BEGIN
      WRITELN(NUMBER);
      BUMP(NUMBER)
    END
END. (* ONE_TO_TEN *)
```

Note the declaration of the formal variable NUM in

```
PROCEDURE BUMP ( VAR NUM : INTEGER )
```

Placing VAR ahead of NUM causes the value of NUM to be assigned to the corresponding actual parameter when BUMP has finished executing. Thus the net result of calling BUMP is increase the value of NUMBER.

Formal parameter declarations which are preceded by VAR are called "VAR parameters". Without the VAR they are called value parameters. The value of a value parameter is not assigned to the corresponding actual parameter when a procedure finishes execution.

What would happen if we make NUM a value parameter by omitting the VAR in its declaration? Because the value is not returned, calling BUMP would have no effect. Consequently, the program variable NUMBER would never change value and we would never exit from the WHILE loop. The value-passing is one way only.

Because values of VAR formal parameters are assigned to the corresponding actual parameter, the actual parameter cannot be a constant or expression. The procedure calls below, for example, are invalid.

```
BUMP(5)              BUMP(M+N)
```

Any or all formal parameters of a procedure can be VAR parameters. The PROCEDURE heading below for example declares A, B and D to be VAR parameters and C to be a non-VAR or value parameter.

        PROCEDURE FRED(VAR A,B:REAL; C:CHAR; VAR D:BOOLEAN)

VAR parameters can also be used in functions thus allowing a function to return more than one value. In such cases, it is more customary and strongly recommended that a procedure be used.

8.4 Retaining Values of Parameters

Occasionally it is necessary to have a PROCEDURE or FUNCTION "remember" a value generated in a previous invocation of that block. Because objects declared in a block are recreated each time the block is invoked (think of the declarations as being "executed") the values of all local variables are lost after a block has finished executing. Two methods are available for remembering what value a variable had when a block was last executed. Both require the use of variables global to the given block. The choice is whether to pass the value of the variable to the block as a parameter or to let the block reference the global variable directly. Both approaches are illustrated in the following problem.

A procedure called HEADER is required to print a heading line at the top of each page. The heading line is to contain the date and a page number. The first time HEADER is invoked, the date must be read from the INPUT file.

Assuming that the date is represented by three integers denoting year, month, and day, these values must be saved so that they are available each time HEADER is invoked. Since the READ is to be done in the procedure, the variables YEAR, MONTH, and DAY cannot be locally-declared variables because their values would be lost the first time the procedure finishes execution. A similar problem occurs with the page number. It must increase by one each time the procedure is invoked. Hence it too must be declared outside the procedure.

Finally, how can the procedure determine whether or not it is being called for the first time? If we set the value of PAGE_NUM to zero in the mainline before invoking HEADER the first time, the procedure logic can determine whether or not to READ the date information based on the value of PAGE_NUM.

In the partial program below, YEAR, MONTH, DAY and PAGE_NUM are declared in the program block and hence are global to the HEADER procedure. PAGE_NUM is passed to the procedure as a parameter. Further comments follow the program.

```
PROGRAM REPORT(INPUT,OUTPUT);

(* THIS PROGRAM SHOWS HOW VALUES CAN BE REMEMBERED
            BY A SUBPROGRAM                               *)

VAR
  YEAR, MONTH, DAY : INTEGER;
  PAGE_NUM         : INTEGER;

PROCEDURE HEADER(VAR PAGE_COUNT : INTEGER);
  BEGIN (* HEADER *)
    IF PAGE_COUNT = 0 THEN
      BEGIN
        WRITELN('ENTER YEAR, MONTH AND DAY');
        READLN(YEAR, MONTH, DAY)
      END;
    PAGE_COUNT := PAGE_COUNT + 1;
    WRITELN('DATE:',YEAR:5,MONTH:3,DAY:3,'  PAGE-',
            PAGE_COUNT:3)
  END; (* HEADER *)

BEGIN (* REPORT *)

  (* MAINLINE STATEMENTS INCLUDING *) PAGE_NUM := 0;

  HEADER(PAGE_NUM)

END. (* REPORT *)
```

Comments

1. When HEADER is invoked, the value of the parameter PAGE_NUM is assigned to the formal parameter PAGE_COUNT. At the first invocation, PAGE_COUNT is zero so HEADER reads three INTEGER values from the INPUT file and assigns them to the program (global) variables YEAR, MONTH and DAY. It then increases the value of PAGE_COUNT, prints the heading line and terminates. The values of the date components are safely stored in global variables and are available on second and subsequent invocations of HEADER.

2. The value of the global variable PAGE_NUM is updated by passing it back and forth using a matching VAR parameter. The page number could also be changed by having the procedure refer directly to the variable PAGE_NUM rather than use the VAR parameter PAGE_COUNT. A further discussion of the advantages and disadvantages of global variables is found in the following paragraphs.

8.5 Global Variables: Good or Bad?

First, some global constants, types and variables are almost always present in a program because all identifiers used in the program body are global. So unless the mainline consists simply of a sequence of procedure invocations, none of which use variables in their parameter lists, a program will contain one or more global variables.

Second, because both the identifiers declared within a block and its formal parameters are destroyed after the block has finished executing, global identifiers are needed when it is necessary to save values generated in a block.

Third, globals are convenient. Their existence means a block can use these identifiers without declaring them in a parameter list. So why not globals all the time? Or, to take it to the extreme case, why not declare all identifiers needed in the entire program in the program block? The answers to these questions are in the next paragraph.

There are some very good reasons for not doing this. In the military and secret service agencies there is a "need to know" rule. It simply says, only tell someone as much as they need to know to do their job. There is no advantage to be gained by giving a person extra information because he or she may pass it on to the wrong person or may even modify it to suit his or her own purposes. The exact same thinking applies within programs. Four important programming guidelines are the following.

Guidelines for Use of Global Identifiers

1. Use parameters to pass all values necessary for a procedure or function to do its job.

2. Do not use a VAR parameter if a value parameter will do.

3. Reduce the number of global variables to those required to save the values generated by a called block.

4. In general, VAR parameters are preferable to direct references to global variables because it makes explicit which values are being modified.

In programming terminology, unnecessary use of global variables often leads to *side effects*. These can occur when one block changes the value of a global variable without other blocks being aware the change has been made. Diagnosing problems resulting from side effects is often very difficult and can be eliminated by minimizing the use of global variables and maximizing the use of value parameters and using VAR parameters where needed. Occasionally, for the sake of execution-time efficiency, these guidelines are ignored.

Is the "need-to-know" rule easily enforced in Pascal? Absolutely not! In fact the most nested block in a program has access to the most variables! That is equivalent to a junior clerk in a company not only having access to all the company data, but the ability to change it as well! This is the reason care must be taken when passing values and results between blocks. It is also a reason for choosing a nesting structure which minimizes potential side effects. This last point is discussed in the final section of this chapter.

8.6 Exercise 8.1

1.   What is the output of the following program?

```
PROGRAM EX8_1_1(INPUT,OUTPUT);
VAR
  C1, C2:CHAR;
PROCEDURE SWITCHO(A, B : CHAR);
  BEGIN
    IF A < B THEN
      B := A; A := B; (* TRICKY *)
    WRITELN(A, B)
  END;
BEGIN
  WHILE NOT EOLN DO
    BEGIN
      READ(C1, C2);
      IF C1 > C2 THEN
        SWITCHO(C2, C1)
      ELSE
        READ(C1,C2)
    END
END.
$ENTRY
1243567798
```

2. What is the output produced by executing the program below?

```
PROGRAM EX8_1_2(OUTPUT);
VAR
  M, N : INTEGER;
PROCEDURE MARTHA(VAR X : INTEGER; Y : INTEGER);
  VAR
    Z : INTEGER;
  BEGIN
    FOR Z := X TO Y DO
      WRITELN(X,Y);
    X := X + 1
  END;
BEGIN
  M := 1; N := 3;
  WHILE M < N DO
    MARTHA(M, N)
END.
```

3. What pattern of values is printed by the following program? (Program execution does not terminate.)

```
PROGRAM EX8_1_3(OUTPUT);
VAR Q : REAL;
PROCEDURE A;
  VAR
    P : REAL;
  PROCEDURE B;
    BEGIN (* B *)
      REPEAT
        WRITELN(P);
        P := P + 2
      UNTIL P >= Q;
      A
    END;
  BEGIN (* A *)
    REPEAT
      P := 1;
      Q := Q + 1;
      B
    UNTIL Q = 4
  END; (* A *)
BEGIN
  Q := 0; A
END.
```

4. For each block in the following program structure, state the variables that are local to the block, those that are global to it, and those that are inaccessible to the block.

```
PROGRAM  BLOCK1;
VAR
   A, B : INTEGER;
PROCEDURE  BLOCK2  (C:BOOLEAN);
   VAR
      D : CHAR;
   PROCEDURE  BLOCK3  (E:REAL);
      VAR
         F : CHAR;
      BEGIN END;
   BEGIN END;
PROCEDURE  BLOCK4;
   VAR
      G : REAL;
   BEGIN END;
BEGIN END.
```

5. For each of the procedures in question 4 above, state which procedures can be invoked. If a procedure cannot invoke another procedure, give the reason.

8.7 Recursive Procedures

This section may be omitted on first reading.

Recursive procedures, like recursive functions, are ones which call themselves. Each time they are invoked, a new set of declarations is created which remain in effect until the block terminates execution. Because these blocks call themselves, these declarations are stacked up, one after the other until finally no more self-calls are made. Then the declarations are released one at a time as each invocation returns control to its calling block.

To illustrate the use of a recursive procedure, consider the problem of determining the minimum number of coins required to pay a given amount of money. In particular, assume the amount must be paid using coins of 25, 10, 5 and 1 cent denominations.

In analyzing this problem, we quickly realize that the answer involves using as many coins of the largest denomination possible; paying what is left using as many of the second largest denomination as possible; and continuing to use successively smaller valued coins to reduce the outstanding balance. The process stops when the amount remaining to be paid is zero. The algorithm is therefore:

1. Get and echo amount to be paid
2. Set coinsize = 25
3. Repeat
    .1 Pay as much as possible using coins of
            value coinsize
    .2 Compute amount left
    .3 If amount left $>$ 0 then set coinsize
            = next lower denomination
  Until amount left = 0

Where is the recursion? Certainly the algorithm can be programmed using a REPEAT-UNTIL or a WHILE loop. The repeat loop can also be transformed into a recursive procedure having two parameters -- the amount to be paid and the coinsize to be used. After paying the maximum possible using the given coinsize, the procedure calculates the amount remaining and the next smaller coinsize. It then calls itself using this new amount and coinsize. This process continues as long as the amount to be paid is greater than zero. The recursive algorithm is therefore:

1. Get the amount
2. Pay amount starting with 25 cent denomination

where Pay has the algorithm

1. Calculate maximum number of coins which
    can be used of the given denomination
2. Calculate the amount still unpaid
3. If amount unpaid $>$ 0 then
    Pay amount remaining starting with
    next smallest denomination

Here is the program showing the output produced for an input value of 87.

```
    PROGRAM CHANGER(INPUT,OUTPUT);

    (* THIS PROGRAM DETERMINES THE MINIMUM NUMBER OF COINS
       REQUIRED TO PAY AN AMOUNT OF $1.00 OR LESS USING
       COINS OF VALUES 25, 10, 5 AND 1 CENT.                    *)

    VAR
      AMOUNT : INTEGER;

    PROCEDURE PAY(AMOUNT, COIN_SIZE:INTEGER);

      VAR
        AMOUNT_LEFT, COINS : INTEGER;

      BEGIN (* PAY *)
        COINS := AMOUNT DIV COIN_SIZE;
        AMOUNT_LEFT := AMOUNT - COINS * COIN_SIZE;
        WRITELN (COINS:3, ' COINS OF VALUE', COIN_SIZE:3);
        IF AMOUNT_LEFT > 0 THEN
          BEGIN
            CASE COIN_SIZE OF
              25: COIN_SIZE := 10;
              10: COIN_SIZE :=  5;
               5: COIN_SIZE :=  1
            END; (* CASE *)
            PAY(AMOUNT_LEFT, COIN_SIZE)
          END (* IF *)
      END; (* PAY *)
    BEGIN (* CHANGER *)
      WRITELN('ENTER AMOUNT TO BE PAID');
      READLN(AMOUNT);
      WRITELN ('THE AMOUNT',AMOUNT:4, ' CAN BE PAID USING:');
      PAY(AMOUNT,25)
    END. (* CHANGER *)
```

The output produced by running the program is shown below.

```
    Execution begins...
    THE AMOUNT  87 CAN BE PAID USING:
       3 COINS OF VALUE 25
       1 COINS OF VALUE 10
       0 COINS OF VALUE  5
       2 COINS OF VALUE  1
```

Recursion is not limited to a procedure or function calling itself directly. For example, if procedure Y is declared within procedure X, it is permissible for Y to invoke X.

It is also permissible for two procedures declared in the same block to invoke each other. If you think about this for a minute, you will realize this means the rule that all identifiers must be declared before they are used is violated since if X is declared before Y it cannot contain a reference to Y. The way around this dilemma is to use a FORWARD directive. The directives FORWARD and EXTERNAL are discussed in the next section.

8.8 The Directives FORWARD and EXTERNAL

This section may be omitted on first reading.

A directive is a word placed after a procedure or function header that informs the compiler that the procedure or function block is found elsewhere. There are two commonly used directives in Pascal. The FORWARD directive says the block is found later in the same program. The EXTERNAL directive says the procedure or function is found in a file of procedures and/or functions stored on some device attached to the computer. We consider each briefly.

8.8.1 The FORWARD Directive

The FORWARD directive has two uses -- one optional, one required. It is required if a procedure or function is referenced before it has been declared. Consider the following program structure in which Function F calls Procedure Y and vice versa.

```
PROGRAM NOGOOD;

FUNCTION F (A,B,C:REAL) : REAL;
  BEGIN (* F *)
    Y (A,B,C) (* AND OTHER STATEMENTS *)
  END; (* F *)

PROCEDURE Y (P,Q,R:REAL);
  VAR
    VALUE : REAL;
  BEGIN (* Y *)
    VALUE := F(P,Q,R)
  END; (* Y *)

BEGIN (* NOGOOD *)
  (* MAINLINE STATEMENTS HERE *)
END. (* NOGOOD *)
```

This structure is invalid because function F contains a reference to Y which appears before Y has been declared. To circumvent this problem we need to put the procedure header for Y ahead of F and specify that the block for Y is FORWARD (comes later). Here is the result.

```
PROGRAM OK;

PROCEDURE Y (P,Q,R:REAL); FORWARD;

FUNCTION F (A,B,C:REAL) : REAL;
  BEGIN (* F *)
    Y (A,B,C) (* AND OTHER STATEMENTS *)
  END; (* F *)

PROCEDURE Y;
  VAR
    VALUE : REAL;
  BEGIN (* Y *)
    VALUE := F(P,Q,R)
  END; (* Y *)

BEGIN (* OK *)
  (* MAINLINE STATEMENTS HERE *)
END. (* OK *)
```

Observe that the procedure header for Y appears ahead of the declaration for F. The directive FORWARD follows the header indicating that the block is found later in the program block. The point chosen to define the missing block is indicated by the word PROCEDURE followed by the procedure name. *The formal parameter list is not repeated in this block header.* The forward block (declarations and body) follows the block header.

Each PROCEDURE or FUNCTION header in a block could include a FORWARD directive meaning its associated block appears later in the same block. Why might you want to do this? A possible advantage is readability. By listing all PROCEDURE and FUNCTION headers prior to defining their blocks, you get an idea of the procedures, functions and their respective parameters that are found in the block. You can then skip over the details of the blocks appearing between the forward directives and the program body. Essentially then, unless required in the circumstances illustrated by the example in the previous subsection, (mutually recursive blocks) the use of FORWARD directives is a matter of personal preference. The important rules are summarized below.

FORWARD Directives

1. The PROCEDURE or FUNCTION header is immediately followed by the FORWARD directive. The directive is separated from the header by a semicolon.

... (continued on the next page)

2.   The block of the procedure or function must appear later in the
     same block containing the directive.

3.   At the location of the block, the block is preceded by a block
     header consisting of the word FUNCTION or PROCEDURE as
     appropriate followed by the function or procedure name and the
     block itself. The formal parameter list, if any, is not repeated.

8.8.2 The EXTERNAL Directive

Many versions of Pascal permit you to invoke Pascal procedures and
functions (even subprograms written in other languages such as FORTRAN)
which are stored in an external file. To do this, the PROCEDURE or
FUNCTION header for the externally-stored subprogram is followed by the
directive EXTERNAL. Here is an example.

```
PROCEDURE  OUTSIDE (X:INTEGER);EXTERNAL
```

This specifies that OUTSIDE exists on some external file and that it expects a
single INTEGER value to be passed to it as a parameter. If a need for
EXTERNAL subprograms exists, read the detailed documentation describing
your Pascal compiler.

8.9 FUNCTIONs and PROCEDUREs : A summary

The purpose of this section is to summarize the rules which apply to function
and procedure definition and use. Each of these rules has been illustrated in
one or more examples in the last two chapters.

1.   Declarations

     A function declaration has the form:

```
     FUNCTION name (formal parameter list): type;
        block
```

     A procedure declaration has the form:

```
     PROCEDURE name (formal parameter list);
        block
```

     where name denotes the name of the function or procedure and the list of
     formal parameters describe the number and type of values passed to
     and/or returned by the function or procedure.

2. Invocation

A function block is invoked by the appearance of

```
function name (actual parameters)
```

in an expression. The values of the parameters are assigned to the corresponding formal parameters which must be variables. Upon return from the function block the value assigned to the function replaces the invoking expression.

A procedure block is invoked by the statement

```
procedure name (actual parameters)
```

The values of the parameters are assigned to the corresponding formal parameters which must be variables. After execution of the procedure block, values of the VAR formal parameters are assigned to the corresponding actual parameters. Execution then continues with the next statement.

3. Nested Blocks

Function and procedure blocks may contain declarations of other functions and procedures. These block declarations follow the LABEL, CONST, TYPE and VAR declarations.

4. Formal Parameters

There are four kinds of formal parameters. They may appear in any order. They are:

value parameters -- each value parameter is an identifier with a type specified by a predefined or previously declared type. The corresponding actual parameter can be any expression with a value which is assignment-compatible with the formal parameter.

variable parameters -- A variable (or VAR) parameter has a VAR declaration. The corresponding actual parameter must be a variable declared with the same type identifier. Values of VAR parameters are assigned to their corresponding actual parameters when the called block terminates execution.

FUNCTION and PROCEDURE parameters -- A FUNCTION or PROCEDURE formal parameter (described in the following section) is identical to a FUNCTION or PROCEDURE heading.

8.10 Procedure and Function Parameters

This section may be omitted on first reading.

Pascal permits the *name* of a function or procedure to be passed as a parameter to another function or procedure. The corresponding formal parameter is a complete function or procedure header. Consider the following example.

If the function F, and the values of LOW and HIGH exist, the procedure below prints the value of F(x) for x= LOW, LOW+1, LOW+2, ...,HIGH.

```
PROCEDURE TABULATE;

  VAR
    X, LOW, HIGH : INTEGER;

  BEGIN (* TABULATE *)
    FOR X := LOW TO HIGH DO
      WRITELN(X:3, F(X):5)
  END (* TABULATE *)
```

Suppose we want to use TABULATE with different functions -- either predefined or user-written ones. The program below passes the user-written function SQROOT to the TABULATE procedure as a parameter. Thus, TABULATE produces a table of square roots.

```
PROGRAM TAB_FUNCTION(OUTPUT);

(* THIS PROGRAM TABULATES VALUES OF THE FUNCTION
   PASSED TO THE PROCEDURE TABULATE OVER A
   GIVEN RANGE OF VALUES                      *)

FUNCTION SQROOT(X:REAL) : REAL;
  BEGIN
    SQROOT := SQRT(X)
  END; (* SQROOT *)
PROCEDURE TABULATE( FUNCTION F(DUMMY:REAL):REAL;
                              LOW, HIGH: INTEGER);
  VAR
    X : INTEGER;
  BEGIN (* TABULATE *)
    FOR X := LOW TO HIGH DO
      WRITELN(X:3, F(X):8:3)
  END; (* TABULATE *)

BEGIN (* TAB_FUNCTION *)
  TABULATE(SQROOT, 10, 20)
END. (* TAB_FUNCTION *)
```

Comments

1. The program has three blocks -- the program block, a function block and a procedure block.

2. The invocation of TABULATE contains three actual parameters, namely: the name of a function, and two INTEGER values delimiting the range of values over which the function is to be calculated.

3. The TABULATE header containing the three matching formal parameters appears below.

```
PROCEDURE TABULATE( FUNCTION F(X : REAL) : REAL;
                    LOW, HIGH : INTEGER )
```

The first formal parameter is an example of a FUNCTION formal parameter. It has the form of a FUNCTION header. The corresponding actual parameter must be a function identifier having the same type of function value and having parameters matching those in the formal parameter header. (In the example, F and SQROOT have the same type and their respective parameters DUMMY and X have the same type.) The name DUMMY was used simply to emphasize that it serves no purpose except to indicate the type of parameter used by SQROOT.

4. Why did we have to create a function called SQROOT? Why not simply pass the function identifier SQRT to TABULATE? The reason is that identifiers corresponding to FUNCTION and PROCEDURE formal parameters must be *declared* in a block global to the block in which the function identifier is used as an actual parameter. The predefined function SQRT is not declared anywhere in the program. Hence it is necessary to create a FUNCTION containing a single executable statement which invokes the SQRT function.

FUNCTION and PROCEDURE formal parameters are the third and fourth kinds of formal parameters, the others being value parameters and VAR parameters. The rules of FUNCTION and PROCEDURE formal parameters follow.

FUNCTION and PROCEDURE Formal Parameters

1. The formal parameter has the form of a FUNCTION header or PROCEDURE header. The corresponding actual parameter is a function or procedure name.

... (continued on the next page)

---

2. The parameter lists of the actual function or procedure and the formal parameter function or procedure must match in number and type.

3. The identifiers known to an actual function or procedure are inherited by the block to which it is passed. (In the example, objects known to SQROOT are also known to TABULATE.)

Passing functions and procedures as parameters is seldom required in most programming problems. The ability to do this in Pascal adds flexibility and generality that may reduce the number of blocks necessary to program an algorithm.

8.11 Program Design
The questions answered in this section include:

● How do you decide what parts of an algorithm to make into procedures?

● When should a pair of procedures be declared one-within-the-other and when should they be declared in the same block?

● If procedures are nested several levels and an error condition is found in an inner level, what should you do?

8.11.1 Algorithm Development

A program involves both data and statements which process the data. More precisely, a program contains variables which are assigned the values of the data to be processed. In Part I of the text we are concerned primarily with the logic used to manipulate the data -- that is the algorithm and its translation into Pascal. In Part II of the book, the focus is on data and how it is structured. Proper choice of suitable data structures is often as challenging a problem as that of developing good algorithms. Data structuring problems are addressed in Part II.

Recall that when developing an algorithm, the "what-how" approach is recommended. The terms "stepwise refinement" and "top down design" are fancy names for the same thing. The steps are simple.

1. Write down what is to be done in a single clear statement.
2. Write down how it is to be done (the steps necessary to accomplish the task).

Each step in the "how" becomes a "what is to be done" at the next level of refinement. The what-how process is repeated until the "how steps" are simple enough to be translated one-for-one into a programming language such as Pascal. As the algorithm develops, it becomes more and more detailed.

Suppose an algorithm involves the three major steps shown below:
1. Read the data
2. Process the data
3. Print the results

Suppose further that the structure of the final algorithm is that shown below.

1. Read the data
    .1_____
    .2_____
        .1____
        .2____
        .3____
2. Process the data
    .1_____
        .1____
        .2____
    .2_____
    .3_____
3. Print the results
    .1_____
    .2_____

To get from the original three-step algorithm to the final algorithm, there are two organized approaches.

- each step can be expanded completely down to the most detailed steps before refining the next step at the same level

- all steps at a given level can be expanded one level of detail before repeating the process

Which is better? In general it doesn't matter much. If the steps are independent and they process different entities, it makes sense to refine a step down to its final level of detail. For example, if the problems of reading the data are completely independent of processing the data, then the read step can be developed in full before expanding the processing step. If, on the other hand, the input logic depends on the result of previous computations then it may be better to expand the steps in parallel.

8.11.2 Partitioning Algorithms Into Procedures

Once an algorithm has been developed, how do you decide how to partition it into functions and procedures? The problem of deciding whether a part of an algorithm should be made into a function or not is relatively easy. If a sequence of steps:

- processes a set of values in order to determine a single value, and

- does not modify other values in the algorithm

then it should be made into a function even if the function is needed only once in the algorithm.

The problem of deciding what steps should be grouped together to form a procedure is more difficult. The basis for forming a procedure can be any of the following. (The justification improves as you go down the list.)

- the steps are all logically related. For example, collecting all input routines into one procedure regardless of where input steps are used in the algorithm.

- the steps are all done at the same time when running the program. For example, an initialization procedure, a final totals procedure, etc.

- the steps all use the same inputs and produce similar outputs but do different things with the input values

- each step is essential to the performance of a well-defined task

The last reason is the best. If, after identifying a potential procedure you can state its purpose, fully and accurately in a simple English sentence having a single transitive verb and a specific non-plural object, then there is excellent justification for making the steps into a procedure. Some example statements are: "get master record", "match transaction and master", "format exception report", "summarize by sales region", "print error message", etc.

How many steps should there be in a procedure? There is no exact best number but most people agree that somewhere between three and seven steps is reasonable. The reason is that the average person can remember about seven ideas at a given time. It is important when studying a procedure that the analyst be consciously aware of all the steps needed to achieve the purpose of the procedure. Procedures of the recommended size have the advantage too that the comments, declarations and body will normally fit onto a single page so that all relevant information is visible at one time.

8.11.3 Should Procedures Be Nested?

When the author first began to use Pascal procedures, the answer to the following question was not immediately obvious. Given two procedures, should one be declared within the other or should they be declared one after the other in the same block? After much experience, the following guidelines are suggested.

1. If a pair of procedures are independent (neither invokes the other), then they can be declared in the same block. The order of declarations doesn't matter.

2. If procedure A is the *only* procedure which invokes procedure B then B should be declared within A.

3. If procedure A *and others* invoke procedure B then B must be declared before A. (If B is declared within A, then nobody but A can invoke B - you can see out but you can't see in.)

4. If A invokes B and B invokes A then the procedures are mutually recursive. This special, infrequently found case is described in Section 8.7.

The basic ideas are: first, do not make a procedure invocable by more procedures than is necesary; and second, if a procedure must be invoked by several other procedures, it must be declared in the same block as those invoking it or in one global to those invoking it.

The comments above apply equally well to functions or mixtures of functions and procedures.

Consider the following situation. The mainline invokes procedures A, B and C. Procedures A and B each invoke D. What is the best block structure for the program? From the description of the invocations, the "invocation tree" below can be constructed.

mainline

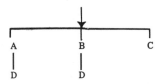

Note that "who-invokes-who" is not necessarily "what-is-declared-within-what". However, declaring procedure D in both procedure A and procedure B is one possible solution. The two disadvantages are that changes to D would have to be made in two places and second, additional memory is used to store a duplicate copy of D.

If D is declared only once, then the fact that A and B both invoke D means that it must be accessible to both and hence declared in the same block as A and B. Therefore the declaration structure should be that shown below.

```
PROGRAM header
PROCEDURE D (* declaration *)
PROCEDURE A (* declaration *)
PROCEDURE B (* declaration *)
PROCEDURE C (* declaration *)
BEGIN (* program body *)
END.
```

Observe that D is declared before A and B because A and B contain references to D. Most Pascal compilers require an identifier to be declared before it is used. Procedure C can be declared before or after any of the other procedures. Could procedures A and B be declared *within* D? Certainly this would allow A and B to invoke D. However, there would be no way for the mainline to invoke either A or B.

A word of caution. Recall that any block has access to all identifiers in every block containing it. Thus nesting, while increasing the independence of unrelated blocks, increases the possibility of side effects. This further emphasizes the importance of using parameter lists to provide communication between blocks.

Determining the nesting structure of blocks is often straightforward. If the same procedure is needed in different parts of an algorithm, the best idea is to construct an invocation tree and perform an analysis similar to that above.

8.11.4 Error Handling

One doesn't write too many programs involving nested blocks before encountering the following problem. An inner block detects an error condition that means no further processing with the given values should be carried out. What should be done? What block should print the error message and take other appropriate action? If the block finding the error prints a message, it may foul up a printout when in fact, a higher level block knows what to do about the error. On the other hand, if a lower level (nested) block simply tells its calling block "I have found an error", the calling block may not have enough information to know what to do.

As with the other questions raised in this section, experience is a great teacher. However, there are principles which can be applied.

In many ways, the structure of a program is much like the organization of a large company. The company has: a president (the mainline in the program); vice-presidents (the first level procedures); managers reporting to the vice-presidents (second-level procedures in a program); and so on down through supervisors to the lowest level of clerk. The organization structure is typically shown as a tree, an example of which is shown in the example below.

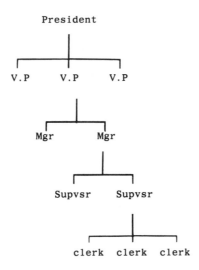

Now, if you were the president of the company and a clerk found a situation not covered by the rules ("his pencil broke"), what should the clerk do? Close the company down? Telephone the president? Ignore the problem? Does it not make sense to:

1.   report that there is a problem and the condition causing the problem to his superior
2.   if the superior does not know what to do (in light of other information available to the superior but not the clerk) then it should be reported up to the next level of authority

The abnormal situation should be reported up the hierarchy to the level at which a particular individual has the responsibility and the knowledge to take appropriate action. This same thinking applies in programming. It is often a good idea for each non-trivial procedure or function heading to contain a formal parameter which acts as a "return code". If the procedure performs normally, the return code is set to zero. If an abnormal condition is found, the return code variable is assigned a value which indicates the nature of the condition found. The first thing a calling procedure should do after invoking a block is check the value of the return code and take appropriate action. In this way an error can be percolated up through procedures until "someone" is competent to deal with it. In Pascal it makes sense to use an enumerated type for the return code values so that the abnormal conditions can be given meaningful names. It may also be a good idea to return the value or values causing the problem.

A somewhat similar kind of situation is encountered when there are many valid arrangements of input values of different types. For example, following an identifier in a line of a Pascal program, there may be any one of: another identifier, a number, an operator such as '+', a delimiter such as '(' or a reserved word. If any one of those sequences may be valid, the best approach is a "guess-if-not-guess-again" strategy. That is, assume the most likely case (say operator) and pass the value to the operator-handling procedure. If that procedure rejects it with an I-don't-understand or not-me kind of return code, then try the next procedure that may be able to make sense of the value. If all procedures reject the value then an error exists.

8.12 Exercise 8.2 Program Design

1. How do the suggested rules for indenting statements help to make the structure of an algorithm clearer?

2. How do the suggested rules for indenting blocks help to show the block structure of a program?

3. Each time a procedure is called, there is a certain amount of overhead in passing values to and from the procedure and in transferring control to, and returning from the invoked procedure. Therefore a program without any procedures runs faster than an equivalent program with procedures. Give two good reasons why the program with procedures is likely better.

4. Suppose a program mainline invokes procedures A and B and A also invokes B. What is a suitable block structure for the program?

5. A program mainline invokes A which invokes B which invokes C which invokes D. Describe two block designs and discuss the merits of each.

6. The invocation tree of a program is shown below.

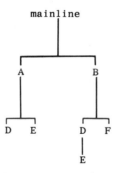

What is a good block structure for the program?

7. Is it ever absolutely necessary to nest block declarations?

8.13 Summary

1. A procedure is a named block (header, declarations and body) which is used to perform one or more steps in an algorithm.

2. Values are passed to a procedure using actual parameters. Through the use of VAR formal parameters, one or more values may be returned from a procedure or function to the calling block.

3. Functions and procedures have many similarities. The important differences are: the way the subprogram is invoked; the replacement of the function expression by a value versus a return to the statement following the procedure invocation; and the purpose of each -- calculate a value versus perform a step in an algorithm.

4. The FORWARD directive is a standard identifier which informs the compiler that the block of a procedure or function is found later in the block. It is required only if two or more procedures or functions are mutually recursive (the invocations form a loop).

5. Algorithm development should be done using a what-how approach. When the algorithm is complete, it is partitioned into procedures and functions. Proper partitioning produces more readable programs having fewer programming errors. You should be able to state the purpose of each procedure in a simple English sentence.

8.14 Programming Problems

8.1   Suppose the equations of two straight lines are

$$A_1x + B_1y = C_1$$
$$A_2x + B_2y = C_2$$

For any given values of A_1, B_1, C_1 and A_2, B_2, C_2 the lines may be parallel, coincident, perpendicular or oblique depending on the values of the A's, B's and C's. The mathematical relationships are as follows.

Orientation	Mathematical Relationship
parallel	$A_1*B_2 = B_1*A_2$
coincident	parallel and $A_1*C_2 = C_1*A_2$
perpendicular	$A_1*A_2 = -B_1*B_2$
oblique	not parallel and not perpendicular

Write a program which reads an unspecified number of A,B,C triples. For each pair of triples read, use a procedure to print the two equations and one to print one of "PARALLEL", "COINCIDENT", "PERPENDICULAR" or "OBLIQUE". Stop when an out-of-data condition is detected. Note that there will be an even number of input lines. Test the program on at least the following four pairs of lines.

```
2x + 3y  =  4        2x - 3y =  4
8x + 12y = 16        6x + 4y = 12


5x + 13y =   0       4x -   y = 8
13x +  5y = -65      64x - 16y = 1
```

In the program, use a procedure to READ each pair of input lines describing the two lines; a procedure to check parallelism and one to process non-parallel lines.

8.2 Write a procedure called TRIAIR to calculate the area of a triangle from the length of the base and the altitude. The procedure will have three parameters -- BASE, ALTITUDE and AREA. The first two values are supplied by the calling statement. The value of AREA is calculated in the procedure. Write a mainline which reads five pairs of REAL values. The values in each pair are the lengths of the base and altitude respectively. The mainline should print the input values and the area for each of the five triangles.

8.3 What triples of integer values (x, y, z) have the property that $x^2+y^2=z^2$? A rigorous way of generating such values is to choose any pair of values m and n such that: m and n are relatively prime (one is not a multiple of the other); m is even and n is odd or m is odd and n is even. If m and n satisfy these conditions then set

$x = 2mn, \quad y = m^2 - n^2, \text{ and } z = m^2 + n^2$

For example, set m=2 and n=1. The values of x, y, and z are x=4, y=3 and z=5. Note that $3^2+4^2=5^2$. Write a program to generate all possible triples using values of m and n of five or less which satisfy the given conditions.

8.4 A ladder of length L leans against a wall. The top of the ladder is initially a distance H above the floor. The top of the ladder starts to slip down the wall. Calculate the position of the mid-point of the ladder when the top is .95H, .90H, .85H, ..., .05H above the floor. Read values of L and H from the input file.

8.5 Suppose a ball dropped from a height H rebounds to a height of .9H. (a) Write a program which determines the number of bounces which the ball must make before its maximum height is 0.1E-10. (b) Add logic to the program for (a) to determine the total length of time the ball is in the air.

8.6   Write a procedure to calculate the value of factorial N where N is an integer in the range 1 .. 10. Program the algorithm first without using recursion, and second with recursion.

8.7   Suppose a brick is eight inches long, four inches wide, two inches thick and weighs 1 kilogram. A number of bricks are piled one on top of the other so that each brick extends to the right of the one below it forming a staircase-like structure. If L denotes the length of the brick suppose the centers of the second, third, fourth, ... bricks are one-half L, three-quarters L, seven-eights L, ... inches to right of the center of the bottom brick. Write a program to determine the horizontal center of gravity of piles of 1 to ten bricks.

8.8   Charlie has just bought a new 10 ounce bottle of shampoo. Each time he shampoos, he uses one-half ounce of liquid. After removing the half-ounce, he replaces it with a half-ounce of water and then shakes the bottle. Thus the shampoo get weaker and weaker after each use. He repeats this procedure until the shampoo is half the original concentration and then uses it at half-strength until it is gone. Determine how many shampoos Charlie gets. Print the concentration and volume remaining after each use.

8.9   Read the dimensions of the sides of an acute-angled triangle. (The square on the longest side is less than the sum of the squares on the other two sides.) Write a program to find the length of the square which can be inscribed in the triangle so that one side of the square is along the longest side of the triangle and the top corners of the square just touch the the other sides as shown below. An example is shown below.

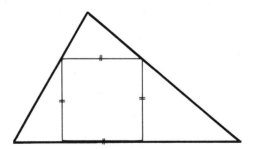

Part II:
Data Structures
and Dynamic Variables

CHAPTER 9: COLLECTIONS OF DATA: AN OVERVIEW

Questions Answered in this Chapter:

1. How can collections of values be defined and named in Pascal?

2. What are the four standard ways of organizing collections of data? In what ways are they similar and how do they differ?

3. What means are available to create unique data structures?

In Part I of the book we described the kinds of *single* values which are used in Pascal programs and the statements used to process these types of values. In Part II, we study the ways of defining and using named collections of values. Many problems would be difficult if not impossible to program without using composite data structures. Hence, knowledge of how to define and process the data stored in them will greatly widen the scope of problems you can solve.

9.1 Attributes of Collections of Data

We use many different adjectives to describe collections of objects and information. Some examples are: a set of marks, a list of cities, a group of animals, a hand of cards, a record of performance, a file of personnel data, a network of pipes, a family tree, a queue of people, a stack of dishes. How do these aggregations differ? In each case, the collection is made up of one or more items or components. The collections differ in the number of components and in the nature of the components. Furthermore, in a list of marks, each component is of the same type -- a number, whereas in others such as an employee record, there are many different types of data. That is, some collections have homogeneous components; others have heterogeneous types of components.

A second difference concerns the structure of the collection. Structure refers to the relationships between components. The simplest structure is one in which the order of the components is unimportant. For example, for some purposes we may consider the set of letters A, B, C to be identical to the set B, C, A. If order is important, they are not equivalent. In the case of a family tree, each person in the tree has a particular relationship to other people in the tree. We use terms like parent, child, grandfather to indicate how two components are related. In a network of pipes, the relationships (structure) may be complex.

A third difference involves the method used to refer to a component in the collection. We sometimes use the position of the component as in "the third city in the list". Other times we give components a unique name and use that name to refer to the component. An example is "Smith's employment record". Finally we may use a relationship to refer to a component, an example being "the wife of Johnson".

Some data structures are open ended or extensible meaning that the number of components may vary. A queue of people may expand or contract for instance whereas a hand of cards in bridge has thirteen cards or components.

Finally, the components in a collection may be collections themselves. For example, in a payroll file, there may be one record or component for each employee. That record however consists of several items of information about the person. Hence each record has several components. One of those components may be a birthdate which itself is a collection of three values representing year, month and day.

Pascal provides four predefined types of data collections. They are called the set, the array, the record, and the file. As well, Pascal provides a type of variable called "pointer" which can be used to create and link variables. A separate chapter is devoted to the details of each type. In the following section the key ideas and concepts of each type are summarized.

9.2 Pascal Data Structures

The four Pascal data structures -- set, array, record and file, have different characteristics. Different terms are used when describing their attributes but each structure is capable of storing a collection of values.

9.2.1 The Set

The simplest data structure is the *set*. It is an unordered collection of scalar values of the same type. An example of a set of integers chosen from the range one thru ten is [2, 9, 5]. It is considered identical to the set [9, 2, 5]. The components of a set are called its *members*. The declaration below declares X to be a set of values chosen from the range one through ten.

```
VAR
   X : SET OF 1 .. 10
```

How many different values could be assigned to X? Since each of the numbers 1 to 10 can either be present or not there are 2^{10} or 1024 different values which X can have. One such assignment is X := [2,7,10].

You can test to see if a value is a member of a set using the IN operator. For example 3 IN [5,9,2] is FALSE. You can create a new set from a pair of sets by intersecting or forming their union. Details and examples of set usage are found in Chapter 13.

9.2.2 The Array

An *array* is an ordered list of components of the same type. A component of an array is called an array *element*. The number of elements in an array must be specified at the time the array is declared. To store the marks of a class of fifty students, we could define an array of fifty REAL-valued elements using a declaration such as

```
VAR
    MARKS : ARRAY [1 .. 50] OF REAL
```

An element of an array is selected by referring to its position within the array. Arrays are the most widely used data structure in almost every programming language. Numerous examples and applications of array usage are found in Chapter 10. A particular kind of array -- a packed array of characters -- is called a *string*. Strings are used in most word processing applications.

9.2.3 The Record

A Pascal *record* is also an ordered collection of components. There are two fundamental differences between arrays and records. First, the components of records (called *fields)* may have different types. Second, each field has a name. Thus each component of a record is referred to by its name rather than its relative position in the record.

An example of a record containing three fields defining a date is the following.

```
VAR
    DATE : RECORD
             YEAR  : 1900 .. 2000;
             MONTH : 1 .. 12;
             DAY   : 1 .. 31
           END
```

A record is a natural structure to store typical data about an employee since it consists of many different kinds of values such as name, employee number, sex code, birthdate and salary.

When defining a record, you can specify that it may have one of several distinct sets of fields. For example, a different family of fields may be required for salaried and wage-earning employees. A record can be defined in which either set of fields can be used. Record applications and their rules of use are found in Chapter 11.

9.2.4 The File

A *file* is similar to an array in that it is an ordered collection of components of the same type. However, the size or length (number of components) of the file does not need to be specified at the time the file is declared. To get this increased flexibility however, we must pay a price. The restriction is that we can only add components to the end of the file. Furthermore, when processing the values of the components, we must start at the beginning and process them in sequence.

An example of a FILE declaration is given below.

```
VAR
    NUMBER_FILE : FILE OF REAL
```

This declaration means that each component of NUMBER_FILE is a single REAL value.

Two files that are used in almost all Pascal programs are INPUT and OUTPUT. Each has the type TEXT which means a sequence of CHAR values. When writing on the OUTPUT file we are really appending one or more characters to the end of the file. We cannot go backwards and overwrite lines created previously. Similarly when reading from the INPUT file, once a character or characters have been read, we cannot back up and re-read those characters. we cannot backup unless we do so from the beginning of the file.

Files are most useful for storing large collections of data. Unlike the other structures which are created when a program begins execution and destroyed when it terminates, a file can exist before, during and after program execution. That is, most files are external to the program and exist independently of it. (It wouldn't do if a company's payroll data was destroyed after the payroll program was run!) Chapter 12 describes file usage in the Pascal programming language.

9.2.5 Pointers

To permit you to create data structures such as trees, networks and rings, Pascal provides a facility for allowing one variable to point to another. A *pointer variable* is a variable whose value is the location of some other variable. By chaining together objects and pointers, many useful data structures can be created.

Using the predefined procedure NEW, variables can be created on an as-needed basis while a program is executing. Furthermore, once created they can be DISPOSEd of when no longer needed. Pointers are described in Chapter 14.

9.3 Summary

1. A collection of data has many characteristics. Some of the more important are the number of components, the type of components, the organization of the components (the structure) and the way the components are referenced.

2. Pascal provides four predefined kinds of data structures which can be used in programs. These are the:

    SET   - an unordered collection of scalar values of the same type.

    ARRAY   - an ordered, fixed length list of elements of the same type.

    RECORD   - a fixed collection of named components of (usually) different types.

    FILE   - an ordered sequence of unspecified length of components of the same type.

3. Pointer values can be used to create unique data structures. They can also be used to create and destroy variables during execution of a block.

4. The characteristics of a particular set, array, record, file or pointer are a type in the same sense as a subrange type or enumerated type. For example, two arrays having identical array characteristics have the same type. If either the number or type of components in a pair of arrays is different, then they have different types.

CHAPTER 10: ARRAYS

Questions Answered in this Chapter:

1. What kinds of problems are difficult to program using scalar variables?

2. How are arrays defined and used?

3. What are string variables?

The preceding chapter presents the important concepts of named collections of values. The array is the most widely used of these types and therefore will be described first.

10.1 An Example Problem

The problem is easy to state. Read five REAL values. Read a value of N between 1 and 5 and print the Nth value. The algorithm for the problem is really found in the problem statement. It is:

1. Read five numbers
2. Get a value for N between one and five
3. Print the Nth value

The data requirements are also easy to describe. Five REAL variables and one INTEGER variable are required. So what is the difficulty? The program below solves the problem and indicates the awkwardness of the solution using our present knowledge.

```
PROGRAM NTH_VALUE(INPUT, OUTPUT);

(* THIS PROGRAM READS 5 REAL VALUES, A VALUE
   FOR N, AND PRINTS THE NTH VALUE. THE LOGIC IS
   A BRUTE-FORCE APPROACH USING A SEQUENCE OF
   ELSE-IFS TO SELECET THE NTH VALUE          *)

VAR
  X1, X2, X3, X4, X5 : REAL;
  N                  : INTEGER;

BEGIN (* NTH_VALUE *)
  WRITELN('ENTER FIVE NUMBERS');
  READLN(X1, X2, X3, X4, X5);
  WRITELN('THE VALUES ARE:', X1, X2, X3, X4, X5);
  WRITELN('ENTER A VALUE BETWEEN 1 AND 5');
  READLN(N);
  WRITE('THE VALUE IN POSITION', N, ' IS');
  IF N = 1 THEN
    WRITELN(X1)
  ELSE IF N = 2 THEN
    WRITELN(X2)
  ELSE IF N = 3 THEN
    WRITELN(X3)
  ELSE IF N = 4 THEN
    WRITELN(X4)
  ELSE IF N = 5 THEN
    WRITELN(X5)
  ELSE
    WRITELN(' OUT OF RANGE')
END. (* NTH_VALUE *)
```

There are two observations to make. First, observe that the five REAL variables must be explicitly named in the READ and WRITELN statements used to read and write their respective values. (If there were a hundred values, we would have to list one hundred variables in each statement!) Second, to select the Nth value it is necessary to use an IF statement containing a sequence of ELSE IFs. A CASE statement could also have been used to perform the selection.

Although we might not mind using this brute force approach for five values, it quickly becomes burdensome for larger numbers of values. What is needed then is an approach that has the following form.

1. For i = 1 to 5 do
    1. Read the ith value
    2. Print the ith value
2. Read value of N
3. Print Nth value.

To read the ith value we need a statement such as

    READ (X_i)

This means we must *change the name of the variable* passed to the READ
procedure each time it is invoked. Until now we haven't been able to do this.
Shown below is a program which declares X to be an array of five REAL
variables. Other comments follow the program.

```
PROGRAM NTH_VALUE(INPUT,OUTPUT);

(* THIS PROGRAM READS AND STORES 5 REAL VALUES
   IN AN ARRAY. IT THEN READS A VALUE FOR N AND
   PRINTS THE NTH VALUE                            *)

VAR
  X      : ARRAY [1..5] OF REAL;
  N, I   : INTEGER;

BEGIN (* NTH_VALUE *)
  WRITELN('ENTER FIVE NUMBERS');
  FOR I := 1 TO 5 DO
    READ(X[I]);
  READLN; (* SKIP THE END-OF-LINE CHAR *)
  WRITELN('ENTER A NUMBER BETWEEN 1 AND 5');
  READLN(N);
  WRITE('THE VALUE IN POSITION', N, ' IS');
  IF (N < 1) OR (N > 5) THEN
    WRITELN(' OUT OF RANGE')
  ELSE
    WRITELN(X[N])
END. (* NTH_VALUE *)
```

This example illustrates the important ideas associated with arrays.
Consider the declaration of the identifier X:

    X : ARRAY [1 .. 5] OF REAL

In English this declares X to be an array of REAL-valued variables having
components designated by members of the subrange type 1..5. Because the
values of the subrange 1..5 are 1,2,3,4,5, the components of the array are
referred to by these values. Specifically, the five components are:

    X[1], X[2], X[3], X[4], and X[5]

Each of these components or *elements* of the array has the type REAL. By
changing the value of the component designator, henceforth called the
subscript, we can refer to any component of the array. This is precisely what
we did in the FOR loop used to read the values, namely:

```
FOR I:= 1 TO 5
  BEGIN
    READ(X[I]);
    WRITELN(X[I])
  END
```

That is, the variable I changes its value each time the body of the loop is
executed. Therefore the array element used as the argument in each
invocation of READ and WRITE is different during each execution of the
loop.

10.2 Basic Rules of Array Usage

The preceding example illustrates the simplest kind of array declaration
and use. The important ideas are summarized below.

Syntax of an ARRAY Declaration

```
ARRAY [index-type] OF element-type
```

where:

- ARRAY and OF are reserved words

- the index-type must be an ordinal type and may take the form of a
  type identifier, an enumerated type or a subrange type. Because
  there is a practical limit on the number of elements in an array,
  an index-type of INTEGER is not permitted. Instead a subrange
  of INTEGERs should be used.

- the element type may be anything except FILE (described in
  Chapter 12) and may be defined in any way. Each element of the
  array has the type specified by the element type.

Elements. An element of an array is referenced by an expression of the form

```
name [ subscript expression ]
```

where

- name is the name of the array

- the subscript expression must result in a value of the index-type

Operations. Except for the assignment operation, values in an array must be
processed element-by-element. For example, suppose we are given the
following pair of arrays to store temperature values:

```
VAR
    JULY, AUGUST : ARRAY [1..31] OF -50..120
```

The following kinds of statements and expressions are *invalid*.

```
READ(JULY)
WRITELN('AUGUST TEMPS ARE', AUGUST)
JULY + AUGUST
```

The only all-array operation permitted is assignment. For the example above,

```
JULY := AUGUST
```

Two arrays are assignment compatible if they are declared in the same declaration (e.g. JULY and AUGUST above) or with the same type name. This automatically means they have the same number of elements and the types of corresponding elements are equal.

Some Pascal compilers permit the value of a function to be an array; standard Pascal does not.

10.3 A Second Example

The following example illustrates two new ideas. The problem is to develop a procedure to reverse the order of elements in an array of N REAL elements. Assume that the value of N and the N REAL values are read from the INPUT file in the program body. Assume further that the result (the reversed set of values) is to be stored in a second array so that the original array is not altered. The mainline algorithm is therefore:

1. Read N
2. Read the values of the N elements
3. Reverse the order of the values
4. Output the original and reversed set of values.

What are the data requirements of the mainline? Aside from the INTEGER variable N, two arrays are needed. (It makes sense to use arrays rather than simple variables because we are processing a number of values of the same type.) The element type is REAL but what should the index-type be? The index-type provides two kinds of information. First, the number of values in the index type automatically determines the number of components in the array. Second, the values of the type are the subscript values used to refer to specific elements. In this example it makes sense to use subscripts 1,2,3,...,N but how big should N be? N cannot be the value of a variable because a type specification requires constants. Since N may vary from one execution of the program to the next we need to have a sufficient number of components to accommodate most values of N which we might be expected. Let us assume N is not greater than 100. The point is that when using arrays, a decision must be made concerning the maximum number of elements that might be required.

The program, except for the procedure to perform the reversal is shown below.

```
PROGRAM REVERSAL(INPUT,OUTPUT);

(* THIS PROGRAM READS A SET OF N REAL VALUES AND
   REVERSES THEIR ORDER                                *)

CONST
  MAX_SIZE = 100;
TYPE
  DATA_ARRAY = ARRAY [1..MAX_SIZE] OF REAL;
VAR
  INDATA, OUTDATA : DATA_ARRAY;
  N, I            : INTEGER;

(* PROCEDURE REVERSE goes here *)

BEGIN (* REVERSAL *)
  WRITELN('ENTER NUMBER OF VALUES TO BE READ');
  READLN(N);
  IF N > MAX_SIZE THEN
    WRITELN('N CANNOT EXCEED', MAX_SIZE)
  ELSE
    BEGIN
      WRITELN('ENTER THE VALUES, ONE PER LINE');
      FOR I:= 1 TO N DO
        READLN(INDATA[I]);
      REVERSE (N, INDATA, OUTDATA);
      WRITELN('   ORIGINAL   REVERSED');
      FOR I := 1 TO N DO
        WRITELN(INDATA[I], OUTDATA[I])
    END (* ELSE *)
END. (* REVERSAL *)
```

When choosing the name of array types, it is a good idea to append "_ARRAY" to the end of the name. This helps to identify the name as an array type. Recall that with scalar types, it was recommended that "TYPE" be appended to an enumerated type name and that RANGE be appended to a subrange type name to clearly distinguish the purpose of the identifier.

Consider now the REVERSE procedure. It will have three formal parameters corresponding to N and the two arrays. Since the values in the second array are to be returned to the mainline, the second array must be a VAR parameter. The logic to perform the reversal is quite simple. The value of the first element in the input array is assigned to the Nth element of the output array; the value in the second element is assigned to the (N-1)th element, etc. Here is the procedure.

```
PROCEDURE REVERSE (N:INTEGER; INPUT:DATA_ARRAY;
                        VAR OUTPUT:DATA_ARRAY);
```

```
(* THIS PROCEDURE REVERSES THE ORDER OF THE
   FIRST N VALUES IN THE ARRAY INPUT. THE
   RESULT IS STORED IN THE ARRAY OUTPUT      *)

VAR
   I : INTEGER;

BEGIN (* REVERSE *)
   FOR I := 1 TO N DO
      OUTPUT[N-I+1] := INPUT[I]
END; (* REVERSE *)
```

There are two important observations to make. First, recall that the types of formal parameters must be specified by type identifiers previously declared in a TYPE declaration. This is why DATA_ARRAY is declared as a type in the PROGRAM declarations. For example, it would be illegal to declare the formal parameter N as being "N: 1..MAX_SIZE" in the procedure header. To do so, a type identifier declared as 1..MAX_SIZE would be needed in the mainline.

Second, the formal parameter INPUT is a value parameter whereas OUTPUT is a VAR parameter. Recall that when a procedure is invoked, for each value parameter such as INPUT, memory locations to store the value(s) of the formal parameter are reserved. The actual parameter values are then assigned to the corresponding formal parameter variables or elements. In this example, one-hundred memory locations and one-hundred assignments are made when REVERSE is invoked. With a VAR parameter such as OUTPUT however, no memory locations are reserved for the formal parameter. Instead, references to VAR-type variables and elements refer directly to the memory locations used by the corresponding actual parameters. This reduces the memory requirements of the program and means that no actual parameter-to-formal parameter copying of values is needed. That is, the use of VAR parameters reduces both memory requirements and program execution time. For this reason, most formal parameters which are arrays are declared as VAR parameters even when the called block is not used to modify the values in the array.

Incidentally, the use of INPUT and OUTPUT as formal parameters does not cause any ambiguity with the standard files INPUT and OUTPUT. Recall that formal parameters are local to the block in which they appear in the header.

10.4 Exercise 10.1

1. What is the output of the following program?

```
PROGRAM TEN_1_1(OUTPUT);
VAR
  A : ARRAY[1..4] OF REAL;
  I : INTEGER;
BEGIN
  A[4] := ORD(4);
  FOR I := 3 DOWNTO 1 DO
    BEGIN
      IF 3*I - SQR(A[I+1]) > 0 THEN
        WRITELN('POSITIVE')
      ELSE
        WRITELN('NON-NEGATIVE');
      A[I] := ORD(I)
    END
END.
```

2. What values are stored in FLAG after executing the following program?

```
PROGRAM TEN_1_2;
TYPE
  FLAG_TYPE = (RED, WHITE, BLUE);
VAR
  FLAG : ARRAY[FLAG_TYPE] OF FLAG_TYPE;
  COLOR: FLAG_TYPE;
BEGIN
  FOR COLOR := BLUE DOWNTO RED DO
    IF ORD(COLOR) <> 0 THEN
      FLAG[COLOR] := PRED(COLOR)
    ELSE
      FLAG[COLOR] := SUCC(WHITE)
END.
```

3. What values are printed by the program. The data is 1 0 1 0 1.

```
PROGRAM TEN_1_3(INPUT,OUTPUT);
TYPE
  SEX_TYPE = (MALE, FEMALE, OTHER);
  KID_ARRAY = ARRAY[-2..+2] OF SEX_TYPE;
  SEX_CODE_RANGE = -1..+1;
VAR
  KID_NUM : INTEGER;
  SEX_CODE : SEX_CODE_RANGE;
  KID : KID_ARRAY;
```

... (continued on the next page)

```
PROCEDURE FLIPPO(VAR DIK : KID_ARRAY);
  VAR
    I : -2..+2;
  BEGIN
    FOR I := 2 DOWNTO -2 DO
      IF DIK[I] = MALE THEN
        DIK[I] := PRED(OTHER)
      ELSE IF DIK[I] = FEMALE THEN
        DIK[I] := SUCC(MALE)
      ELSE
        DIK[I] := PRED(FEMALE)
  END; (* FLIPPO *)
BEGIN
  FOR KID_NUM := -2 TO +2 DO
    BEGIN
      READ(SEX_CODE);
      CASE SEX_CODE OF
        -1 : KID[KID_NUM] := OTHER;
         0 : KID[KID_NUM] := FEMALE;
        +1 : KID[KID_NUM] := MALE
      END; (* CASE *)
    END; (* FOR *)
  FLIPPO(KID);
  FOR KID_NUM := -2 TO 2 DO
    CASE KID[KID_NUM] OF
      MALE   : WRITELN('MALE');
      FEMALE : WRITELN('FEMALE');
      OTHER  : WRITELN('OTHER')
    END (* CASE *)
END.
```

4. What is the output from the following program when used the input values 5 4 3 2 1?

```
PROGRAM EX10_1_4(INPUT,OUTPUT);
VAR
  LIST : ARRAY[1..5] OF INTEGER;
  I : INTEGER;
BEGIN
  FOR I := 1 TO 5 DO
    READ(LIST[I]);
  FOR I := 2 TO 5 DO
    BEGIN
      IF I = 5 THEN
        LIST[I] := LIST[1]
      ELSE
        LIST[I+1] := LIST[I];
      WRITELN(LIST[I])
    END
END.
```

5.   What is the error in each of the following?

```
a)   TYPE   X = ARRAY [1,2,3] OF CHAR
b)   TYPE   Y = ARRAY [(A,B,C)] OF (A,B,C)
c)   TYPE   Z = ARRAY [-5..5] OF Z
d)   TYPE   W = ARRAY [10] OF BOOLEAN
e)   TYPE   DOG = ARRAY[(TRUE,FALSE)] OF (BOXER,POOCH)
f)   TYPE   LONG = ARRAY[INTEGER] OF BOOLEAN
g) Given:
   VAR
      A :   ARRAY [1..10] OF REAL;
      B :   ARRAY [1..10] OF REAL;
   Then
      A := B
h)   PROCEDURE A (P:ARRAY [1..10] OF INTEGER)
```

6.   Is there any purpose in defining an array with one element as opposed to a simple variable? For example:

```
VAR
   NEXT: ARRAY [1..1] OF CHAR
```

7.   Given the type

```
TYPE
   WEATHER_TYPE = (HOT, COLD, NICE);
```

You want to keep track of how many days in a month are of each type. Which of the following would you recommend and why?

```
ARRAY [1..31] OF WEATHER_TYPE   or
ARRAY [WEATHER_TYPE] OF 1..31
```

8.   Suppose elements of the array BAC declared by

```
BAC : ARRAY[1..5] OF INTEGER
```

have been assigned values using the FOR statement below.

```
FOR N:= 1 to 5 DO
   BAC[6 - N]:= N
```

What is the value of the following?

```
a)   BAC[2]* 3 DIV BAC[3]
b)   BAC[4]MOD 3 + 3 MOD BAC[4]
c)   BAC[3]-BAC[2] < BAC[1] DIV 4
d)   BAC[BAC[BAC[BAC[1]]]]
```

9.   For each of the following, define an array then write a FOR statement to assign the values shown to the elements of the array.

a) 2, 5, 8, 11, 14, 17
b) 1, 3, 7, 15, 31, 63
c) TRUE, FALSE, TRUE, FALSE, TRUE, FALSE
d) 1, 0, -1, 1, 0, -1

10. In processing a true-false test of N questions suggest a use for the following arrays.

```
ONE:   ARRAY [BOOLEAN] OF 1..N
TWO:   ARRAY [1..N] OF BOOLEAN
```

11. You are given the following declarations:

```
CONST
  SIZE = 100;
TYPE
  N_RANGE = 1..SIZE;
  X_ARRAY = ARRAY [N_RANGE] OF REAL;
VAR
  N: N_RANGE;
  X: X_ARRAY
```

Suppose each of the elements of X has been assigned a value in the program body. For each of the following write a PROCEDURE having a header of the form:

```
PROCEDURE name ( N:N_RANGE; VAR X:X_ARRAY)
```

a) SHIFT. If N is positive, the values in X are shifted right N positions and the leftmost N elements are set to zero. If N is negative, the element values are shifted left N elements and the rightmost N elements are set to zero. If N is 0, no change is made in X.

b) ROTATE. If N is positive, rotate the element values right N positions. A right rotation of N means values in positions X[1] thru X[SIZE-N] are assigned to elements X[N+1] thru X[SIZE] and values in X[N+1] thru X[SIZE] are assigned to X[1] thru [N]. If N is negative, an analogous rotation to the left is made. If N is 0 or equal to SIZE, no change is made. Note that ROTATE (N,X) is equivalent to ROTATE (N-SIZE,X).

12. Write three FUNCTIONs each of which is passed an array of CHAR values having a type declared by

```
TYPE  LINE_ARRAY= ARRAY[1..LINESIZE] OF CHAR
```

and each of which returns a function value representing the first subscript of an element containing a blank. If no blank is present, the function returns 0. In the first, use a WHILE loop, in the second a REPEAT-UNTIL loop and in the third, a FOR loop.

10.5 Two Dimensional Arrays

So far, arrays consisting of an ordered list of simple values have been used. The word "vector" is often used to describe these one-dimensional arrays. Frequently, however, it is natural to store the values processed by a program in a table or matrix. For example, suppose a door-to-door survey of six houses is conducted with the purpose of determining for each house: the number of pre-school children, elementary school children, high school children and adults. The results of the survey might be recorded as shown below.

	PRE–SCHOOL	ELEMENTARY	HIGH SCHOOL	ADULTS
House 1	0	1	2	2
House 2	2	0	0	2
House 3	0	0	0	1
House 4	1	2	0	2
House 5	1	0	1	2
House 6	0	2	3	2

In this table of numbers there are six horizontal *rows,* one for each house, and four vertical *columns,* one for each type of information collected. A rectangular array of numbers such as this is often called a *matrix.* We can refer to any element in a matrix by specifying its row and its column. For example, the value of the element in row 5 and column PRE-SCHOOL is 1. The sum of the values of the elements in row 3 represents the total number of people in house 3.

If we want to use the information in the array to answer questions such as "Which houses have no pre-school children?", "How many adults are there in the six houses?", and "Which house has the most children?", then we must be able to define an array of twenty-four elements. Furthermore, we would like to use a pair of subscripts -- a row designator and a column designator to reference each of these twenty-four elements.

In Pascal, a suitable array variable can be created with the following declarations:

```
CONST
  MAX_HOUSE = 6;
TYPE
  AGE_TYPE = (PRE_SCHOOL, ELEMENTARY, HIGH, ADULT);
VAR
  S: ARRAY [1..MAX_HOUSE, PRE_SCHOOL..ADULT] OF INTEGER
```

The variable S (short for "survey") is a *two-dimensional array* having rows designated by values in the subrange 1..MAX_HOUSE and columns designated by the values in PRE_SCHOOL..ADULT. Since the subrange PRE_SCHOOL..ADULT includes all the constants of AGE_TYPE, the column type could also have been specified more simply by the type identifier AGE_TYPE.

The array S has twenty-four elements each of which is an INTEGER variable. To refer to a particular element in the table, two subscripts are used -- the first designates the row, and the second designates the column. For example, if the survey results are those shown previously then S[1, PRE_SCHOOL] has a value of 0; S[5,HIGH] has a value of 1, and S[6,ADULT] has a value of 2.

The commonly used syntax of a two dimensional array type specification is shown below.

```
ARRAY [row type, column type] of element type
```

Elements of a two-dimensional array are referenced by an expression of the form

```
array name [row subscript, column subscript]
```

The row and column subscripts may be any expressions which yield a value in the row type and the column type respectively.

10.5.1 A Program to Process the Survey Data

Suppose the twenty-four values of the survey data have been recorded in the INPUT file such that the four values for the nth house are found in the nth line of the file. The task is to read the data and answer the question "Which house has the most people?"

The algorithm for answering this question is straightforward. It involves the following steps:

1. Initialize
   .1 Set Bighouse = 0
   .2 Set Most-people = 0
2. For each house do
   .1 Count # people in the house
   .2 If Count > Most-people then
      .1 Set Bighouse = house
      .2 Set Most-people = Count
3. Output Bighouse and Most people.

The program uses an array to store the survey data, INTEGER variables for Bighouse, Most-people and the Count.

```
PROGRAM SURVEY(INPUT,OUTPUT);

(* THIS PROGRAM READS FOUR ITEMS OF SURVEY DATA
   FOR EACH OF SIX HOUSES AND THEN ANSWERS THE
   QUESTION "WHICH HOUSE HAS THE MOST PEOPLE?"  *)

CONST
  MAX_HOUSE = 6;

TYPE
  AGE_TYPE = (PRE_SCHOOL, ELEMENTARY, HIGH, ADULT);

VAR
  S : ARRAY [1..MAX_HOUSE, AGE_TYPE] OF INTEGER;
  HOUSE : 1..MAX_HOUSE;
  AGE   : AGE_TYPE;
  BIG_HOUSE, MOST_PEOPLE, COUNT : INTEGER;

BEGIN (* SURVEY *)
  (* 1 - INITIALIZE *)
      FOR HOUSE := 1 TO MAX_HOUSE DO
        FOR AGE := PRE_SCHOOL TO ADULT DO
          BEGIN
            READ(S[HOUSE, AGE]);
            WRITE(S[HOUSE, AGE]);
            IF AGE = ADULT THEN WRITELN
          END; (* HOUSE DATA *)
      BIG_HOUSE := 0;
      MOST_PEOPLE := 0;

  (* 2 - DETERMINE BIG_HOUSE AND MOST_PEOPLE *)
      FOR HOUSE := 1 TO MAX_HOUSE DO
        BEGIN
          COUNT := 0;
          FOR AGE := PRE_SCHOOL TO ADULT DO
            COUNT := COUNT + S[HOUSE, AGE];
          IF COUNT > MOST_PEOPLE THEN
            BEGIN
              MOST_PEOPLE := COUNT;
              BIG_HOUSE := HOUSE
            END
        END; (* HOUSE LOOP *)

  (* 3 - OUTPUT THE RESULTS *)
      WRITELN('THE HOUSE WITH THE MOST PEOPLE IS',
              BIG_HOUSE:3,' WHICH HAS',MOST_PEOPLE:3,
              ' PEOPLE.')
END. (* SURVEY *)
```

Comments:

1. To read the twenty-four values of the array elements, a pair of nested
    FOR statements is used. The index of the outer loop is HOUSE. For each
    value of HOUSE the body of the inner loop is executed for each of the
    four age groups. To read the values column-by-column, the order of the
    FOR statements should be interchanged as shown below.

```
FOR AGE := PRE_SCHOOL TO ADULT DO
   FOR HOUSE := 1 TO MAX_HOUSE DO
      BEGIN
         READ(S[HOUSE,AGE]);
            .
      END
```

    This of course would mean the twenty-four data values would need to be
    in the following order: six pre-school values, six elementary school values,
    six high-school values, and six adult values.

2. Do we really need a two-dimensional array to solve this problem? Observe
    that once the count for a particular house has been calculated, there is no
    need to refer to the values in that row again. Thus, it would be sufficient
    to use a one-dimensional array called HOUSE_DATA declared as follows.

```
HOUSE_DATA: ARRAY[PRE_SCHOOL..ADULT] OF INTEGER
```

    The point is this. Even though input data to a program may be viewed in
    the form of a table, it may not be necessary to have all the values
    simultaneously available if it is possible to do all the processing required
    for one row independently of the values in other rows. Note however, there
    are many queries concerning the survey data which would require the
    entire matrix of values to be available. An example is "How many
    elementary school children are there in houses having more than the
    average number of people?" We would need to keep the values because we
    can't answer the question about a house until the average has been
    computed and this requires reading all the values.

3. What happens if there is a tie for the house with the most people? As
    written, the variable BIG_HOUSE changes only if the count is greater
    than the largest value to date. Hence the program outputs the first house
    found with the greatest number of people. A programming problem at the
    end of the chapter asks you to modify the program to output all houses
    having the greatest number of people.

10.6 Exercise 10.2

1. Suppose a two-dimensional array has been declared as follows.

        DATA : ARRAY[0..2, 0..3] OF INTEGER

    Suppose the values assigned to the elements are as shown below:

        2 5 -7 3
        4 8 22 7
        5 9 -8 3

    a) How many rows and columns are there?
    b) What is the element in position [2,1]?
    c) What are the subscript pairs of the prime numbers?
    d) What is the sum of the elements in the third row?
       The second column?

2. Suppose A and B are two matrices of six INTEGER values each. The array A has two rows and three columns; B has three rows and two columns.

    a) Define the arrays such that the first row and first column has a subscript of 1 in each array.

    b) What subscript pairs appear in A but not in B?

    c) Suppose the value assigned to A[I,J] is I+J for all elements in A and the value of B[I,J] is I-J for all elements in B. Then:

            i) What pairs of I and J values are such that B[I,J]
               +A [I,J] = 2•I?
           ii) What pairs of I and J values are such that B[I,J]
               - A[I,J] =-2•J?
          iii) What is the value of:
                   1. A[B[2,1],A[1,2]]?
                   2. B[A[2,B[3,1]]-1,B[A[1,B[3,1]],1]]?

    d) Write three statements -- two FORs and an assignment statement which will assign the values of A to the elements of B such that B[I,J] is given the value of A[J,I].

    e) Is an array necessary to perform the processing in the SURVEY program? Explain.

10.7 Higher Dimensioned Arrays

Suppose the house survey referred to in the preceding section is taken in two different years for the same six houses. This means we have two tables of data each of which contains twenty-four values organized into six rows and four columns. A single array of forty-eight elements can be defined to store the values as follows.

```
SURVEY: ARRAY[1..MAX_HOUSE, AGE_TYPE, 1..2] OF INTEGER
```

The third dimension of the array has the type 1..2 and denotes the year of the survey. Each element in this three-dimensional array has three subscripts. For example the number of adults in house 4 in the second year is the value of

```
SURVEY [4, ADULT, 2]
```

The typical method used to display all the values in a three-dimensional array is to use three nested FOR loops. For example, to print two tables on separate pages, one for each year, the following program fragment can be used.

```
FOR YEAR:= 1 TO 2 DO
  BEGIN
    PAGE (OUTPUT);
    FOR HOUSE:= 1 TO MAX_HOUSE DO
      BEGIN
        FOR AGE:= PRE_SCHOOL TO ADULT DO
          WRITE(SURVEY[HOUSE,AGE,YEAR]);
        WRITELN (* OUTPUT THE LINE OF VALUES *)
      END (*HOUSE LOOP*)
  END(*YEAR LOOP*)
```

Arrays having four, five or more dimensions can also be created. The limit on the number of dimensions depends on the Pascal compiler used and on the amount of memory available to store the array values. The principles and rules for higher dimensioned arrays are the same as for one and two-dimensional arrays.

10.8 An Alternate Syntax of Array Declarations

This section may be omitted on first reading.

In an array declaration, the type of each element is not restricted to a simple type. For example in the survey data, it may be more natural to think of the data as an array of six items each of which is a four-value array. This is permissible and can be defined in the following way.

```
SURVEY:ARRAY[1..MAX_HOUSE] OF ARRAY[PRE_SCHOOL..ADULT] OF INTEGER
```

Although defined differently this declaration is equivalent to the one used previously which is:

SURVEY:ARRAY[1..MAX_HOUSE, PRE_SCHOOL..ADULT] OF INTEGER

Because these array definitions are equivalent, any element can be referenced using a pair of subscripts. However, there is also an alternate way of referencing an element. Specifically, if the data is viewed as an array of six elements, each of which contains the four values associated with a single house then SURVEY[1] is the array of data for the first house. More generally, an element SURVEY[i] is an array of the type:

ARRAY[PRE_SCHOOL..ADULT] OF INTEGER

If SURVEY[3] is an array, it follows that we can reference an element of that array by enclosing a subscript expression in brackets after the array. More particularly, the number of high school students in house 3 can be referenced by the expression

SURVEY[3][HIGH]

When the compiler processes this expression, it first encounters SURVEY which is recognized as an array name. The "[3]" which follows indicates the third element of SURVEY and the [HIGH] indicates that the element having the subscript HIGH of the third element of the SURVEY[3] array is wanted.

In general, this method of referencing elements in arrays having more than one dimension is *not* recommended. Most people prefer to enclose all the subscripts within a single pair of brackets. One instance where it may seem more natural occurs when each row is a string of CHAR values. This use is discussed more fully in the section of this chapter called "Strings".

The array SURVEY could also be declared as an array of four column vectors. The statement below shows how:

SURVEY: ARRAY[PRE_SCHOOL..ADULT]OF
        ARRAY[1..MAX_HOUSE] OF INTEGER

If done this way, SURVEY[PRE_SCHOOL] is the six-element array of the counts of pre-school children. This declaration of SURVEY is *not* equivalent to the preceding one because the first subscript refers to the age group and the second to the house number.

10.9 PACKED Data

10.9.1 Concepts

The concept of packed data is simple. Each value stored in the computer memory requires a certain number of bits to represent the value. Different numbers and patterns of bits can be used to represent a given value. Some representation schemes are very efficient in that fewer bits are required per value compared to other schemes which may use more bits per value. Like many other things however, there is a tradeoff. A sophisticated, clever scheme for minimizing the number of bits per value may require extra execution time to decipher the bit patterns in order to determine the value or values being represented. Thus the saving achieved in the memory required may be offset by an increase in execution time.

In Pascal, you can opt for relatively efficient memory utilization by specifying that the values in an array are to be packed. Packing is also possible with record, set and file structures which are discussed in the next three chapters. One particular kind of packed array is deserves special attention. It is an array in which each element has a CHAR value. These so-called string variables are the subject of Section 10.10. However, before examining string variables, we shall consider the general techniques for defining packed data structures.

10.9.2 Declaration of Packed Arrays

To specify that an array is to be stored in packed form, the reserved word PACKED is placed ahead of the word ARRAY. Some examples are:

```
VAR
    A1 : PACKED ARRAY[1..10] OF CHAR;
    A2 : PACKED ARRAY[(RED,WHITE,BLUE)]OF(FLAG1,FLAG2);
    A3 : PACKED ARRAY[1..5]OF PACKED ARRAY[1..2]OF REAL;
    A4 : ARRAY[BOOLEAN]OF PACKED ARRAY[BOOLEAN] OF CHAR
```

A3 illustrates a packed array of packed arrays. In A4, the array elements are packed but the array itself is not.

10.9.3 PACK and UNPACK

This subsection can be omitted on first reading.

PACK and UNPACK are complementary standard procedures for packing and unpacking arrays. Most people work with unpacked values since memory requirements are not usually a limiting factor in running a program. If there is a need to change from one to the other, the procedure PACK and UNPACK can be used according to the rules given below.

The PACK Procedure

General Form

> PACK (source, offset, target)

Notes

1. The source must be an unpacked array and the target must be a packed array. The elements in the two arrays must have identical types.

2. Offset must be a valid subscript of the source array.

3. The value of source[offset] is assigned to the first element of the target array. The value of source[SUCC(offset)] is assigned to the second element of the target and so on. The assignments continue until the last element of the target array has been assigned a value. The number of assignments made equals the number of elements in the target array.

The rules for UNPACK are similar. They are summarized on the following page.

The UNPACK Procedure

General Form

> UNPACK (source, target, offset)

1. The source must be a packed array and the target an unpacked array. The elements in the two arrays must have identical types.

2. Offset must be a valid subscript of the target array. (This is the reverse of PACK).

3. The first element of source is assigned to target[offset]. The second element of source is assigned to target[SUCC(offset)], and so on until each element of source has been assigned to an element of the target array. Thus the number of assignments made is the number of elements in the source array.

10.10 STRINGS

The word "string" has a specific meaning in Pascal. It means a PACKED ARRAY of CHAR values. It is singled out for special attention because sequences of characters are read, processed and output in most applications of non-numeric computing. There are string constants, string types and string variables. Although a string is an array, there are two operations that can be done with a string that are not allowed for any other type of array. These are:

- a string can be output using WRITE and WRITELN (Components in non-string arrays must be written element-by-element).

- The relational operators $<$, $=$, $>$, etc. can be used to compare two strings of the same length.

10.10.1 String Constants, Types and Variables

A string constant is a sequence of characters enclosed within single quotes. Examples are: 'HELLO-THERE', '123', 'IT''S'. If a quote is one of the characters in the constant, two successive quotes are used. The word "literal" is a synonym for string constant. The length of a literal or string constant is the number of characters between the quotes and two successive quotes are counted as one. Shown below is a string constant declaration.

```
CONST
    DATE_PATTERN = 'XX/XX/XX'
```

A string type must have the following kind of declaration.

```
PACKED ARRAY[1..n] OF CHAR
```

That is, the first subscript must be 1 and the last a positive INTEGER constant. The number of elements in the array determines the length of the string. In the example above 'n' denotes the length of the string.

If you anticipate needing strings of various lengths in a program, it is a good idea to define the string types at the beginning of the program in the manner shown below.

```
TYPE
    STRING1 = PACKED ARRAY[1..1] OF CHAR;
    STRING2 = PACKED ARRAY[1..2] OF CHAR;
    STRING3 = PACKED ARRAY[1..3] OF CHAR;
    STRING4 = PACKED ARRAY[1..4] OF CHAR
```

A *string variable* is simply a variable having a string type.

10.10.2 Operations with strings

Assignment. As with other arrays, two strings of the same length are assignment compatible. If X and Y are of the type STRING4 defined above, then the following assignment statements are valid.

```
X := 'ABCD'
Y := '1234'
X := Y
X := X
```

Note that "X := '2'" and "Y := '12345'" are invalid because the lengths are different.

Comparison. Two strings of the same length may be compared using any of the six relational operators. The comparison is made character-by-character starting from the left. For example

'A' < 'B' is   true because 'A' precedes 'B' in the collating sequence of CHAR values. (More precisely because ORD('A') < ORD('B')).

'23' > '24' is false because ORD('3') < ORD('4')

'PQR' <> 'PRS' is true because ORD('R') <> ORD('S')

'123' = 123 is invalid because strings and INTEGERs are different types and cannot be compared.

The fact that strings of the same length can be compared directly means that sorting a sequence of words into alphabetical order can be done relatively easily.

Input and Output. If the values in a string are to be obtained from the INPUT file, they must be read character-by-character. The procedures READ and READLN cannot have string parameters.

On the other hand, strings can be written on the output file using WRITE and WRITELN. In fact, this has been done many times already in statements containing literals such as:

```
WRITE('THE ANSWER IS':20, ANSWER)
```

If a format specifier is not used, each character in a string occupies one position in the OUTPUT line. If the format specifier is greater than the length of the string, the string is right-justified in the space provided and blanks are appended to the left of the first character. If the format specifier is less than the length of the string, the rightmost characters in the string are truncated to produce a string having a length equal to the format specifier. One way to remember this rule is simply to remember the word POT. In "POT" the 'O' stands for output; the 'P' is on the left and that is where Padding (with blanks) occurs. 'T' stands for Truncation and it occurs on the right.

Other operations with strings are governed by the same rules that apply to packed arrays.

10.10.3 An Example

The task is to produce a list of the days of the week in alphabetical order. That is, we want to output a single line containing:

FRIDAY MONDAY SATURDAY SUNDAY THURSDAY TUESDAY WEDNESDAY

Assume that the INPUT file contains the seven names in their usual sequence. The mainline algorithm involves three steps

1. Read the names
2. Sort them
3. Output the result

We already have the knowledge to read the data and to write the results. How can they be sorted into alphabetic order? There are many ways of sorting a set of values. Some are relatively efficient and some are not. When the number of values to be sorted is small the choice of method is not very critical so we shall use the following very simple algorithm called an exchange sort. Given an array of values it is:

1. Find the lowest value in the array and exchange with the value of the first element.

2. Of those remaining, find the next lowest value and exchange with the value of the second element.

3. Of those remaining, find the next lowest value and exchange it with the value in the third element.

4. etc.

When converted to an iterative algorithm, the sorting routine is therefore:

For Pos = 1 to the maximum subscript less 1
    .1 Find largest value between element
              Pos and the end of the array
    .2 Exchange the value with that in element Pos

In the given problem, different days of the week must be compared. This means the days should be stored in strings of the same length. Since Wednesday has the most letters we need STRING9 variables.

Aside from the SORT procedure, the program appears as follows.

```
PROGRAM SORT_DAYS(INPUT,OUTPUT);

(* THIS PROGRAM READS THE DAYS OF THE WEEK FROM
   THE INPUT FILE AND SORTS THEM INTO ALPHABETICAL
   ORDER                                              *)

CONST
  BLANK = ' ';
  BLANKS = '         ';  (* NINE BLANKS *)
  WEEK_LENGTH = 7;

TYPE
  STRING9 = PACKED ARRAY [1..9] OF CHAR;
  WEEK_ARRAY = ARRAY [1..WEEK_LENGTH] OF STRING9;

VAR
  WEEK_DAY : WEEK_ARRAY;
  DAY_NUM, CHAR_NUM : INTEGER;
  NEXT_CHAR : CHAR;

PROCEDURE SORT(VAR X : WEEK_ARRAY);
  (* sort block goes here *)

BEGIN (* SORT_DAYS *)
  (* 1 - READ THE NAMES OF THE DAYS OF THE WEEK *)
     FOR DAY_NUM := 1 TO WEEK_LENGTH DO
       BEGIN
         WEEK_DAY[DAY_NUM] := BLANKS;
         CHAR_NUM := 0;
         READ(NEXT_CHAR);
         WHILE NEXT_CHAR <> BLANK DO
           BEGIN
             CHAR_NUM := CHAR_NUM + 1;
             WEEK_DAY[DAY_NUM,CHAR_NUM] := NEXT_CHAR;
             READ(NEXT_CHAR)
           END
       END; (* DAY_NUM LOOP *)

  (* 2 - SORT THE VALUES *)
     SORT(WEEK_DAY);

  (* 3 - OUTPUT THE RESULTS *)
     FOR DAY_NUM := 1 TO WEEK_LENGTH DO
       WRITELN(WEEK_DAY[DAY_NUM])
END. (* SORT_DAYS *)
$ENTRY
MONDAY TUESDAY WEDNESDAY THURSDAY FRIDAY SATURDAY SUNDAY
```

Comments: Some of these points simply reinforce ideas introduced previously.

1. By declaring WEEK_LENGTH as a constant, the program can be easily modified to adapt to a different number of names.

2. It is necessary to make WEEK_ARRAY a named type because a variable having this type is passed to a procedure; recall that a formal parameter must have its type specified by name.

3. The logic required to read the names of the days of the week from the INPUT file is complicated by the fact that the names have different lengths and care must be taken to prevent a subscript from exceeding its upper bound.

4. The variable WEEK_DAY is an array of arrays having the following type.

        WEEK_DAY : ARRAY[1..WEEK_LENGTH] OF STRING9

    If a single subscript is used as in WEEK_DAY[3], it refers to the third element which has a type of STRING9. That is the third element of WEEK_DAY is a packed array of characters. If a second subscript is used, it refers to an element in the particular STRING9 array. Thus WEEK_DAY[5,2] refers to the second character in the fifth element of WEEK_DAY. Put another way, WEEK_DAY can be viewed as a single two-dimensional array having one row for each day and one column for each character in the name.

5. The FOR loop to output the days in sorted order illustrates the use of a string variable as a parameter to WRITELN. In the statement

        WRITELN(WEEK_DAY[DAY_NUM])

    the parameter has the type STRING9.

    The SORT procedure is shown on the following page.

```
PROCEDURE SORT(VAR X : WEEK_ARRAY);

   (* THIS PROCEDURE SORTS THE ROWS IN THE PARAMETER
      ARRAY INTO ALPHABETICAL SEQUENCE USING AN
      EXCHANGE SORT ALGORITHM                        *)

   VAR
    NEXT_POS, I, LOW_POS : 1..WEEK_LENGTH;
    TEMP                 : STRING9;

   BEGIN (* SORT *)
     FOR NEXT_POS := 1 TO WEEK_LENGTH - 1 DO
       BEGIN
         LOW_POS := NEXT_POS;
         FOR I := NEXT_POS + 1 TO WEEK_LENGTH DO
           IF X[I] < X[LOW_POS] THEN
             LOW_POS := I;
         IF LOW_POS <> NEXT_POS THEN (* EXCHANGE *)
           BEGIN
             TEMP := X[NEXT_POS];
             X[NEXT_POS] := X[LOW_POS];
             X[LOW_POS] := TEMP
           END (* EXCHANGE *)
       END (* NEXT_POS LOOP *)
   END; (* SORT *)
```

The upper limit on the outer FOR loop is 6 rather than 7 because by the time six exchanges have been made, the seventh element must necessarily have the highest value.

Similarly the lower limit of the loop which examines names not already positioned correctly can begin at NEXT_POS +1 rather than NEXT_POS by initially assuming the element at NEXT_POS has the lowest value of those remaining.

10.10.4 Useful String Operations

When working with strings, one quickly finds the requirement that strings must be the same length, a real nuisance when comparing or assigning them. Although some versions of Pascal support variable length strings, standard Pascal does not. The string processing extensions which are supported by Waterloo Pascal and serveral others are described in Appendix C. There are several string operations which are needed frequently but for which predefined functions and procedures are not generally provided. The list below outlines some that are useful. You may want to consider developing a library of these routines if you do a lot of string processing.

In the following, STRINGm and STRINGn denote string types of length m and n respectively.

- FUNCTION STRING_LENGTH (s: STRINGm):INTEGER
  - returns the position of the last non-blank character in the parameter string.

- FUNCTION INDEX (s1: STRINGm;s2:STRINGn):INTEGER
  - if the string s2 is not found in s1 then
          return 0
    else
          return the subscript of the element in
          s1 where s2 starts
    For example, if s1 is 'ABCDEF' and s2 is 'DE'
    then INDEX (s1,s2) returns 4

- PROCEDURE TRIM (VAR s: STRINGm)
  - removes leading blanks in s by shifting all characters left. If there are k leading blanks, the rightmost k elements are set to blanks.

- PROCEDURE STRING (s1:char_array_of_length_M; var s2:STRINGm)
  - converts the unpacked array of characters of size m to the type STRINGm by using the PACK procedure

- PROCEDURE SUBSTRING (s1:STRINGm; i:INTEGER;
                                    VAR s2: STRINGn)
  - assigns the characters in elements i, i+1, i+2, ..., i+n-1 to elements of s2

- PROCEDURE CONCAT (s1:STRINGm; s2:STRINGn;
                                 VAR s3: STRING(m+n))
  - the characters in s3 contain those in s1 followed by those in s2

- PROCEDURE READSTRING (s:STRINGm)
  - fills s with the next m characters from the INPUT file

- PROCEDURE TOKEN(s:STRINGm;VAR start,stop:INTEGER)
  - beginning with the element in s having the subscript start, sets start equal to the subscript of the first non-blank character found; sets stop equal to the subscript of the character to the left of the next blank following start which is found

- PROCEDURE TRANSLATE (C1,C2:CHAR; VAR s: STRINGm)
  - replaces all instances of the character C1 in s with the character C2

- PROCEDURE TRUNC_STRING (VAR s: STRINGm; i:INTEGER)
  - assigns a blank to elements of s having a subscript greater-than-or-equal-to i.

10.11 Exercise 10.3 Strings

1. Which of the following are string types? If not a string, which are invalid in any case?

    a) PACKED ARRAY[1..5] OF CHAR
    b) ARRAY[1..5] OF PACKED CHAR
    c) PACKED ARRAY[0..10] OF CHAR
    d) ARRAY[1..1] OF PACKED ARRAY[1..10] OF CHAR
    e) PACKED ARRAY[1..1] OF PACKED ARRAY[1..1] OF CHAR

2. Given the declarations below, what is the error in each of the assignment statements which follow?

    ```
    VAR
        S1 : PACKED ARRAY[1..1] OF CHAR;
        S2 : PACKED ARRAY[1..2] OF CHAR;
        A1 : ARRAY[1..1] OF CHAR;
        A2 : ARRAY[1..2] OF CHAR;
         C : CHAR
    ```

    a) S1 := S2
    b) S1 := A1
    c) S1 := C
    d) S2 := A2
    e) A2[1]:= S1

3. Write and test a Pascal subprogram for each of functions and procedures that were given in the previous subsection. In each case choose appropriate values of m and/or n. Make sure your subprogram prints a suitable message if a value passed to the subprogram is out of range. The names of the subprograms are:

    a) STRING_LENGTH
    b) INDEX
    c) TRIM
    d) STRING
    e) SUBSTRING
    f) CONCAT
    g) READSTRING
    h) TOKEN
    i) TRANSLATE
    j) TRUNC_STRING

4. Write a procedure called DIGITIZER which has the header

    ```
    PROCEDURE DIGITIZER (number:INTEGER;
                            VAR numstring:STRING 10)
    ```

The procedure produces the string equivalent of an integer value. For example -123456789 becomes '-123456789'. If fewer than 10 characters are needed in the result, the leftmost characters in the string should be set to blanks.

10.12 Summary

1. An array in Pascal is a named collection of components of the same type. Each component (element) has a unique subscript which is used to reference the component.

2. The number of elements (size) of an array must be specified by a constant when the type is declared.

3. An array may have one-dimension (a vector), two-dimensions (a matrix) or several dimensions.

4. Arrays of the same type may be assigned one to the other but not compared, read or written except on an element-by-element basis. This rule is relaxed for strings (See rule 6 below).

5. Arrays can be packed which may decrease the memory requirements for storing the values of the array elements. The use of packed arrays may increase the time taken to execute a program.

6. The word string denotes a type which is a packed array of CHAR values having 1 as the first subscript. Unlike other arrays, strings can be used as parameters to WRITE and WRITELN. They can also be compared using the relational operators if they have the same length.

10.13 Programming Problems

10.1   Read five INTEGER values from a single input line and store them in an array of variables called K. On four successive lines print the values; the subscripts of the variables which have positive values, negative values, and zero values.

10.2   Read a set of ten INTEGER values from a single line. Print all pairs of values which add up to twelve.

10.3   Read ten INTEGER values each of which represents some person's age. Determine which two persons are: closest in age; farthest apart in age.

10.4   Suppose A and B are arrays of eight INTEGER values each. Read
the two sets of values using FOR-loops. Print those values which are in:
both A and B; either A or B or both; A but not B; B but not A; either
A or B but not both. Test your program using the following sets of
values.

$$A = (2, 5, 8, 4, 7, 1, 6, 10)$$
$$B = (9, 8, 4, 10, 3, 5, 12, 11)$$

10.5   Read four lines of data each of which contains seven REAL values
representing daily temperatures (one line per week). For each week,
calculate the average temperature and the maximum and minimum
temperatures. Calculate the average, high and low temperatures for the
four week period. Display your results as shown below.

				TEMPERATURES						
	M	T	W	TH	F	S	S	AVG	HI	LO
WEEK 1	XX	XX	XX	XX	XX	XX	XX	XX.X	XX.	XX.
WEEK 2	XX	XX	XX	XX	XX	XX	XX	XX.X	XX.	XX.
WEEK 3	XX	XX	XX	XX	XX	XX	XX	XX.X	XX.	XX.
WEEK 4	XX	XX	XX	XX	XX	XX	XX	XX.X	XX.	XX.
								----	--	--
FOUR WEEK STATISTICS								XX.X	XX.	XX.

10.6   Add additional statements to the program for the previous problem so
that the average, high and low temperatures for each day of the week
are calculated.

10.7   Start with any four digit INTEGER value in which at least two of
the digits have different values. Form the largest and smallest possible
numbers from the digits. Subtract them to give a new number.
Compare the number to 6174. If equal, stop. If not, repeat the entire
process until the number 6174 is obtained. (It will show up in at most
seven steps regardless of the number you start with!) For example, if
you start with 1998 you get successively: 8082 (from 9981 - 1899);
8532 (from 8820 - 0288); 6174 (from 8532 - 2358). Print your starting
value and each number obtained during the procedure.

10.8   Write a program which reads an INTEGER value and finds all of its
divisors. For example, the divisors of 6 are 1, 2, 3, and 6. Store the
divisors in an array called VEC. For each element of VEC, determine
how many divisors it has. (For the example, these would be 1, 2, 2, and
4. Store these values in a vector called NDIVS. Find the sum of cubes
of the elements of NDIVS and compare this with the square of the
sum of the elements of NDIVS. They will be equal! This is a general
procedure for finding sets of numbers having this property. Write a
program which reads several values and generates the set of values
associated with each input number according to the rules above.

10.9   Read an unknown number (less than fifty) of INTEGER values one at a time. Stop when any value occurs for the second time. Print the message "THE VALUE XX WAS THE XX AND XX VALUE IN THE SEQUENCE".

10.10   Write a program which reads in the house survey data shown in the table at the begining of Section 10.4. Record the data for each house on a separate line. Answer the following questions. Which house has the most children? Which houses have more than one child in high school? What is the ratio of children to adults in each house? In the houses containing no children in elementary school or at least one pre-school child, what is the average number of high-school children?

10.11   The input data contains twenty INTEGER values each of which is zero or some positive value. Read the values and store them in a vector called DATA. Print the values in DATA. Create a new set of values called DENSE from the elements of DATA as follows. If there are N consecutive zero values in DATA, store a value of -N in the next element of DENSE. If an element of DATA is positive, store its value in the next element of DENSE. (See example below.) Print the values in DENSE. Finally use the elements of DENSE to generate the original set of values by reversing the logic used to create DENSE. Store the re-created set of values in COPY and print its values. For example:

DATA   2 3 0 0 0 0 1 5 7 0 0 8 4 0 9 6 0 0 3 0

DENSE 2 3 -4 1 5 7 -2 8 4 0 9 6 -2 3 0

COPY   2 3 0 0 0 0 1 5 7 0 0 8 4 0 9 6 0 0 3 0

10.12   Read ten INTEGER values and store them in the first row of a table having two rows and ten columns. Find the smallest value and store its column number in a variable called ORIGIN. Find the second smallest value and store its column number in row two of the column containing the smallest value. Continue to find successively larger values and store their column numbers in row two of the column containing the previously found value. Finally, in row two of the column containing the largest value, store a zero. (See the example below.) Having done this use the value of ORIGIN and the row two values to print the original set of values in order of smallest to largest. For example:

column	1	2	3	4	5	6	7	8	9	10
Row 1	15	-10	12	-19	8	45	-11	66	30	-2
Row 2	9	10	1	7	3	8	2	0	6	5

and   ORIGIN = 4 (points to column 4)

Write the program in such a way that it will work for any ten INTEGER values.

10.13 The Ackermann function ACK[i,j] is defined as follows. ACK[0,j]=j+1; ACK[i,0]=ACK[i-1,1]; ACK[i,j] = ACK[i-1, ACK[i,j-1]]. Write a program which stores the values of ACK[0,0] thru ACK[9,9] in a ten-by-ten table. The element in the ith row and jth column should be the value of ACK[i-1,j-1].

10.14 Write a function called DETERMINANT which calculates the value of the determinant of a two-by-two matrix. The function will have a single parameter, the name of the two-by-two matrix of REAL values.

10.15 Write a procedure called RANDOM to generate a set of 100 "random" INTEGER numbers R[1], R[2], R[3],... in the range J thru K. Use the following method. Set R[1] equal to any positive INTEGER value. For N=2, 3, ..., 100, set R[N]=25173*R[N-1] MOD 65536. This will generate 100 random numbers in the range 0 thru 65535. To reduce the range to that of J thru K, replace R[I] by

$$R[I] \ / \ 65535.0 \ * \ (K-J+1) \ + \ J$$

The parameters of the procedure will be R, J, and K. Test your procedure by writing a mainline which prints the one hundred numbers generated by RANDOM on ten lines of ten values each.

10.16 Use the procedure RANDOM written for the previous problem in this problem. Generate two hundred random INTEGER values in the range one thru six. Use these numbers to represent the outcome on one hundred throws of a pair of dice. That is, if the values of R[1] and R[2] were 3 and 6 respectively, this would mean the dice on the first throw showed 3 and 6. Write a program which answers the following two questions about the hundred throws of the dice. (a) How many times did each of the 36 possible results occur? Print the data in a table having six rows and six columns where the row indicates the value on the first die. The column indicates the value on the second die. (b) What percentage of the time did each of the eleven possible totals 2, 3, 4, ..., 12 occur in the hundred throws? Print suitable headings followed by eleven lines of statistics.

10.17   Write a procedure which has two parameters -- K, an array of twenty INTEGER values, and INSERT. Values in K and the value of INSERT are passed to the procedure. The procedure should insert the value of INSERT into the array K so that values in K are non-decreasing (increasing order of magnitude except for ties) and then return control to the calling block. Write a mainline which initializes an array of twenty INTEGER values called DATA to zero and then reads one INTEGER value from each of twenty input lines. After each value is read, use the procedure to insert the value in the proper position in DATA. After the twenty values have been read, print the values in DATA and verify that they have been stored in order of increasing magnitude.

10.18   Write a procedure to assign an array of M*N REAL values stored in a vector to the first M rows and N columns of a matrix. Assume M and N are less than ten. The mainline should read values of M and N, then MN more values. The procedure should assign the first N values to row one of the parameter matrix, the next N values to row two, etc.. The procedure will have four variables in the parameter list: the values of M and N; the vector containing the MN values; the matrix in which the values are to be stored.

10.19   A programming project. Suppose a fifty-by-fifty matrix contains elements having values of zero or one. Suppose less than twenty percent of the elements have a value of one and all the rest are zeros. Design any scheme you like for reducing the memory required to store the array values. Make sure your technique will work for an arbitrary set of values and does not depend on the array values having a particular pattern.

10.20   Suppose a sentence on an input line has less than fifty characters and contains N words (where N is determined by the program). Write a program which reads the sentence and prints it N times such that on the first line the first word starts in print position 60, on the second line the second word starts in print position 60, etc.. For example, if the sentence is "PROGRAMMING IS EASY", the following output would be produced.

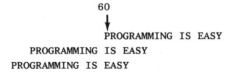

```
                    60
                    ↓
                    PROGRAMMING  IS  EASY
          PROGRAMMING  IS  EASY
          PROGRAMMING  IS  EASY
```

10.21   Modify the survey program so that if there is a tie for the most number of people in a house, all houses satisfying that criterion are listed.

10.22   A 5 by 5 matrix and its inverse are shown below.

```
1 1 1 1 1              2 -1  0  0  0
1 2 2 2 2             -1  2 -1  0  0
1 2 3 3 3              0 -1  2 -1  0
1 2 3 4 4              0  0 -1  2 -1
1 2 3 4 5              0  0  0 -1  1
```

The pattern shown for the inverse may be extended to any N by N matrix having the form of the matrix on the left. Read a value for N (assume N is 8 or less); generate the matrix and its inverse and then multiply them to test the correctness of the pattern generation routines. (The product must have ones down the diagonal, and zeros elsewhere.) Use separate procedures called GEN_MATRIX, GEN_INVERSE, PRINT_MATRIX and TEST in your program.

10.23   Write a function called PERCENTILE having parameters X, N and K where X is a set of N REAL values in order of increasing magnitude and K is one of 10, 20, 30, ..., 90. The value of PERCENTILE calculated in the procedure should be the Kth percentile of the values in X. The Kth percentile is a value such that K percent of the values are less than it and 100-K percent of the values are greater. Use PERCENTILE to calculate the tenth thru ninetieth percentiles of a set of fifteen typical marks out of one-hundred.

10.24   The Arithmetic Mean (AM), Geometric Mean (GM) and Harmonic Mean (HM) of a set of N values X1, X2, X3, ..., Xn are defined as:

$$AM = \frac{X1 + X2 + X3 + \ldots + Xn}{N}$$

$$GM = \sqrt[N]{X1 \; X2 \; X3 \; \ldots \; Xn}$$

$$HM = \frac{N}{\dfrac{1}{X1} + \dfrac{1}{X2} + \dfrac{1}{X3} + \ldots + \dfrac{1}{Xn}}$$

Write a program called MEANS in which AM, GM, and HM are functions used to calculate the corresponding means of a set of N numbers. The functions should have two parameters -- the value of N and the array of values.

10.25   Solve the same problem as above but have the mainline pass a value to a MEANS function which is one of the values in the enumerated type (AM, GM, HM). The MEANS function should contain three function blocks called AM_MEAN, GM_MEAN and HM_MEAN. One of these is invoked to obtain the required value.

10.26   Binary Search. Suppose you have a vector X of 100 REAL values
ordered such that X[I] $\leq$ X[I+1] for I=1,99. A value of Y is read and
you want to determine if the value of Y is already stored in X.
Naturally you could use the brute force method of comparing Y with
X[1], Y with X[2], etc. looking for a match. A more efficient way is to
compare Y with the middle element of X, X[50] and if Y < X[50]
search X[1] thru X[49]; if equal the search is over; if Y > X[50]
search X[51] thru X[100]. If not equal, continue with the same
technique (compare Y to the middle element of the elements
remaining). By repeatedly dividing any remaining interval in two, either
a match will be found or all possibilities will have been exhausted. This
method is known as a binary search.

Write a program which reads a value of N, then N more values
and stores them in a vector X. Assume N is 25 or less. Read ten more
values and for each determine if it matches one of the N values
previously read using a procedure called BIN_SEARCH. Second,
modify the procedure so that it is recursive. That is BIN_SEARCH
calls itself to search a sub-array. Do you think this is a good use of
recursion? What are its advantages and disadvantages?

10.27   The N coefficients of an (N-1)th degree polynomial f(x) can be
chosen so that the curve will pass thru any N points in the XY plane.
Suppose (X_1,Y_1), (X_2,Y_2), ..., (X_n,Y_n) are N points in the XY plane.
The value of f(x) which passes thru all N points is given by

$$f(x) = \frac{\sum y_i L_i(x)}{L_i(x_i)}$$

where $L_i(x) = \pi (x - x_j)$ (π means product of)

$$j \neq i$$

Write a procedure called interpolate which has three items in the
parameter list -- the value of N, the value of X for which the function
value is to be calculated, and VAR parameter to store the function
value. Declare a global array containing a table of two rows and fifty
columns. The row one values are the values of the X coordinates, those
in row two, the corresponding Y coordinates. To test the function, use
eight data points generated in the following way. In row one store
values of 0, 45, 90, 135, ..., 315. In row two, store values of the sine of
the corresponding angle in row one. Assume the row one values are in
degrees. Use the procedure INTERPOLATE to calculate estimates of
the sine of angles of 15, 60, 105, 150, 195, 240, 285 and 330 degrees.
For each of these print the estimated sine value, the true sine value,
and the percent error resulting from using the approximating function.

10.28   A programming project. In physics, there are five commonly used
equations which describe the relationships between distance (s),
acceleration (a), final velocity (v), time (t) and initial velocity (u) of a
moving body. Each of the five equations can be identified by the
variable which does not appear in the equation. For this reason, they
are sometimes known as the "SAVTU" equations. The equations are as
follows.

"S" equation: $a = (v-u)/t$

"A" equation: $v = t(u+v)/2$

"V" equation: $s = ut + (at^2)/2$

"T" equation: $v^2 = u^2 + 2as$

"U" equation: $s = vt - (at^2)/2$

Write a procedure called SAVTU which has the parameters DATA and
CODES defined by:

```
VAR
    DATA : ARRAY[1..5] OF REAL;
    CODE : ARRAY[1..5] OF INTEGER
```

Let the values in DATA be the values of distance, acceleration, final
velocity, time and initial velocity. The values in CODE indicate which
values are known and which are to be calculated. If CODE[I] is zero it
means the value of DATA[I] is to be calculated by the procedure and
stored in DATA[I]. If CODES[I] is 1, it means DATA(I) can be used
in the calculation of the unknown values. Note that in any call to the
procedure, that at least three values in CODE must equal one. Use any
method you like in the procedure to calculate the unknown values. Test
your procedure on at least the ten different ways that three values of
the five can be specified as known. Include in your procedure a return
code which indicates if fewer than three of the CODE values are 1.

CHAPTER 11: RECORDS

Questions Answered in this Chapter:

1. What are Pascal records? How are they defined and used in programs?

2. How can a single record have one of several different structures?

Records provide an easy-to-use method of defining and processing collections of heterogeneous data. Next to the array, records are the most widely used data structures.

11.1 Concepts and Record Declarations

In many computer applications, the information describing a person, event, system or process of interest consists of several different descriptors or characteristics. Some examples follow:

- a person has a name, address, sex, age, height, weight, and marital status

- an election has a winner, one or more losers and the votes obtained by each

- a system of city streets has roads, intersections, traffic volumes

- an item in inventory has a part number, description, quantity on hand, quantity on order

In Pascal, collections of heterogeneous (different) types of data can be grouped to form a record. When this is done, the entire collection can be referred to by a record name. In addition, the individual components which are called *fields* can be accessed and processed separately.

There are two important differences between arrays and records. First the elements of an array must all have the same type. In a record on the other hand, the components or fields may have different types. Second, a component of an array is referenced by its position in the array whereas each field of a record has a unique name. Records and arrays are similar in that both must be defined with a finite number of components.

Examples of record declarations. Shown below are declarations of three record types. A summary of the important ideas follows the examples.

```
TYPE
  POINT_REC = RECORD
                  X:REAL; (* X coordinate *)
                  Y:REAL  (* Y coordinate *)
              END

  DATE_REC =  RECORD
                  YEAR : 1900..2000;
                  MONTH: 1..12;
                  DAY  : 1..31
              END;

  PERSON_REC =   RECORD
                     NAME: PACKED ARRAY[1..30]OF CHAR;
                     SEX : (MALE,FEMALE,OTHER);
                     BIRTH_DATE: RECORD
                                     YEAR : 1900..2000;
                                     MONTH: 1..12;
                                     DAY  : 1..31
                                 END
                 END
```

When declaring a record type, the convention used for the type name is to append "_REC" to a descriptive name. This emphasizes the structure of the type and allows the root part of the identifier to be used as a variable name.

As illustrated above, a record declaration consists of the reserved word RECORD followed by declarations of the fields of the record followed by the reserved word END. The type POINT_REC is a record type having two REAL fields. A record of type DATE_REC has three fields, each of which has a type specified by a different subrange of integers. PERSON_REC shows that a field of a record can be a structured type. For example, the field called NAME has a string type, SEX has an enumerated type, and BIRTH_DATE has a record type.

A summary of the declaration syntax can be found at the end of the next section.

11.2 Using Fields

How do you refer to a field in a record? Suppose we are given the declaration below.

```
VAR
   POINT: RECORD
            X:REAL;
            Y:REAL
          END;
```

To read the values of the X and Y coordinates from the INPUT file, the following READ invocation can be used.

```
READ (POINT.X, POINT.Y)
```

POINT.X and POINT.Y are the two fields in the POINT record. In general, a field is designated by the sequence

```
record name    .    field name
```

Because the names of fields within a record must be unique, a field name appended to the record name is sufficient to uniquely identify each component of a record.

If a field is a structure, its components can be selected by appending either the subscript, if an array, or field identifier, if a record. For example, consider the following declaration.

```
VAR
   PERSON: RECORD
            NAME:PACKED ARRAY [1..20] OF CHAR;
            SEX :(MALE,FEMALE,OTHER);
            BIRTH_DATE: RECORD
                          YEAR : 1900..2000;
                          MONTH: 1..12;
                          DAY  : 1..31
                        END (*BIRTH_DATE*)
          END(*PERSON*)
```

The three fields of PERSON are PERSON.NAME, PERSON.SEX and PERSON.BIRTH_DATE. Since PERSON.NAME is an array of twenty characters, it follows that PERSON.NAME[I] denotes the Ith element of the PERSON.NAME array. Thus to read the name from the INPUT file, the following FOR loop can be used.

```
FOR I:= 1 TO 20 DO
   READ(PERSON.NAME[I])
```

In the PERSON record, the field PERSON.BIRTH_DATE is a record having the following three fields: PERSON.BIRTH_DATE.YEAR, PERSON.BIRTH_DATE.MONTH and PERSON.BIRTH_DATE.DAY.

Operations which can be performed on a field are the same as those that can be performed with any variable having that field type. For example, because PERSON.SEX has the enumerated type (MALE, FEMALE, OTHER), it cannot be read or written using READ and WRITE. On the other hand ORD(PERSON.SEX) will be 0 if the field value is MALE, 1 if FEMALE and 2 if OTHER. Similarly because PERSON.NAME is a string, the statement below is perfectly valid.

```
WRITELN (PERSON.NAME)
```

The only operation that can be performed with an entire record is the assignment operation, and then only if the target and source records have the same type. For example, given the declaration

```
VAR
    JOHN, TOM, MARY : PERSON_REC
```

where PERSON_REC is the record type defined above, then the following two statements are examples of valid record-to-record assignments.

```
JOHN := TOM
MARY.BIRTH_DATE := JOHN.BIRTH_DATE
```

Why is the following fragment *not* valid?

```
VAR
    A : RECORD
            I: INTEGER
        END;
    B : RECORD
            I: INTEGER
        END;

BEGIN
        .
    B := A
        .
END
```

The error is not that the field name I is used in both declarations. This is perfectly acceptable. The only requirement is that fields *within* a record have unique identifiers. (Technically, the scope of a field identifier is the record in which it appears). The error is in the assignment statement B:=A. Although you and I can see that A and B have equivalent types, it is difficult for the compiler to determine this. To be assignment compatible, two records must be declared: with the same type name; or with type names defined equal to each other; or in the same VAR declaration. None of these conditions is satisfied by A and B above. The simplest remedy is to use the following declaration

```
VAR
   A,B : RECORD
               I : INTEGER
         END
```

When this is done, the statements A:=B and B:=A are valid. Note that if a pair of records are assignment compatible, of necessity the fields within them must be assignment compatible.

Some Pascal compilers permit a function "value" to be an entire record; standard Pascal does not.

11.3 The WITH Statement -- A convenience

Motivation: When choosing names for identifiers in a program, there is often a tradeoff. Longer and more English-like names make a program easier to read and debug. On the other hand, long names take extra time to write and enter into the computer and therefore increase the probability of making typographical errors. The length problem is compounded in the case of records because both the record name and field name must be explicitly stated each time a field reference is needed. As a convenience to the programmer the Pascal language contains a WITH statement having the following form.

```
WITH record identifier DO
     statement
```

The idea is that field names used in the statement can be used without the record name prefix.

An example. We are given the following declaration.

```
VAR
   PERSON: RECORD
             NAME: PACKED ARRAY[1..20] OF CHAR;
             SEX : (MALE, FEMALE)
             BIRTH_DATE: RECORD
                            YEAR  : 1900..2000;
                            MONTH : 1..12;
                            DAY   : 1..31
                         END; (*BIRTH_DATE*)
             HIRED_DATE:  RECORD
                            YEAR : 1900..2000;
                            MONTH: 1..12;
                            DAY  : 1..31
                         END(*HIRED_DATE*)
          END (*PERSON*)
```

The following are examples of explicit field designators.

```
PERSON.NAME - the person's name
PERSON.BIRTH_DATE - the person's birthdate
PERSON.BIRTH_DATE.MONTH - the month of the person's
                                 birthdate
PERSON.HIRED_DATE.YEAR - the year the person was hired
```

The statement below shows how assignments could be made to components of the record using a WITH statement to save writing.

```
WITH PERSON DO
  BEGIN
    NAME:= 'FREDDY FUDPUCKER     ';
    SEX:= MALE;
    BIRTH_DATE.YEAR:= 1965;
    HIRED_DATE.MONTH:= 7
  END (*WITH PERSON*)
```

When used in the body of a WITH statement, a field name has precedence over any other identical identifier. For example, suppose the identifier NAME is declared as a string variable in the same block in which the PERSON record is declared. Then references to NAME outside the WITH statement refer to the NAME string. References to NAME within the WITH statement refer to the field called NAME.

The WITH statement can refer to records within a record. For example, the record PERSON.BIRTH_DATE can be used in a WITH specification as shown below.

```
WITH PERSON.BIRTH_DATE DO
   YEAR:= 1965
```

A more general form of WITH is summarized on the following page.

The WITH Statement

General Form

>   WITH rec1, rec2, ..., recN DO
>   body statement

Notes

1. rec1, rec2, ... must be record variables

2. Each record in the list must have been declared previously or be
    a field of some record preceding it in the list.

3. The form above is equivalent to the following sequence of nested
    WITH statements

>   WITH rec1   DO
>   WITH rec2   DO
>
>   .
>   .
>
>   WITH recN   DO
>   body statement

4. In the body statement, the field name of any field belonging to a
    record in the list may be used without prefixing the name with
    the record name. If the same field name occurs in more than one
    of the records in the list, it is assumed to be associated with the
    record nearest the end of the list.

5. The record references are evaluated only at the time the WITH
    statement is encountered. Thus if a record in the WITH list is
    subscripted with a variable, then changing the value of the
    subscript in the body statement does not change the record
    reference. (See example (ii) below.)

Example(i). Using the PERSON record declared previously, the following is
valid.

```
WITH PERSON, HIRED_DATE DO
   BEGIN
      NAME:= '_____';
      YEAR:= 1979; (* refers to HIRED_DATE.YEAR *)
      BIRTH_DATE.MONTH:= 5
   END
```

References to BIRTH_DATE fields must include the record name BIRTH_DATE explicitly. References to fields in HIRED_DATE however can be made using just the field name.

Example (ii). Rule 5 states that a record reference in a WITH statement is evaluated only at the time the WITH statement is encountered. To see the implication of this suppose variable X is an array of records declared by:

```
X: ARRAY[1..10] OF RECORD
                    M : INTEGER
               END
```

That is, each element of X is a record containing a single INTEGER field. Consider the following fragment. (Assume I is an INTEGER variable.)

```
I:= 1;
WITH X[I] DO
  BEGIN
    WRITELN (M);
    I:= 2;
    WRITELN (M)
  END
```

Both WRITELN invocations print the value of the field X[1].M. Changing I to 2 in the body of the WITH statement does not change the record reference to X[1] in the WITH statement.

One last point. Assuming Y to be a record within X, what is the difference between

```
WITH X, Y  DO      and      WITH X.Y  DO
```

The first allows fields of either X or X.Y to be referenced by name alone. The second means that only fields of the record X.Y can be referenced by name.

11.4 Exercise 11.1

1. Write appropriate record declarations for each of the following:

   a) A student record containing a name, address, sex and an array of 10 marks.
   b) A complex number containing a real and an imaginary component which are REAL numbers.
   c) A piece of art containing descriptors for its: author, date, period (middle ages, renaissance, modern), size (a pair of integers), owner's name, coloured or black and white (boolean value).

2. Given the declarations below, write statements to perform the assignments requested.

```
TYPE
  DATE_REC = RECORD
                  YEAR  : 1900..2000
                  MONTH : 1..12
                  DAY   : 1..31
               END;
  PERSON_REC = RECORD
                   NAME: PACKED ARRAY[1..20] OF CHAR;
                   BIRTH_DATE : DATE_REC;
                   EMPLOYMENT_DATE: RECORD
                                        HIRED:DATE_REC;
                                        FIRED:DATE_REC
                                     END
                END; (*PERSON_REC*)
VAR
  DATE:DATE_REC;
  EMPLOYEE: ARRAY[(TOM,JOHN,ANN,SUE)] OF PERSON_REC;
  PERSON: PERSON_REC
```

a) Assign DATE to Tom's birthdate
b) Assign Sue's record to Ann's record
c) Make John's fired date equal to his hired date
d) Assign the year of Ann's birthdate to the year
      of Tom's hired date

3. Given the declarations in the previous question:

a)   For each of the following, write the explicit full-field designator of all fields referenced

```
      i) WITH PERSON DO
             WRITELN (NAME)

     ii) WITH EMPLOYEE[TOM] DO
             WRITELN (BIRTH_DATE.YEAR)

    iii) WITH PERSON.EMPLOYMENT_DATE DO
             WRITELN (FIRED.MONTH)

     iv) WITH EMPLOYEE[ANN], BIRTH_DATE, EMPLOYMENT_DATE,
             HIRED DO
         WRITELN (NAME, MONTH)
```

b) For each of the following write a WITH statement so that field designators can be used as described.

      i) BIRTH_DATE refers to the birth date of PERSON
     ii) MONTH refers to the month of Tom's birth_date
    iii) DAY refers to the day Ann was fired
     iv) NAME refers to Sue's name and HIRED refers
         to her hiring date
      v) BIRTH_DATE refers to John's birth_date, FIRED to
         his firing date and YEAR to the year he was hired.

4.   Under what circumstances is "WITH a,b DO" equivalent in every way to "WITH a.b DO"?

5.   Sometimes when choosing a data structure to store the data associated with a particular problem, one has a choice between an array of records and a record of arrays. What factors should be considered in making this choice?

11.5 Variant Records

Concepts. There are many instances where the characteristics of an object of interest fall into several distinct classes or groups. For example, the payroll information needed for a wage-earning employee is different from that required for a salaried employee; the descriptors of a vehicle will be different if the vehicle is a car, truck or bus; the data describing a football running play is different from that describing a passing play.

In each case a separate record structure could be declared to accommodate the differences. However, along with the differences, one frequently finds one or more fields which are common to each case. For example, regardless of whether salaried or wage earning, an employee has a name and address. In Pascal, a record can be defined which includes a fixed part for fields which are part of every record and a variant part which can be defined in different ways. We can learn all that is necessary by studying a simple example.

An Example. The data necessary to describe four geometrical figures is shown below.

```
1. square    - length of side
2. rectangle - length and width
3. triangle  - lengths of the three sides
4. circle    - radius
```

A record to store *any one* of the four kinds of figures can be declared as shown below.

```
TYPE
    FIGURE_REC = RECORD
                    FIG_NAME : PACKED ARRAY[1..9] OF CHAR;
                    CASE FIG_CODE: 1..5 OF
                        1: (SIDE : REAL);
                        2 : (LENGTH,WIDTH : REAL);
                        3: (SIDE1,SIDE2,SIDE3 : REAL);
                        4: (RADIUS: REAL);
                        5: ( ) (*EXTRA*)
                 END (*FIGURE_REC*)
```

There are several important observations to make.

First, the FIG_NAME field precedes the CASE specification and is therefore common to all forms of the record. All common fields are declared before the first variant.

Second, the five variants of the record are defined using a CASE construct which is similar to, but has three important differences from, a CASE statement. Consider the line

```
CASE FIG_CODE : 1 .. 5 OF
```

Between the reserved words CASE and OF, FIG_CODE is declared as a variable which can take on values in the subrange 1..5. The variable following the word CASE is called the tag field. The tag field belongs to every record. The value assigned to the tag field indicates which of the structures that follow is being used. In this example a tag field value of 1 indicates a square, a value of 2 indicates a rectangle, 3 a triangle, and 4 a circle. The value 5 is used in the example to show that a particular case can be empty. That is, no fields are defined for a tag field value of 5.

Third, note that the field declarations of each case are enclosed in parentheses. Note further that there is no END to denote the end of the CASE. The END is unnecessary because the variant part of a record must follow the fixed part and therefore the END which ends the entire record declaration automatically terminates the last variant.

Finally, the field names in the variants must be unique. (The same field name cannot be used as a field in two different variants.)

The single record declaration of FIGURE_REC above is equivalent to declaring the following five record types.

```
RECORD ( *SQUARE* )
   FIG_NAME: PACKED ARRAY[1..9] OF CHAR;
   FIG_CODE: 1..5;
   SIDE : REAL
END

RECORD ( *RECTANGLE* )
   FIG_NAME: PACKED ARRAY[1..9] OF CHAR;
   FIG_CODE: 1..5;
   LENGTH,WIDTH : REAL
END

RECORD ( *TRIANGLE* )
   FIG_NAME: PACKED ARRAY[1..9] OF CHAR;
   FIG_CODE: 1..5;
   SIDE1, SIDE2, SIDE3 : REAL
END

RECORD ( *CIRCLE* )
   FAG_NAME: PACKED ARRAY[1..9] OF CHAR;
   FIG_CODE: 1..5;
   RADIUS : REAL
END

RECORD ( *EXTRA* )
   FIG_NAME: PACKED ARRAY[1..9] OF CHAR;
   FIG_CODE: 1..5
END
```

We shall use this declaration in solving the following problem.

Read a value from one to four denoting one of square, rectangle, triangle or circle respectively. Obtain the dimensions of the figure and compute its area and perimeter.

Solution. A procedure should be used to perform the processing of the different figures. The procedure should be passed a record containing the value of the figure code. It then should read the corresponding dimension information and return the computed area and perimeter. The procedure PROCESS_FIG follows.

```
PROCEDURE PROCESS_FIG(VAR FIG : FIGURE_REC;
                      VAR AREA, PERIM: REAL);

   VAR
      SIDE, LENGTH, WIDTH, SIDE1, SIDE2, SIDE3,
      RADIUS, HALF  : REAL;

   BEGIN (* PROCESS_FIG *)
      WITH FIG DO
        BEGIN
          CASE FIG_CODE OF
            1: BEGIN (* SQUARE *)
                 FIG_NAME := 'SQUARE    ';
                 WRITELN('ENTER THE LENGTH OF A SIDE');
                 READLN(SIDE);
                 AREA := SQR(SIDE);
                 PERIMETER := 4 * SIDE
               END;
            2: BEGIN (* RECTANGLE *)
                 FIG_NAME := 'RECTANGLE';
                 WRITELN('ENTER THE LENGTH AND WIDTH');
                 READLN(LENGTH, WIDTH);
                 AREA := LENGTH * WIDTH;
                 PERIMETER := 2 * (LENGTH + WIDTH)
               END;
            3: BEGIN (* TRIANGLE *)
                 FIG_NAME := 'TRIANGLE ';
                 WRITELN('ENTER THE LENGTHS OF THE SIDES');
                 READLN(SIDE1, SIDE2, SIDE3);
                 PERIMETER := SIDE1 + SIDE2 + SIDE3;
                 HALF := PERIMETER / 2;
                 AREA := SQRT(HALF * (HALF-SIDE1) *
                            (HALF-SIDE2) * (HALF-SIDE3))
               END;
            4: BEGIN (* CIRCLE *)
                 FIG_NAME := 'CIRCLE    ';
                 WRITELN('ENTER THE RADIUS');
                 READLN(RADIUS);
                 AREA := PI * SQR(RADIUS);
                 PERIMETER := 2 * PI * RADIUS
               END;
          END (* CASE STATEMENT *)
        END (* WITH *)
   END; (* PROCESS_FIG *)
```

The program except for PROCESS_FIG is shown below.

```
PROGRAM FIGURES(INPUT,OUTPUT);

(* THIS PROGRAM READS INFOMATION ABOUT ONE OF
   FOUR DIFFERENT GEOMETRIC FIGURES AND COMPUTES
   THE AREA AND PERIMETER OF THE FIGURE            *)

CONST
  NUMBER_OF_FIGURES = 4;
  NAME_LENGTH = 9;
  PI = 3.14159;

TYPE
  STRING9 = PACKED ARRAY[1..NAME_LENGTH] OF CHAR;
  FIGURE_REC =
    RECORD
      FIG_NAME : STRING9;
      CASE FIG_CODE : INTEGER OF
        1 : (* SQUARE *) (SIDE : REAL);
        2 : (* RECTANGLE *) (LENGTH, WIDTH : REAL);
        3 : (* TRIANGLE *) (SIDE1, SIDE2, SIDE3 : REAL);
        4 : (* CIRCLE *) (RADIUS : REAL);
        5 : (* EXTRA *) ()
    END;

VAR
  FIGURE           : FIGURE_REC;
  AREA, PERIMETER : REAL;

PROCEDURE PROCESS_FIG(VAR FIG : FIGURE_REC;
                      VAR AREA, PERIM: REAL);

     (* block of procedure goes here *)

BEGIN (* FIGURES *)
  WITH FIGURE DO
    BEGIN
      WRITELN(OUTPUT,'ENTER THE FIGURE CODE WHERE: 1=SQUARE,');
      WRITELN('  2=RECTANGLE, 3=TRIANGLE, 4=CIRCLE');
      READLN(FIG_CODE);
      IF (FIG_CODE >= 1) AND (FIG_CODE <= 4) THEN
        BEGIN
          PROCESS_FIG(FIGURE, AREA, PERIMETER);
          WRITELN(' THE AREA OF THE ',FIG_NAME,' IS ',AREA);
          WRITELN(' THE PERIMETER IS',PERIMETER)
    END (* WITH FIGURE *)
          END (* IF *)
END. (* FIGURES *)
```

This example clearly points out the differences between the CASE construct used to declare different sets of fields in a record and the CASE statement which performs different actions based on the value of the expression following the word CASE.

11.6 Record Declaration Syntax: A Summary

The complete syntax of a record declaration is one of the most complex of all type specifications. It is summarized below.

Record Declarations

General Form

> PACKED RECORD field list END

Notes

1. PACKED is optional. If present, an attempt is made to minimize the memory required to store the values in the record.

2. The field list consists of two optional parts: a fixed part and a variant part. If both are present the fixed part must precede the variant part.

3. The fixed part consists of a sequence of field declarations similar to variable declarations in a block. That is, each field declaration consists of one or more identifiers followed by a colon followed by a type specification. A field cannot have a file type (files are described in CHAPTER 12).

4. The variant part has one of the following two forms:

> CASE tag-field : tag-field-type OF variants

> or

> CASE tag-type OF variants

where:

- the tag field is an identifier having an ordinal type.

- each variant has the form:

> constant list : (field list)

> where the constant list is a list of one or more constants of the
> tag field type separated by commas. The field list is that
> described in note 2 above. (A field of a record can itself be a
> record meaning that a record can have fields which are records
> having fields which are records ...).
>
> • Variants are separated by a semicolon.

11.6.1 Omitting a Tag Field

This subsection may be omitted on first reading.

Consider the second form of the tag specification which is:

```
CASE type OF variants
```

That is, no tag field is specified. As an example, consider the following
declaration which contains only three variants and no tag field.

```
TYPE
    FAMILY_REC = RECORD
                    CASE (MOM, DAD, CHILD) OF
                    MOM   : (MOM1, MOM2 : REAL);
                    DAD   : (DAD1, DAD2, DAD3: INTEGER);
                    CHILD : (CHILD1: BOOLEAN)
                 END
```

There is one variant for each value in the tag-type (MOM, DAD, CHILD) but
the record does not contain a field in which the tag value is stored.

The omission of a tag field can cause problems. For example, suppose a
program contains several variables of type FAMILY_REC. Further suppose
some contain MOM data, others DAD data and still others CHILD data. How
would you know which records contained which type of data? Specifically,
suppose an array called FAMILY is declared as

```
FAMILY : ARRAY[1 .. 100] OF FAMILY_REC
```

You would need some method of remembering which records used the MOM
variant, which used the DAD variant and which the CHILD variant.
Occasionally there are circumstances which justify the omission of a tag field
but in general it is not a good idea.

11.6.2 Tag Field Control

For most Pascal compilers the presence of a tag field does not restrict the field names that can be used. Any field name in any variant can be used regardless of the tag field value. The tag field value is used only to help you remember which variant is desired. For example, if a figure record contains a figure code of 1 (a square), you can still process the variant as if it were a triangle. Naturally the results are garbage.

When the compiler encounters a variant part in a record declaration, it keeps track of the amount of memory needed to store each of the variants. After the last variant declaration has been processed, it determines which variant requires the greatest amount of memory and allocates that amount of memory to store the values in the record. That is, the memory used is the same for all variants even though some variants require less memory than others.

The program below makes these ideas clear.

```
PROGRAM VARIANT_USE(OUTPUT);

(* EQUIVALENCING A REAL AND INTEGER VALUE *)

VAR
  INTREAL : RECORD
                CASE TAG : BOOLEAN OF
                   TRUE : (X : REAL);
                   FALSE: (Y : INTEGER)
            END; (* INTREAL *)

BEGIN (* VARIANT_USE *)
  INTREAL.TAG := TRUE;
  INTREAL.X    := 1.5;
  INTREAL.TAG := FALSE;
  WRITELN(INTREAL.Y)
END. (* INTREAL *)
```

The program executes without errors! The value printed is 1092091904. Why? When the assignment of the value 1.5 to X is made, the bit pattern representing the REAL value 1.5 is assigned to the memory locations reserved for the variant part of the record. When the value of Y is written, this same bit pattern is retrieved from memory and because Y is of type INTEGER, it is interpreted as representing an INTEGER value. This results in the value shown. That is, the bit patterns for the REAL value 1.5 and the INTEGER value 1092091904 are the same. The existence of the tag field has no effect.

Some Pascal processors check at execution-time that a field name belongs to the variant specified by the current setting of the tag field. Such processors will not execute the example above.

11.6.3 Using Variants to Save Memory

This subsection may be omitted on first reading.

The computer used to run a Pascal program which contains large arrays may not have sufficient memory to execute the program. For example, suppose the program contains

```
VAR
    X: ARRAY[1..10000] OF INTEGER;
    Y: ARRAY[1..10000] OF REAL
```

If values in X and Y are not needed at the same time, then the memory requirements can be cut in half by defining a record with two variants as follows.

```
VAR
    NUMBERS: RECORD
                CASE IN_USE : (INTS, REALS) OF
                    INTS: (X : ARRAY[1..10000] OF INTEGER);
                    REALS:(Y : ARRAY[1..10000] OF REAL)
             END
```

The tag field IN_USE can be used to help remember which of the variants is being used. If the value of IN_USE is INTS, the integer array is in use; if the value is REALS, then a REAL array is being used.

11.7 Summary

1. A record is a suitable vehicle for grouping related values having different types.

2. Each component of a record is called a field. Fields are referred to by name. Names of fields within a record must be unique. A field can be of any type except a file.

3. The WITH statement is a convenience which permits fields of the records named in the WITH header to be used without the record name prefix.

4. A single record structure can contain several alternative collections of fields. To help remember which set of fields (which variant) is being used, a value is normally assigned to a tag field to identify the variant in use.

5. The amount of memory reserved to store the values in a record is sufficient to store the data in the fixed part plus that of the largest variant.

11.8 Programming Problems

The following ideas may be helpful in solving some of the problems which follow. A pair of values (x,y) can represent a directed line segment (a vector) from the origin to the point (x,y) in the xy plane. Two vectors having the same length and direction but different initial points are considered equal. Thus, in the diagram below, the vectors OP and AB are considered equal.

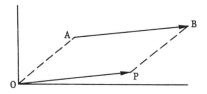

In Pascal, it is common to use a record to store the coordinates of a point using the type declaration:

```
TYPE
   POINT_REC = RECORD
                   X : REAL;
                   Y : REAL
               END
```

11.1   The game of Tic-Tac-Toe is well known. Suppose the elements of a three-by-three matrix called BOARD contain values of -1, 1, or 0 where: -1 indicates Player One has chosen the square; +1 indicates Player Two has chosen the square; 0 indicates neither player has chosen the square. Write a program which reads values for BOARD and prints one of "PLAYER ONE WINS", "PLAYER TWO WINS", or "UNDECIDED".

11.2   Most credit cards have an account number in which the last digit is called the "check digit". Its value depends on the values of the other digits. When the account number is read from a card, the last digit is compared with what it should be based on the other digits in the number. Suppose an account number has ten digits (including the check digit). One method of calculating the check digit is as follows. Find the sum of the 2nd, 4th, 6th and 8th digits (beginning from the left). Call this total SUM1. Form a number consisting of the first, 3rd, 5th, 7th and 9th digits. Multiply this value by two and add the digits in the result. Call this total SUM2. Add SUM1 and SUM2 and subtract the last digit from ten to obtain the check digit. For example, to see if the number 2520764263 is valid: we have SUM1=5+0+6+2=13; now 2*22746 = 45492 and therefore SUM2=4+5+4+9+2 = 24; thus SUM1 + SUM2 = 37 and so the check digit should be 10-7=3. Thus the account number is valid. Write a program which reads an unknown number of ten digit account numbers and determines which are valid (the check digit agrees with that calculated according to the rules above). When testing your program use at least two valid account numbers. Note that to obtain SUM2 you will need to extract the individual digits in a number. This can be done by repeatedly dividing the number by ten and using the remainder as the value of the next digit.

11.3   Write a program which reads in three pairs of X-Y values representing the coordinates of the vertices of a triangle. Read the coordinates of a fourth point. Determine if the fourth point lies inside, on the edge of, or outside the triangle defined by the first three points. Print the coordinates of all four points along with an appropriate message.

11.4   Suppose values of the function $(x^2-2x+3)/(3x^3-2x^2+5)$ are to be calculated for various values of x. The values of x to be used are obtained in the following way. The first input line contains a value of N indicating the number of *ranges* of values of x to be used. Assume N is twenty-five or less. Beginning on the same line containing the value of N, N pairs of numbers are recorded. The first number in each pair denotes the lowest value in the range of integer values to be used. The second number in the pair denotes the highest value in the range. For example, if there were two pairs of numbers say 2,5 and 11,15, the values of x to be used would be 2,3,4,5 and 11,12,13,14,15. Print out "UNDEFINED" if the denominator has a value of zero.

11.5   Here is a game you can try with a friend. Each player writes down three non-negative integer numbers which add up to five. Examples are (0 0 5), (1 3 1) and (2 2 1). Compare your numbers with those of your opponent. The person who has the higher first number gets seven points (no points if a tie). The higher second number is worth five points and the higher third number is worth four points. Play ten times. The winner is the one with the highest total number of points. Write a program which generates all possible triples of numbers which can be used in the game. Use these to identify the rows and columns of a matrix. In the (i,j)th element of the matrix, store the point value which would be obtained by someone who chose the triple associated with row i if his opponent chose the triple associated with column j. Print the values in the matrix with appropriate row and column headings.

11.6   The game of ten-pin bowling is divided into ten "frames". In each frame, the player has at most two chances to knock down all ten pins. The score in any frame is determined as follows.

name	# of balls thrown	pins knocked down	score
strike	1	10	10 + pins knocked down on next 2 throws
spare	2	10	10 + pins knocked down on next throw
open frame	2	<10	# of pins knocked down

Should a bowler get a spare or strike in the 10th frame he throws one or two additional balls respectively in order to obtain his score for the tenth frame. The largest number of balls a player can throw in one game is therefore 9*2+3=21.

Write a program which reads the number of pins knocked down on each throw and prints the frame-by-frame score. Use at least one non-trivial procedure in the program. Test your program on the following three cases.

```
 8  1  7  3  9  1  9  0  9  1 10 10  7  1  7  3  9  1  9
 9  1  9  0  8  2  8  2  7  2 10  6  0 10  9  0  9  0
10 10  7  2  9  1 10 10 10  7  0  8  2 10 10  4
```

11.7   Write a procedure called MERGE to "merge" two arrays of names. Each name is stored in a record containing a name field and an age field. (The array elements are records.) The number of records used in each array should be passed to the procedure. If the names of the two arrays are "S1" and "S2" and if they have M and N records respectively, the procedure should create a third array of M+N records made up of the union of the values in S1 and S2. The values in the merged array should also be in alphabetical order. For example, if the records in the first array contain Ann, Charlie, Ted and Zeke, and if those in the second contain Dave, Pat and Tom, then the merged records will contain Ann, Charlie, Dave, Pat, Ted, Tom and Zeke. The merging process can be done efficiently by processing elements in S1 and S2 in order and selecting the lower value of the two being considered as the next value to be put in the merged set. In the mainline, assume M and N are less than ten.

11.8   Use the procedure written to solve the previous problem to merge K sets of values. Assume K is five or less. This can be done by having the mainline: read the value of K; read the data for the first pair of arrays; merge them using the procedure; read the next array of values; merge it with the previous result; read the next array; etc. The input data should each contain the number of records in the array followed by the values. (The first input value contains the number of sets.)

11.9   If several forces are acting on a body at rest, they can be replaced by
a single equivalent force. Suppose each force is represented by a value
(x,y) where the magnitude of the force is given by the distance between
the origin and the point (x,y). The direction of the force is represented
by the angle between the x-axis and the ray thru the origin and the
point (x,y). Assume the body upon which the forces are acting is at the
origin. The resultant force is simply the sum of the force vectors. Write
a program which reads a value of N and then N pairs of REAL
numbers representing the magnitude and direction of the forces.
Calculate the resultant force and print its magnitude and direction.

11.10   At time zero, Fifi, the cat, is located at point (0,10) in the xy plane.
Fido, the dog, is at the origin. Fifi runs parallel to the x-axis at a rate
of 0.8 units per second. Fido runs at a rate of 1 unit per second with
his head down in the direction of Fifi. At the end of each second he
lifts his head up, sees where Fifi is, and runs in that direction during
the next second. How long, to the nearest second, does it take Fido to
catch Fifi? Print the positions of Fifi and Fido at one second intervals
during the chase.

11.11   A wooden equilateral triangle is used to hold balls on a pool table. If
the rack is positioned in the corner of the pool table as shown in the
following diagram, what is the distance X? Use any method you like to
solve the problem.

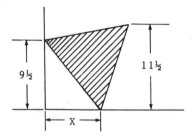

11.12   The angle between the line from the origin to the point (x,y) and the
x-axis can be calculated from the following formula.

$$\cos^{-1}\left(\frac{x}{\sqrt{x^2 + y^2}}\right)$$

Write a function called ANGLE to calculate this value. The procedure
will have only one parameter, an array containing the x-y coordinates.

11.13   The dot (scalar) product of two complex numbers u and v is denoted by u●v and has a value of |u| |v| cos(x) where x is the angle between the vectors. The cross product of u and v has a value of |u| |v| sin(x). Write a pair of functions called DOT and CROSS to compute these values. Each will have two x-y coordinates as parameters. Two vectors in the xy plane are perpendicular if, and only if, their dot product is zero. They are parallel if, and only if, their cross product is zero. Write a mainline which reads the end coordinates of an unspecified number of pairs of vectors and for each, prints one of "PARALLEL", "PERPENDICULAR", or "OBLIQUE". Use the procedures DOT and CROSS.

11.14   A man travels 24 miles northwest, 40 miles 35 degrees east of north and then 36 miles 20 degrees south of east. How far and in what direction is he from his starting point?

11.15   Write a function called MEDIAN which has three points A,B,C as its parameters where A,B and C represent the coordinates of the vertices of a triangle. The function value should be the length of the median from the vertex A to the side BC.

11.16   Suppose each student's answers to a true-false test of ten questions have been recorded on the input file, one line per student. On each line, positions one to six contain the student's ID number; positions seven to ten are blank and positions eleven thru twenty contain "T's" and "F's" indicating the student's answers. Assume twelve students took the test. Preceding the first student record is a line containing the correct answers. This answer line has an ID number of zeros and the correct answers in columns eleven thru twenty. Write a program which:

a) Lists each student's answers and calculates the percentage of
     right answers.

b) Calculates the average mark on the test.

c) Prints the percentage of right answers for each question.

d) Determines how many students answered both of questions 3
     and 7 correctly.

e) Determines those questions for which the students in the
     bottom half of the class did as well as students in the top
     half of the class.

The foregoing problem should be solved making the assumption that each student answered all questions. Suppose now that a blank in an answer column means that the student did not answer the question. Explain why this makes the programming problem more difficult. Can you solve the problem with this new assumption?

11.17   Input consists of 10 pairs of numbers representing the coordinates of 10 points. Store the coordinate of each point read in a record having three fields -- POINT.X, POINT.Y, POINT.LENGTH where LENGTH is the square root of x^2+y^2. After the data has been read, read a value for N and print the coordinates of the point having the Nth largest LENGTH value.

11.18   One method of storing a list of words in alphabetical sequence consists of prefixing each word with a number indicating how many characters from the previous word are used at the beginning of the current word. For example, to store the words APPLE, APPLICANT, APPLICATION, APPRAISE, BOX, BOXER, the following string would be used.

OAPPLE4ICANT7TION3RAISE0BOX3ER$

Assume that a dollar sign follows the last character of the last word. Problem: Create an appropriate string to store the following words: atom, atomic, backtracking, body, boundary condition, box model, call, catchall, character, circular definition. Write a program which prompts for a word or phrase as input and prints a line of the following form:

_____ IS (NOT) IN THE LIST

Assume that case is not significant. That is "Cat" and "cat" are the same. The program should terminate when a null (empty) string is entered. Test your program on at least the following words: boundary, boxmodel, a, characters, boxing, atom, catch.

CHAPTER 12: FILES

Questions Answered in this Chapter:

1. What are files? What is the difference between external and internal files? How are they defined and used in Pascal programs?

2. How can the READ and WRITE procedures be stated in terms of the basic procedures GET and PUT?

3. What is a file update? How can a file be sorted using a sequence of merges?

12.1 File Concepts

A file is a sequence of components of the same type. Unlike an array however, the number of components in a file is not specified when the file is defined. That is, the size of a file is open-ended. There is a price which must be paid to obtain this freedom. First, the only way to increase the size of the file is to add a component to the end of the file. Secondly, the components can only be processed (read or written) starting from the beginning and proceding sequentially. That is, you cannot read or write the tenth component, then the seventh, then the twenty-third or whatever. A third restriction is that one file cannot be made equal to another using an assignment statement.

In spite of these three significant limitations there is an advantage that files have over other data structures. They can exist independently of the program which creates or uses the data in the file. If these so-called external files did not exist, it would mean that the payroll data for a company would have to be defined as program constants or recreated using thousands of assignment statements each time the payroll was needed. Changes to payroll data could only be made by changing the payroll program - hardly a desirable situation. Consequently, files are kept on an external medium such as a reel of tape, a deck of cards, or a magnetic disk. The reasons are: it is cheaper; the data isn't lost when the program finishes execution; the size is not usually a limiting factor; and the program logic and data can be kept separate and independent.

The two external files used in almost every Pascal program are INPUT and OUTPUT. Each is a sequence of characters. (Each component of the file is a CHAR value.) To process the INPUT file, components are read one after the other, starting with the first. Similarly, values in the OUTPUT file are written character-by-character.

12.2 An Example

The problem is simple to state. Read an unspecified number of integer values and determine how many are equal to the last value read. When considering how to solve the problem, one quickly realizes that it is necessary to store all the values because no comparisons can be done until the final value has been read. Furthermore because the number of values is unspecified, a file is an appropriate vehicle for storing the values as they are read. The algorithm is shown below.

1. Read and place all values in a file
2. Save the last value read
3. For each value in the file
   .1 Read it and compare its value to last
   .2 If equal then add one to count
3. Print the result.

The program below translates this algorithm into Pascal. It illustrates most of the important features of files and shows how the standard procedures RESET and REWRITE are used.

```
PROGRAM EQUAL_LAST(INPUT,OUTPUT);

(* THIS PROGRAM DETERMINES HOW MANY NUMBERS IN A
   SEQUENCE OF INTEGER VALUES OBTAINED FROM THE
   INPUT FILE EQUAL THE LAST VALUE IN THE SEQUENCE *)

VAR
  NUMFILE      : FILE OF INTEGER;
  NEXT         : INTEGER; (* THE VALUE BEING PROCESSED *)
  LAST         : INTEGER; (* THE LAST VALUE IN THE INPUT *)
  COUNT        : INTEGER; (* HOW MANY EQUAL LAST *)

BEGIN (* EQUAL_LAST *)
  (* READ AND STORE VALUES IN A FILE *)
    REWRITE(NUMFILE); (* PREPARE THE OUTPUT FILE FOR WRITING *)
    WRITELN('ENTER VALUES ONE PER LINE, EMPTY LINE TO EXIT');
    WHILE NOT EOLN DO (* READ, ECHO AND WRITE *)
      BEGIN
        READLN(NEXT);
        WRITELN(NEXT);
        WRITE(NUMFILE, NEXT) (* APPEND TO NUMFILE *)
      END;
```

... (continued on the next page)

```
    (* PREPARE TO READ AND COMPARE *)
        LAST := NEXT; (* REMEMBER LAST VALUE *)
        COUNT := 0;
        RESET(NUMFILE); (* READY FILE FOR READING *)
    (* READ AND COMPARE *)
        WHILE NOT EOF(NUMFILE) DO
          BEGIN
            READ(NUMFILE, NEXT);
            IF NEXT = LAST THEN
              COUNT := COUNT + 1
          END;
        WRITELN((COUNT - 1):3,' OTHER VALUES EQUAL THE LAST VALUE')
    END. (* EQUAL_LAST *)
```

The program declares NUMFILE as a FILE having INTEGER components.
If more than one identifier has the type FILE OF INTEGER or if the file is
being passed to a procedure or function, a file type should be declared as
shown below.

```
    TYPE
        INTEGER_FILE = FILE OF INTEGER
```

A file declaration has the form

```
    FILE of component-type
```

where the component-type may be anything except another file type. (You
can't have a file of files.) Files are also not permitted as components of arrays,
records and sets (Sets are described in Chapter 13.) There are two further
restrictions. First, a file passed to a procedure or function must be a VAR
parameter. Second, a file cannot be assigned to another file using an
assignment statement.

Once a file has been declared, it may be used for either input or output
but not both simultaneously. In the example, the first step consists of reading
values from the INPUT file and writing (appending) them to NUMFILE.
Before a file can be used for output, the standard procedure REWRITE must
be invoked. It has the general form

```
    REWRITE (filename)
```

Execution of REWRITE means the next value written to the file will be the
first component of the file. Any components already in the file are erased
when a REWRITE is executed.

To append a component to the file, the WRITE procedure is used. Because the data is not being stored on the standard OUTPUT file, the first argument of the WRITE procedure must specify the name of the file. In the example, the statement used is

    WRITE (NUMFILE, NEXT)

After all the values have been written on NUMFILE, the components must be read. The RESET procedure is used to ready a file so that READ will obtain the first component. It has the general form

    RESET (filename)

Once a file has been reset, components can be read using a READ invocation of the form below

    READ (filename, param1, param2, ..., paramN)

The parameters denote the entities to receive the values of the next N components in the file. Note that if there are no components, EOF is set equal to TRUE. Unlike values of the type TEXT however, components are not partitioned into lines. Hence EOLN cannot be used.

12.3 File Buffers, GET and PUT

The purpose of this section is to describe the two-step nature of READ and WRITE operations. The concept of a file buffer is explained and use of the standard GET and PUT procedures is illustrated.

12.3.1 The File Buffer

For any file including the standard files INPUT and OUTPUT, an area of memory is automatically set aside to store the value of a single component. This area is called the *file buffer*. A file buffer is a variable with a type which is the same as that of the components of the file. Thus both the INPUT file buffer and the OUTPUT file buffer have the type CHAR, These buffers can be used like any other variables of the component type once we know how to refer to them.

The name of the buffer consists of appending the symbol '↑' to the file name. Because most keyboards do not have an up arrow symbol, the at sign '@' is used. For example, the INPUT buffer is INPUT@; the OUTPUT buffer is OUTPUT@, and the buffer for NUMFILE used in the previous example is NUMFILE@. In Chapter 14 we will see that the '@' has uses other than specifying file buffers.

12.3.2 Input Buffers and GET

Suppose data required by a program is stored in a file. To transfer a value from the file to a variable involves two steps. The first is to transfer the value from the device to the file buffer. This operation is called a "get". The second is to assign this buffer value to the target variable.

Keyboard Input. When you type a line of input at the keyboard, the first character typed i Keyboard Input. When you type a line of input at the keyboard, the first character typed is put in the keyboard file buffer. Each time you READ a character, the buffer value is assigned to the target variable and the next character in the line is then placed in the buffer. That is the buffer always contains the next character to be read. If the buffer contains the end-of-line character, EOLN has a value of TRUE.

Non-keyboard Input. In the case of non-keyboard input, the first component of the file is placed in the buffer *when a RESET is executed.* From then on the process is similar to keyboard input in that each READ causes the buffer contents to be assigned to the READ parameter following which the next component of the file is placed in the buffer. If there are no components to put in the buffer, EOF has a value of TRUE.

You can explicitly transfer the next component of a file to an input buffer using the standard procedure GET. It has only one parameter -- the file name. For example

```
GET (INPUT)
```

causes the next character in the INPUT file to be assigned to INPUT@. EOLN is set to TRUE if this character is the end-of-line character.

In summary, the procedure invocation

```
READ (filename, x)
```

does two things. First it assigns the contents of the file buffer to the READ parameter. Second, it executes a GET. Hence the following are equivalent.

```
READ(INPUT,X)        and      { X := INPUT@;
                              { GET(INPUT)
```

You can use an assignment and a GET to replace any operation that uses a READ. For example, to skip all characters in the input file up to the next end-of-line character either of the following WHILE loops can be used.

```
WHILE NOT EOLN(INPUT) DO      WHILE NOT EOLN(INPUT)DO
    GET(INPUT)                    READ(INPUT,X)
```

The only difference is that the READ approach executes an assignment of INPUT@ to X prior to each GET. Both loops end with an end-of-line character in the buffer INPUT@. Note that the READLN procedure (usable only with TEXT files) is not equivalent to either of these loops because at the termination of READLN the buffer contains the first character in the next line of input rather than the end-of-line character. That is READLN executes a GET after EOLN is true.

12.3.3 Output Buffers and PUT

The predefined procedure PUT appends the contents of the file buffer to the end of the file. The file name is the PUT parameter. An example is

```
PUT (OUTPUT)
```

What does the WRITE procedure do? WRITE performs both an assignment and a PUT as shown below.

```
WRITE(OUTPUT, x) is equivalent to    OUTPUT@ := X;
                                     PUT(OUTPUT)
```

If you wish you can use buffer assignments and PUTs instead of WRITEs. For example, to write sixty asterisks on the OUTPUT file the statements below can be used.

```
OUTPUT@ := '*';
FOR I := 1 to 60 DO
   PUT (OUTPUT)
```

If output characters are directed to a display screen rather than a printer, there are some automatic enhancements which make it easier to view the output. The following kinds of things are typically done.

- a pause occurs after each screenful of data has been sent to allow you time to read it before continuing

- long lines which exceed the width of the screen are "folded" at the screen boundary. The characters which would be truncated appear on the line below.

- page numbers and headings are removed from the output.

The use of GET and PUT provide a degree of control over input-output operations not available using READ and WRITE. In general however, the use of READ and WRITE is recommended because they are "higher level" and thus reduce the opportunity to make mistakes. In addition when used with TEXT files, READ includes the logic necessary to assemble characters to form a number whereas GET (INPUT) only gets the next character. Similarly on output WRITE creates the appropriate sequences of characters to represent numbers, BOOLEAN values and strings. PUT, on the other hand, can only transfer a single character to a TEXT file.

12.4 Internal and External Files

An external file is one whose components are stored on a storage device other than the memory occupied by the program while it is executing. Examples of external files are a payroll file residing on a reel of tape, a set of experimental results recorded on punched cards or a file of printed output. Some versions of Pascal require that all files be external files. The standard files INPUT and OUTPUT are two external files which are automatically available to the Pascal programmer.

When an external file is used, two things must be done. First, the file name must appear in the PROGRAM header. Second, the compiler must be told where an input file is physically located or where the data in an output file is to be stored. A program header has the following general form:

        PROGRAM name (names of external files)

For example, if a payroll program contains declarations for the external files OLD_PAYROLL and NEW_PAYROLL and uses the standard files INPUT and OUTPUT, the program header, relevant declarations and RESET and REWRITE invocations appear as shown below.

```
PROGRAM PAYROLL(INPUT, OUTPUT, OLD_PAYROLL, NEW_PAYROLL);
TYPE
  PAY_REC = RECORD
                NAME       : PACKED ARRAY[1..20] OF CHAR;
                WAGE_RATE  : REAL;
                REG_HOURS  : REAL;
                OVERTIME   : REAL
            END;
  PAY_FILE = FILE OF PAY_REC;
VAR
  OLD_PAYROLL, NEW_PAYROLL : PAY_FILE;
BEGIN (* PAYROLL *)
    .
  RESET(OLD_PAYROLL);
  REWRITE(NEW_PAYROLL);
    .
END. (* PAYROLL *)
```

The second requirement -- that of linking the file name with the specific external device containing the file -- depends on the Pascal compiler used. Some compilers require the information to be placed in job-control statements which precede the PROGRAM statement; others use a second argument in the RESET and REWRITE procedures to specify this information; others use an ASSIGN or OPEN procedure. An example is the following

```
RESET (OLD_PAYROLL, 'OLDPAY TAPEIN')
```

You should read the reference material describing your compiler to find out how to associate a file identifier with an external file of data. The information relevant to Waterloo Pascal is described in section 2.2 of Appendix C.

12.5 TEXT Files : A Summary

TEXT is one of the five standard types in Pascal (the others being INTEGER, REAL, CHAR and BOOLEAN). Although discussed in some detail in Chapter 5 the explanations which appear there simply alluded to the nature of files. Variables may have the type TEXT. This is *not* equivalent to declaring them as a FILE OF CHAR A TEXT file has some unique characteristics which are: Specifically these are:

- A TEXT file can be partitioned into lines using end-of-line characters.

- The function EOLN is set equal to true if a TEXT file buffer contains the end-of-line character.

- For an input TEXT file the READ procedure permits parameters of the types INTEGER and REAL as well as CHAR to be used as parameters. Character sequences in the input file representing these kinds of values are assembled to form the values.

- When READLN is used, then following the assignment of values to parameters, the TEXT file buffer contains the first character following the next end-of-line character.

- For an output file of type TEXT, arguments may have the types INTEGER, REAL, BOOLEAN and PACKED ARRAY [1..N] OF CHAR as well as CHAR. For numeric and Boolean values, the WRITE procedure generates the characters necessary to represent each value. WRITELN appends an end-of-line character to the TEXT file after the parameter values have been written.

- The PAGE procedure can be used with a TEXT file directed to a printer. It causes a skip to the top of the next page.

- The standard files INPUT and OUTPUT have the type TEXT. REWRITE(OUTPUT) is automatically performed prior to the first WRITE or PUT and RESET(INPUT) is automatically performed prior to the first READ or GET.

Knowing how Pascal files are processed and the special considerations which apply to TEXT files, the reader is advised to re-read Section 4 in Chapter 5. The rules for what-happens-when during input and output operations are stated there using explanations which appeal intuitively. However, INPUT and OUTPUT are files just like other Pascal files. The explanations given previously can be better understood using the knowledge gained from this chapter.

12.6 Exercise 12.1

1. What is the error in each of the following?

   a) VAR X = FILE OF REAL
   b) VAR Y : FILE OF TEXT   (dec as type)
   c) PROCEDURE OOPS(VAR ZFILE :FILE OF BOOLEAN)
   d) TYPE
           SALES_FILE = FILE OF SALES_REC;
           SALES_REC = RECORD
                           PART_NUM: INTEGER;
                           QUANTITY: INTEGER
                       END
   e) VAR A, B : FILE OF INTEGER;
        BEGIN A := B END.

2. If A has the type FILE OF CHAR and B has the type TEXT, are A and B assignment compatible?

3. What are the errors in each of the following? For each assume the following declarations have been made.

        PROGRAM EX12 (AFILE, BFILE);

        VAR
           AFILE, BFILE : FILE OF REAL;
           A, B : REAL

```
a)   BEGIN
        GET (AFILE,A);
        B := A;
        PUT (BFILE,B)
     END


b)   BEGIN
        REWRITE (AFILE);
        FOR I := 1 TO 10 DO
           GET (AFILE)
     END


c)   BEGIN
        RESET (AFILE);
        WHILE NOT EOLN(AFILE)DO
           GET(AFILE)
     END
```

4. Suppose the file NUMFILE declared as FILE OF REAL has been previously created and exists on an external storage device. The input to the program consists of NUMFILE and several integer values in the INPUT file not necessarily in increasing order. The object is to write a program which will read each value N in the INPUT file and print the value of the Nth component in NUMFILE. Use GETs instead of READs in your program. (You will have to RESET the file more than once.)

5. Suppose you are reading a file and are somewhere in the middle. You decide at that time, one or more components must be added to the file. Develop a procedure for doing this.

6. Write a FUNCTION to count the number of lines in the INPUT file.

7. Write a PROCEDURE to put N blank lines in the OUTPUT file. Use PUT and not WRITE or WRITELN.

12.7 File Updates

Every organization that uses a computer to perform record keeping functions maintains one or more files of data. In a typical business there is a personnel file, an accounts receivable file, an accounts payable file, an inventory file and general ledger files. The process of keeping the data in a file up-to-date is called updating the file.

The inputs to the simplest kind of program that performs a file update consist of the file which needs updating (called the *master file*) and a file of changes to be made to the master file (called the *transaction file*). The file update program produces two outputs: a new, updated master file and a report of the changes made. The inputs and outputs are often shown in a diagram called a system flowchart. An example appears below.

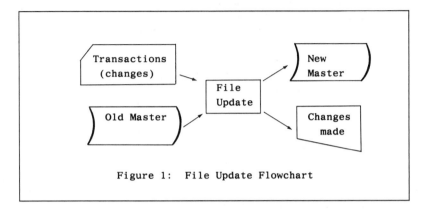

Figure 1:   File Update Flowchart

There are three kinds of transactions -- additions, changes, and deletions. An addition specifies that a new master record is to be inserted in the file. A change transaction specifies a change to be made to a value in an existing master file record. A deletion transaction causes a master file record to be removed from the file.

How do transactions indicate which master file record is to be affected? The usual and best method is to associate a unique identifier or *key* with each record (component) in the master file. Then by putting the key of the master file record affected in each transaction, it is relatively straightforward to match transactions and master file records.

One more idea is needed before proceding to an update algorithm and example. If the transactions are not ordered by key values, we would need the ability to read the master file record having a particular key. For example, if the key of the first transaction was 37, we would have to find the record having that key in order to make the changes. The next transaction might contain a key of 15, the next 249 etc. Consequently, a great deal of time could be spent searching for the master file record which matches a given transaction key.

Fortunately, there is a better way. It consists of ordering the records in the transaction file and those in the master file by increasing key values prior to performing the file update. By sorting the two input files, each record in the file only needs to be read once.

Shown below is the mainline logic for a file update for which it is assumed there are only changes and deletions in the transaction file. (The logic to allow for the creation of new master records is left as an exercise to the reader).

1. Open (reset) the Transaction file and Old Master file
2. Open (rewrite) the New Master file
3. While not at the end of the Transaction file
 .1 Read the next Transaction record
 .2 Read the next Old Master record
 .3 If the Old Master-key less than the Transaction-key
  Repeat
   .1 New Master record = Old Master record
   .2 Write New Master record
   .3 Read Old Master record
  Until Old Master-key = Transaction-key
 .4 If the transaction is a change then
  .1 New Master record = Old Master record + changes
  .2 Write New Master record
  .3 Report changes made
 .5 If the Transaction is a deletion then
  .1 Report deletion
4. While not end of Old Master file do
 .1 Read Old Master record
 .2 New Master record = Old Master record
 .3 Write New Master record
5. Stop

Step 4 in the algorithm copies all records in the old master file having keys higher than the highest key in the transaction file to the new master file.

The algorithm does not include logic to: a) create new master file records; b) process more than one change to the same master record; c) process the error condition of a transaction record having a key which does not match a master record key. (What does it do in this case?) Nonetheless it does contain the basic logic of a sequential file update which is now illustrated using a concrete example.

12.7.1 An Example File Update

Suppose the master file contains one record for each person in a company. Assume each record has five fields and is declared as follows.

```
MASTER_REC = RECORD
                ID_NUM     : INTEGER; (* THE RECORD KEY *)
                NAME       : PACKED ARRAY[1..20] OF CHAR;
                WAGE_RATE  : REAL;
                HOURS      : REAL;
                PAY        : REAL
              END; (* MASTER_REC *)
```

The employee's identification number (ID_NUM) is used as the record key. Assume that a transaction record has the following type:

```
TRANS_REC = RECORD
                ID_NUM     : INTEGER; (* KEY *)
                TRANS_CODE : CHAR; (* 'C'=CHANGE, 'D'=DELETE *)
                HOURS      : REAL (* USED IN CHANGE RECORD *)
              END; (* TRANS_REC *)
```

If you have studied the section on variant records in Chapter 11, you will realize the transaction record could be defined as a variant record using TRANS_CODE as the tag field.

Before the old master file can be updated, it must first be created. Shown below is a program to create a master file of ten PERSON_REC records. Data defining the master records is obtained from the INPUT file and written on the OLDMASTER file.

```
PROGRAM CREATE_OLDMASTER(INPUT,OUTPUT,OLDMASTER);

(* THIS PROGRAM CREATES A MASTER FILE OF TEN RECORDS
   FROM DATA IN THE INPUT FILE                      *)

CONST
  NAME_LENGTH = 20;
TYPE
  MASTER_REC = RECORD
                  ID_NUM     : INTEGER; (* THE RECORD KEY *)
                  NAME       : PACKED ARRAY[1..20] OF CHAR;
                  WAGE_RATE  : REAL;
                  HOURS      : REAL;
                  PAY        : REAL
                END; (* MASTER_REC *)
  MASTER_FILE = FILE OF MASTER_REC;
VAR
  OLDMASTER : MASTER_FILE;
  WORK_REC  : MASTER_REC;
  I         : INTEGER;
```

... (continued on the next page)

```
PROCEDURE PRINT_MASTERS( VAR MASTERS : MASTER_FILE);
  BEGIN (* PRINT_MASTERS *)
    WRITELN('    MASTER RECORD DATA');
    WHILE NOT EOF(MASTERS) DO
      BEGIN
        WRITELN(MASTERS@.ID_NUM:4, ' ', MASTERS@.NAME:20,
                MASTERS@.WAGE_RATE:6:2, MASTERS@.HOURS:5:1,
                MASTERS@.PAY:6:2);
        GET(MASTERS)
      END (* WHILE *)
  END; (* PRINT_MASTERS *)

BEGIN (* CREATE_OLDMASTER *)
  REWRITE(OLDMASTER,'OLDMAST DATA');
  WITH WORK_REC DO
    BEGIN
      WHILE NOT EOF(INPUT) DO
        BEGIN
          READ(ID_NUM);
          FOR I := 1 TO NAME_LENGTH DO
            READ(NAME[I]);
          READLN(WAGE_RATE, HOURS, PAY);
          WRITE(OLDMASTER,WORK_REC)
        END (* WHILE *)
    END; (* WITH WORK_REC *)
  RESET(OLDMASTER, 'OLDMAST DATA');
  PRINT_MASTERS(OLDMASTER)
END. (* CREATE_OLDMASTER *)
```

Comments

1. The file of master records is called OLDMASTER. Because it is an external file, it appears along with INPUT and OUTPUT in the program header.

2. The mainline opens the OLDMASTER file using the procedure invocation

    ```
    REWRITE (OLDMASTER, 'OLDMAST DATA')
    ```

    The second parameter is used by the Waterloo Pascal compiler as the symbolic name of the device on which the data is physically stored. Other compilers may use a different method.

3. In the PRINT_MASTERS procedure, note that the formal parameter is a
    VAR parameter. This illustrates the rule that files can only be passed as
    VAR parameters; and further that parameter types must be specified by
    an identifier. For example "MASTERS : FILE OF MASTER_REC" is
    invalid.

4. Why is the GET the last step in the WHILE loop rather than the first?
    Recall that for non-keyboard files a RESET automatically GETs the first
    component of a file. Hence, the first record is already in the buffer when
    the WHILE-loop is entered. Compare this with the placement of the
    READ in the mainline WHILE-loop. Remember that a READ simply
    assigns the buffer contents to a variable and then does a GET. A more
    important reason for using READs in the mainline however, is to use the
    built-in logic for assembling INPUT characters to form numbers.

Suppose the master file records produced by the CREATE_MASTERS
program contain the data shown below.

```
171Jay Moore            9.50   0.0   0.0
294George Graham        4.75   0.0   0.0
295Al Barnhill          4.75   0.0   0.0
302Bill Lawson         50.00   0.0   0.0
417Gloria Smith         4.75   0.0   0.0
484Barb Gilleland       6.80   0.0   0.0
499Pat Griggs           9.50   0.0   0.0
500Fiona Davidson       9.50   0.0   0.0
603Don Stewart         25.00   0.0   0.0
758John Bassett        12.50   0.0   0.0
```

Further, suppose that five transactions containing the data below have
been recorded in a file called TRANS using a program similar to the
CREATE_MASTER program above.

ID_NUM	TRANS_CODE	HOURS
171	C	40.0
294	C	42.0
302	D	
499	C	61.5
500	D	

Once the master file and transaction file have been created, the update
program should read the two files and for each employee in the transaction
file, update the HOURS_WORKED filed in the master record and calculate
the amount of pay. Records of employees for which there are no transactions
are simply copied to the new master file.

The program to update the OLDMASTER file with the transactions in TRANS file will have the following program header and declarations.

```
PROGRAM UPDATE(INPUT,OUTPUT,OLDMASTER,NEWMASTER,TRANS);

(* THIS PROGRAM UPDATES THE OLDMASTER FILE WITH THE
   CHANGES AND DELETIONS SPECIFIED IN THE TRANS FILE.
   THE UPDATED FILE IS CALLED NEWMASTER               *)

CONST
  CHANGE = 'C';
  DELETE = 'D';

TYPE
  MASTER_REC = RECORD
                 ID_NUM    : INTEGER; (* THE RECORD KEY *)
                 NAME      : PACKED ARRAY[1..20] OF CHAR;
                 WAGE_RATE : REAL;
                 HOURS     : REAL;
                 PAY       : REAL
               END; (* MASTER_REC *)

  TRANS_REC = RECORD
                ID_NUM     : INTEGER; (* KEY *)
                TRANS_CODE : CHAR; (* 'C' = CHANGE, 'D' = DELETE *)
                HOURS      : REAL (* USED IN CHANGE RECORD ONLY *)
              END; (* TRANS_REC *)
  MASTER_FILE = FILE OF MASTER_REC;

VAR
  OLDMASTER, NEWMASTER : MASTER_FILE;
  TRANS                : FILE OF TRANS_REC;
  WORK_REC             : MASTER_REC;

PROCEDURE PRINT_MASTERS( VAR MASTERS : MASTER_FILE);

  (* THIS PROCEDURE PRINTS THE CONTENTS OF A MASTER FILE *)

  BEGIN (* PRINT_MASTERS *)
    WRITELN('    MASTER RECORD DATA');
    WHILE NOT EOF(MASTERS) DO
      BEGIN
        WRITELN(MASTERS@.ID_NUM:4, ' ', MASTERS@.NAME:20,
                MASTERS@.WAGE_RATE:6:2, MASTERS@.HOURS:5:1,
                MASTERS@.PAY:7:2);
        GET(MASTERS)
      END (* WHILE *)
  END; (* PRINT_MASTERS *)
```

The body of the UPDATE program is shown below. GET and PUT are used to perform input-output operations. READs and WRITEs could be used instead.

```
BEGIN (* UPDATE *)
  (* 1 - OPEN FILES *)
      RESET(OLDMASTER, 'OLDMAST DATA');
      RESET(TRANS, 'TRANS DATA');
      REWRITE(NEWMASTER, 'NEWMAST DATA');
  (* 2 - MAIN PROCESSING LOOP *)
      WHILE NOT EOF(TRANS) DO
        BEGIN
          IF OLDMASTER@.ID_NUM < TRANS@.ID_NUM THEN
            REPEAT
              NEWMASTER@ := OLDMASTER@;
              WRITELN(NEWMASTER@.ID_NUM:4,' COPIED');
              PUT(NEWMASTER);
              GET(OLDMASTER)
            UNTIL OLDMASTER@.ID_NUM = TRANS@.ID_NUM;
          IF TRANS@.TRANS_CODE = CHANGE THEN
            BEGIN
              NEWMASTER@ := OLDMASTER@;
              NEWMASTER@.HOURS := TRANS@.HOURS;
              NEWMASTER@.PAY := NEWMASTER@.HOURS *
                                    NEWMASTER@.WAGE_RATE;
              PUT(NEWMASTER);
              WRITELN(OLDMASTER@.ID_NUM:4,' CHANGED')
            END (* CHANGE *)
          ELSE (* DELETE *)
            WRITELN(OLDMASTER@.ID_NUM:4,' DELETED');
          GET(OLDMASTER);
          GET(TRANS)
        END; (* WHILE *)
  (* 3 - COPY ANY REMAINING OLDMASTERS TO NEWMASTER *)
      WHILE NOT EOF(OLDMASTER) DO
        BEGIN
          NEWMASTER@ := OLDMASTER@;
          WRITELN(NEWMASTER@.ID_NUM:4,' COPIED');
          PUT(NEWMASTER);
          GET(OLDMASTER)
        END; (* WHILE *)
  (* 4 - PRINT NEW MASTER FILE *)
      RESET(NEWMASTER,'NEWMAST DATA');
      PRINT_MASTERS(NEWMASTER)
END. (* UPDATE *)
```

used with the old master and transaction data shown previously, the
out appears as shown below.

```
on begins...
    ANGED
    ANGED
    ᴜᴜᴜ COPIED
302 DELETED
417 COPIED
484 COPIED
499 CHANGED
500 DELETED
603 COPIED
758 COPIED
    MASTER RECORD DATA
171 Jay Moore              9.50 40.0 380.00
294 George Graham          4.75 42.0 199.50
295 Al Barnhill            4.75  0.0   0.00
417 Gloria Smith           4.75  0.0   0.00
484 Barb Gilleland         6.80  0.0   0.00
499 Pat Griggs             9.50 61.5 584.25
603 Don Stewart           25.00  0.0   0.00
758 John Bassett          12.50  0.0   0.00

...execution ends
```

12.8 Sorting Using File Merges

The purpose of this section is to describe what is meant by a file merge
and to show how file merges are used in arranging a set of values into either
ascending or descending sequence.

12.8.1 Merging Files

A file merge is a simple form of file update. Starting with two files having
components which are already in sequence according to the value of some key,
a new output file is produced by merging the components of the two input
files so that the resulting file has all components in sequence. For example, if
the input files contain the component keys below

File A : 9 12 13 22 37

File B : 4 5 10 25

Then the output file would contain components with the following keys:

4   5   9   10   12   13   22   25   37

An arbitrary rule can be used to break ties. The example illustrates a *two-way merge*. In general, there can be N input files which are merged to form a single output file. This is called an N-way merge.

The algorithm below can be used to perform a two-way merge. The input files are called File A and File B; the ouput file is File C. Assume that READ_FILE is a procedure which, when the end-of-file is encountered, assigns the value of 9999 to the variable Low Key. 9999 is assumed to be higher than any key in the file.

Merge Algorithm

1. Initialize
    .1 Open File A, File B, File C
    .2 READ_FILE (A)
    .3 READ_FILE (B)
    .4 Compute Low Key (See note below)
2. While Low Key $\neq$ 9999 do
    .1 if A-key = Low key then
            .1 write File A record on File C
            .2 READ_FILE (A)
        else
            .1 write File B record on File C
            .2 READ_FILE (B)
    .2 Compute Low Key
3. Stop

12.8.2 Sorting Using A Sequence of Merges

This section describes how a two-way merge can be used to sort a file. Suppose that each component in a file is a record and that each record has a key field. Assume that the values of the keys are randomly ordered. The goal is to create a new file in which the keys of the records are in order of increasing value. There are many algorithms for sorting a set of values -- some efficient, some inefficient. A simple but relatively inefficient technique called the exchange sort is described and programmed in Chapter 10. Many methods rely on the ability to have the entire set of records in memory at the same time. This allows the records, or the keys at least, to be stored in an array, thus giving direct access to any record or key. If the number of items to be sorted is too large to be kept in memory, the following procedure is often used. It is called a *sort-merge*.

1.   Create sorted sequences of records and write these sequences alternately on Files A and B.

... (continued on the next page)

2. Merge sequences from A and B to form longer sequences alternately writing them on Files C and D.

3. Merge pairs of sequences from C and D writing them alternately on Files A and B.

4. Repeat steps 2 and 3 until a single output sequence is obtained. The file is then sorted.

How should the sorted sequences referred to in step 1 be created? The simplest approach is to use whatever sequences happen to be found in the input data! For example, suppose the INPUT file contains the following twenty integers. An asterisk separates the naturally found sequences of sorted values. (Each sequence terminates when the next value decreases.)

68●53●26 83●22 76●15●11●0 70●22 95●54 66●47●29 73●7 23 72●

In this collection of values there are five runs (sequences) of length one, six runs of length two and one run of length three. The objective is to create one run of length twenty.

The results of applying the algorithm to the data is shown below.

After Step 1: (Distribute Input To Files A and B)

    A: 68 ● 26 83 ● 15 ● 0 70 ● 54 66 ● 29 73
    B: 53 ● 22 76 ● 11 ● 22 95 ● 47 ● 7 23 72

After Step 2: (Merge A and B to form C and D)

    C: 53 68 ● 11 15 ● 47 54 66
    D: 22 26 76 83 ● 0 22 70 95 ● 7 23 29 72 73

After Step 3: (Merge C and D to form A and B)

    A: 22 26 53 68 ● 0 22 47 54 66 70 95
    B: 11 15 76 83 ● 7 23 29 72 73

After Step 2: (Merge A and B to form C and D)

    C: 11 15 22 26 53 68 76 83
    D: 0 7 22 23 29 47 54 66 70 72 73 95

After Step 3: (Merge C and D to form A and B)

    A: 0 7 11 15 22 22 23 26 29 47 53 54 66 68 70 72 73 76 83 95
    B: empty

Shown below is a program to perform the sort merge. The headers for the procedures DISTRIBUTE and MERGE appear on the following page.

```
PROGRAM SORT_MERGE(INPUT,OUTPUT,FILEA,FILEB,FILEC,FILED);

(* THIS PROGRAM SORTS A FILE OF INTEGER VALUES OBTAINED FROM
   THE INPUT FILE. A SERIES OF 2-WAY MERGES IS USED AFTER
   DISTRIBUTING THE RUNS FOUND IN THE INPUT TO FILES A AND B *)

TYPE
  INT_FILE = FILE OF INTEGER;
VAR
  RUN_COUNT : INTEGER; (* NUMBER OF SEQUENCES WRITTEN *)
  FILEA, FILEB, FILEC FILED : INT_FILE;
  ABINPUT : BOOLEAN; (* TRUE IF FILES A ND B HAVE THE INPUT *)

  (* procedures DISTRIBUTE and MERGE go here *)

BEGIN (* SORT_MERGE *)
  DISTRIBUTE (FILEA, FILEB, RUN_COUNT);
  ABINPUT := TRUE;
  WHILE RUN_COUNT > 1 DO
    IF ABINPUT THEN
      BEGIN
        MERGE((* FROM *) FILEA, FILE B, (* TO *) FILEC, FILED,
              RUN_COUNT);
        ABINPUT := FALSE
      END
    ELSE
      BEGIN
        MERGE((* FROM *), FILEC, FILED, (* TO *) FILEA, FILEB,
              RUN_COUNT);
        ABINPUT := TRUE
      END; (* WHILE *)
  IF ABINPUT THEN
    WRITELN('THE SORTED VALUES ARE IN FILE A')
  ELSE
    WRITELN('THE SORTED VALUES ARE IN FILE C')
END. (* SORT_MERGE *)
```

The headers for DISTRUTE and MERGE are shown below.

```
PROCEDURE DISTRIBUTE(VAR FILE1, FILE2 : INT_FILE;
                     VAR RUN_COUNT    : INTEGER);

   (* THIS PROCEDURE READS INTEGERS FROM THE INPUT FILE
      AND WRITES THE SEQUENCES OF INCREASING VALUES FOUND
      ALTERNATELY ON FILES 1 AND 2. RUN_COUNT IS SET
      EQUAL TO THE NUMBER OF RUNS WRITTEN                  *)

PROCEDURE MERGE(VAR FILE1, FILE2, FILE3, FILE4 : INT_FILE;
                VAR RUN_COUNT                  : INTEGER);

   (* THIS PROCEDURE READS RUNS OF INTEGER VALUES FOUND IN
      FILES 1 AND 2 AND WRITES THE MERGED SEQUENCES ON
      FILES 3 AND 4. RUN_COUNT EQUALS THE NUMBER OF RUNS
      CREATED                                             *)
```

A slight variation of the program logic for performing a sort-merge allows only three files to be used. Following the creation of Files A and B containing runs of values, the pairs of runs are merged but each merged sequence is written on File C. File C can then be viewed as a file to be sorted and processed in the same way as the original input. That is, the runs on C are distributed alternately between A and B. Files A and B are again merged to form a new C. File C is redistributed until File C contains only a single run. The basic algorithm is shown below.

```
1. Copy input data onto file C
2. Repeat
   .1 Distribute data on C to files A and B
   .2 Merge A and B to form a new C
   Until number of runs on C = 1
```

The algorithm has the advantages that it uses one less file and that the final output is always found on File C. It is less efficient than the four-file merge because a distribute step precedes each merge.

When sorting very large files, it is wise to increase the number of files used to six (three in, three out), eight (four in, four out) or more during each merge. This is because for N input files, the length of each output sequence is on the average N times the length of the average input sequence. For example, if there were a quarter of a million runs after the first distribution, it would take eighteen merges using a two-way merge because $2^{18} > 250,000$; twelve merges using a three-way merge ($3^{12} > 250,000$); and only seven merges using a six-way merge ($6^7 > 250,000$).

12.9 Exercise 12.2

1. Consider the program fragments below. Assume INPUT is a non-keyboard
    file.

```
GET (INPUT);                      READ(INPUT,X);
WHILE NOT EOF DO                  WHILE NOT EOF DO
  BEGIN                             BEGIN
    WRITELN(INPUT);                   WRITELN(X);
    GET(INPUT)                        READ(INPUT,X)
  END                               END
```

   a) Why do they produce different results?

   b) If the INPUT file contains 'ABCD', what output is produced in each
       case?

   c) Change the GET fragment to produce the same output as the READ
       fragment.

   d) Change the READ fragment to produce the same output as the GET
       fragment.

2. Complete the programming of the SORT_MERGE program and test it
    using the example data shown.

12.10 Summary

1. A file is an open-ended sequence of components of the same type. At any
    point in time a file is either available for input operations or output
    operations but not both.

2. A file type is declared using the construct

    ```
    FILE OF component-type
    ```

    Associated with each file is a file buffer designated by appending the '@'
    character to the file name. A file buffer is an area of memory used for
    storing the value of a single component.

3. A file is either internal or external. An internal file is created by the
    program and exists only while the program is executing. An external file
    exists independently of the program. Names of external files must appear
    in the program header. Different computers have different requirements
    for linking the name of the file with the external medium on which the
    data is recorded.

4. To use a file as a source of input data the RESET procedure must be

executed. For non-keyboard files RESET causes the first component of the file to be transferred to the file buffer. GET places the next component of any input file in the file buffer. The following are equivalent.

```
READ (filename, X)                    X : = filename@;
                                       GET (filename)
```

5. To use a file for storing data the REWRITE procedure must be executed. It erases all existing components of the file. The PUT procedure appends the contents of the file buffer to the end of the file. The following are equivalent

```
WRITE (filename, X)                    filename@ := X;
                                       PUT (filename)
```

6. TEXT is a predefined type meaning FILE OF CHAR. The standard files INPUT and OUTPUT have the type TEXT. It is not necessary to RESET the INPUT file or REWRITE the OUTPUT file before they are used. When READ and WRITE are used with a TEXT file, conversion of CHAR values to numbers (when READ is used) and conversion of numbers, BOOLEAN and string values to CHAR values (when WRITE is used) is performed automatically.

7. A file update is one of the most common of all kinds of computer programs. It involves a file containing data to be changed (the master file), a file of changes (the transaction file) and an updated file (the new master file).

8. Given two ordered sequences of values, a merge of the sequences produces a single sequence containing all the values in order. Merging is used extensively when sorting large files.

12.11 Programming Problems

12.1   Write a program which reads a set of twenty INTEGER values; sorts them into increasing order of magnitude; and writes them in four groups of five values each on a file. Repeat this process for a second set of values and write the output on a different file. Using these two sets of values as input, perform a merge of the two files of values to produce one string of forty non-decreasing values. Write the merged values on a third file in records of four values per record. Print the values in the original sets and in the merged set.

12.2   Prepare a file of twenty-five records each of which has the following
         information. Assume the marks are integer values.

```
         positions            item

            1-5        student number
             6         year of studies (1,2,3 or 4)
            7-9        mark in course 1
           10-12       mark in course 2
           13-15       mark in course 3
           16-18       mark in course 4
           19-21       mark in course 5
```

   a) Arrange the lines in order of increasing student number and write
      them on a file -- one record per student. Call this the student
      master file.
   b) Read the student master file and: (i) print the student number, marks,
      and average of each student. (ii) While reading the data from the
      file, accumulate statistics required to print the report shown
      below. Print the report at the end of the run. One page should be
      printed for each year. Assume a pass requires a 60 percent
      average.

                            PASS/FAIL REPORT

	YEAR OF STUDIES				
	1	2	3	4	OVERALL
NUMBER OF STUDENTS	XX	XX	XX	XX	XX
PERCENT WHO PASSED	XX.X	XX.X	XX.X	XX.X	XX.X
PERCENT WHO FAILED	XX.X	XX.X	XX.X	XX.X	XX.X
AVERAGE MARK	XX.X	XX.X	XX.X	XX.X	XX.X

12.3   Prepare several data records of each of the following types. Each
         record is either an "add" or "delete" transaction which refers to the
         student master file created in problem 3 above. Add records have the
         same data as the student records described in problem 3 but in
         addition, have a "1" in position 25. Delete records have a student
         number in positions 1-5 and a "0" in position 25. Arrange the
         add/delete records in order of increasing student number. The inputs to
         the program are the student master file and the set of add/delete
         records. The output is a new student master file (written on a file
         which is different from the old student master file). The new master
         file should reflect the changes specified by the add/delete records. The
         program should detect and print error messages for the following
         conditions: an attempt to delete a student record which is not on the
         old student master file; an attempt to add a student who is already on
         the old student master file; an add or delete record which is out of
         sequence -- the student number on the add/delete card is less than the
         student number on the previous add/delete card. Once the new student
         master file has been written, reset the file and print the same two
         reports described in the previous problem.

12.4   Assume that each of twelve students takes two courses -- Math and English. Prepare a file of twelve records containing the following data.

```
positions    data
    1-2      student number (range 01-99)
    3-24     student name
    25-26    math mark
    27-28    English mark
```

Write a program which reads the twelve records and records the information on a file so that the information about the student having a student number of K is found in the Kth record of the file. On a second file write a single record containing the twelve valid student numbers in order of increasing magnitude. Display the contents of each record for future reference.

12.5   Using the data files created in the previous problem, print a report which, for each student, displays the student number, name, math mark, English mark, and average. Rewrite each student's record to include his average in the information kept in the file.

12.6   Given a file that contains one-hundred-thousand integers in the range one to one million, find an integer that is not in the file. Develop two algorithms. First assume you have lots of main memory. Second, assume you have very little memory but lots of file space. Test your algorithms using a small number of values.

12.7   Anagrams. Given a dictionary of words and a reference word, find all words in the dictionary which are formed by permuting the letters of the reference word. For example, given "stop" you would find "pots", "spot" and "tops".

12.8   Moving Billboard. An input file contains several messages -- one message per line. After each message is read display it on the screen as though it appeared on a moving billboard. That is it starts at the right edge of the screen and moves across the screen from right to left. Use a constant SCREEN_WIDTH in your program to define the width of the display window.

CHAPTER 13: SETS

Questions Answered in this Chapter:

1. What is a set?

2. How are sets defined and used in Pascal?

13.1 Concepts

In many ways, a set is the simplest of the four predefined data structures available in Pascal. In English we use the word set to describe many different collections such as: a set of people, a set of marks, a set of traffic lights, a set of elevator stops, a set of colors, or a set of axioms. In each instance, a set has associated with it the notion of a collection or group of objects, people or ideas. In Pascal, a *set* is an unordered collection of values all chosen from the same reference set.

For example, suppose an elevator stops at floors 1, 2 and 3. At any point in time, there may be people waiting for the elevator's arrival at any, all or none of the floors. There are eight possibilities. They are:

[1]	waiting at floor 1 only
[2]	waiting at floor 2 only
[3]	waiting at floor 3 only
[1,2]	waiting at floors 1 and 2
[1,3]	waiting at floors 1 and 3
[2,3]	waiting at floors 2 and 3
[1,2,3]	waiting at floors 1, 2 and 3
[ ]	no one waiting (the empty set)

In Pascal, components of a set are called *members*. Members must belong to an ordinal type such as CHAR, BOOLEAN, enumerated type or a subrange of INTEGERs. The order in which members of a set are listed is not important. For example, shown below are six equivalent sets.

[1,2,3], [1,3,2], [2,1,3], [2,3,1], [3,1,2], [3,2,1]

Because a member can be listed more than once without changing the set, there are in theory at least an infinite number of ways of constructing a Pascal set equivalent to [1,2,3]. Two examples are [1,2,2,1,3] and [2,3,3,1,3,3,2,2]. Each has three members. Two of the many useful applications of sets are illustrated later in the chapter.

13.2 Set Declaration and Construction

13.2.1 Declarations

A set is a family of types just like other structured types in Pascal. Shown below is an example of a variable declaration which can be used to define sets of any or all of the weekdays.

```
VAR
    WEEKDAYS: SET OF (MON, TUES, WED, THURS, FRI)
```

Recall that the list of values in an enumerated type must be enclosed in parentheses. This declaration means that WEEKDAYS can be assigned any one of thirty-two possible sets of MON..FRI. For example, the following assignment is valid:

```
WEEKDAYS: = [TUES, THURS, MON]
```

The general form of a set type specification is as follows.

SET Declarations

General Form

      SET OF base-type

Notes

1. The base-type must be BOOLEAN, CHAR, an enumerated type, a subrange of INTEGERS, or an identifier declared as one of these types.

2. Each compiler has a limit on the number of values permitted in the base-type. For example, SET OF 1..10 may be acceptable for a given compiler but SET OF 1..1000 may not.

3. The word PACKED may optionally precede the reserved word SET. If present, an attempt may be made to minimize the memory required to store the values in a set.

You cannot define a set of arrays, set of records, set of files or set of sets. Members of a set must be scalar non-REAL values.

13.2.2 Constructing Sets

A set is constructed by enclosing the members of the set within brackets. The members may be listed explicitly or the subrange operator may be used to specify the members. Given the declaration

```
VAR
    ONETEN: SET OF 1..10
```

Then the following four expressions are examples of sets which can be assigned to ONETEN:

$$[1,3], \; [2,2..5, \; 3..6], \; [\;], \; [1..10]$$

Note that the empty set (containing no members) can be assigned to, and is a member of, every set.

The following sets can not be assigned to ONETEN.

$$[1..11], \quad [1, \; [2]]$$

The first is invalid because 11 is not a value in the base-type. The second set is invalid because [2] is a set and not a scalar value. A set can be assigned to a variable declared as a set if the base-types of the source and target sets are assignment compatible.

13.3 Operations With Sets

Aside from assignment, there are three kinds of operations that can be performed with sets. They are comparisons, membership testing and "arithmetic". We consider each in turn.

13.3.1 Comparison of Sets

Two sets may be compared using the relational operators <=, =, >= and <>. The base-types must be the same or be subranges of the same type.

The tests for equality and inequality operate as you would expect. Thus

```
[1,2,3] = [3,1,2] is TRUE
[2,3] <> [1,2]    is TRUE
```

When used with sets, the less-than-or-equal and greater-than-or-equal operators have a different meaning from that when used to compare two scalar values. The "<=" means "is included in" or "is contained by". The ">=" means "contains". Some examples follow.

[2,3] <= [1,2,3] is TRUE because each member of the set in the left argument is also a member of the right argument set.

[4,1,5] >= [1,5] is TRUE because the set which is the left argument contains every member of the set which is the right argument.

Unlike the comparison of two scalars where either X <= Y is true or X >= Y is true, it is quite possible that opposite comparisons for a pair of sets are false. For example:

```
[1,2,3] <= [4,5,6] is FALSE
[1,2,3] >= [4,5,6] is FALSE
```

The empty set [ ] is included in every set. Thus:

[ ] <= any set is TRUE

[ ] >= any set is FALSE unless the right argument is also an empty set

Note that the strong inequality operators '<' and '>' cannot be used to compare two sets. In mathematics however, the notion of a proper subset is well-defined. That is, X < Y if all members of X are members of Y but not vice-versa. An exercise question asks you to write expressions for these relationships.

13.3.2 Arithmetic Operations With Sets

There are three standard "arithmetic operations" which can be performed with sets. They are called union, difference and intersection. Each specifies a rule for constructing a new set from a pair of given sets. Rather than invent new symbols to denote these operations, the arithmetic operators +, - and * are used. Hence these are often called arithmetic operations. Members of the sets used as arguments must have the same base-type or be subranges of the same base-type.

Union

The union of two sets A and B is the set consisting of all members belonging to A or B or both of A and B. In Pascal the '+' symbol denotes union. Some examples follow.

```
  i) [1,2,3] + [2,3,4] → [1,2,3,4]

 ii)  A + [] = [] + A = A for any set A

iii)  A + B  = B + A for all sets A and B
```

Difference

The difference of two sets A and B is the set consisting of members of A not in B. The minus sign denotes set difference. Some examples are:

    i) `[1,2,3] - [3,1]` ➜ `[2]`

    ii) `[1,2,3] - [4 .. 10]` ➜ `[1,2,3]`

    iii) `A - []` ➜ `A for any set A`

    iv) `[] - A` ➜ `[] for any set A`

Intersection

The intersection of two sets A and B is a set consisting of members belonging to both A and B. The multiplication operator '`*`' denotes intersection. Three examples follow.

i) [1,2,3] * [2,3,4] ➜ [2,3]

ii) [1,2,3] * [4,5,6] ➜ []

iii) A * [] = [] * A ➜ [] for any set A

13.3.3 Priority of Set Operations

The priority of set operations is the same as that of the operators in non-set operations. Therefore

```
* (intersection) has the highest priority
+ - (union, difference) have equal priorities
<=, =, >=, <> (comparison) have the lowest priorities
```

The following example illustrates these priorities.

```
[1,2,3] + [2,3,5] * [4,2] - [1,5] <= [1..3]
 ➜ [1,2,3] + [2] - [1,5] <= [1..3]
 ➜ [1,2,3] -[1,5] <= [1..3]
 ➜ [2,3] <= [1..3]
 ➜ TRUE
```

13.3.4 Identities Using Set Operations

There are several expressions involving set operations which are true regardless of the values of the sets used as arguments. In the following, let A, B, and C denote sets of the same base-type.

i) Commutative Laws

```
A * B = B * A
A + B = B + A
```

Note: A-B is not equal to B-A unless A=B

ii) Associative Laws

```
A + (B+C) = (A+B) + C
A * (B*C) = (A*B) * C
```

Note: A - (B - C) is not equal to (A - B) - C but is equal to (A - B) + C as you would expect.

iii) Distributive Laws

```
A * (B + C) = A * B + A * C
(A + B) * C  = A * C + B * C
```

iv) DeMorgan's Laws

Given the base-type of a set, the complement of the set consists of the set of values not in the set. For example, if the base-type contains the values 1..5, then the complement of [2,3] is [1, 4, 5]. In the next section a simple procedure for producing the complement is provided. Letting COMPL denote the operation of taking the complement of a set, the following two identities, known as DeMorgan's Laws are true for every pair of sets X and Y.

```
COMPL (X + Y) = COMPL (X) * COMPL (Y)
COMPL (X * Y) = COMPL (X) + COMPL (Y)
```

For example, if A = [1,2,3,4,5] and B = [4,5,6,7] are sets chosen from the base type 1..10, then:

```
COMPL(A + B)  →  COMPL(1,2,3,4,5,6,7)
              →  [8,9,10]

COMPL(A)  *  COMPL(B)  →  [6,7,8,9,10] * [1,2,3,8,9,10]
                       →  [8,9,10]
```

13.3.5 The Membership Operator (IN)

How do you determine if a particular value belongs to a set? One way is to intersect the value and the set and test if the result is empty. For example, given a value for X, the Boolean expression ([X] * [1,2,3,4,5] <> []) can be used to determine if X is in [1,2,3,4,5]. Parentheses are not required since intersection has a higher priority than the relational operators. The expression has a value of TRUE if X is in [1,2,3,4,5] and FALSE otherwise. As an alternative, the IN operator can be used. The expression X IN [1,2,3,4,5] has the same truth value as the intersection expression. Note that X is not enclosed in brackets. The expression has the form "value IN set".

The IN operator has the same priority as other relational operators (the lowest). For a value X and a set A, X IN A is TRUE if X is a member of A and FALSE otherwise.

Although in English we say "if X is not in A', the priority of operators in Pascal is such that the corresponding expression must be written NOT (X IN A). This is necessary because X IN A produces a BOOLEAN value. The expression X NOT IN A contains two operators in succession and is therefore invalid.

13.4 Exercise 13.1

1. Define a type called STOPLIGHT_SET which may have any of the following values: GREEN, RED, YELLOW, GREEN_YELLOW. How many different sets can be assigned to a variable of the type STOPLIGHT_SET?

2. Given the program fragment below, what are the values of the expressions which follow?

    ```
    VAR
      S1, S2, S3, S4 : SET OF (A, B, C, D);
    BEGIN
      S1 := [A, B, C];
      S2 := [];
      S3 := [A, B];
      S4 := [B, C]
    END
    ```

    a) S1 + S2

    b) S1 * S2 = S2

    c) S3 - (S1 + S2) >= S3 - S4

    d) A IN (S4 - (S3 - (S2)))

3.   What is the error in each of the following?

   a)   [1, 2, 3] + 4

   b)   TYPE   INT_SET = SET OF (1,2,3)

   c)   VAR X : SET OF (1..5, 10..15)

   d)   [3] IN [1, 2, 3]

   e)   NOT 2 IN [1, 2, 3]

   f)   TYPE
        JANE_SET = SET OF CHARLIE_RANGE;
        CHARLIE_RANGE = 'A' .. 'Z'

4.   Square brackets are used to enclose subscripts of array elements. Is there
     any possible confusion with using them to enclose members of a set?

13.5 Four Useful Extensions of Set Operations

When working with sets, there are several commonly performed operations
for which no operator, standard function or procedure is provided. The purpose
of this section is to provide prototypes of expressions, functions and procedures
which are useful when manipulating sets.

In the following discussion assume the global declarations below are in
effect.

```
CONST
  LOW = 1;
  HIGH = 10;

TYPE
  RANGE = LOW .. HIGH;
  LOW_HI_SET = SET OF RANGE;

VAR
  S : LOW_HI_SET
```

That is S is a subset of the integers in the range one to ten.

i) Complement

The complement of a set is a set consisting of members of the base-type
which are not members of the given set. Using the declarations above, suppose
S has been assigned the set [2,4,6,8,10]. Then the complement of S is the set
[1,3,5,7,9].

A procedure to produce the complement of a LOW_HI_SET set is shown below. It is easily modified to apply to any other base-type.

```
PROCEDURE COMPLEMENT(INPUT      : LOW_HI_SET;
                     VAR OUTPUT : LOW_HI_SET)
   BEGIN
      OUTPUT := [LOW .. HIGH] - INPUT
   END (* COMPLEMENT *)
```

Some versions of Pascal permit FUNCTIONs to have a set value. If so, it is more natural to make COMPLEMENT a function which returns a set as the result. Standard Pascal does not allow a function value to be a set.

ii) Cardinality

The *cardinality* of a set is the number of members in the set. For example the cardinality of [4,22,5] is 3 and that of [] is 0. The function below returns the cardinality of a set constructed of values chosen from the range 1..10.

```
FUNCTION CARDINALITY(S : LOW_HI_SET) : INTEGER;
   VAR
      MEMBER : RANGE;
      COUNT  : INTEGER;
   BEGIN
      COUNT := 0;
      FOR MEMBER := LOW TO HIGH DO
         IF MEMBER IN S THEN
            COUNT := COUNT + 1;
      CARDINALITY := COUNT
   END (* CARDINALITY *)
```

It is necessary to use a variable such as COUNT because a function name appearing on the right side of an assignment statement results in an attempted function invocation. In this example, this is certainly not wanted.

iii) An IN Loop

It would be nice to have a loop of the form "FOR x IN s DO" causing the body of the loop to be executed once for each member of the set s. Given the preceding declarations such a loop can be simulated by a FOR loop as shown below.

```
FOR X := LOW TO HIGH DO
   IF X IN S THEN
      BEGIN
         body of loop
      END
```

iv) Proper Subsets

Given two sets X and Y, a function to determine if X is a proper subset of Y (all members of X belong to Y but not vice-versa), is shown below.

```
FUNCTION PROPER(X, Y : LOW_HI_SET) : BOOLEAN;
  BEGIN
    PROPER := (X * Y = X) AND (X <> Y)
  END (* PROPER *)
```

13.6 Two Applications of Sets

This section illustrates two ways that sets can be used effectively in programs. The first is a simple problem but the ideas can be easily extended to more complicated situations. The second problem demonstrates a method for generating all possible sets of the base-type values.

13.6.1 Example 1: Character Analysis

Suppose the problem is that of reading a single line of input and determining how many letters, digits, punctuation symbols and other characters are present. To solve the problem seven sets of characters are needed. Three define what is meant by a letter, a digit and a punctuation symbol; three more contain the input characters belonging to these reference sets; the seventh set will contain the characters in the input which are not members of any of the three reference sets.

The main loop consists of reading each character; determining which set it belongs to and then adding it to that set.

Once the sets of characters found in the input have been created, the members of each must be printed. Since there are four sets, it makes sense to write a procedure to print members of a CHAR set. It has the following header.

```
PROCEDURE PRINT_SET (S: CHAR_SET)
```

How do you print the members of a set? *If* it is relatively easy to define the *possible* members of the set, each can be tested to see if it is *actually* a member. Specifically in the case of CHAR values, the ORD values go from 0 to either 127 or 255 (for the ASCII and EBCDIC character sets respectively). Assuming the EBCDIC character set is used, the logic is a simple FOR loop of the form below.

```
FOR I = 0 to 255
  IF CHR(I) IN S THEN WRITE CHR(I)
```

Note that each possible character is tested to see if it is in S and if so, it is printed.

Global declarations for the program and the PRINT_SET procedure are shown below.

```
PROGRAM CHARACTERS(INPUT,OUTPUT);

(* THIS PROGRAM PRINTS THE SETS OF LETTERS, DIGITS
   PUNCTUATION SYMBOLS AND OTHER CHARACTERS FOUND
   IN THE INPUT FILE                              *)

TYPE
  CHAR_SET = SET OF CHAR;

VAR
  LETTERS, DIGITS, PUNCS, OTHER : CHAR_SET;
  LETTERS_USED, DIGITS_USED, PUNCS_USED, OTHERS : CHAR_SET;
  NEXT : CHAR;

PROCEDURE PRINT_SET(S : CHAR_SET);
  CONST
    MAX_ORD = 255; (* largest ORD value *)

  VAR
    I : 0 .. MAX_ORD; (* range of ORD values *)

  BEGIN (* PRINT_SET *)
    FOR I := 0 TO MAX_ORD DO
      IF CHR(I) IN S THEN WRITE(CHR(I))
  END; (* PRINT_SET *)

BEGIN (* CHARACTERS *)
  (* mainline body goes here *)
END. (* CHARACTERS *)
```

In the mainline which follows, examine the statement used to define the set of letters. Because the upper and lower case letters in the EBCDIC collating sequence are not contiguous ranges, it is necessary to break them up into six subranges as shown. If the ASCII system is used, LETTERS can be initialized using the statement "LETTERS : = ['A'..'Z', 'a'..'z']".

```
BEGIN (* CHARACTERS MAINLINE *)
   (* 1. INITIALIZE REFERENCE SETS *)
        LETTERS := ['A'..'I', 'J'..'R', 'S'..'Z',
                    'a'..'i', 'j'..'r', 's'..'z'];
        DIGITS := ['0'..'9'];
        PUNCS  := [',', '.', '!', ';', ':', '?', ''''];
        LETTERS_USED := [];
        DIGITS_USED  := [];
        PUNCS_USED   := [];
        OTHERS       := [];
   (* 2. READ AND ASSIGN EACH CHARACTER TO A SET *)
        WRITELN('ENTER A LINE OF TEXT');
        WHILE NOT EOLN DO
          BEGIN
            READ(NEXT);
            IF NEXT IN LETTERS THEN
              LETTERS_USED := LETTERS_USED + [NEXT]
            ELSE IF NEXT IN DIGITS THEN
              DIGITS_USED := DIGITS_USED + [NEXT]
            ELSE IF NEXT IN PUNCS THEN
              PUNCS_USED := PUNCS_USED + [NEXT]
            ELSE
              OTHERS := OTHERS + [NEXT]
          END; (* WHILE *)
   (* 3. DISPLAY THE RESULTS *)
        WRITELN;
        WRITELN('THE FOLLOWING LETTERS WERE FOUND');
          PRINT_SET(LETTERS_USED);
          WRITELN;
        WRITELN('THE FOLLOWING DIGITS WERE FOUND');
          PRINT_SET(DIGITS_USED);
          WRITELN;
        WRITELN('THE FOLLOWING PUNCTUATION WAS FOUND');
          PRINT_SET(PUNCS_USED);
          WRITELN;
        WRITELN('THE FOLLOWING OTHER CHARACTERS WERE USED');
          PRINT_SET(OTHERS);
          WRITELN
END. (* CHARACTERS *)
```

When used with the declarations and PRINT_SET procedure above the program produces the output shown below. The input data is shown on the first line of output.

```
Execution begins...
Twenty-three dollars ($23.00) is not much money, John.

THE FOLLOWING LETTERS WERE FOUND
acdehilmnorstuwyJT
THE FOLLOWING DIGITS WERE FOUND
023
THE FOLLOWING PUNCTUATION WAS FOUND
. ,
THE FOLLOWING OTHER CHARACTERS WERE USED
 ($)-
```

Question. The input line contains several blanks. Where does the blank appear in the output produced? Since it is not a letter, digit or punctuation symbol, it must be in OTHERS. A close look at the output verifies that indeed a blank space occurs at the beginning of the characters in OTHERS. It comes first because it has a lower ORD value than the remaining characters in OTHERS.

13.6.2 Example 2: Powersets

Give a base-set, its *powerset* consists of all possible sets of members chosen from the base-type. If there are N values in the base-type, there are two-to-the-Nth sets in the powerset. For example, the powerset of the base-type BOOLEAN consists of the following four sets.

[ ], [FALSE], [TRUE], [FALSE, TRUE]

Frequently, a means of generating the powerset of a given base-type is required in order to evaluate all possible sets of the component values. This is often desirable when testing a program in order to insure the program correctly processes every combination of a set of input values.

Several algorithms exist for generating the sets in a powerset. One is the following. It operates by transforming any set in the powerset into another set according to the following algorithm.

```
If the cardinality is even then
    Flip (see below) the lowest value in the set
Else
    .1 Find the lowest value currently in the set
    .2 If this is less than the high value in the base-type
        Flip the successor of the lowest value found
    Else
        Flip the high value, this will result in the empty set
```

Flipping a value means that if the value is in the set, remove it; if not in the set, make it a member of the set. The algorithm above changes only one member at each iteration. The cardinality (number of elements in the set) alternates between odd and even. Starting from any set, by applying the algorithm repeatedly, all sets in the powerset are generated before the cycle is repeated.

We will apply the algorithm to the following problem. The chairman of an organization wishes to form a committee consisting of himself and one or more of Tom, John, Ann, and Sue. He wants a list of the possible committees. Since there are sixteen sets in the powerset of four values, the output will have fifteen combinations. (The null set is not feasible since the chairman wants at least one member.)

The mainline logic is straightforward and is shown below.

1. S = null set
2. Repeat
      .1 generate next set from S
      .2 print the new set
    Until the next set is null

Let us make the program work for any base-type having up to ten values. Suppose the name of each value in the base-type can be stored in a string variable of length eight and that the number of values in the base-type and the name of each is obtained from the input data. If there are N values, we can then generate the powerset of values chosen from 1..N and use the array of names to print meaningful lists of of the members in each set.

The global declarations used in the program which follows have the following uses:

```
CONST
  HIGH = 10; (* MAX NUMBER OF VALUES IN THE BASE-TYPE *)
  NAME_LENGTH = 8;

TYPE
  RANGE = 1..HIGH;
  RANGE_SET = SET OF RANGE;
  STRING8 = PACKED ARRAY[1..NAME_LENGTH] OF CHAR;
  NAME_ARRAY = ARRAY [1..HIGH] OF STRING8;

VAR
  S       : RANGE_SET; (* CONTAINS A SUBSET OF THE BASE-TYPE *)
  CARD    : 0..HIGH; (* NUMBER OF MEMBERS IN S *)
  NAME    : NAME_ARRAY; (* NAMES OF BASE-TYPE VALUES *)
  N       : RANGE; (* ACTUAL NUMBER OF VALUES IN BASE-TYPE *)
  I, J    : 1..MAXINT; (* LOOP INDICES *)
```

The INITIALIZE procedure shown below: reads the number of values in the base-type; reads and stores the names of the values in the array NAME; and makes the starting set equal to the empty set.

```
PROCEDURE INITIALIZE(
            VAR N : RANGE; (* COUNT OF REFERENCE SET *)
            VAR NAME : NAME_ARRAY; (* NAMES OF VALUES *)
            VAR S : RANGE_SET; (* SUBSET OF VALUES *)
            VAR CARD : INTEGER (* CARDINALITY OF S *) );

  (* THIS PROCEDURE OBTAINS THE NUMBER OF VALUES IN THE
     REFERENCE SET & THEIR NAMES, AND INITIALIZES THE
     SUBSET TO AN EMPTY SET WITH CARDINALITY 0            *)

VAR
  I : RANGE;
  J : 1..NAME_LENGTH;

BEGIN (* INITIALIZE *)
  WRITELN('HOW MANY VALUES IN THE REFERENCE SET');
  READLN(N);
  WRITELN('ENTER THE NAMES OF THE VALUES, ONE PER LINE');
  FOR I := 1 TO N DO
    BEGIN
      FOR J := 1 TO NAME_LENGTH DO
        IF NOT EOLN THEN
          READ(NAME[I,J])
        ELSE
          NAME[I,J] := ' ';
      READLN (* SKIP END-OF-LINE CHAR *)
    END;
  S := []; (* INITIAL SET IS EMPTY *)
  CARD := 0
END; (* INITIALIZE *)
```

The procedure to generate the next set in the powerset is shown below. NEXT contains FLIP as an imbedded procedure.

```
PROCEDURE NEXT(VAR S:SET_TYPE; VAR CARD:INTEGER);

  (* THIS PROCEDURE MODIFIES THE PARAMETER SET S
     AND RETURNS ITS CARDINALITY IN CARD *)

VAR
  MEMBER : RANGE;

PROCEDURE FLIP(VALUE:RANGE);

  (* IF VALUE IS IN THE SET S, IT IS REMOVED.
     IF NOT, IT IS ADDED TO S                  *)

  BEGIN (* FLIP *)
    IF VALUE IN S THEN
      BEGIN
        S := S - [VALUE];
        CARD := CARD - 1
      END
    ELSE (* VALUE NOT IN S *)
      BEGIN
        S := S + [VALUE];
        CARD := CARD + 1
      END
  END; (* FLIP *)

BEGIN (* NEXT *)
  IF ODD(CARD) THEN
    BEGIN
      MEMBER := 1;
      WHILE NOT (MEMBER IN S) DO
        MEMBER := SUCC(MEMBER);
      IF MEMBER = N THEN
        FLIP(N)
      ELSE
        FLIP(SUCC(MEMBER))
    END
  ELSE (* EVEN CARDINALITY *)
    FLIP (1)
END; (* NEXT *)
```

Finally, a print routine is useful to display the values in a set. It is shown below.

```
PROCEDURE PRINT(S: RANGE_SET);

  (* THIS PROCEDURE PRINTS THE MEMBERS IN THE SET S *)

VAR
  MEMBER : RANGE;

BEGIN (* PRINT *)
  IF S <> [] THEN
    BEGIN
      FOR MEMBER := 1 TO N DO
        IF MEMBER IN S THEN
          WRITE(NAME[MEMBER]:NAME_LENGTH, ' ');
      WRITELN
    END (* NONEMPTY *)
END; (* PRINT *)
```

The remainder of the program and example input appears below. Comments appear where the blocks of the three preceding procedures are inserted when running the program.

```
PROGRAM POWERSET (INPUT, OUTPUT);

(* THIS PROGRAM GENERATES AND DISPLAYS THE POWERSET
   OF A REFERENCE SET OF UP TO TEN VALUES              *)

CONST
  HIGH = 10; (* MAX NUMBER OF VALUES IN THE BASE-TYPE *)
  NAME_LENGTH = 8;

TYPE
  RANGE = 1..HIGH;
  RANGE_SET = SET OF RANGE;
  STRING8 = PACKED ARRAY[1..NAME_LENGTH] OF CHAR;
  NAME_ARRAY = ARRAY [1..HIGH] OF STRING8;

VAR
  S    : RANGE_SET; (* CONTAINS A SUBSET OF THE BASE-TYPE *)
  CARD : INTEGER; (* NUMBER OF MEMBERS IN S *)
  NAME : NAME_ARRAY; (* NAMES OF BAS-TYPE VALUES *)
  N    : RANGE; (* ACTUAL NUMBER OF VALUES IN BASE-TYPE *)
  I, J : 1..MAXINT; (* LOOP INDICES *)
```

... (continued on the next page)

```
(* PROCEDURE INITIALIZE
       - block of INITIALIZE goes here              *)

(* PROCEDURE NEXT(VAR S:RANGE_SET; VAR CARD:INTEGER);
       - block of NEXT goes here                    *)

(* PROCEDURE PRINT(S: RANGE_SET);
       - block of PRINT goes here                   *)

BEGIN (* MAINLINE *)
  INITIALIZE (N, NAME, S, CARD);
  REPEAT
    NEXT(S,CARD);
    PRINT(S)
  UNTIL S = [ ]
END. (* POWERSET *)
```

Shown below is the output produced when N=4 and when the names of the four values are Tom, John, Mary, and Ann.

```
Execution begins...
Tom
Tom       John
John
John      Mary
Tom       John      Mary
Tom       Mary
Mary
Mary      Ann
Tom       Mary      Ann
Tom       John      Mary      Ann
John      Mary      Ann
John      Ann
Tom       John      Ann
Tom       Ann
Ann
```

13.7 Exercise 13.2

1. Earlier in the chapter, the following statement was made: "If it is relatively easy to define the possible members of a set, then ...". Given the restrictions on sets in Pascal, how easy is it? Use examples to defend your point of view.

2. Modify the algorithm and procedure for generating a powerset so that it generates only subsets having a given number of members. Do you think this is an efficient algorithm for doing this?

3. Use the powerset algorithm as the basis for generating all permutations of all subsets of a given base-type. (In a permutation, the order in which values are listed is important.)

13.8 Summary

1. A set is an unordered collection of ordinal values of the same type. The declaration takes the form

    ```
    SET OF base-type
    ```

    There is a compiler-defined limit on the number of values permitted in the base-type.

2. Three kinds of operations can be performed with sets. These are denoted by the following operators.

    arithmetic operations: + (union), - (difference), * (intersection)

    comparisons : = (equality), <> (inequality), <= (subset),
                                  and   >= (contains)

    membership test: IN

3. Other useful operations with sets which are easy to program include: the cardinality of a set; the complement of a set; a test for a proper subset; and a simulated "FOR x IN s" loop.

4. There are many uses for sets. Frequently a means of generating a powerset is helpful in creating an exhaustive list of sets of the base-type values.

13.9 Programming Problems

13.1   Write a program to count the number of occurrences of each letter of the alphabet in a sentence contained on a single input line.

13.2   Create two FILEs each of which contains twenty records of one INTEGER value each. The values in each file should be in order of non-decreasing magnitudes. Using these files as input, use sets to determine how many values are present in both sets an how many unique values there are in total. Use an algorithm such that each record needs to be read only once.

13.3   Write a procedure called FLIPSET which, given two sets A and B produces a set with the common members removed. Use the procedure to solve the following problem.

Suppose a set of doors numbered 1 to 25 are initially closed. Twenty-five people successively pass down the line of doors and reverse the status (open or closed) of one or more doors according to the following rules. The first person reverses every door; the second person then flips the status of the even-numbered doors; the third person flips every third door, and so on. (The 25th person will simply change the status of the 25th door.) What doors are open after the 25th pass? What is the general rule that determines the status of any given door after N passes?

13.4   The game of Keno is a popular gambling game in many places. A player pays $1.20 for each game and then chooses eight numbers in the range 1 .. 80. The house randomly picks twenty numbers in the same range. If the player matches five numbers, he wins $10; if he matches six, he wins $100; seven is worth $2200 and matching all eight wins $25000. Write a program to play ten games of Keno. The first ten lines of input data contain the players guesses. Use either of the random number generator described in the problems of Chapters 7 and 10 to generate the house numbers. Assume the player starts with $25. Print a report showing the cumulative position of the player after each game.

13.5   The input file contains a number of lines describing the characteristics of individuals as follows.

```
positions      data

    1-3        ID #
    4-12       name
   13-14       age
     15        sex ('M' or 'F')
     16        hair color (1=brunette, 2=blonde,
                            3=redhead, 4=bald)
     17        eye color (1=brown, 2=blue, 3=hazel)
   18-19       height
     20        blank
   21-23       weight
```

Prepare an input file containing several records. Read the data into an array of records and print a report with appropriate headings showing the data in the file.

Answer the following questions using set operations. Hint: For each question, build one or more sets of ID#s and perform the set operations with these. When the resultant set has been found, its members to search for the names in the array of data.

a) Who are the males?

b) What brown-eyed individuals are females?

c) Which people under 50 have either red hair and hazel eyes or blonde hair and blue eyes?

d) For the first male, print the names of females who are within five years of his age, not taller than he is, and do not have red hair.

13.6   Acme parking lots charges $0.50 per hour for a parking space. Suppose a line of data is recorded for each car using the lot. It contains: the license number (an INTEGER), the arrival time (a pair of INTEGERs denoting hours and minutes), and a departure time in hours and minutes. Assume that hours range from 0 to 24 and that no one leaves after midnight. (The departure time is always greater than the arrival time).

a) Develop an algorithm and write a program to read each line of data (stop when a license number of zero is found); compute the charges for each car and print a report in the form below.

```
            ACME PARKING LOT
      LICENSE #       TIME IN       TIME OUT       CHARGE

        XXXXX         XX  XX         XX  XX         X.XX
        XXXXX         XX  XX         XX  XX         X.XX
          .
          .
        XXXXX         XX  XX         XX  XX         X.XX

      TOTAL NUMBER OF CARS = X
      TOTAL CHARGES          = $ XXX.XX
```

Test your program using the following lines of data.

```
        3527      8       0      11      0
        1469     10      15      14     45
        2750      0      27      20     27
        1986     17      53      18     45
        7787     15      15      15     59
           0
```

b)   Assume the parking charge should be rounded to the nearest five
     cents. Modify and run the program.
c)   Assume the charge is "$0.50 per hour or any fraction thereof".
     Modify and run the program.
d)   Use a set to keep track of the number of cars in the lot at any
     given time. Print a report showing the cars in the lot at the end of
     each hour. Assuming the parking lot has 25 spaces, calculate the
     percent utilization of the lot for the periods midnight to 8 a.m., 8
     a.m. to 6 p.m. and 6 p.m. to midnight.

13.7   A real estate firm wants to be able to match clients searching for
       homes with appropriate houses for sale. To do this, two files have been
       prepared -- a client file, and a house file. Information in these files
       consist of the following record types.

```
CLIENT_REC = RECORD.
                  REF_NUM      : INTEGER;
                  BEDROOMS     : 1..6;
                  PRICE_CODE : 1..10;
                  WOODED       : -1..+1;(*see note below*)
                  POOL         : -1..+1;
                  SCHOOL       : -1.._1
             END
```

Note: A preference code of -1 means the feature is not wanted; zero
means the client is indifferent and +1 means the client must have it.

The House file has records of the following type

```
HOUSE_REC = RECORD
                  REF_NUM      : INTEGER;
                  BEDROOMS   : 1..6;
                  PRICE_CODE: 1..10;
                  WOODED       : BOOLEAN;
                  POOL         : BOOLEAN;
                  SCHOOLS      : BOOLEAN
             END
```

For example if SCHOOLS is TRUE it means there are schools nearby.

        The problem. Create a client file and a house file containing a
mixture of client preferences and house characteristics. Then, for each
client list the houses which are suitable, meaning that the house must
have:

- at least the number of bedrooms needed
- a price code no greater than that specified by the client
- all of the features required by the client and none of the features not
    wanted by the client

CHAPTER 14: POINTERS AND DYNAMIC STRUCTURES

Questions Answered in this Chapter:

1. What are the most important limitations of the data structures and types described previously?

2. How can the pointer type be used to overcome these limitations?

3. What are the three basic linked list structures?

4. How are tree structures defined and used?

14.1 Motivation

When an array is defined in a program, the number of elements in the array is fixed. In this sense an array is a static (unchanging) structure. Suppose for example, all components of an array are used in some application. Suppose further that because of a value found in the input data it is necessary to add a component to the array. How would you do this? With our present knowledge we could not because a *dynamic* structure is needed.

A second example. Suppose it is necessary to store and process data about the descendants of a particular individual. The typical way of showing such information is to draw a "family tree". Although this data could be stored in an array, record or file, none of these structures is tree-like. Furthermore, different people have different tree structures depending on the number of offspring each person has. Hence a means of creating and processing different structures is needed.

A third example. Suppose you want to process a large but unknown number of values. After each value is read it is necessary to process the previous values. An array is unsuitable because it must be declared with a fixed number of components. Furthermore memory restrictions may mean insufficient memory is available to define a large enough array. A file is unacceptable from a practical standpoint because of the necessity of alternating between input and output operations.

Fortunately, the programming difficulties outlined in these scenarios can be overcome using the facilities available through *pointer variables*. Essentially their use permits:

- the creation of variables at execution-time

- the chaining or linking of variables to form structures needed to store and retrieve data

The next section explains the vocabulary associated with pointer variables and illustrates the mechanics of their use by means of a simple example. The remainder of the chapter shows how pointer variables are used in creating and manipulating two of the most commonly found dynamic structures -- trees and linked lists.

14.2 Vocabulary and Concepts

14.2.1 An Example Problem

Suppose a program is required to process either an array of one-thousand REAL values or an array of four-thousand INTEGER values but not both. The first character in the input file is an 'I' or an 'R' indicating which is required. The values of the corresponding type follow the indicator. Suppose further that the computer used to run the program only has enough memory to store one of the arrays but not both. How can the problem be solved? One approach is to write two separate programs! However, this would not solve the problem if it were necessary to process several arrays of different types.

Analysis. We need to be able to create *at execution-time* an array of variables of the appropriate type. Thus the algorithm is:

    1. Read the type ('I' or 'R')
    2. If 'I' then
            1. Create an array of 4000 INTEGER variables
            2. Read and process the values
        Else
            1. Create an array 1f 1000 REAL variables
            2. Read and process the values
    3. Stop

Until now, all variables used in a program had to be declared at the time
the program was written. When the compiler processes a variable declaration
it allocates sufficient memory to store the value of the variable. The amount of
memory reserved for a variable depends on its type. The compiler must
remember the location of the area of memory reserved for the variable so that
references to the variable will refer to the correct memory location. The
location is called the *address* of the variable.

The above steps which are performed by the compiler for declared
variables are precisely what we want to do at execution-time. That is, at
execution-time we need to request that an area of memory be reserved to store
one of the following types.

```
TYPE
  REAL_ARRAY     = ARRAY [1..1000] OF REAL;
  INTEGER_ARRAY = ARRAY [1..4000] OF INTEGER
```

The address of the array needs to be known so that the READ procedure can
assign each value in the input file to the appropriate area of memory. If we
know the address, we can refer to the array and/or its elements.

The term *buffer* means an area of memory. Recall that associated with
every file is a buffer -- namely an area of memory large enough to store one
component of the file. A pointer variable points to a buffer. That is, the value
of a pointer variable is a memory address. In the program below, INT_PTR
and REAL_PTR are pointer variables which point to buffers of the types
INTEGER_ARRAY and REAL_ARRAY respectively. The value of
INT_PTR is the address of the INTEGER array; the value of REAL_PTR is
the address of the REAL array. At execution-time, the program uses the
standard procedure NEW to create a buffer of the appropriate type. The
address of the newly-created variable is returned via the NEW parameter.
Further comments follow the program.

```
PROGRAM ONE_ARRAY(INPUT,OUTPUT);

(* THIS PROGRAM PROCESSES AN ARRAY OF 1000 REAL
   ELEMENTS OR 4000 INTEGER VALUES. THE ARRAY IS
   CREATED AFTER READING THE FIRST DATA VALUE  *)

CONST
  MAX_INTS = 4000;
  MAX_REALS = 1000;

TYPE
  INTEGER_ARRAY   = ARRAY [1 .. MAX_INTS] OF INTEGER;
  REAL_ARRAY      = ARRAY [1 .. MAX_REALS] OF REAL;

VAR
  INT_PTR : @INTEGER_ARRAY; (* points to an INTEGER_ARRAY *)
  REAL_PTR : @REAL_ARRAY; (* points to a REAL_ARRAY *)
  FLAG : CHAR; (* CONTAINS 'I' OR 'R' *)
  I    : INTEGER; (* LOOP INDEX *)

BEGIN (* ONE_ARRAY *)
  READLN(FLAG); (* DETERMINE THE TYPE OF BUFFER NEEDED *)
  IF FLAG = 'I' THEN
    BEGIN
      NEW(INT_PTR); (* CREATE AN INTEGER_ARRAY BUFFER *)
      FOR I := 1 TO MAX_INTS DO
        BEGIN
          READ(INT_PTR@[I]); (* READ THE I'TH VALUE *)
          WRITELN(INT_PTR@[I])
        END
    END (* INTEGER PROCESSING *)
  ELSE
    BEGIN
      NEW(REAL_PTR); (* CREATE A REAL_ARRAY BUFFER *)
      FOR I := 1 TO MAX_REALS DO
        BEGIN
          READ(REAL_PTR@[I]); (* READ THE I'TH VALUE *)
          WRITELN(REAL_PTR@[I])
        END (* FOR *)
    END (* REAL PROCESSING *)
END.
```

Comments.

1. Declaring Pointer Variables. Consider the VAR declaration in the
    program.

    ```
    VAR
        INT_PTR : @INTEGER_ARRAY; (* address of INTEGER buffer *)
        REAL_PTR: @REAL_ARRAY; (* address of REAL buffer *)
    ```

    The type of the variable INT_PTR is "@INTEGER_ARRAY" which
    means "a pointer to an INTEGER_ARRAY buffer". The values which
    can be assigned to INT_PTR are addresses of INTEGER_ARRAY
    variables. Similarly REAL_PTR can be assigned the address of a
    REAL_ARRAY buffer. The '@' symbol specifies a pointer type in a type
    declaration. Some compilers recognize other characters as the pointer
    character. Commonly used symbols are '↑' (up arrow) and '∧' (hat, carrat
    or circumflex) as well as the '@'.

2. In general, a pointer type has the form

    ```
    @ type-identifier
    ```

    where the type identifier specifies the type of variable which will be
    created by the NEW procedure. The buffer type may be any type except
    a FILE. You can even point to a pointer. A pointer type may be given a
    name as in

    ```
    TYPE
        INT_ARRAY_POINTER = @INT_ARRAY
    ```

    Alternately the type specification may appear in a VAR declaration as
    was done in the example.

3. Operations with pointers. Variables which are pointers cannot be used in
    arithmetic operations because Pascal does not permit you to add and
    subtract memory addresses. Furthermore, because a particular program
    may occupy different areas of memory when it is run at different times,
    most compilers prohibit pointer variables from being stored in external
    files. Pointer variables can be compared with each other to determine if
    they are equal or not. Less than and greater than have no meaning.

14.2.2 Assigning Values to Pointer Variables

There are two ways to give a value to a pointer variable such as INT_PTR. The first is to use an assignment statement; the second uses the standard procedure NEW.

An assignment statement has one of the forms below:

```
pointer variable := pointer variable
```

or

```
pointer variable := NIL
```

In the first case, the variables must be pointers to buffers of the same type.

NIL. Although not used in the example, the reserved word NIL denotes a special constant which can be assigned to a pointer variable and means "no address". If a pointer has a value of NIL it is not pointing to anything. In the example, both INT_PTR and REAL_PTR could be initialized to NIL but it would serve no useful purpose.

NEW. The second method of assigning a value (an address) to a pointer variable is to use the NEW procedure. NEW requires a pointer variable as a parameter and does two things.

1. It creates a buffer to store a value of the type associated with the parameter.

2. It assigns the address of the buffer to the parameter.

For example, NEW (INT_PTR) reserves an area of memory large enough to store an array of 4000 INTEGER values. The address of this buffer is assigned to INT_PTR.

14.2.3 Using The Buffer

If you know the address of a buffer, the buffer itself is referred to by appending the pointer symbol '@' to the buffer address. Thus:

- INT_PTR@ is the INT_PTR buffer. INT_PRT@ has the type INTEGER_ARRAY.

- REAL_PTR@ is the REAL_PTR buffer. REAL_PTR@ has the type REAL_ARRAY.

In the example problem however, we wanted to process the elements of an array, not the array in its entirety. Since an element of an array is referenced by appending a subscript to the array reference, it follows that:

```
INT_PTR@[1] is the first element in the INT_PTR@ array,
INT_PTR@[I] is the Ith element in the INT_PTR@ array, and
INT_PTR@[4000] is the last element in the INT_PTR@ array
```

When you see the sequence "X@" where X is a pointer variable, mentally replace the pointer symbol with the word "buffer". That is, X is the pointer or address of the X-buffer X@.

Releasing Buffers. A new buffer can be created dynamically using the NEW procedure. There may also be a requirement to get rid of buffer when it is no longer needed. In the example, it could be that an array of INTEGER values is followed by an array of REAL values.

DISPOSE is a standard procedure which is used to release a buffer. Its general form is

```
DISPOSE (pointer variable)
```

After execution of the DISPOSE procedure the buffer addressed by the pointer variable becomes inaccessible. The Pascal processor may reassign and/or reuse the area for other purposes. Once its associated buffer is DISPOSEd of, the value of a pointer variable is indeterminate and cannot be used again until it is reassigned a value using either an assignment statement or as a parameter of NEW.

14.2.4 The Basic Ideas Summarized

The important ideas associated with pointer variables are:

1. The value of a pointer variable is a memory address. The type of value found at this address is that found in the declaration of the pointer variable. The range of values which can be assigned to a pointer variable is the range of memory addresses controlled by the Pascal processor.

2. The area of memory addressed by a pointer variable is called a buffer. A buffer is referred to by appending the pointer character to a pointer variable name.

3. NIL is a special pointer constant denoting no-address. NIL can be assigned to any pointer variable.

4. The expression "NEW(pointer)" creates a buffer and assigns its address to the pointer variable parameter.

5. The invocation "DISPOSE (pointer)" de-activates the buffer associated with the parameter.

14.3 Exercise 14.1

1. What is the output from the following program?

```
PROGRAM EX14_1_1(OUTPUT);
VAR
  X, Y, Z : @INTEGER;
BEGIN
  NEW(X); NEW(Y); NEW(Z);
  X@ := 5; Y@ := 7; Z@ := 12;
  IF SQR(Z@) > SQR(X@) + SQR(Y@) THEN
    WRITELN(Z@ * X@+Y@)
  ELSE
    WRITELN(Z@, ABS(Y@-X@))
END.
```

2. What is printed by the following program?

```
PROGRAM EX14_1_2(INPUT,OUTPUT);
TYPE
  CHAR_POINTER = @CHAR;
VAR
  C     : PACKED ARRAY [1..5] OF CHAR;
  C_PTR : PACKED ARRAY [1..5] OF CHAR_POINTER;
  I     : INTEGER;
BEGIN
  FOR I := 1 TO 5 DO
    BEGIN
      NEW(C_PTR[I]);
      READ(C[I], C_PTR[I]@);
      IF C[I] > C_PTR[I]@ THEN
        C_PTR[I] := NIL
    END;
  FOR I := 1 TO 5 DO
    IF C_PTR[I] = NIL THEN
      WRITE(C[I])
    ELSE
      WRITE(C_PTR[I]@);
  WRITELN
END.
$ENTRY
ABCCEDFG4X
```

3. Given the declarations below, what is the error in each of the following?

```
TYPE
  COLOR_TYPE = (RED, GREEN, BLUE);
  COLOR_POINTER = @COLOR_TYPE;
VAR
  COL_PTR1, COL_PTR2, COL_PTR3 : COLOR_POINTER;
a) NEW(COLOR_POINTER)
b) RED := COL_PTR1@
c) DISPOSE(COL_PTR2@)
d) COL_PTR3@ = GREEN OR COL_PTR1@ = GREEN
e) IF COL_PTR1 > COL_PTR2 THEN
f) PROCEDURE COLORS(VAR A : @(RED,GREEN,BLUE))
g) DISPOSE(COL_PTR1); IF COL_PTR1 = NIL THEN
```

4. Can you think of any use for:
    a) an array of pointer variables?
    b) a pointer variable which points to a pointer variable? For
       example:

```
TYPE
  BOOL_POINTER = @BOOLEAN;
  BOOL_POINTER_POINTER = @BOOL_POINTER
```

14.4 Pascal Data Structures: A Review

The example in the preceding section shows how the procedures NEW and DISPOSE are used to create and destroy variables at execution-time. The most important use of pointer variables, however, is in the creation of data structures other than the array, record, file and set. In some cases, the required data structure may be static such as one which represents a network of highways (highways are not created and destroyed frequently). In other cases such as a queue of people waiting for a bus, the structure changes as the queue expands and contracts. Pointer variables permit static structures to be created easily and, when coupled with NEW and DISPOSE, dynamic structures are also relatively easy to create and modify.

Let us first review the structures of the predefined types available in Pascal.

A single value has no structure because structure depends on the relationships among the component parts. Hence there must be more than one value or component for a structure to exist.

Although a set has multiple values, it is likewise unstructured because it is simply a collection of scalar values in which the components (the members of the set) are not individually accessible. For example, you cannot process the third component of a set because the members of the set are unordered.

Arrays and records are examples of direct access data structures. A direct access structure is one in which the components can be referred to directly by specifying either the name of the component in the case of a record, or by the component subscript in the case of an array.

A Pascal file structure is a special instance of the family of linked list structures. Consider the diagram below in which each box represents a component in a linked list.

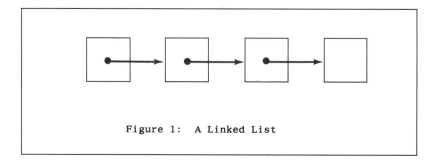

Figure 1:   A Linked List

The arrows connecting pairs of successive components indicate that each component contains a pointer to the next component in the list. In order to find a particular component you must start at the beginning of the list and follow the arrows until the desired component is found.

A Pascal file is a restricted form of linked list in that:

● A component can only be added to the end of a file and cannot be inserted at the beginning or between two existing components.

● At any point in time a file is either available for reading (retrieving components) or writing (appending components) but not both.

● The REWRITE procedure deletes all components in a file. There is no way to delete a single component without making a copy of the entire file excluding the particular component.

These restrictions can be overcome using pointer variables to connect components in various ways. Examples follow.

14.5 Linked Lists

A *linked list* is a sequence of components in which each component except the last contains a pointer to the next component in the list. The last component typically contains a NIL pointer. In Pascal, the components are almost always records. Records are used because fields in a record may have different types and for a linked list, one of the fields must be a pointer to the next record in the list. A diagram of a linked list is shown below:

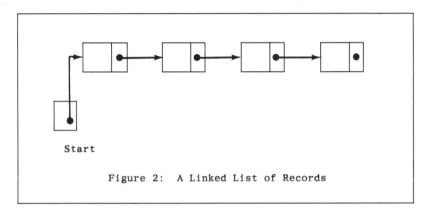

```
    Start
```

Figure 2:   A Linked List of Records

The partitioned boxes represent records. The last partition of the box denotes the field in the record which points to the next record in the list. The box labelled Start is a pointer variable which points to the first record in the list. The last record in the list does not point to any other record. The value of its pointer field is NIL.

A list can be modified by adding a component at the beginning, middle or end; deleting a component; or changing the value of one or more fields.

If components are added and removed only at one end of the list, it is called a *stack* or *push-down list*. If components are added at one end and removed at the other, it is called a *queue*. Other special cases have also been given names such as rings and doubly-linked lists but in this text they are lumped together under the general heading linked lists.

14.6 Stacks

A stack is a list in which components are added and removed from the same end of the list. If the records are "piled vertically" or stacked, a new record is stacked on top of the other records. Stacks occur in the real world in many places. Railway cars pushed onto a dead-end siding form a stack; a pile of plates in a cafeteria forms a stack because clean plates are added to and removed from the top. Because one end of a stack serves both as the entrance and exit, any item removed must will have been on the stack a shorter length of time than those below it. For this reason, stacks are sometimes called LIFO (Last-In-First-Out) lists.

In the world of programming, compilers use stacks extensively. At execution time, recursive functions and procedures stack the values needed for each invocation of the subprogram.

An example. The lines of input data consist of either a plus sign followed by an integer or a minus sign. If a plus sign is found, the number which follows is to be pushed onto the stack. If a minus sign is present, the number on the top of the stack is to be "popped". (To "pop" a stack means to remove the topmost element. The problem is to read the input lines and perform the push and pop operations indicated.

Analysis. At any point in time the stack will consist of one or more records. The first field will contain the data of interest which in this example is an integer. The second field will point to the record below it in the stack. Thus the following types are needed.

```
TYPE
  INFO_TYPE = INTEGER; (* data of interest *)
  STACK_REC_POINTER = @STACK_REC; (* pointer type *)
  STACK_REC = RECORD (* buffer type *)
                INFO       : INFO_TYPE;
                NEXT_REC   : STACK_REC_POINTER
              END
```

In keeping with the convention for naming types, the suffix "_POINTER" is appended to a meaningful type name. Note that it is impossible to satisfy the requirement that an identifier be declared before it is used. Specifically STACK_REC refers to STACK_REC_POINTER and STACK_REC_POINTER refers to STACK_REC. Most Pascal compilers require the pointer variable to be declared first.

To keep track of the stack we need a variable to point to the top record in the stack. In the case of an empty stack, this TOP variable will have the value NIL.

The mainline algorithm for the problem is straightforward:

1. Create an empty stack
2. While data exists
   .1 Read the action code
   .2 If the action code is '+'
      .1 Read the number
      .2 Push it onto the stack
   Else if the action code is '-'
      .1 Pop the last value

It is clear we should use two procedures -- one to push items onto the stack and one to perform the pop operation. Here is the PUSH procedure.

```
PROCEDURE PUSH ( VAR TOP : STACK_REC_POINTER; DATA : INFO_TYPE);

   (* THIS PROCEDURE PUSHES THE DATA ONTO THE STACK *)

   VAR
     NEW_TOP : STACK_REC_POINTER; (* ADDRESS OF THE NEW RECORD *)

   BEGIN (* PUSH *)
     NEW (NEW_TOP); (* CREATE A NEW RECORD *)
     NEW_TOP@.INFO := DATA;
     NEW_TOP@.NEXT_REC := TOP; (* LINK NEW REC TO OLD TOP *)
     TOP := NEW_TOP (* UPDATE THE TOP POINTER *)
   END; (* PUSH *)
```

Note the construction of the expression "NEW_TOP@.INFO". NEW_TOP is a pointer to a record; NEW_TOP@ *is* that record; NEW_TOP@.INFO is the first field in the record.

To pop (remove) a record, requires the following three steps to be executed.

1. Save the pointer to the current top record
2. Cause Top to point to the second record
3. Dispose of the former top record

The POP procedure follows.

```
PROCEDURE POP (VAR TOP : STACK_REC_POINTER;
               VAR DATA: INFO_TYPE          );

  (* THIS PROCEDURE REMOVES THE TOP RECORD FROM THE
     STACK AND RETURNS ITS INFO IN DATA                *)

  VAR
    OLD_TOP : STACK_REC_POINTER; (* TOP BEFORE THE POP *)

  BEGIN (* POP *)
    OLD_TOP := TOP; (* SAVE THE TOP ADDRESS *)
    DATA := TOP@.INFO;
    TOP := TOP@.NEXT_REC; (* NEW TOP IS SECOND RECORD *)
    DISPOSE (OLD_TOP); (* RELEASE THE OLD RECORD *)
  END; (* POP *)
```

What would happen if POP were invoked and there were no records in the
stack? Technically speaking, this is called a "stack underflow" and indicates a
logic error. To avoid stack underflows an IF statement of the form below
should be used.

```
IF top ≠ NIL then
  POP ( ....)
ELSE
    WRITELN (' ERROR *** STACK UNDERFLOW', ...)
```

The complete program excluding the PUSH and POP procedures is shown
below.

```
PROGRAM STACK(INPUT,OUTPUT);

(* THIS PROGRAM DEMONSTRATES THE PRINCIPLES OF DEFINING AND
   MANAGING A STACK. IT STACKS POSITIVE NUMBERS ENTERED FROM
   THE KEYBOARD AND REMOVES THE TOP ELEMENT OF THE STACK IF
   A MINUS SIGN IS ENTERED                                    *)

CONST
  PLUS = '+';
  MINUS = '-';

TYPE
  INFO_TYPE   = INTEGER; (* TYPE OF DATA IN STACKED RECORDS *)
  STACK_REC_POINTER = @STACK_REC;
  STACK_REC   = RECORD
                  INFO      : INFO_TYPE;
                  NEXT_REC  : STACK_REC_POINTER
                END;
```

... (continued on the next page)

```
VAR
   TOP        : STACK_REC_POINTER; (* POINTS TO TOP OF STACK *)
   ACTION     : CHAR; (* PLUS OR MINUS *)
   VALUE      : INFO_TYPE; (* DATA PUT IN STACK RECORDS *)

(* PROCEDURE PUSH ( VAR TOP : STACK_REC_POINTER;
                     DATA : INFO_TYPE );
        - block of PUSH goes here                         *)

(* PROCEDURE POP (VAR TOP : STACK_REC_POINTER;
                   VAR DATA: INFO_TYPE          );
        - block of POP goes here                          *)

BEGIN (* STACK *)
   WRITELN('ENTER ''+'' AND A NUMBER TO ADD A RECORD');
   WRITELN('ENTER ''-'' TO REMOVE A RECORD');
   WRITELN('ENTER AN EMPTY LINE TO EXIT');
   TOP := NIL; (* INITIALIZE THE STACK *)
   WHILE NOT EOLN DO
     BEGIN
       READ(ACTION);
       IF ACTION = PLUS THEN
         BEGIN (* add a record *)
           READ (VALUE);
           PUSH (TOP, VALUE);
           WRITELN(VALUE,' HAS BEEN PUSHED')
         END
       ELSE IF ACTION = MINUS THEN
         BEGIN (* remove a record *)
           POP (TOP, VALUE);
           WRITELN(VALUE,' HAS BEEN POPPED')
         END;
       READLN (* SKIP THE END-OF-LINE CHARACTER *)
     END (* WHILE *)
END. (* STACK *)
```

One final point. What is the advantage of declaring INFO_TYPE equivalent to INTEGER? Why not use INTEGER every place INFO_TYPE appears? The advantage is that by giving a name to the type of data in the records, PUSH and POP are more general and may be used without modifications in many programs. That is, only the declaration of INFO_TYPE may have to be changed.

14.7 Queues

The word queue is synonymous with waiting line. Examples are a queue of people waiting for a bus, a queue of jobs waiting for processing on the computer, or a queue of buy/sell orders at the stock exchange. The simplest representation of a queue which can be manipulated on a computer is a linked list of records in which records are added at the back of the queue and removed from the front. This queue discipline is called FIFO which stands for first in, first out. Recall that a stack is LIFO -- last in, first out.

The figure below is a schematic representation of a queue.

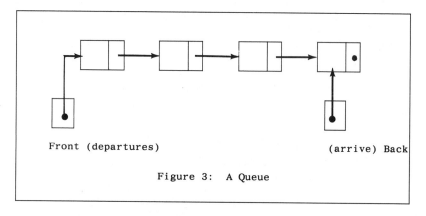

Front (departures)   (arrive) Back

Figure 3:   A Queue

Each "person" in the queue points to the person behind.

An Example Problem. A number of people arrive, join a queue and subsequently leave. Each arrival or departure is indicated by a line of input data where: a plus sign followed by a name denotes an arrival; a minus sign denotes a departure. When a departure takes place, the name of the person leaving does not need to be specified because the queue discipline requires the first item in the the queue to be removed. The problem is to read the data and print a sequence of messages indicating the activity taking place such as:

RALPH	ARRIVED
SUE	ARRIVED
RALPH	DEPARTED
DIANE	ARRIVED
etc.	

Analysis. The items in the queue will be records containing two fields -- an "info" field containing a name and a pointer to the next record in the queue. We will use the following types.

```
TYPE
  INFO_TYPE = PACKED ARRAY [1..NAME_LENGTH] OF CHAR;
  Q_REC_POINTER = @Q_REC;
  Q_REC = RECORD
              INFO      : INFO_TYPE;
              NEXT_REC  : Q_REC_POINTER
          END
```

The use of INFO_TYPE is recommended as it makes the procedures for manipulating queues more general. To keep track of the queue we need two pointers declared as follows:

```
VAR
  FRONT, BACK : Q_REC_POINTER
```

What logic routines are required in the program? The mainline logic is straightforward. After creating an empty queue we should read each input line and either create and append a record to the back of the queue or remove a record from the front of the queue. An error condition is present if an attempt is made to remove a record when the queue is empty. It is natural therefore to use three procedures:

EMPTY - a function which is true if the queue is empty

ARRIVAL - a   procedure which adds a record to the back of the queue

DEPARTURE - a procedure which removes the record at the front of the queue

The EMPTY function is simply:

```
FUNCTION EMPTY (FRONT : Q_REC_POINTER) : BOOLEAN;

  (* RETURNS TRUE IF Q IS EMPTY *)

BEGIN (* EMPTY *)
  EMPTY := FRONT = NIL
END; (* EMPTY *)
```

The ARRIVAL logic should: create a new record; store the data in the new record; cause the current last record to point to the new one; and cause BACK to point to the newly-created record. If the queue is empty at the time of an arrival, then FRONT must be updated as well. Here is the ARRIVAL procedure.

```
PROCEDURE ARRIVAL (VAR FRONT, BACK : Q_REC_POINTER;
                       DATA : INFO_TYPE      );

  (* THIS PROCEDURE ADDS A RECORD TO THE BACK OF THE Q *)

  VAR
    NEW_BACK : Q_REC_POINTER;

  BEGIN (* ARRIVAL *)
    NEW (NEW_BACK); (* CREATE A NEW RECORD *)
    NEW_BACK@.INFO := DATA; (* STORE THE DATA *)
    NEW_BACK@.NEXT_REC := NIL; (* DENOTES LAST REC *)
    IF NOT EMPTY(FRONT) THEN
      BACK@.NEXT_REC := NEW_BACK (* LINK OLDBACK *)
    ELSE
      FRONT := NEW_BACK;
    BACK := NEW_BACK (* CHANGE POINTER TO BACK OF Q *)
  END; (* ARRIVAL *)
```

The DEPARTURE actions involve changing FRONT to point to the second record (if there is one) and disposing of the old front record.

```
PROCEDURE DEPARTURE (VAR FRONT : Q_REC_POINTER;
                     VAR DATA  : INFO_TYPE      );

  (* THIS PROCEDURE REMOVES THE RECORD AT THE FRONT *)

  VAR
    OLD_FRONT : Q_REC_POINTER;

  BEGIN (* DEPARTURE *)
    OLD_FRONT := FRONT;
    DATA := FRONT@.INFO; (* RETURN DATA BEING REMOVED *)
    FRONT := FRONT@.NEXT_REC; (* 2ND REC BECOMES FRONT *)
    DISPOSE (OLD_FRONT) (* RELEASE RECORD *)
  END; (* DEPARTURE *)
```

The mainline excluding the EMPTY, ARRIVAL and DEPARTURE
procedures is shown below.

```
PROGRAM QUEUE(INPUT,OUTPUT);

(* THIS PROGRAM DEMONSTRATES THE PRINCIPLES OF DEFINING AND
   MANAGING A QUEUE. IT ADDS PEOPLE TO THE BACK OF THE QUEUE
   AND REMOVES THEM FROM THE FRONT                         *)

CONST
  PLUS = '+'; (* DENOTES A QUEUE ARRIVAL *)
  MINUS = '-'; (* DENOTES A QUEUE DEPARTURE *)
  NAME_LENGTH = 10; (* MAX LENGTH OF NAME *)
  BLANK = ' ';

TYPE
  INFO_TYPE = PACKED ARRAY [1..NAME_LENGTH] OF CHAR;
  Q_REC_POINTER = @Q_REC;
  Q_REC  = RECORD
                  INFO       : INFO_TYPE;
                  NEXT_REC   : Q_REC_POINTER
              END;

VAR
  FRONT, BACK : Q_REC_POINTER; (* FRONT AND BACK OF Q *)
  ACTION      : CHAR; (* PLUS OR MINUS *)
  NAME        : INFO_TYPE; (* DATA PUT IN Q RECORDS *)
  I           : 1..NAME_LENGTH; (* NAME ARRAY INDEX *)

(*  FUNCTION EMPTY (FRONT : Q_REC_POINTER) : BOOLEAN;
        - block of EMPTY goes here               *)

(* PROCEDURE ARRIVAL (VAR FRONT, BACK : Q_REC_POINTER;
                    DATA : INFO_TYPE    );
        - block of ARRIVAL goes here                *)

(* PROCEDURE DEPARTURE (VAR FRONT : Q_REC_POINTER;
                    VAR DATA  : INFO_TYPE    );
        - block of DEPARTURE goes here        *)
```

... (continued on the next page)

```
BEGIN (* QUEUE *)
  FRONT := NIL; BACK := NIL; (* INITIALIZE Q *)
  WRITELN('ENTER ''+'' AND A NAME TO JOIN Q');
  WRITELN('ENTER ''-'' TO DEPART FROM THE Q');
  WRITELN('ENTER AN EMPTY LINE TO EXIT');
  WHILE NOT EOLN DO
    BEGIN
      READ(ACTION);
      IF ACTION = PLUS THEN (* arrival *)
        BEGIN
          FOR I := 1 TO NAME_LENGTH DO
            IF NOT EOLN THEN
              READ(NAME[I])
            ELSE
              NAME[I] := BLANK;
          ARRIVAL (FRONT, BACK, NAME);
          WRITELN (NAME,' HAS JOINED THE QUEUE')
        END (* ADD TO Q *)
      ELSE IF ACTION = MINUS THEN (* departure *)
        BEGIN
          IF NOT EMPTY(FRONT) THEN
            BEGIN
              DEPARTURE(FRONT, NAME);
              WRITELN(NAME,' HAS LEFT THE QUEUE')
            END
          ELSE
            WRITELN('QUEUE EMPTY, DEPARTURE NOT PERMITTED')
        END; (* ELSE *)
      READLN (* SKIP END-OF-LINE-CHARACTER *)
    END (* WHILE *)
END. (* QUEUE *)
```

14.8 General Linked Lists

A general linked list is a sequence of components linked by pointers. The words "head" and "tail" are often used to denote the first and last items in the list. Unlike a stack in which items are added and removed at the same end, or a queue in which items are added at one end and removed at the other, in a general linked list items can be inserted at or removed from any location in the list.

14.8.1 Maintaining an Ordered List

An example problem. The input data consists of several lines containing one word per line. The objective is to read the words which are in random alphabetical order, and store them in a linked list so that they are maintained in dictionary sequence. Thus after reading each word, the list must be searched to find the correct location to insert the new record.

Analysis. The type declarations needed are the following.

```
TYPE
  INFO_TYPE = PACKED ARRAY [1..WORD_LENGTH] OF CHAR;
  LIST_REC_POINTER = @LIST_REC;
  LIST_REC = RECORD
               INFO      : INFO_TYPE;
               NEXT_REC  : LIST_REC_POINTER
             END
```

The mainline logic is:

1. Create an empty list
2. While data exists
    .1 Create a new record and store the word
    .2 Find out where the record goes in the list
    .3 Insert the record in the list
3. Print the contents of the list

Based on the algorithm, we should use four procedures to perform the create, find, insert and print actions. The following four subsections discuss each in turn.

Creation. The creation procedure simply obtains the data and stores it in a newly-created record. It returns the address of the new record and is

```
PROCEDURE CREATE (VAR NEW_REC : LIST_REC_POINTER);

  (* THIS PROCEDURE CREATES A NEW RECORD FOR THE LIST *)

VAR
  I : INTEGER; (* FOR LOOP INDEX *)

BEGIN (* CREATE *)
  NEW (NEW_REC); (* CREATE AN EMPTY RECORD *)
  FOR I := 1 TO WORD_LENGTH DO
    IF NOT EOLN THEN
      READ(NEW_REC@.INFO[I])
    ELSE
      NEW_REC@.INFO[I] := ' ';
  NEW_REC@.NEXT_REC := NIL;
  READLN; (* SKIP END-OF-LINE CHAR *)
END; (* CREATE *)
```

Find. The FIND procedure should return the address of the record which the new record is to follow. This makes it easy to perform the insertion. If the new word belongs at the head of the list, FIND returns a value of NIL. Here it is.

```
PROCEDURE FIND ( HEAD : LIST_REC_POINTER;
                 DATA : INFO_TYPE;
                 VAR AFTER_REC : LIST_REC_POINTER);

(* THIS PROCEDURE DETERMINES THE POSITION IN THE LIST
   AFTER WHICH A NEW RECORD CONTAINING 'DATA' SHOULD
   BE INSERTED. 'AFTER_REC' IS NIL IF THE NEW DATA
   BELONGS AT THE FRONT OF THE LIST                     *)

VAR
   LOOPING : BOOLEAN; (* CONTROLS SEARCH LOOP *)
   CURRENT, NEXT : LIST_REC_POINTER;

BEGIN (* FIND *)
   IF HEAD = NIL THEN (* empty list *)
      AFTER_REC := NIL
   ELSE IF DATA < HEAD@.INFO THEN (* insert at front *)
      AFTER_REC := NIL
   ELSE (* location is after some existing record *)
      BEGIN (* SEARCH *)
         LOOPING := TRUE;
         CURRENT := HEAD;
         WHILE LOOPING DO
            BEGIN
               NEXT := CURRENT@.NEXT_REC;
               IF NEXT = NIL THEN
                  LOOPING := FALSE (* END OF LIST *)
               ELSE IF DATA < NEXT@.INFO THEN
                  LOOPING := FALSE (* LOCATION FOUND *)
               ELSE (* KEEP GOING *)
                  CURRENT := NEXT
            END; (* WHILE *)
         AFTER_REC := CURRENT
      END (* SEARCH *)
END; (* FIND *)
```

Insertion. Given the result of FIND, the logic to insert a record has three separate cases namely: the list is empty; the record goes at the head of a non-empty list; the record follows some other existing record. The INSERT procedure is shown below.

```
PROCEDURE INSERT (VAR HEAD : LIST_REC_POINTER;
                     NEW_REC, AFTER_REC: LIST_REC_POINTER );

  (* THIS PROCEDURE INSERTS A NEW RECORD IN THE LIST
     FOLLOWING AFTER_REC. IF AFTER_REC IS NIL, THE NEW
     RECORD IS PUT AT THE HEAD OF THE LIST            *)

  BEGIN (* INSERT *)
    IF HEAD = NIL THEN (* list was empty *)
      HEAD := NEW_REC
    ELSE IF AFTER_REC = NIL THEN (* insertion is new head *)
      BEGIN
        NEW_REC@.NEXT_REC := HEAD;
        HEAD := NEW_REC
      END
    ELSE (* follows some other record *)
      BEGIN
        NEW_REC@.NEXT_REC := AFTER_REC@.NEXT_REC;
        AFTER_REC@.NEXT_REC := NEW_REC
      END
  END; (* INSERT *)
```

Print. The procedure to print the data in the list is:

```
PROCEDURE PRINT_LIST ( HEAD : LIST_REC_POINTER );

VAR
  CURRENT : LIST_REC_POINTER;

  BEGIN (* PRINT_LIST *)
    WRITELN('THE INFORMATION IN THE LIST IS:');
    CURRENT := HEAD;
    WHILE CURRENT <> NIL DO
      BEGIN
        WRITELN(CURRENT@.INFO);
        CURRENT := CURRENT@.NEXT_REC
      END
  END; (* PRINT_LIST *)
```

The complete program excluding the four procedures follows.

```
       PROGRAM WORD_LIST (INPUT, OUTPUT);

       (* THIS PROGRAM BUILDS A LIST OF WORDS IN ALPHABETICAL
          ORDER AND THEN PRINTS THE LIST                        *)

       CONST
         WORD_LENGTH = 15;

       TYPE
         INFO_TYPE = PACKED ARRAY [1..WORD_LENGTH] OF CHAR;
         LIST_REC_POINTER = @LIST_REC;
         LIST_REC = RECORD
                      INFO : INFO_TYPE;
                      NEXT_REC : LIST_REC_POINTER
                    END;

       VAR
         HEAD, NEW_REC, AFTER_REC : LIST_REC_POINTER;

       (* PROCEDURE CREATE (VAR NEW_REC : LIST_REC_POINTER);
            - block of CREATE goes here             *)

       (* PROCEDURE FIND ( HEAD : LIST_REC_POINTER;
                           DATA : INFO_TYPE;
                           VAR AFTER_REC : LIST_REC_POINTER);
            - block of FIND goes here               *)

       (* PROCEDURE INSERT (VAR HEAD : LIST_REC_POINTER;
                         NEW_REC, AFTER_REC: LIST_REC_POINTER );
            - block of INSERT goes here          *)

       (* PROCEDURE PRINT_LIST ( HEAD : LIST_REC_POINTER );
              - block of PRINT_LIST goes here        *)

       BEGIN (* WORD_LIST *)
         HEAD := NIL; (* AN EMPTY LIST *)
         WRITELN('ENTER WORDS ONE PER LINE, EMPTY LINE TO EXIT');
         WHILE NOT EOLN DO
           BEGIN
             CREATE(NEW_REC); (* BUILD A WORD RECORD *)
             FIND(HEAD, NEW_REC@.INFO, AFTER_REC); (* LOCATION *)
             INSERT(HEAD, NEW_REC, AFTER_REC) (* INSERT IT *)
           END;
         PRINT_LIST(HEAD)
       END. (* WORD_LIST *)
```

Observe that the procedures FIND and INSERT have similar structures. Should they be combined into a single procedure? It does make sense for the given problem because a new item is always put in the list. However FIND can also be used to determine if a word is already in the list. In this case it returns the address of the record containing the word. Hence FIND is useful for answering queries as well as a prelude to list insertion.

14.8.2 Other Linked Lists

There are many other kinds of linked lists. A *ring* is a linked list in which the last item in the list points to the first. A *doubly - linked* list is one in which each record contains pointers to the record preceding and the record following it. Insertion and deletion of records in a doubly-linked list is slightly more complicated than the logic to update a singly-linked list but in some instances, the ability to search forward and backwards is important. The doubly-linked ring also has some useful applications. A D-queue (double queue) is one in which additions and deletions can take place at either end.

14.8.3 Networks

The most general linked structure is called a *network* or *plex*. A network consists of a number of nodes linked together by arcs or edges. To store the data about the distances between towns in the network below, a linked list structure could be used in which the information about each town is kept in a single record.

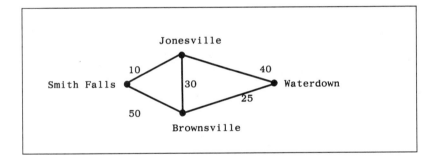

Suppose the data to be kept about each town includes its name, population, and distance to each adjacent town. Because each record must have the same type (a pointer can only point to one type of value or record) and because Jonesville and Brownsville are adjacent to three other towns, each town record must have provision for pointing to as many as three other towns. Suitable declarations are shown below.

```
CONST
  NAME_LENGTH   = 20;  (* CHARACTERS IN A NAME *)
  MAX_NEIGHBORS=  3;  (* MAX NUMBER OF ADJACENT TOWNS *)

TYPE
  TOWN_REC_POINTER = @TOWN_REC;
  TOWN_REC = RECORD
               NAME : PACKED ARRAY[1..NAME_LENGTH] OF CHAR;
               POPULATION : 0..MAXINT;
               NEIGHBOR : ARRAY [1..MAX_NEIGHBORS] OF
                          RECORD
                            DISTANCE : 1..MAXINT;
                            NEXT_TOWN : TOWN_REC_POINTER
                          END
             END (* TOWN RECORD *)
```

If a town has only one neighbor, the pointers in the second and third elements of its NEIGHBOR array are set to NIL. Using the above definitions, questions such as: "What is the closest town to Jonesville?" and "What towns have only two neighbors?" can be answered easily. More complicated questions such as "What is the shortest route between Smith Falls and Waterdown?" or "What towns are within X miles of Brownsville?" require more complex algorithms.

In general, if the data in a network is static (does not change frequently) the use of arrays to store the data is often preferable. In cases where the network requires updating regularly, a linked list approach is likely better.

14.9 Trees

A data structure has a tree-structure if it has the properties illustrated in the diagram below.

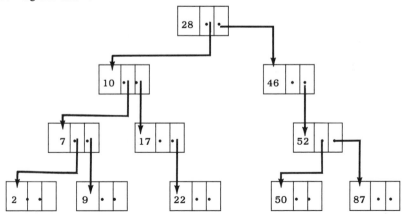

The reason for using the word "tree" is clear even though the tree is drawn upside down. In such a tree, the *root node* is the one at the top. The root node does not have any pointers to it. Observe also that there is a path from the root node to every other node in the tree. Nodes which do not point to any other node are called *leaf nodes*. The '87' node is an example of a leaf node.

If each node in a tree contains pointers to at most two other nodes, it is called a *binary tree* or *B-tree*. The example tree is a binary tree. Binary trees have many useful applications. One is sorting numbers or other values. This application is illustrated later in this section.

The data in a binary tree is most easily stored by using records containing fields which have the data of interest and a pair of pointers to the nodes (records) below them in the tree. In many applications each node has a unique value called its *key*. The example tree can be represented by records using the types below.

```
TYPE
  KEY_TYPE = REAL;
  (* INFO_TYPE = other data in a node record *)
  NODE_POINTER = @NODE_REC;
  NODE_REC = RECORD
                KEY : KEY_TYPE;
                (* INFO : INFO_TYPE *)
                LEFT, RIGHT : NODE_REC_POINTER
             END
```

Family terminology is frequently used when describing trees. In a binary tree, nodes have a left son and right son. Each son has a parent node. Terms such as ancestors, descendants, uncles, offspring and even cousins may be used to describe the relationship among nodes in a tree. In the example the '7' and '17' nodes are brothers; '28' is the parent of the '10' and '46' nodes; '17' and '52' are first cousins.

14.9.1 Displaying the Contents of Tree

In what sequence should the values in the nodes of a tree be printed? Three common orderings are used. Observe that any node in a tree can be viewed as the root of a *subtree* containing the nodes below it. For example, the 10 node is the root of the tree containing the 10, 7, 17, 2, 9 and 22 nodes. Similarly for a given node the terms left subtree and right subtree refer to the subtrees of which the left son and right son are the roots. The three systematic orderings of the nodes are as follows:

1. Preorder : root node, left subtree, right subtree
2. Inorder   : left subtree, root node, right subtree
3. Postorder : left subtree, right subtree, root

The prefix "pre", "in" or "post" indicates whether the root node is printed before, between or after the subtree nodes. By applying the same rule to print the subtree values as is used to print the entire tree, a complete, unambiguous algorithm is available for displaying the node values. For example, the three orderings applied to the example tree result in the following sequences.

Preorder (root first)
   28, 10, 7, 2, 9, 17, 22, 46, 52, 50, 87

Inorder (root between subtrees)
   2, 7, 9, 10, 17, 22, 28, 46, 50, 52, 87

Postorder (root last)
   2, 9, 7, 22, 17, 10, 50, 87, 52, 46, 28

You probably observed that the inorder sequence results in a list of increasing values! This is not a coincidence. In the example tree, the value of the left son of every node is less than the root node value, and the value of the right son is greater than the root value. In this situation, printing the node values in inorder sequence produces an ascending sequence of values. This is the property which is exploited when using a binary tree to sort values.

A procedure to print the node values in inorder sequence is shown below. The procedure is recursive because it invokes itself to print the values in the left and right subtrees.

```
PROCEDURE PRINT_TREE (ROOT : NODE_POINTER);

   (* THIS PROCEDURE PRINTS THE KEY VALUES IN THE
      TREE IN INORDER SEQUENCE (LEFT SUB-TREE, ROOT,
      RIGHT SUB-TREE). THE PROCEDURE IS RECURSIVE. *)

BEGIN (* PRINT_TREE *)
  IF ROOT <> NIL THEN
    BEGIN
      PRINT_TREE (ROOT@.LEFT);
      WRITELN (ROOT@.KEY:6:2);
      PRINT_TREE (ROOT@.RIGHT)
    END
END; (* PRINT_TREE *)
```

14.9.2 Finding A Value In A Tree

Given a tree in which each node has a unique value called its key, a procedure can be written which returns a pointer to the node in the tree containing the key. If the key is not present, the procedure can return a pointer to the node which would be the parent if a node containing the key were added to the tree. Shown below is a procedure which can be used with a tree containing numeric keys.

```
PROCEDURE FIND ( VAR PARENT : NODE_POINTER;
                 SEARCH_KEY : KEY_TYPE);

 (* FIND DETERMINES IF THE SEARCH_KEY IS IN THE TREE. IF SO,
    PARENT IS THE NODE CONTAINING THE KEY. IF NOT FOUND,
    PARENT IS THE NODE WHICH SHOULD BE USED AS THE PARENT *)

BEGIN (* FIND *)
  IF PARENT <> NIL THEN
    BEGIN
      IF (SEARCH_KEY < PARENT@.KEY) AND
                  (PARENT@.LEFT <> NIL) THEN
        BEGIN (* SEARCH LSEFT SUBTREE *)
          PARENT := PARENT@.LEFT;
          FIND (PARENT,SEARCH_KEY)
        END
      ELSE IF (SEARCH_KEY > PARENT@.KEY) AND
                     (PARENT@.RIGHT<>NIL) THEN
        BEGIN (* SEARCH RIGHT SUBTREE *)
          PARENT := PARENT@.RIGHT;
          FIND(PARENT,SEARCH_KEY)
        END
    END
END; (* FIND *)
```

Searching for a key in a binary tree requires relatively few comparisons to be made. For this reason, many collections of data which are searched frequently are kept as binary trees. The next subsection illustrates the use and construction of a binary tree.

14.9.3 Building A Sorted Binary Tree

Suppose the input data contains a number of REAL values to be arranged in ascending sequence. To perform the sort, a binary tree is to be built such that when the nodes are visited in inorder sequence (left tree, root, right tree),, they will be in order of increasing values. Duplicate values in the input should be ignored. The algorithm is given below.

1. Create an empty tree
2. While data exists
    .1 Find its location of the key value in the tree
    .2 If not found
        .1 Create a node record
    .3 Insert it into the tree
3. Print the key values in inorder sequence

Node Creation. The logic to create a node record involves using NEW to get a new record; storing the key value in the data field; and assigning NIL to the left and right sons. The CREATE procedure is shown below.

```
PROCEDURE CREATE ( VAR NEW_NODE : NODE_POINTER;
                       KEY : KEY_TYPE        );

  (* THIS PROCEDURE CREATES AND INITIALIZES A NODE RECORD *)

  BEGIN (* CREATE *)
    NEW (NEW_NODE);
    NEW_NODE@.KEY := KEY;
    NEW_NODE@.LEFT := NIL;
    NEW_NODE@.RIGHT := NIL
  END; (* CREATE *)
```

Node Insertion. Given a pointer to the parent node, the logic to insert a new node as either the left son or right son is straightforward. A special case occurs when the tree is empty prior to insertion. This empty-tree condition is indicated by assinging NIL to the parent parameter.

```
PROCEDURE INSERT (VAR PARENT : NODE_POINTER;
                      NEW_NODE : NODE_POINTER);

  (* THIS PROCEDURE INSERTS THE NEW INTO THE TREE AS
     EITHER THE LEFT SON OR RIGHT SON OF THE PARENT NODE *)

  BEGIN (* INSERT *)
    IF PARENT = NIL THEN (* EMPTY TREE *)
      ROOT := NEW_NODE
    ELSE
      IF NEW_NODE@.KEY < PARENT@.KEY THEN
        PARENT@.LEFT := NEW_NODE
      ELSE
        PARENT@.RIGHT := NEW_NODE
  END; (* INSERT *)
```

The complete program to build and print the key values follows.

```
PROGRAM TREE_SORT(INPUT, OUTPUT);

(* THIS PROGRAM READS A SEQUENCE OF NUMBERS AND BUILDS A
   A BINARY TREE SUCH THAT WHEN THE LEAF NODE ARE VISITED
   IN INORDER SEQUENCE, THE VALUES INCREASE IN MAGNITUDE *)

TYPE
  KEY_TYPE = REAL; (* NODE KEY *)
  (* INFO_TYPE = OTHER DATA PRESENT IN NODE *)
  NODE_POINTER = @NODE_REC;
  NODE_REC = RECORD
                KEY : KEY_TYPE;
                (* INFO : INFO_TYPE *)
                LEFT, RIGHT : NODE_POINTER
             END;

VAR
  ROOT, PARENT, NEW_NODE : NODE_POINTER;
  KEY_VALUE              : KEY_TYPE;
  FOUND                  : BOOLEAN;

(* PROCEDURE CREATE ( VAR NEW_NODE : NODE_POINTER;
                     KEY : KEY_TYPE     );
     - block of CREATE goes here              *)

(* PROCEDURE FIND ( VAR PARENT : NODE_POINTER;
                   SEARCH_KEY : KEY_TYPE);
     - block of FIND goes here                  *)

PROCEDURE INSERT (VAR PARENT : NODE_POINTER;
                  NEW_NODE   : NODE_POINTER);
     - block of INSERT goes here              *)

(* PROCEDURE PRINT_TREE (ROOT : NODE_POINTER);
     - block of PRINT_TREE goes here        *)
```

... (continued on the next page)

```
BEGIN (* TREE_SORT *)
  ROOT := NIL; (* EMPTY TREE *)
  WRITELN ('ENTER KEY VALUES, EMPTY LINE TO EXIT');
  WHILE NOT EOLN DO
    BEGIN
      READLN (KEY_VALUE);
      PARENT := ROOT;
      FOUND := FALSE; (* ASSUME NOT FOUND *)
      IF ROOT <> NIL THEN
        BEGIN
          FIND (PARENT, KEY_VALUE);
          FOUND := KEY_VALUE = PARENT@.KEY
        END;
      IF NOT FOUND THEN
        BEGIN
          CREATE (NEW_NODE, KEY_VALUE);
          INSERT (PARENT, NEW_NODE);
        END
    END; (* WHILE *)
  PRINT_TREE (ROOT)
END. (* TREE_SORT *)
```

14.9.4 Deleting a Node From A Tree

The procedure used to delete a node from a binary tree is in general more complicated than that to add a node. The reason is that because a new node is always a leaf node, it is simply a matter of finding which position preserves the ordering of the key values. Similarly when deleting a leaf node or a node with only one son, the procedure is likewise simple. Consider the number tree used previously as an example.

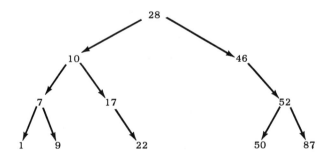

For example to delete the '9' node, the right pointer from '7' is set to NIL and the '9' node DISPOSEd of. Similarly, to delete the '46' node, the '52' node simply moves up to take its place. (The right son of '28' becomes the '52' node.) Complications arise however when deleting a node with two non-NIL sons such as the 10, 28, or 52 nodes. For example, if the 10 node is deleted, what is the left son of 28? In order to preserve the relationship:

```
left son ≤ father ≤ right son
```

the node which replaces a father node must have a value between the two sons. It follows that this value can be either the largest value less than the father or the smallest value greater than the father. If 10 is being deleted for example, either 9 or 17 could be used as the replacement node. The result in the two cases is shown below.

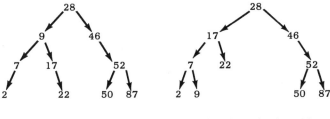

         With 9 Replacing 10   With 17 Replacing 10

Similarly if the root node 28 is deleted, it can be replaced by either the largest value in the left subtree (the 22 node) or the smallest value in the right subtree (the 46 node).

Details of the algorithm are left to the reader. An example of a recursive algorithm for performing node deletion can be found in Chapter 4 of Niklaus Wirth's book *Algorithms + Data Structures = Programs*.

14.9.5 Analysis of Tree Search and Insertion

Does the shape of the tree make any difference in the performance of routines which build or examine nodes in the tree? Most definitely. Suppose the input data happens to be in increasing sequence prior to building the tree. What shape will the tree have? With a little thought you will realize that every node including the root will only have a right son. Hence the result is simply a linked list. The power of the tree structure to efficiently sort and find particular values depends to what extent the tree is balanced. A perfectly balanced tree is one in which for every node the difference between the number of nodes in the left subtree and the right subtree is at most one. With respect to the example tree for instance, the tree is not perfectly balanced because there are six nodes in the left subtree of the root node and four in its right subtree. Note however, that four of the subtrees in the example tree are perfectly balanced.

The efficiency of a balanced tree results from the fact that you don't need to go very far down the tree to either add, locate or find a replacement node.

Since in general the order of input values cannot be controlled when building a tree, several algorithms exist for balancing a tree after it has been created. Algorithms also exist for maintaining balance when adding or deleting nodes. These can be found in the aforementioned reference.

14.10 Summary

1. Pointer variables are used to create variables at execution-time and to link together variables (usually records) to form various data structures.

2. The value of a pointer variable is a memory address of a variable of a given type. Pointer variables can be assigned the value of another pointer variable or NIL. Pointer values can only be compared for equality.

3. Variables of the same type can be linked together by defining a record having two or more fields. Some fields contain data; others are pointers to other records of the same type.

4. One of the most commonly-used data structures is a linked list. Stacks and queues are particular kinds of linked lists.

5. A tree is a suitable vehicle for storing data having a hierarchical structure. A binary tree is an efficient way to create, maintain and retrieve data having a natural ordering.

14.11 Programming Problems

14.1   Modify the first example program in the chapter to permit a series of INTEGER and REAL arrays to be processed. When testing the program, use values of 5 and 3 for MAX_INTS and MAX_REALS rather than 4000 and 1000.

14.2   The input consists of the surnames of a number of individuals. Read the names and put each one in a record which is appended to the end of a linked list. After the last name has been read, point the last record to the record containing the first name thus forming a ring. Assuming clockwise to mean the original order of the data, print the name of: the second person clockwise from the first person; the fifth person counterclockwise from the last person.

14.3   Draw a circle. Write the letters of the alphabet and a blank around the outside of the circle in a clockwise direction. Write a program which reads in a value of N and then a sentence. (a) Translate the sentence into a coded message by replacing each symbol in the sentence by the symbol which is N positions clockwise around the circle. Print the coded message. (b) Print the original message by decoding the message produced in part (a). Use a ring of records to store the letters. Make use of the logic developed for the previous question.

14.4   Add to the general linked-list program found in Section 14.8 logic to print the list in reverse order. This permits an ordered list of values to be displayed in either ascending or descending sequence.

14.5   Develop algorithms and procedures for creating, searching and updating a doubly linked list. A doubly linked list is one which contains two pointer fields -- one to the next record in the list and one to the previous record. Test your program using the names of people as the data field in the record. Print the names in forward and reverse order after the list has been constructed. What are the advantages and disadvantages of doubly linked lists?

14.6   A factorial value can be calculated recursively. If Pascal did not have recursive functions, recursion could still be performed using pointer variables to control a stack. Write a program which uses a stack to calculate the value of the factorial for an integer between one and ten.

14.7   The first line of input consists of a number of people's names. Read the names, storing them in a binary tree. Print the names in reverse alphabetical order. The second input line also contains several names. For each name found, print a message of the type: "CHARLIE NOT FOUND" or "CHARLIE EXISTS".

14.8   Assume the tree used in the previous problem represents a genealogical (family) tree in which the root node represents the first generation. (Because it is a binary tree, it implies no individual can have more than two children!) Answer the following questions. Who are the second generation. For each third generation person, print the name of his or her aunt or uncle (there can only be one) and the names of all his or her first cousins. Who has the most grandchildren?

14.9   A consumer has $15,000 and is debating whether to buy a small foreign car or a large domestic car. The relevant data is as follows.

	Small	Large
purchase price	$10,000	$15,000
miles/gallon	35	22
annual maint. cost	400	350
depreciation/year	15%	10%

Assume that: the car will be driven 12,000 miles per year; the cost of gas is currently $2.00/gal and will increase ten percent per year; the difference in purchase prices ($5,000) could be invested at 8 percent per year; the depreciation applies to the value of the car at the start of each year.

Write a program which determines the net position of the consumer at the end of each of the next five years.

14.10   Suppose, while practicing your basketball shooting you perform the following drill. Starting one foot away from the basket you take a shot. If you make the shot, you step back one foot and shoot again. As long as you keep making the shot you move back one more foot for the next shot. As soon as you miss, you return to the one-foot mark and start again. Suppose the probability of making a shot from N feet away is (1 - 0.01N). Use simulation to answer the following questions.

   a)   During 100 shots, how many are taken from 1 foot, 2 feet, 3 feet, ...?

   b)   What is the average number of shots which must be taken before being successful at a distance of fifteen feet. (Run the simulation ten times, stopping each time the first successful shot from fifteen feet occurs. Average the ten counts.)

   c)   Given that a shot has just been successful from five feet away, what is the probability of making an eight foot shot without any intervening misses.

   d)   Answer questions (a), (b), (c) above using the rule that when a miss occurs, you move one foot closer rather than return to the start. Assume that if you miss at one foot, you stay there until a shot is made.

14.11   A friend has watched you play the game described n the previous question and offers you the following bet. *After* each of your shots, he will take one shot from the foul line which is twelve feet from the basket. If he misses before you do, he will pay you $5. If you miss any shot up to and including a shot from the foul line, you pay him $10. Suppose the probability of him making a foul line shot is 0.9. Should you take the bet? Does it make any difference if he has to shoot first? How would you determine a fair payoff for the game?

Part III:
Appendices

APPENDIX A: CHARACTER SETS AND STANDARD IDENTIFIERS

A.1 Character Sets

The characters used to construct identifiers in Pascal programs consist of the letters, the digits and the underscore (in some compilers). Upper and lower case letters are equivalent.

The characters have an ordering called the collating sequence. The two most common collating sequences are the ASCII and EBCDIC orderings which are defined below.

A.1.1 ORD values of the ASCII Characters

32	blank	48	0	64	@	80	P	96	`	112	p
33	!	49	1	65	A	81	Q	97	a	113	q
34	"	50	2	66	B	82	R	98	b	114	r
35	#	51	3	67	C	83	S	99	c	115	s
36	$	52	4	68	D	84	T	100	d	116	t
37	%	53	5	69	E	85	U	101	e	117	u
38	&	54	6	70	F	86	V	102	f	118	v
39	'	55	7	71	G	87	W	103	g	119	w
40	(	56	8	72	H	88	X	104	h	120	x
41	)	57	9	73	I	89	Y	105	i	121	y
42	*	58	:	74	J	90	Z	106	j	122	z
43	+	59	;	75	K	91	[	107	k	123	{
44	,	60	<	76	L	92	\	108	l	124	|
45	-	61	=	77	M	93	]	109	m	125	}
46	.	62	>	78	N	94	^	110	n	126	~
47	/	63	?	79	O	95	_	111	o		

A.1.2 The EBCDIC Characters

Letters.

129	a	145	j			193	A	209	J		
130	b	146	k	162	s	194	B	210	K	226	S
131	c	147	l	163	t	195	C	211	L	227	T
132	d	148	m	164	u	196	D	212	M	228	U
133	e	149	n	165	v	197	E	213	N	229	V
134	f	150	o	166	w	198	F	214	O	230	W
135	g	151	p	167	x	199	G	215	P	231	X
136	h	152	q	168	y	200	H	216	Q	232	Y
137	i	153	r	169	z	201	I	217	R	233	Z

Digits.

The digits 0 through 9 have ORD values of 240 through 249

Special Characters.

ORD	Character	ORD	Character	ORD	Character
64	blank	74	cent sign	75	period
76	less than	77	(	78	plus
79	vertical bar	80	ampersand		
90	exclamation	91	dollar sign	92	asterisk
93	)	94	semicolon	95	not sign
96	hyphen	97	slash	107	comma
108	percent	109	underscore	110	greater than
111	question mark	122	colon	123	number sign
124	at sign	125	single quote	126	equal sign
127	double quote				

A.2 Special Symbols

Certain characters and character-sequences are called special symbols. Some Pascal implementations recognize equivalent characters or character pairs.

Special Symbols (Other than Reserved Words)

```
+      -      *      /      =      <      >
.      ,      ;      :      (      )      ↑
[      ]      <=     >=     <>     :=     ..
       and blank
```

The following equivalences are recognized by some compilers.

```
≤      and    <=             ≥      and    >=
≠      and    <>
(*     and    {              *)     and    }
(.     and ⌐ [               .)     and    ]
'↑'    and    '@'    and    '∧'
```

Special Symbols (Reserved Words)

AND	ARRAY	BEGIN	CASE	CONST
DIV	DO	DOWNTO	ELSE	END
FILE	FOR	FUNCTION	GOTO	IF
IN	LABEL	MOD	NIL	NOT
OF	OR	PACKED	PROCEDURE	PROGRAM
RECORD	REPEAT	SET	THEN	TO
TYPE	UNTIL	VAR	WHILE	WITH

A.3 Standard Identifiers

The following identifiers are recognized by all Pascal compilers. They are not reserved words. They can be declared as having a different meaning from the standard.

```
Constants
      TRUE        FALSE       MAXINT

Types
      BOOLEAN      CHAR       INTEGER      REAL       TEXT

Files
      INPUT       OUTPUT

Procedures
      DISPOSE      GET        NEW        PACK       PAGE       PUT
      READ         READLN     RESET      REWRITE    UNPACK     WRITE
      WRITELN

Functions
      ABS         ARCTAN      CHR        COS        EOF        EOLN
      EXP         LN          ODD        ORD        PRED       ROUND
      SIN         SQR         SQRT       SUCC       TRUNC

Directive
      FORWARD
```

A.4 Operators

A.4.1 Arithmetic operators

Operator	Operation	Type of operands	Type of result
+	addition	INTEGER/REAL	INTEGER/REAL
−	subtraction	INTEGER/REAL	INTEGER/REAL
*	multiplication	INTEGER/REAL	INTEGER/REAL
/	division	INTEGER/REAL	REAL
DIV	integer division	INTEGER	INTEGER
MOD	modulo reduction	INTEGER	INTEGER

For any arithmetic operator, the result is REAL if either operand is REAL.

A.4.2 Boolean operators

Each Boolean operator requires its operand(s) to be of type BOOLEAN and produces a result of type BOOLEAN.

```
Operator      Number of operands        Operation

  NOT               1                logical negation
  AND               2                logical and
  OR                2                logical or
```

A.4.3 Relational operators

Each relational operator requires two operands and produces a result of type
BOOLEAN. With the exception of IN, both operands must have the same
type unless one is REAL and the other is INTEGER.

```
Operator     Operation              Type of operands

= <>         equal to, not equal to REAL, ordinal, string,
                                              set, pointer
< >          less than, greater than REAL, ordinal, string
<=           less than or equal to  REAL, ordinal, string, set
>=           greater than or equal to REAL, ordinal, string, set
IN           set membership         left: ordinal type
                                    right: set of the same
                                              ordinal type
```

When applied to sets, the operators <= and >= mean "is contained within"
and "contains" respectively.

A.4.4 Set Operators

Each set operator requires two operands of the same set types and produces a
result of the same type.

```
Operator        Operation

  +           set union
  -           set difference
  *           set intersection
```

A.4.5 Priorities of Operators (highest to lowest)

```
1.  NOT
2.  *   /   DIV   MOD   AND
3.  +   -   OR
4.  =   <>   <     >    <=   >=    IN
```

Within a level, operators have equal priority and are applied left to right.

APPENDIX B: PASCAL SYNTAX DIAGRAMS

The following three pages contain syntax diagrams for standard Pascal.

Names within rectangular boxes refer to other syntax diagrams. Words and symbols within rounded enclosures must be used exactly as written.

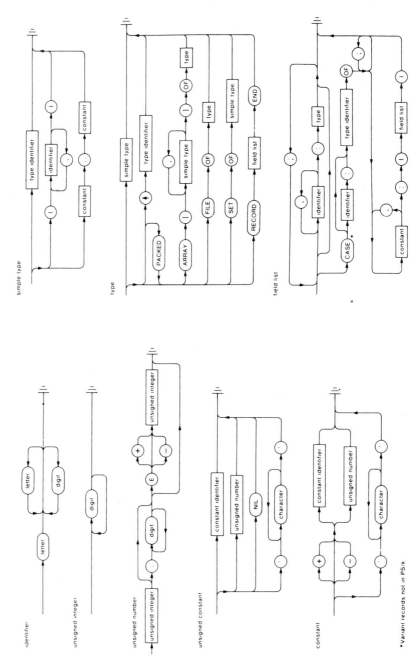

*Variant records not in PS/k

Reprinted with permission from: Holt, R.C., and Hume, J.N.P. Programming Standard Pascal. Reston, VA: Reston Publishing Company, Inc., 1980.

348

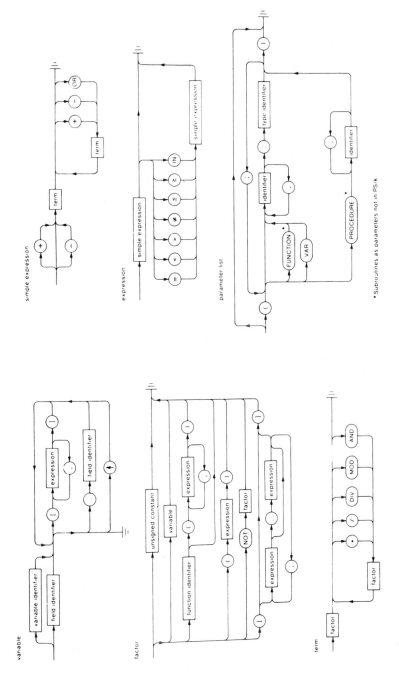

Reprinted with permission from: Holt, R.C., and Hume, J.N.P. Programming Standard Pascal. Reston, VA: Reston Publishing Company, Inc., 1980.

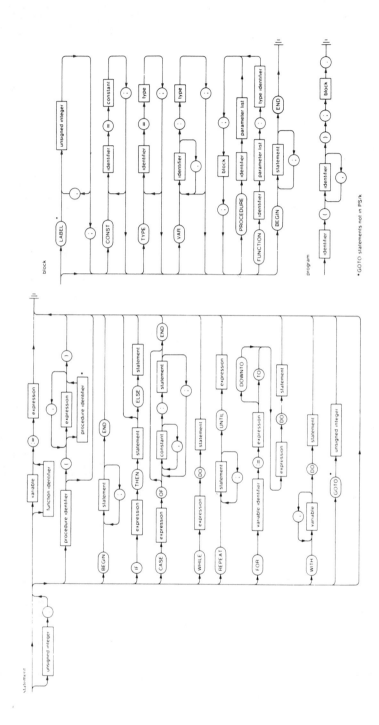

Reprinted with permission from: Holt, R.C., and Hume, J.N.P. *Programming Standard Pascal*. Reston, VA: Reston Publishing Company, Inc., 1980.

350

APPENDIX C: WATERLOO PASCAL

C.1 Introduction

This appendix provides information about the Waterloo Pascal implementation of the Pascal language. It is adapted from the material in Appendix G of *Waterloo Pascal Users Guide* by Boswell, Welch, and Grove, published by WATFAC Publications Ltd. Permission from the authors and the publisher to reproduce this material is gratefully acknowledged.

The first section provides an overview of the language, its running environment and important features. The remainder of this Appendix has four sections: a description of the language supported by the Waterloo Pascal compiler, including minor language extensions, I/O facilities, and various system-dependent attributes; a description of the debugging facilities that are available with interactive versions of the compiler; a description of the multiprocessing extensions; and a description of the string extension.

C.1.1 Overview

At the University of Waterloo, it became apparent that a "debugging" Pascal compiler was needed in the same spirit as the WATFIV and WATBOL compilers. Such a compiler has a special set of objectives, including:

1. a fast compilation rate:

2. a comprehensive set of readily-understandable compile-time diagnostics, in full English text (as opposed to error codes or numbers);

3. a run-time environment that ensures that all run-time violations are detected and meaningfully diagnosed; and

4. facilities which enable a programmer to debug programs quickly and efficiently.

Such a "teaching" compiler may tend to sacrifice execution speed in order to meet these objectives, as compared to "production" compilers. This, however, is an acceptable tradeoff, since most student programs are not usually executed more than a few times (it has been observed that once a student obtains a working program, it is rarely run again).

Work on the compiler began in May, 1979, and a prototype version has been in use by undergraduate students at the University of Waterloo since September, 1979. This section describes version V3.1 which became available in 1984. A VAX VMS version should also be available.

C.1.2 Environments - Availability

The Waterloo Pascal compiler was designed to be portable, and is written in a portable systems-implementation language called WSL (Waterloo Systems Language). The current implementation of Waterloo Pascal is for the IBM /370 architecture. The compiler was developed on an IBM 4331 under the VM/CMS operating system, and is currently running under both the VM/CMS and OS (MVT, VMS, TSO) operating systems. The VM/CMS version has been implemented in such a way as to take full advantage of the interactive capabilities of that system, whereas the OS version is oriented more towards a batch environment.

C.1.3 Features of Waterloo Pascal

In order to achieve a reasonable compilation rate, it was decided to implement a one-pass, "compile and execute" processor, eliminating the overhead associated with such things as temporary work files, and the "linkage edit" step.

Interactive versions of Waterloo Pascal include a debugger which may be used to oversee a program during execution. The debugging facilities include temporary execution suspension ("breakpoints"), control flow tracing, and variable examination. The debugger may be activated when a program begins execution, or by causing an attention interrupt at any point during execution.

The compiler produces two output files: a LISTING file, and a diagnostics (DIAGS) file. The LISTING file contains a list of the source program statements (with any compile-time error messages inserted into the listing at the point of error), followed by the program output (with any run-time error messages), followed by some statistical information.

The DIAGS file is a summary of all diagnostic and statistical information. Error messages contain a line number reference to the source file. If the interactive debugger is used, the DIAGS file will also contain a copy of all the debugger output. This feature is useful for producing hard copies of program traces.

Particular attention is paid to the problem of "cascading error messages" (that is, where one error may cause many other error messages) which seems to plague many compilers of Pascal-like languages.

The classes of run-time errors that Waterloo Pascal detects are:

● attempt to use a variable that has not been assigned a value;

● attempts to assign a value that is outside the declared range of a variable;

- array subscripting errors;

- attempts to use a NIL pointer, or to use previously "disposed" memory;

- dynamic storage resources exhausted;

- run-stack overflow (for example, infinite recursion detection);

- attempt to violate variant record rules; and

- control statement semantics: branching into an inactive FOR or WITH statement; no case match in a CASE statement. no case match in a CASE statement.

It is important that these conditions are detected and diagnosed "gracefully"; not simply indicated by an operating-system-dependent error message. In the event of any run-time error, Waterloo Pascal displays:

- the name of the variable involved (if any);

- the source-file line number where execution was taking place when the error occurred; and

- a traceback of all functions and procedures and their points of activation.

In the event of a run-time error in interactive environments, the debugger may be used to perform a post-mortem examination of the state of the program. In batch environments (or interactive environments where the debugger is not used) a list of scalar and string variables and their values is given at each level of the procedure/function traceback.

C.2 Waterloo Pascal Language Description

C.2.1 The Pascal Language

Unlike many other programming languages, there is no universally-accepted standard for the Pascal language. The *Pascal User Manual and Report* by Jensen and Wirth, published by Springer-Verlag, is the original definition of the Pascal language. The International Organization for Standardization (ISO) is currently preparing a standard for Pascal; its latest draft is the 97/5 N 678 - Third Draft Proposal ISO/DP 7185, Specification for the Computer Programming Language Pascal. The language accepted by the Waterloo Pascal compiler corresponds quite closely with these two documents.

C.2.2 Particulars of the Waterloo Pascal Implementation

Implementation-defined Attributes

The ISO draft standard requires an implementor to define certain attributes of an implementation. Those that are noted here pertain to the IBM/370 architecture versions of Waterloo Pascal.

1. The type CHAR is defined to be all 256 EBCDIC characters. This includes all uper and lower case letters, and all special characters. Note that the alphabetic characters are not contiguous in the collating sequence.

2. MAXINT is defined to be 2,147,483,647 (that is, 2^{31} -1).

3. The largest REAL value is approximately 7.2E+75, and the smallest positive REAL value (machine epsilon) is approximately 5.4E-79.

4. The default field widths used by procedures WRITE and WRITELN are 12, 5, and 16 for INTEGER, BOOLEAN, and REAL, respectively. The default number of decimal places displayed by WRITE and WRITELN for a REAL number in exponential notation is 9.

5. The exponent character used by WRITE and WRITELN for a number in exponential notation is "E", although both "E" and "e" may be used in program constants.

6. The BOOLEAN constants TRUE and FALSE are written as "TRUE" and "FALSE", respectively.

7. The standard procedure PAGE puts an ASA control character "1" on any file with a record length of 121 or 133 characters (these record lengths imply a printable file). Note that this includes the compiler's LISTING file (which contains the standard file OUTPUT).

8. The effect of RESETting or REWRITEing the standard files INPUT or OUTPUT is the same as for any file.

9. Any PROGRAM parameters (parameters to the program statement) other than INPUT and OUTPUT are ignored.

Implementation-dependent Attributes

The ISO draft standard also allows an implementor to specify various other attributes about its implementation.

1. The only procedure directive in Waterloo Pascal is the FORWARD directive (there is no EXTERNAL directive).

2. Declaring a structured type to be PACKED has no effect on the internal representation.

3. The operands of a dyadic operator are evaluated left-to-right so that in the following expression, the left-operand-expression is evaluated first:

    left-operand-exprn   operator   right-operand-exprn

    This includes the assignment operator. Also, BOOLEAN expressions are always evaluated completely (there is no partial expression optimization).

4. The order of evaluation and binding of function and procedure actual parameters is strictly left-to-right.

5. Reading from a file to which PAGE was applied has no special effect.

6. There are some additional standard functions and procedures (see Section 2.5).

7. Sets may have a maximum of 50,000 elements.

8. The default size of the run stack is 10,000 bytes (all variables, both global and local, are allocated from this area).

9. Data items of the type CHAR are stored in one byte.

10. INTEGER, enumerated types, and subrange types are stored in four bytes.

11. Data items of the type REAL are stored in eight bytes.

File I/O Considerations

This subsection outlines some of the specifics of the operating-system interfaces as they apply to file input/output in the VM/CMS environment.

Source files. Waterloo Pascal will accept source files in either fixed-length or variable-length record formats. The filetype of source files must be "PASCAL", and they may reside on any accessed mini-disk (Waterloo Pascal will search all disks according to the CMS search order).

Standard Output Files. The compiler output files (LISTING and DIAGS) are created on the A-disk, and are fixed-length files with record lengths of 121 and 80 bytes, respectively.

The standard file OUTPUT is written onto both the LISTING file and the user's terminal (see Section C.1.3 of this Appendix). If the source program is contained in a file with a CMS filename of "MYPROG", then the LISTING and DIAGS files are called "MYPROG LISTING A" and "MYPROG DIAGS A", respectively.

Input Files. Suppose a the file MYPROG PASCAL A contains the following lines:

```
PROGRAM PROGNAME ( ... , X);
       .
       .
VAR X : FILE OF ....;
       .
       .
RESET( X );
       .
       .
```

Waterloo Pascal will attempt to open the file "X FILE A" for input. For the same program segment, the standard TEXT file INPUT would have the VM/CMS filename "MYPROG INPUT A". As an alternative, the data for INPUT may be placed in the program source file following a line containing "$ENTRY" (the "$ENTRY" is understood by the compiler to separate the program and the data). If a "$ENTRY" line is present, the data following it is used, and the VM/CMS file is not opened.

Terminal Input/Output. Since VM/CMS is an interactive system, it is natural to write interactive programs that communicate with a terminal. For this, Waterloo Pascal recognizes the special filename "terminal": thus,

```
RESET( TERM_IN, 'TERMINAL' );   and
REWRITE( TERM_OUT, 'TERMINAL" );
```

open a user's terminal for input and output, respectively. Note that the names TERM_IN and TERM_OUT are not special; they are simply Pascal variable names. The inherent problem with interactive I/O in Pascal (due to the language definition) has been solved by means of a technique known as "lazy I/O", so that interactive I/O works as one would expect.

The special names "READER", "PRINTER", and "PUNCH" are also recognized and refer to VM/CMS virtual devices.

General File Specification. Waterloo Pascal allows more general forms of the standard functions RESET and REWRITE so that VM/CMS files may be accessed by name during execution. For example, either

```
RESET( X, 'MASTER DATA A' );   or   REWRITE( X, 'MASTER DATA A' )
```

would open the VM/CMS file "MASTER DATA A". It is also possible to use

```
RESET( X, FILENAME );    or    REWRITE( X, FILENAME )
```

where FILENAME is a PACKED ARRAY OF CHAR containing a VM/CMS filename.

File Attributes. When Waterloo Pascal creates a file with an activation of REWRITE, the default file attributes of that file are:

- fixed-length records of 80 bytes for TEXT files, and

- whatever is required for all other types of files (for example, a FILE OF INTEGER requires a fixed-length record of four bytes).

These default attributes may be over-ridden by placing the desired attributes ahead of the CMS file name in the extended forms of the RESET and REWRITE statements. The attribute specification has the form "(type : component length)" where:

- type is "T" for TEXT files and "F" for all other files

- component length is the *maximum* length in characters (bytes) in a TEXT file or the number of bytes required for a component for any other file

For example,

```
RESET (TRANSACTIONS,  '(T:40)TRANS DATA A')
REWRITE (MASTER_FILE,  '(F:800)MASTER DATA A')
```

specifies that the input file with the variable name TRANSACTIONS is a TEXT file with a maximum length of 40 characters and that MASTER_FILE components are to be written with 800 byte records. The record length should match the the number of bytes required by a component. Component lengths can be determined from the information in subsection C.2.2 above.

Options

Options in Waterloo Pascal are specified by means of a special type of comment. The first character in the comment must be a dollar-sign ($). A list of one or more options, separated by commmas may then be specified. The options implemented are:

1. L+,L-   source listing control. The default is "L+" (list the source).

2. C+,C-   compiler output case control. Since some I/O devices may not support lower case alphabetic characters, Waterloo Pascal will translate all compiler output (the DIAGS file, the source listing portion of the LISTING file, and terminal messages) into upper case. The default is "C-" (do not translate).

3. S n   run stack size control. The default is n = 10000 bytes, and the minimum allowed is 1000 bytes.

4. X n   statement execution control. Waterloo Pascal limits the

number of statements that a program may execute. The default is n = 25000. Each installation sets an absolute limit for this option; it may be specified as n = 0.

5. P n   standard output control. The "P" option controls the number of physical lines that may be written (by a program) on the LISTING file. The default is n = 1000. Like the "X" option, there is an installation maximum for the "P" option which may be specified as P = 0.

6. W+,W-   warning message control. There are a few situations where Waterloo Pascal will issue a warning, rather than an error (for example, a ";" detected inside a comment). These messages may be controlled with the "W" option; "W+" for notification, "W-" for no notification. The default is "W+".

7. T+,T-   trailing blanks control. The option is used to control whether or not trailing blanks will be removed from TEXT file input lines. The default is T- meaning that trailing blanks are removed (the last non-blank character in the line is immediately followed by the end-of-line character). T+ means that lines are not modified in any way.

The "S", "X", "P" and "T" options have no effect until the program begins execution. Thus, if they are specified more than once, the last textual occurrence in the source program is the one used. The "C" and "W" options have effect during both the compilation and execution of a program. During compilation, they may be changed as desired, but it is the last textual occurrence of the option that is used throughout the execution of the program.

Standard Functions and Procedures Waterloo Pascal provides several additional standard routines beyond those specified for standard Pascal.

a) Procedure RTOS

RTOS ("Real To String") converts a REAL or INTEGER value to a sequence of characters. There are two or three parameters, as follows:

Parameter 1:   - the value to be converted
                      - may be INTEGER or REAL

Parameter 2:   - the string variable containing the result
                      - the result is right justified and padded with blanks on the left

Parameter 3:   - optional
                      - if specified, must be an INTEGER value giving the number of decimal places in the result

The format of the result depends on the expression type and whether the number of decimal places in the result (Parameter 3) is specified. For example, given

        VAR S : PACKED ARRAY [1..12]

the table below shows the result in the four cases and illustrates each with an example.

Expr'n Type	Precision Given	Resulting Format	Example Expression	Result 123456789 12
REAL	no	exponential	RTOS(123.45, S)	0.12345E 03
REAL	yes	fixed point	RTOS(123.45,S,1)	123.4
INTEGER	no	integer	RTOS(123,S)	123
INTEGER	yes	fixed point	RTOS(123,S,2)	123.00

b) Function STOR

STOR ("String To Real") converts a string representing a REAL or INTEGER number into a REAL number (which may be converted into an INTEGER by use of the ROUND or TRUNC standard functions). It takes one parameter, namely the string to be converted. For example, if X is REAL then

        X := STOR('12.34E+5')

causes the variable x to have the correct internal representation of the given REAL number. The format of the numbers that may be converted is the standard (usual) Pascal number format.

c) Function ARCTAN2

ARCTAN2(y, x) computes the inverse tangent of y/x, where x and y may be either INTEGER or REAL. The only values for which ARCTAN2 is not defined are $y = x = 0$.

   The motivation for ARCTAN2(y, x) (as opposed to ARCTAN(y/x)) is that given y and x separately, it is possible to determine the sign of the result).

d) Procedures TRACEON and TRACEOFF

TRACEON may be used to "trace" the execution of a program. If it is invoked, all subsequent invocations of user procedures and/or functions cause a line to be displayed indicating the name of the routine being invoked, plus the value of any scalar or string parameters to the routine. TRACEOFF is used to disable the tracing feature. Neither procedure requires any parameters.

e) Procedures START, RECEIVE, SEND, REPLY

Waterloo Pascal supports simulated multiple concurrent processes by means of two standard functions (START and RECEIVE) and two standard procedures (SEND and REPLY). The syntax and semantics of these routines is described in detail in *Multiple Concurrent Processes in Waterloo Pascal* in section 4 of this Appendix.

f) String Extension Functions and Procedures

Most of the function provided by the string extension is achived through a set of standard functions and procedures, including STRCONCAT, STRDELETE, STRINSERT, STRLEN, STRSCAN, STRSIZE and SUBSTR. The string extension is described in detailin section 5 of this Appendix.

g) Procedures CHECKOFF and CHECKON

Normally, Waterloo Pascal will detect the use of a variable which has not been assigned a value. Occasionally, however, it is desirable to disable this checking. Procedures CHECKOFF and CHECKON are provided to allow the user to disable (with "CHECKOFF") and re-enable (with "CHECKON") the uninitialized variable checking.

Neither procedure requires any parameters.

Character-set Extensions

Because some of the special characters used in the Pascal language may not be available on some I/O devices, Waterloo Pascal recognizes the following escape sequences:

```
(*    . . .          opening brace bracket
*)    . . .          closing brace bracket
).    . . .          opening square bracket
.)    . . .          closing square bracket
@     . . .          upward-pointing arrow
```

In addition, the cent-sign and not-sign (or tilde) may be used instead of the upward-pointing arrow.

Miscellaneous Considerations

All identifiers are case-insensitive. For example, mydata, MyData and MYDATA are equivalent variable identifiers.

The underscore character "_" is permitted in identifiers.

Instead of the "$ENTRY" used for separating the program source and the standard INPUT file, a "%EOF" may be used. The batch versions of Waterlo Pascal permit an installation to define various other "control" records for use in source files. Users of the batch versions should consult their systems personnel for information regarding their installation.

The "$PAGE" directive is available to force the compiler to begin the next line of the LISTING file at the top of a new page.

The compiler should not be used with source files that have a record length greater than 100.

Sequence numbers are not part of the Pascal language; thus, the compiler will not accept programs that have them.

Permanent Restrictions

In order to ensure the security of the run-time environment of Waterloo Pascal (that is, to allow complete run-time semantic checking), the restriction that file types may not contain pointer types is enforced.

The uninitialized variable checking in Waterloo Pascal is implemented by setting all variables to a special "uninitialized" value prior to their use by a program. Occasionally, this special value will interfere with a legitimate Pascal program. The following table shows the special values used by the compiler for uninitialized variable checking which might conflict with a legitimate value.

```
        variable type          "uninitialized" value

        CHAR                  CHR( 254 )
        INTEGER               -16,843,010
        REAL                  -4.50539073E+74 (approx.)
```

The uninitialized value checking may be controlled with the CHECKOFF and CHECKON standard procedures.

ISO Third DP 7185 Discrepancies

At the time of writing, the ISO Third DP 7185 was the most up-to-date Pascal Standards document. This section lists all of the known items in which the standard and Waterloo Pascal differ. The numbers following each item refer to the appropriate section in the ISO Third DP 7185.

• With the exception of the following items, Waterloo Pascal conforms to Level 0 of the standard. This means that conformant arrays are not implemented. Level 0 is equivalent to the Pascal standard proposed by the "Joint ANSI/X3J9-IEEE Pascal Standards Committee".[5]

• The underscore character "_" is allowed in identifiers. [6.1.3]

• The syntax of string constants is extended to permit string constants to be enclosed in double-quotes ("). This change is necessitated by the string extension. [6.1.7]

• Waterloo Pascal does not permit "FILE OF POINTER" types. [6.4.3.5]

- It is possible for a program to generate its own line markers (that is, the end-of-line character is a value in the standard type CHAR. [6.4.3.5]

- The implementation of the string extension requires the relaxation of the type compatibility rules for string types (that is, PACKED ARRAY [1 .. n] OF CHAR. The relaxation applies to value parameters, relational operators and assignment statements. [6.4.6; 6.6.3.2; 6.7.2.5; 6.8.2.2]

- The restriction on passing components of a PACKED type as VAR parameters is not enforced. [6.6.3.3]

- The special variant parameters of NEW AND DISPOSE are ignored. [6.6.5.3]

- Integer arithmetic expression results outside the range -MAXINT..MAXINT do not cause an error (INTEGER overflow is not detected). [6.7.7.2]

- The alteration of a FOR index variable because of a function or procedure side-effect is not detected. [6.8.3.9]

- The standard procedures READ and READLN are modified to permit the reading of variables of the generic string type. This change is necessitated by the string extension. [6.9.1; 6.9.2]

C.3 Waterloo Pascal Interactive Debugging Facility

C.3.1 Introduction

The VM/CMS version of Waterloo Pascal supports an interactive debugger. It has three classes of debugging facilities:

1. temporary execution suspension ("breakpoints").

2. control flow tracing, and

3. examination of variables.

A breakpoint is defined as a place in the program at which execution is to be suspended temporarily. When a breakpoint is reached, the debugger is invoked and the prompt "debug?" is displayed, soliciting a command from the terminal. The user may then set or remove breakpoints, set or remove trace ranges, or examine the contents of variables.

To invoke Waterloo Pascal with the debugger, use the command:

```
PW   -D filename
```

Where "PW" represents whatever command is used to invoke the Waterlo Pascal compiler. The debugger will be invoked just before execution of the program begins so that breakpoints and/or trace ranges may be set. If a run-time error occurs, the debugger will be invoked one final time so that the user may perform a post-mortem examination of the variables in the program.

Alternately, the debugger may be invoked at any time by causing an attention interrupt. Causing such an interrupt depends upon the particular system and type of terminal being used. It may be a break key, return key, attention key, enter key, PA1 key, or some other key. When the attention is created, the debugger will be invoked, and will display a message such as:

Interrupt at line 20 in body of program 'demo'

This interrupt feature is independent of whether or not the "-d" was specified on the command line used to invoke the compiler.

C.3.2 Debug Commands

All commands are specified by their first letter (in either upper or lower case). The commands are as follows:

1. Breakpoint

    The breakpoint command is used to specify locations in a program where execution is to be suspended and the debugger is to be invoked. Breakpoint uses the following subcommands (only the first letter need be specified):

    • Set *range*

      - set breakpoints for the special *range*

      - a *range* is defined to be:

              line1   - at *line1* only
              line1 *line2* - from *line1* to *line2* inclusive
              *   - all lines
              **line2*   - from the first line to *line2*
              line1 *   - from *line1* to the end of the program
              routine-name   - at entry to routine *routine-name*

      - note that *line1* must be less than or equal to *line2*

      - example:

              B S 45 50 - set breakpoints on lines 45 through 50

- Reset *id-number*
    - clears a previously-set *range*

    - *id-number* is an identification number as determined by the list subcommand ("*" may be used to clear all ranges)

    - examples:

        B R 2   - removes the second breakpoint range
        B R *   - removes all breakpoints

- List
    - lists all of the ranges that are set, with their respective identification numbers

2. Trace

The trace command may be used to observe the flow of execution of a program. When trace is active, each time that a line from any trace range is executed, a message is displayed indicating the current point of execution.

Trace uses the same subcommands as the breakpoint command.

3. Display

The value of program variables may be displayed with the display command. The command requires one parameter: either the name of the variable to be displayed, or an asterisk "*". In the case of an asterisk, the values of all active scalar and string variables are displayed.

Only variables that are known (in the Pascal scope sense) at the given point of execution may be displayed.

4. Quit

The quit command immediately terminates the execution of a program.

5. Help

The help commands displays a brief summary of all the debugger commands and their operands.

6. Go

The go command is used to resume execution after a breakpoint. If single-step mode is active, the "enter" (or "return", etc.) key maybe used instead (that is, one line will be executed each time the key is depressed).

7. Single-step

The single-step command may be used to tell the debugger to suspend
execution at each line of the program. It is similar to the breakpoint
command "B S *", the advantage being that the "enter" or "return" key
may be used to resume execution, rather than the go command.

The command requires one parameter, as follows (only the first letter
of the parameter need be specified):

● Set   - enables single-step mode

● Reset   - disables single-step mode

C.4 Multiple Concurrent Processes in Waterloo Pascal

C.4.1 Introduction

Extensions have been added to Waterloo Pascal which support the use of
multiple concurrent processes.

A process may be defined loosely as a "thread of execution". When a
standard Pascal program is executed, only one process (thread of execution)
exists; execution of the program proceeds in the usual fashion. The extensions
for multiple concurrent processes permit more than one process (thread of
execution) to be active as the program is executed. A program which is made
up of a number of these concurrent processes may be viewed as a collection of
the single threads of execution, all of which are executing at the same time.
Facilities are provided so that concurrently-executing processes may
communicate with each other.

Numerous models of concurrent processes have been proposed; the scheme
used by Waterloo Pascal is based upon *Toth, A Portable Real-Time Operating
System* by Cheriton et al in CACM V22, Feb. 79. This particular model was
chosen because it requires minimal perturbation to the Pascal language (no
syntax changes are necessary, and no new keywords are required), and because
it has proven to be highly satisfactory in practical applications. The
implementation of the scheme required the addition of one standard type
(PROCESS_ID), plus the addition of two standard functions and two standard
procedures (START and RECEIVE, SEND and REPLY).

C.4.2 Process Creation

A Pascal program begins execution as a single process; the initial process
is created which starts executing at the beginning of the program body.
Subsequently, ore processes may be created and various parts of the program
may be executed concurrently. When a process is created it is said to be a
"child" of the process which created it. Similarly, the process which created
the child is said to be the "parent" of the child.

Every process is identified by a unique value of type PROCESS_ID. A new process maybe created by a function activation of the form:

new_id:= START(procedure_name) where

- new_id is a variable of type PROCESS_ID to contain the id of the newly-created process, and

- procedure_name is the name of a procedure where execution of the newly-created process is to begin. This procedure is called the "main procedure" of the newly-created process.

Notes:

1. An arbitrary number of processes may be active in any part of a program at the same time.

2. Variables which are known to several procedures will be available to all processes active in those procedures. Such shared variables may be used to communicate between processes. Each process will have its own private copies of all variables defined inside its main procedure.

3. A procedure may be passed as a parameter to START provided that the procedure is visible (in terms of scope) in the main procedure of the process executing the START.

4. A process dies (terminates) 'when its main procedure exits. If there are any local variables of the main procedure which are being used as shared variables by any children, then the parent will not in fact die until the children die.

C.4.3 Inter-process Communication

Processes communicate by means of the the standard routines SEND, RECEIVE and REPLY. A process can send a message to another process by a procedure activation of the form:

```
SEND( message_buffer, id );
```

where:

- message_buffer is the name of a variable containing the message which is to be sent (and is also where the reply to the message will be placed), and

- id is a value of type PROCESS_ID which identifies the process to which the message is directed.

The process sending the message is called the "sender" and the process receiving the message is called the "receiver". The sender is blocked from execution (may not execute) until the receiver receives, and replies to the message. A message is received by a function activation of the form:

```
sender_id := RECEIVE( message_buffer, id );    or
sender_id := RECEIVE( message_buffer );
```

where:

- sender_id is a variable of type PROCESS_ID which is assigned the id of the process which sent the message,

- message_buffer is a variable which is to receive the message being sent (it must be of the same type as the message specified by the sender), and

- id is a value of type PROCESS_ID which explicitly specifies the process from which the message is to be received. If this is not specified, a message will be accepted from any process sending a message to the receiver. If id is specified then the value returned by RECEIVE (that is, sender_id) will be the same as the value of id.

If a process executes a RECEIVE when no process is trying to SEND to it, then the receiver will be blocked from execution until some other process does execute a SEND to it.

After a process has received a message, the sender is still blocked from execution until the receiver executes a procedure activation of the form:

```
REPLY( message_buffer, id );
```

where:

- message_buffer is a variable containing a message which is to be returned to the sender, and

- id is a value of type PROCESS_ID which specifies the process to which the reply is directed. Normally, it would be the value returned by RECEIVE.

Notes:

1. Using the id of a deceased process as a parameter to SEND, RECEIVE or REPLY is an error.

2. All storage allocated by NEW is shared between all processes, and pointers may be passed im messages. Storage allocated by NEW, and not freed by DISPOSE may still be referenced after the death of the process which allocated it.

3. A common expression is:

> REPLY(message RECEIVE(message));

A situation that sometimes arises in program with multiple concurrent processes is "deadlock": each process is waiting for some event to happen (each process is blocked on some other process). If deadlock occurs, Waterloo Pascal will diagnose it as an error, and provide status information about each process.

The example program below provides a simple illustration of the concurrent processing facilities. A message is passed from the sending process to the receiving process and a reply is received.

```
PROGRAM MPDEMO( OUTPUT );

  TYPE
   MSG = PACKED ARRAY(.1..11.) OF CHAR;

  PROCEDURE RECEIVER;
   VAR
    SENDER_ID : PROCESS_ID;
    MESSAGE   : MSG;
   BEGIN
    SENDER_ID := RECEIVE( MESSAGE );
    WRITELN( MESSAGE );
    MESSAGE :='HI THERE ';
    REPLY( MESSAGE, SENDER_ID );
   END;

  PROCEDURE SENDER;
   VAR
    RECEIVER_ID : PROCESS_ID;
    MESSAGE     : MSG;
   BEGIN
    RECEIVER_ID := START( RECEIVER );
    MESSAGE :='HELLO THERE';
    SEND( MESSAGE, RECEIVER_ID );
    WRITELN( MESSAGE );
   END;

  BEGIN
   SENDER;
  END.
```

When executed, the following two lines are printed.

```
Hello there
Hi there
```

C.5 Waterloo Pascal String Extension

C.5.1 Introduction

The Waterloo Pascal string extension provides a convenient facility for string processing in Pascal. The Pascal language, as described by Jensen and Wirth or the proposed ISO standards, defines a string type as

```
PACKED ARRAY   [1 .. N]   OF CHAR
```

where N is the length of the string.

C.5.2 The Problem With Standard Pascal Strings

String types are compatible only if they are of exactly the same length, making it inconvenient to render common string-processing algorithms in Pascal. For example, in standard Pascal, 'abc' could not be assigned or compared to a string variable of any length except three.

Single character constants such as 'a' are of type CHAR and are therefore not compatible with any string types, even

```
PACKED ARRAY [ 1 .. 1 ] OF CHAR
```

In standard Pascal, there is no way to represent the null string with a constant. The zero length string constant is not allowed.

C.5.3 The Waterloo Pascal Extension

The extensions for string processing in Waterloo Pascal provide the following facilities:

1. type compatibility for unequal length strings;

2. a simple and efficient mechanism for variable length strings;

3. a method for representing string constants which are only one character long, as well as the null string;

4. a library of routines for manipulating strings;

5. a method of reading string input.

The following sections describe the various extensions in detail. They are designed in such a way as to allow standard-conforming Pascal programs to behave as always, without interference.

C.5.4 String Type Compatibility

The extension defines all string types to be uniformly compatible, without regard to their length. For example, suppose the following declarations are made:

```
VAR
    STR1 : PACKED ARRAY [ 1 .. 10 ] OF CHAR;
    STR2 : PACKED ARRAY [ 1 .. 5 ] OF CHAR:
```

The Waterloo Pascal string extension allows the following assignment statements, which would not be allowed in standard Pascal.

```
STR1 := STR2;
STR2 := STR1;
STR1 := 'ABCDEFG';
STR2 := 'ABCDEFG';
```

When a string is assigned to a variable which is not of sufficient length, the string is truncated to the appropriate length. This extension also applies to value parameter passing which has the same type compatibility rules as assignment.

The extension also allows the relational operators to be applied to strings of unequal length; for example:

```
STR1 = STR2
STR2 <= 'AB'
STR1 > 'ABCDEF'
```

C.5.5 String Constants

The usual Pascal representation for string constants, using single quotes, is of course supported. Note that a string constant of length 1 is given type CHAR. The extension provides that strings may be enclosed in double quotes. When double quotes are used, a string constant of length 1 will be given a string type, as distinct from type CHAR. The null string may be represented by two adjacent double quotes (""). The following examples illustrate this:

```
STR1 := "";
STR1 := "A";
STR1 := "AB";
STR1 := "ABC";
STR1 = ""
STR1 > "A"
STR1 <= "ABCD"
```

A convenient convention, which is used in the remainder of this section, is to use double quotes for all string constants and single quotes for single character constants.

C.5.6 Variable Length Strings

Strings may be thought of as variable length up to some fixed maximum which is specified in their declaration. A string variable of length 10, such as STR1 declared above, may contain any string from 0 to 10 characters in length. A special character value, STREND, is used to mark the end of a string which occupies less than the maximum length of a string variable. When the following assignment is executed:

```
STR1 := "abc"
```

the individual components of variable STR1 have the following values:

```
STR1[ 1 ] = 'a'
STR1[ 2 ] = 'b'
STR1[ 3 ] = 'c'
STR1[ 4 ] = STREND
STR1[ 5 ] = is undefined
STR1[ 6 ] is undefined

...

STR1[ 10 ] is undefined
```

If STR1 were assigned a string constant of length 10 then no STREND character would be stored in STR1.

C.5.7 Procedures and Functions For Use With Strings

Generally, those procedures and functions which take string arguments, such as WRITE, RESET and REWRITE, take the extended string parameters. In the descriptions that follow, the identifiers string, str1, str2 and dest represent strings, and the identifiers length and offset represent integers.

C.5.8 Procedures

STRCONCAT(str1, str2)
    Procedure STRCONCAT concatenates str2 to str1. Str1 must be a string variable. For example, if

```
str1 := "ab";
STRCONCAT( str1, "cd" );
```

were executed, str1 would contain "abcd".

STRDELETE(string, length, offset)

    Procedure STRDELETE removes length characters from string starting at index offset. String must be a string variable. For example:

```
str1 :="abcxxxdef";
STRDELETE( str1,3,4 );
```

leaves str1 containing "abcdef".

STRINSERT(str1,str2,offset)

    Procedure STRINSERT inserts str2 into str1 at index offset. Str1 must be a string variable. For example:

```
str1 :="abcdef";
STRINSERT( str1,"xxx",4 );
```

leaves str1 containing "abcxxxdef".

SUBSTR(str, length, offset, dest)

    Procedure SUBSTR assigns the segment of str starting at offset, of the specified length, to the string variable dest. For example:

```
str1 :="abcdef";
SUBSTR( str1, 3, 3, str2 )
```

leaves "cde" in str2.

C.5.9 Functions

STRLEN(string) : INTEGER

    Function STRLEN returns the length of a string. For a string constant this is the length of the string, and for a string variable it is the length of the string which currently is contained in the variable. For example:

```
STRLEN ( "abc" ) = 3
```

If the following assignment were executed:

```
str1 :="abc";
```

then STRLEN(str1) would be 3.

STRSCAN(str1,str2) : INTEGER

    Function STRSCAN searches str1 for an occurrence of str2. If found, the index of the first matching character in str1 is returned, otherwise 0 is returned to indicate no occurrence. For example:

```
STRSCAN( "123abcd","abc" ) = 4
STRSCAN( "bc","abc" ) = 0
```

STRSIZE(string) : INTEGER
> Function STRSIZE returns the upper bound of the index type of string. For a string constant this is the length of the string, and for a string variable it is the maximum length string which the variable can store.

```
STRSIZE ( "abc" ) = 3
STRSIZE ( str1 ) = 10
```

C.5.10 String I/O

The standard procedures WRITE and WRITELN have been extended to handle variable-length string parameters. Only the used portion of a string variable (that is, up to a STREND character, if any) is written.

Similarly, the standard procedures READ and READLN have been extended to allow variable-length string data to be read. Characters are read into a string variable until it is full (that is, STRSIZE characters have been read), or end-of-line is encountered.

APPENDIX D: PASCAL-VS

Pascal-VS is a Pascal compiler operating in the MVS and VM/CMS environments. The language recognized by the compiler adheres to the currently proposed ISO standards and includes many important extensions. These extensions include: separate compilation, dynamic character strings and extended input-output capabilities. Two manuals available from IBM, describe the complete language and its use. They are the *Pascal-VS Language Reference Manual,* publication number SH20-6168 and the *Pascal-VS Programmers' Guide* (SH20-6162).

The purpose of this appendix is to summarize the extensions of standard Pascal which are found in Pascal-VS.

D.1 Declaration Extensions

Pascal-VS includes five kinds of declarations other than LABEL, CONST, TYPE, VAR, PROCEDURE, FUNCTION. They are:

STATIC -   An alternative to VAR. Declares variables whose values are preserved over separate invocations of the block in which they are declared. Can be used to have a procedure or function "remember" a value of a local variable from the most recent invocation.

DEF and REF - These declarations declare variables used in external modules so that proper communication with external routines is possible. Differences between DEF and REF are found in the Pascal-VS Reference Manual.

VALUE -   The VALUE declaration can be used to specify an initial value for DEF and STATIC variables. It contains a series of ordinary assignment statements to perform the initializations.

SPACE -   The SPACE declaration provides control over the use of memory for storing variables.

Pascal-VS permits a CONST declaration to be an array or record as well as a scalar value.

D.2 Type Extensions

As well as the standard five types, PASCAL/VS permits the following types.

SHORTREAL - similar to REAL but each value uses less memory with a resulting decrease in the number of significant digits which a number may have.

STRING - declarations of the form PACKED ARRAY[1..n]OF CHAR can be lumped together as the type STRING meaning that different declarations are not required for different values of n. A maximum length can be assigned. Any variable of type STRING is compatible with any other variable of type STRING. Numerous functions are available for processing STRING values.

ALFA and ALPHA - these types are STRINGs of length 8 and 16 respectively.

STRINGPTR - a pointer to a STRING type with the added flexibility that the maximum length does not have to be specified until execution time

D.3 Formal Parameters

As well as value, VAR, PROCEDURE and FUNCTION parameters, Pascal-VS allows CONST parameters and conformal STRING parameters.

A CONST formal parameter indicates the value passed by the calling routine cannot be changed by the called routine.

A STRING parameter does not need to have its maximum length match that of the corresponding argument.

D.4 Directives

Pascal-VS includes the following directives as well as FORWARD.

INTERNAL - an internal routine can only be invoked from within the block that contains the routine declaration

EXTERNAL - an external routine is a procedure or function that can be invoked from outside its normal scope

FORTRAN   -   similar to EXTERNAL but indicates the routine has been (will be) compiled by a FORTRAN compiler and that appropriate parameter-passing conventions should be used

MAIN   -   allows a Pascal procedure to be used as the mainline and/or invoked from a non-Pascal program

REENTRANT - similar to MAIN but causes the routine to be reentrant (interruptable without loss of data)

D.5 Statements

Pascal-VS includes the ASSERT, CONTINUE, LEAVE and RETURN statement as well as permitting an OTHERWISE option in the CASE statement.

ASSERT   -   is used to assert that a Boolean expression has a value of true. If false, an execution-time error is generated.

CONTINUE - used to continue a WHILE or REPEAT loop from a point inside the loop body. Means a GOTO need not be used to test the loop termination condition.

LEAVE   -   used to exit from a FOR, WHILE or REPEAT loop without checking the termination condition

RETURN   -   used to exit from a procedure or function from a point within the body of the block

OTHERWISE - (CASE statement extension). If the value of the case selector expression does not match any of the values in the case label lists, an OTHERWISE following the last case specifies that the statement between it and the END is to be executed.

D.6 Input-Output Extensions

A number of procedures for handling files are available in Pascal-VS. The purpose of each is summarized below.

TERMIN   -   permits the terminal to be used as a source of input data

TERMOUT   -   permits the terminal output device to be used as an output text file

PDSIN   -   specifies that a Pascal input file is stored as a partitioned
              data set on an external device

PDSOUT   -   specifies that a Pascal output file is to be stored as a
              partitioned data set on an external storage device

UPDATE   -   allows a partitioned data set to be used as both an input
              and an ouput file

CLOSE   -   terminates processing of a file

SEEK   -   used to specify the next component of a direct access file
              which will be processed with a GET or PUT

READ extensions
> a) string data can be read with a READ or READLN
> procedure
>
> b) A field length specifier can be associated with a variable in
> a read list. It specifies the number of characters to be
> searched in the input file to find the value of the variable.

WRITE extensions
> a) a negative field specifier causes the value to be left-justified
> in the field
>
> b) a COLS procedure is provided which returns the position of
> the next character in the output file would occupy. When
> used with an appropriate expression as a format specifier,
> direct control over the horizontal positioning of output items
> can be done.

D.7 Standard Procedures and Functions

Pascal-VS has many built in procedures and functions beyond those in
standard Pascal. These include:

D.7.1 General Routines

TRACE procedure - displays the current list of procedures and functions
which are active. Helpful as a debugging tool.

HALT procedure - stops further execution of Pascal statements

DATETIME procedure - returns the current date and time of day

CLOCK function - returns the number of microseconds the program has
been executing

PARMS function - returns a string containing the parameter values passed to the main program

RETCODE procedure - returns a value to the system program when the mainline ceases execution

D.7.2 Memory Management Routines

MARK procedure - can create a pointer to a block of memory from which NEW buffers are assigned

RELEASE procedure - releases a MARKed area of memory

NEW extensions - a buffer for a particular variant can be created thus minimizing memory usage. A string buffer can also be created.

D.7.3 Limit Routines

LOWEST, HIGHEST functions - return the smallest and largest value of the type of the argument. For example because 17 is an INTEGER, HIGHEST(17) is MAXINT.

LBOUND, HBOUND functions - return the smallest and highest subscript values of the argument element

SIZEOF function - returns the number of bytes used to store the argument value

D.7.4 Conversion Routines

scalar conversion function - the inverse of ORD which can be used with any scalar type. (Standard Pascal only has CHR which is the inverse of ORD for CHAR values.)

FLOAT function - explicitly converts an INTEGER value to a REAL value

STR function - converts either a CHAR value or a PACKED ARRAY[1..n]OF CHAR to the Pascal-VS type STRING

D.7.5 Mathematical Routines

MIN function - returns the smallest of the argument values

MAX function - returns the largest of the argument values

RANDOM function - returns a "random" number in the range zero to one

D.7.6 String Routines

LENGTH function - returns the number of characters in a string value

MAXLENGTH function - the maximum number of characters that can be stored in the string variable

SUBSTR function - extracts a subsequence of characters in the string argument

DELETE function - returns the string argument minus the specified substring

TRIM function - removes trailing blanks from the string argument

LTRIM function - removes leading blanks from the string argument

COMPRESS function - replaces multiple blanks in a string with a single blank

INDEX function - returns a subscript indicating where in a given string a second string begins

TOKEN procedure - returns the next identifier, number or delimiter in an argument string

READSTR procedure - simulates the action of READing from a string instead of a file

WRITESTR procedure - WRITEs the arguments to a string instead of a file

D.8 Other Extensions

Pascal-VS includes a number of compiler options which provide control over: imbedding groups of source statements found in other files; checking for use of variables and functions which have not been assigned a value; printing page titles and listing source statements during the compile time of the job; spacing the listing of source statements.

APPENDIX E: IBM PERSONAL COMPUTER PASCAL

The Pascal compiler for the IBM Personal Computer is designed to process standard Pascal (as defined in the International Standards Organization draft ISO/TC 97/SC5 N595). It supports numerous extensions of the standard which make it suitable for writing compilers, operating systems and interpreters as well as application programs.

The purpose of this appendix is to summarize the language extensions in IBM Pascal. Detailed information can be found in the publication "Pascal Compiler", publication number 6172272 in the IBM Personal Computer Language Series.

E.1 Summary of Extensions

1. Metacommands

    Metacommands are used to control compiler debugging, listing files and source file execution. Thirty commands are available. They can be grouped into three general categories:

    - Debugging and Error Handling. Fourteen commands provide the ability to check for unassigned variables, subscript out of range, stack overflow and other error conditions.

    - Listing and File Format. Ten commands are available to control the existence, spacing and formatting of the listing file produced by the compiler.

    - Source File Control. Six metacommands can be used to: imbed source files, ignore lines in the source file depending on the value of a constant, print messages on the screen during compilation and save and restore the settings of metacommands.

    Metacommands begin with a '$' and are placed inside Pascal comments as in (*$PAGE*) which causes the next line of the listing file to be written at the top of a page.

2. Units

    A unit is a set of declarations plus an initialization procedure which can be separately compiled and used by other programs and units. The availability of units result in significant reductions in compile times for large programs. It also provides a structured way of breaking a program into modules which is preferable to the use of external procedures and variables.

3. Super Array

   IBM Pascal provides a super array type which allows the number of components in an array to vary. The lower bound of a super array is specified and the upper bound is denoted by an '*'. The existence of super arrays reduces problems associated with processing arrays of different but unknown lengths.

4. Strings

   Strings in standard Pascal are fixed length. The type SUPER ARRAY referred to above allows strings to have variable lengths. A number of string handling procedures and functions are provided with the language. String assignment, comparison and READ/WRITE are done automatically.

5. Constants

   Constant values can be declared as an expression of other constant values.

   Numbers can be expressed in binary, octal, decimal or hexadecimal notational. READ and WRITE can be used with non-decimal numbers.

   Variables can be initialized with a constant value at compile time.

   A CONST formal parameter is allowed which means the procedure or function invoked cannot modify the value.

   Array and record constants are allowed.

6. Systems Implementation Features

   Several features are available which make the job of writing language translators and operating systems much easier. These include: the types WORD and ADDRESS, extended input-output capabilities, random files and file modes, and intrinsic procedures and functions.

7. Control Statements and Operators

   The statements BREAK, CYCLE and RETURN exit from an interative statement, begin the next iteration, and exit from a block respectively.

   The CASE statement can be ended with an OTHERWISE clause containing statements which are executed if the value of the case selector expression is not associated with any of the cases.

There are two sequential control operators - AND THEN and OR ELSE. When evaluating X AND THEN Y, if X is false, Y is not evaluated. For the expression X OR ELSE Y, if X is true, Y is not evaluated. The first is useful if X being false implies the evaluation of Y should give an execution-time error. The OR ELSE avoids an error if X being true implies Y would generate a run-time error.

8. Input-Output Extensions

Text files can be given a fixed line length automatically.

READ can be used with Boolean, pointer, and STRING types.

Format specifiers may be negative causing left justification in the output values.

Direct access files and a SEEK procedure are supported.

9. Error Conditions Not Recognized

ISO Pascal defines many conditions which are errors. The standard permits an implementation to state that certain errors are not detected. There are a few error conditions that IBM Pascal does not diagnose. These are described explicitly in the reference manual for IBM Pascal.

APPENDIX F: DEBUGGING HINTS, EFFICIENCY AND GENERALITY

F.1 Debugging Hints

1. Echo your input data. That is, print the input values as soon as they are read.

2. Use meaningful variable names.

3. Use lots of comments and blanks.

4. Indent the program statements to clearly show the logical structure of the program.

5. Print intermediate results until you are sure that the program logic is correct.

6. Use a BOOLEAN variable called "DEBUG" and statements of the type "IF(DEBUG) WRITELN(...)" .

7. Carefully check your program logic after the program has been written and before it is entered. Carefully check your source file before running the program.

8. Use the tracing option if available to trace through complex sequences of statements.

9. If you make a change in program logic, satisfy yourself that it will not affect other parts of the program.

10. During the debug phase, print any values which will eventually be written in a file to insure that the correct values are being generated.

11. What not to do. Don't plan. Assume your logic is correct. Assume your input data is correct. If an error occurs, don't make any changes -- run the program again -- it must have been the computer's mistake.

F.2 Program Efficiency

What is meant by an efficient program? Efficiencies can be achieved in the following areas: memory requirements; compile time; execution time; programming and entry time. Usually however, there is a tradeoff. That is, efficiency in one area means inefficiencies result in another area. The following list is not suggested as being complete. The suggestions in the list may decrease the execution time of a Pascal program. Compile time may or may not be a significant factor in running Pascal programs.

1. Loops

a) A subscripted variable which is used more than once in the body of a loop should be assigned to a simple variable.

b) To reduce the number of times the decision to repeat the loop must be made, processing two or more subscript values within the loop may be desirable. For example, the left fragment below is more efficient than the right.

```
I := 1                          I := 1
REPEAT                          REPEAT
  X[I] := 0;                      X I  := 0;
  X[I+1] := 0;                    I := I + 1
  I := I + 2                    UNTIL I > 100
UNTIL I > 100
```

c) If possible, nested loops should have the innermost loops with the most repetitions. For example:

```
FOR I := 1 TO 10 DO            FOR I := 1 TO 100 DO
  FOR J := 1 TO 100 DO           FOR J := 1 TO 10 DO
    X := 0                         X := 0
```

2. Subscripted Variables

a) Avoid using arrays having many dimensions.

b) Assign subscripted variables used more than once in a loop to a simple variable.

c) Use records instead of arrays.

3. Conditional Control

a) In an IF statement, use a BOOLEAN expression which makes the most likely result FALSE.

b) An IF is faster for a two-way branch than a CASE statement.

c) A CASE is faster than a sequence of ELSE IFs.

d) Use a BOOLEAN variable called LOOPING as a test to continue a WHILE loop.

e) Use the IN operator instead of IFs or CASEs.

4. Expressions

   a) Avoid mixing two types of values. If X is REAL then "X+2.0" is better than "X+2".

   b) Addition is usually faster than multiplication. "X+X" is better than "2.0*X".

   c) To evaluate a polynomial such as $Ax^3 + Bx^2 + Cx + D$, write it as

   $$(((A * X + B) * X + C) * X + D).$$

5. Input-Output

   a) A single READ is better than two separate READs.

   b) Use default field widths.

   c) Use WRITE instead of WRITELN.

6. Memory Requirements

   a) Use PACKED for arrays, records, and sets.

   b) Use VAR parameters instead of value parameters for arrays and records.

   c) Use variants to define two or more data structures not needed simultaneously.

   d) Use sets.

   e) Use pointers.

   f) DISPOSE of buffers when no longer needed.

F.3 Generalization Hints

   A generalized program is one which can be used to solve a wide variety of problems without making changes in the program. This is usually done by reading data from the input file which defines the characteristics of the problem to be solved. A generalized program will solve many problems and it will also permit someone with no programming knowledge to use the program simply by preparing an appropriate set of input data. Some generalization hints are:

1. Check for error conditions which although not present in the problem for which the program was written, could be present using different data.

2. Use constant declarations.

3. Use statements which are acceptable to almost all Pascal compilers.

4. Read the number of problems to be solved from the input data.

5. Read loop control values.

6. Use end-of-line and end-of-file tests instead of sentinel values.

INDEX OF APPLICATIONS

Index

S

T

U

V

W